Also by John S. Peart–Binns

Blunt (Bishop Alfred Blunt of Bradford)
Ambrose Reeves
Cornish Bishop (J.W. Hunkin of Truro) with
Alan Dunstan
Eric Treacy
Defender of the Church of England (Bishop Ronald
Williams of Leicester)
Living with Paradox (Archbishop John Habgood
of York)
Wand of London
Joost de Blank
Maurice B. Reckitt
Graham Leonard
Edwin Morris

Bishop Hugh Montefiore

John S. Peart-Binns

An Anthony Blond Book
London   New York

First published in Great Britain by Quartet Books Limited 1990
A member of the Namara Group
27/29 Goodge Street
London W1P 1FD

British Library Cataloguing in Publication Data

Peart-Binns, John S. (John Stuart)
  Hugh Montefiore, Bishop of Birmingham
  1. Church of England. Montefiore, Hugh, 1920
  I. Title
  283'.092'4

ISBN 0-7043-2714-7

Typeset by MC Typeset Ltd, Gillingham, Kent
Printed and bound in Great Britain by
BPCC Hazell Books Ltd
Member of BPCC Ltd
Aylesbury, Bucks

For Christopher

Acknowledgements

The help I have received from a large number of people, covering all aspects of Hugh Montefiore's life, work and thought, is massive. It has been as generously given as it has been gratefully received. It is said that if you want a job doing give it to a busy person. My correspondents are all busy people and the rapidity and quality of their responses have proved the truth of the saying.

Many people wrote in confidence to assist me with background material or foreground detail rather than for direct quotation. It seems wrong to name only some of the people who have assisted me in my undertaking. So I offer a HUGE thank you to everyone who has contributed or helped in any way. Without such assistance my offering would have been partial and stunted.

There would have been no book at all if it had not been for the willing and active co-operation of Hugh Montefiore at all stages of research and writing. The floorboards of my home creaked when he arrived with a complete car load of his papers. No file or letter has been closed to me. Biographers are professional pryers. Hugh and I have explored themes with my rigour and his vigour. There have been subjects he would have preferred to leave untouched and unmentioned yet he has never tried to act as censor. Mutual trust must be the relationship between biographer and subject. Naturally, he has read the manuscript and offered his detailed comments, leaving the final judgement to me. He may not agree with every word that is written but he is an honest man who recognizes himself in the biography – 'warts and all'.

Eliza and Hugh Montefiore welcomed me into their home with joy and graciousness. The combination of generous hospitality and mental virility has been both stimulating and pleasurable. The probing in the study and the fellowship at mealtimes have been wonderfully complemented and sustained by prayers and Holy Communion each morning in his chapel. To miss the spiritual dimension of Hugh's life (wonderfully supported by Eliza) is to miss almost everything. Thank you for agreeing that this biography should be written.

Finally, my thanks go to my publisher Anthony Blond who at all times is encouraging and helpful as well as being persuasive and persistent.

JSP-B

Contents

Introduction   xi

1 Enduring Roots   1
2 The Vision   17
3 War   27
4 Oxford and Colloquy   37
5 Ordination and Restlessness   47
6 Fellow and Dean   59
7 'Everything I've Got'   79
8 Squalls and Tempests   103
9 Constraining the Waters   133
10 Mr Johnson Arrives   157
11 The Future – Apocalypse or Concorde?   185
12 Prince of the Church   205
13 Style and Substance   217
14 Contrasts   235
15 National and Ethical   245
16 Theologian – Explorer and Stabilizer   271
17 Living Tornado with a Human Face   295

Notes   315

Appendix A: 'What I Believe'   337

Appendix B: Select Bibliography   350

Index   357

Introduction

Writing biographies of living subjects is a perilous activity. There is no corpse, but a living entity, and in this case an animated one. An undefiled objective approach is impossible. Yet some evaluation is both desirable and necessary and critical appraisal is neither inopportune nor invalid.

The biographer calls and assembles the witnesses. They tell what they know. Whilst aiming for a degree of objectivity, even with a living subject, he must in some sense be biased. But he must not be an advocate for the subject's views, to some of which he may hold different and contrary ones. None the less the biographer must have a feeling for the subject which makes him take on the case in the first place.

The readers form the jury. There is no judge. The life goes on. And what a vigorous life it is. Hugh Montefiore is able to be with and near his wife whilst undertaking an amazing variety of work. He is as exhaustingly busy as ever, though in some new ways. With a word processor to hand he is producing articles, sermons, lectures and publications as fast as paper can be released from the machine.

Amongst other activities Montefiore is Chairman of Transport 2000, which is an important body as transport takes a prominent place in any headline for the future, and of the Homes for Homeless People Trust, the financial trust for the central Cyrenians. He also chairs the Luthuli Cultural and Welfare Services Trust, which was set up through the African National Congress. Montefiore was asked to chair it after

Oliver Tambo had had dinner with a group of the 'urban' bishops. Scholarships are given to South African students for higher education in Africa and elsewhere.

Montefiore is President of the Gaia Trust, which James Lovelock set up to further his cause. It is said that Lovelock's books have been responsible for greening the 'Iron Lady'. In April 1989 Montefiore lectured at the Wrekin Trust Conference in Winchester on 'The Bearing of the Gaia Hypothesis on Christian Theology'.

An important venture which Montefiore chairs is The Gospel and Our Culture, which has been set up by the British Council of Churches. He will be editing a weighty book by academics, analysing various aspects of our culture from a missionary point of view, to be published in 1991 in time for a National Consultation at Swanwick in 1992.

He is also a vice-president of the Town and Country Planning Association and also of the Pedestrian Association. He is a trustee of Friends of the Earth, the Mobility Trust (which makes grants to the physically disabled who fall outside the National Health Service net), and of the South African Townships Health Trust.

In 1989 he delivered the Drummond Lectures at Stirling University on 'Christianity and Politics' (to be published by Macmillan) and is the 1989 Bishop Williams Lecturer at Rikkyo University, Tokyo; his subjects include Church and State, abortion and IVF, geriatrics, the ordination of women, the environment and Christian values in a technological society.

During February 1989 Montefiore went on a preaching and lecture tour in seminaries and parishes in America, visiting St Louis, Berkeley, California, Boston, New York, Alexandria, Washington, Ambridge, Sewannee and Denver. Whilst there he attended the consecration of Barbara Harris as the Anglican Communion's first woman bishop, not as an officiating bishop (which he would have liked) but as a correspondent for *The Times*. *The Times* then 'lost' his article so it did not appear. Montefiore is not one of those who think this consecration will irrevocably divide the Anglican Communion and he is not much bothered how the Church of Rome reacts. Indeed, he thinks it 'could well turn out to herald a future blessing of wholeness for the entire Church of God'.

Immediately after being consecrated, in accordance with American custom, Bishop Harris celebrated Holy Communion. Whenever I see a woman actually functioning as a priest, the whole controversy about women's ordination seems to me absurd. I looked at Barbara Harris officiating. She was habited in the traditional vestments of the Church. Her words and actions were the same as those of men. She celebrated with reverence and concentration. She resembled her fellow bishops in every way, except for her sexuality. Womanhood seemed in no way to impede her symbolic role: on the contrary, it added a wholeness to the episcopate.

Montefiore has never lived in the past and the mental virility and physical pace of his continuing life suggests there will be many new ideas and initiatives in the future. So – why a biography now? Montefiore retired in 1987, aged sixty-six, before his statutory time (bishops have to retire at seventy), whilst still at the height of his powers and near the zenith of his influence. Of what interest and lasting effect are his words and works? There can be no complete answer to these questions now. None the less there is some value in a biographical portrait which attempts to be partially objective. When contemporaries die, particles of history vanish and perspectives change. Time can obscure as well as illuminate issues of the day.

The Church of England is in danger of being rent asunder from within and any sense of unity in diversity in the Anglican Communion can seem like a forlorn hope. There are few leading churchmen who are prepared to voice their belief in the strength of Anglicanism, stoutly defending its distinctive position. Montefiore does, even when bewailing its manifold defects.

As Montefiore looks back on his 'professional' life in the Church, his major anxiety concerns the General Synod. It somehow seems right that his swashbuckling approach should have been embodied in his synodical number. In accordance with practice, when speaking he had to preface his speech with both name and number. His number was 7, or, as he used to put it, 007. He considers that the General Synod meets too often and too long and attempts too much. It is like a sponge absorbing all the issues of the age, religious and secular, setting up working parties *ad nauseam* and then squeezing the results on an unnoticing Church. His major criticism relates to the futility of so much that a rather self-important General Synod does.

> Within three groups of midweek sessions a year the Synod attempts to pass new legislation (largely on the parliamentary model), to make decisions needed by the Church, to advise Her Majesty's Government on matters of moment (not that Her Majesty's Government takes the slightest notice: it only does that, as with the Shops Bill, when men and women in the pews are aroused), and also to stage what I can only call 'educational' debates on any matters put forward by the various Boards, whether they be matters of ministry, baptism and confirmation, worship or the like. I do not myself believe that 'educational' debates have any place in the system – they are singularly ineffective – and I believe there are more effective ways of putting pressure on the Government.

The paradox of synodical government with its semblance of democracy is that it is leading to a greater emphasis on the bishops as a whole on matters of doctrine. Montefiore thinks it intolerable that a non-representative body (and despite elections, that is what General Synod is) should have the power to decide the doctrine of the Church of England. Surely in an episcopal church it is the task of the House of Bishops, who are still guardians of the faith, to deliberate, debate and decide what is and what is not consonant with the doctrine of the Church of England. Montefiore wants the roles to be reversed. The bishops acting collegially should agree what needs to be done and then should seek the approval of the clergy and laity, who would have the power of veto or amendment if they wished to exercise it. (He can be assured they would!)

The real affliction of General Synod results from its parliamentary procedure leading to its partisan composition and polarized convictions. Montefiore expresses his own position in this way:

I have never fully understood those who put their allegiance to catholicism or to evangelicalism or to radicalism above their allegiance to their Church. I myself abhor all labels, and I am very proud simply to be regarded as a Church of England man. I do not mean by that that I am a broad churchman, or that churchmanship does not matter to me. On the contrary, I have a very high doctrine of the Church (and of course an even higher doctrine of God's Kingdom). I am proud to belong to a Church which is, as I believe, truly catholic, and truly evangelical and at the same time makes a genuine appeal to reason and sound learning. I must seek the truth as I see it, and I regard that as a sacred vocation. At the same time it is unlikely that I shall be much wiser than my elders or my contemporaries, and so I have a great respect for tradition. And at the same time I hear the Word of God through the Bible, and I have found that through it God not only strengthens me but also disturbs me; and so I hold to the protestant principle.*

On this basis history is likely to shew that Montefiore, far from being a firebrand radical, was one who firmly belonged to the middle ground, which he tried to defend and strengthen against the threatened and actual vandalism caused by people on the extreme perimeters. In a House of Lords debate (28 November 1985) he quoted with approval some words from the preface to the Book of Common Prayer: 'It hath been the wisdom of the Church of England ever since the first compiling of her public liturgy, to keep the mean between two extremes.' To attempt to do this whilst holding and expressing strong convictions is not easy. To attempt it at all is courageous and worthwhile.

The present Archbishop of Canterbury (Robert Runcie) observes:

We missed Hugh Montefiore at the 1988 Lambeth Conference because his all-round ability would have been noticeable there. Though he was not a distinguished

* Lecture, 'The Future of the Church of England', Sion College, London, 1988.

philosopher or writer, he was the bishop most like William Temple in the modern period. He had an ability to be courageous and to be full of ideas about a wide range of subjects and had that happy knack of producing a Christian angle on almost anything. My only anxiety about Hugh concerned his judgement. His knowledge, fluency and courage often seemed to outstrip his judgement, but this was even more true of William Temple when it came to making appointments.

Like William Temple, Montefiore has the ability to be priest, preacher, pastor and prophet. Prophets are not frequently pastors. They are single-minded, tend to brush opposition aside, which can mean a lack of consideration towards people. They are uneasy people to live with. Montefiore is saved from apocalyptic apoplexy by his strong desire to be a pastor. Yet this does not mute his voice.

'Conservation', 'environment', 'ecology' are words that have become both overworked and abused. They have fallen into the hands of pressure groups and party politicians who sometimes flog all meaning out of them. Montefiore was using and acting on these words long before they became fashionable. We will see how he was an early and lonely voice speaking and writing about ecological perils ahead. It has never been an hysterical voice. His arguments have been balanced by evidence and reliable statistics. More than thirty years since his ecological warnings in the 1950s, Montefiore places in the second league the terrible violence that is being done to the environment, yet may not cause irrevocable harm to the planet earth. Now he places in the first league some real dangers to the future of life on earth, or at least to the future of *Homo sapiens*, which are caused by present practices.

Consider what are the essentials for life, or at least for human life. We need a consistent and equable climate. We need protection against harmful rays from outside our planet. We need sufficient water for our needs. We need a sufficiently fertile soil to produce our food. We need the right kind of atmosphere in which to breathe. We need the appropriate circulation of those trace elements which are necessary for our health. We need healthy oceans which play a vital ecological role. All these are beginning to be at risk through human activity.★

If Montefiore paused or stopped at that stage it could be regarded as the thinking of a humanist, as someone hoping for a secular Utopia where all is light and goodness and where justice reigns supreme on earth. But as a Christian who searches the Scriptures, Montefiore knows that God gives no sign that things are going to improve *ad infinitum*. That is the secular idea of progress for the world. He thinks the Anglican Communion as well as other parts of Christendom has an opportunity to chart the way ahead with grounded hope and exploratory faith. He may have been involved in all the internal controversies of the Church (some of which he caused) but they are not what chiefly concerns him. If he had been invited to give the keynote speech at the 1988 Lambeth Conference on 'The Unity We Seek', he would have lifted sights from parochial concerns, ecumenical jitters and the possibility or probability of internal fragmentation, to a larger vision of God's creation, greater than the community of men and women, even though mankind is the crown of creation.

Here on Planet Earth we have a great variety of plants and animal life, on the earth and in the oceans and in the air. Man has emerged as a kind of steward, the only creature on earth able to reflect on God's creation, and to take thought for it. But his stewardship is uncertain and often profligate. Without man there is a natural kind of harmony in the world. There is a struggle for life and the survival of the fittest; but there is co-operation also and an ecological balance which is naturally achieved. Left to itself, without the interference of man, the earth naturally reaches a climax of fertility. Man can impose order on this earth, he can act as the gardener, but more often he uses it as he wishes for his own devices without thought of consequences. God has purposes for man, so that all through the centuries of evolution conditions have been

★ Lecture on conservation, Ripon Town Hall, 1989.

optimal for the emergence of intelligent life. Conditions are maintained by natural checks and balances; and if man interferes with them wantonly, the evidence suggests that God has so arranged it that Gaia will continue on its way, but mankind will perish from the earth.

This is the worst case; and if it takes place, it will be due to man's failure, and this will involve the failure of the Church. But there is still time; time to mend our ways, time for the Church to help in enabling man to fulfil his proper role in creation, using it of course for his own purposes, admiring its beauty, but respecting it for its own intrinsic worth, and taking positive steps not to disrupt its natural harmonies. We can even picture a new humanity in Christ using our God-given intelligence, our moral sense and our imagination to set forward the unity of all creation in Christ.

The story, however, begins not with a Christian bishop but with a Jewish boy.

1 Enduring Roots

In the beginning was Sir Moses Haim Montefiore (1784–1884). He was in fact not the first Montefiore, but he was, without question, the most influential. He was an icon in his lifetime and his portrait was to be found in all kinds of Jewish homes. It was also seen in the Christian home of his great-great-great-nephew Hugh William Montefiore. Over Hugh Montefiore's study mantelpiece throughout his Christian ministry, from Newcastle curacy to Birmingham see, hung a striking picture of Moses Montefiore.

Even in old age, the picture portrays an amazing, larger than life Jew, six feet three inches tall. He was said to combine in his own person the resources of Croesus, the vitality of Methuselah and the zeal of Dr Livingstone. In one testimonial he was referred to as a 'king, helper and shield',[1] and his life bore witness to these epithets. Even nearer the mark are words on a memorial plaque on the house where he was born in Leghorn, Italy: 'Honoured by the powerful, blessed by the poor'.

The character and personality of the great-great-great-nephew, Jew turned Christian, cannot be properly understood nor appreciated without an examination of the roots which have never been severed and which, in a strange but calculable way, still support him.

The oldest Jewish families in England were Sephardi, that is, of Spanish and Portuguese origin. The Montefiores were such. There was always a taint of easy superiority about them, particularly when compared with the later Jewish arrivals in England, the Ashkenazi Jews from Central and Eastern Europe.

The Ashkenazi spoke with that mixture of Hebrew and German called Yiddish. They were much more a people set apart and pushed apart. Historically they were more familiar with the ghetto mentality and attitude of suffering than were the Sephardi Jews. And the differences between the two were not superficial. The Sephardi Jews of earlier times in Spain differed little from their Gentile counterparts. They absorbed the cultural background against which they lived and, apart from their religious beliefs and some knowledge of Hebrew, there was little to distinguish them from the Gentiles. The gap between the two was less than that between Church and Chapel in Victorian England.

There was almost a class distinction between Sephardi and Ashkenazi Jew in England – never more manifest than in the places where they lived. Sephardi Jews were well-established and well-heeled. They lived in comfortable circumstances and were often leading lights in the City, where they acquired fortunes. The Ashkenazi settled in the East End of London, in Whitechapel and Mile End.

Sephardi Jews came to England in the eighteenth century, not solely as a result of harassment. England was seen as a land of the free where hard work and initiative would be rewarded. Chaim Bermant puts it well:

> Persecution in Eastern and Central Europe had occasioned
> a movement of Jews towards the West, but neither Cohens
> nor Goldsmids, neither Rothschilds nor Montefiores were
> victims of oppression or hunger. They had done well in
> Europe and hoped to do better in England, and they had
> chosen their country well.[2]

Moses Montefiore married Judith, a daughter of Levi Barent Cohen the first really rich English Jew – an Ashkenazim and merchant from Amersfort in Holland who had settled in London. He also set up an endowment fund to provide dowries for poor Ashkenazi girls marrying Sephardi.

Moses Montefiore had a cushioned beginning and there were few clues to his future commanding stature in a secular education that was scanty and a religious education that was devout but limited. His aim was to become a stockbroker, which he did in partnership with his brother Abraham. They prospered and increased. By marriage, links were formed with other great names of Anglo-Jewry: for example, Moses became a brother-in-law to Nathan Mayer Rothschild, who had married another daughter of Levi Barent Cohen.

In the nineteenth century there were many legal disabilities for Jews. Indeed, Moses was fortunate to be a broker, for the number of Jewish brokers at any one time was limited to twelve and Moses had had to buy a licence from the Lord Mayor of London, costing about £1,200. The universities were closed to Jews and in many spheres entry was either legally barred or precluded because a Christian oath was required. It was questionable whether Jews were legally entitled to own real estate. What could be done about this unsatisfactory state of affairs, a blemish on a so-called enlightened country? Denzil Sebag-Montefiore (Hugh Montefiore's brother) supplies the answer:

Moses set himself to change this situation, no doubt reflecting that he could not hope to improve conditions of oppressed Jews in other countries unless conditions first improved at home; although I must emphasize that oppression was not the problem in Britain, just these widespread disabilities. He had the satisfaction of seeing the achievement of Jewish emancipation in Britain during his lifetime. He was an idealist, but his idealism was linked to practical genius. He knew when to push for the removal of Jewish disabilities and the obtaining of full civil rights, and when to pause for public opinion to catch up. His idealism and philanthropy found an answering spark in the humanitarianism and idealism of Victorian Britain. His personal conduct was an example to the Gentiles, many of whom tended to regard Jews as mean, avaricious, revengeful and not to be trusted; they found it both novel and surprising for a Jew to be held up as a philanthropist, a patriot and an apostle of altruism in its broadest sense, and as a pattern of all that is good and true and noble.

Moses was fortunate to become acquainted with the young Princess Victoria, before she became Queen of England. This arose because, when she was in lodgings in Ramsgate with her impecunious mother, it was only natural that Moses, as owner of a great house nearby, should offer her the freedom of his grounds and gardens. He is credited with having given her a golden key to open the door made for her in the garden wall. It led to the association – quite intimate at times – of the royal uncles with a number of Jewish causes. It ultimately led to the assistance of some Foreign Ministers and the Foreign Office, which opened the doors of British embassies to Sir Moses when on his missions abroad. He was not only frequently invited to stay at the embassy, but officials often prepared the ground for him beforehand, and kept an eye on Jewish interests after his departure.[3]

By a combination of a towering personality, persistent persuasiveness and beneficent contacts, he was more instrumental than any other individual in changing the climate to allow Jews to emerge from the shadows into the brightest light of day. Yet this remarkable man, who was received with esteem wherever he went, by Tsars Nicholas I and Alexander II and by Sultans, was not exotically flamboyant but rather paternalistic: the kind of man whose word was trusted because it was matched by deeds. Israel Finestein portrays him accurately:

> He had the pragmatism of the cautious business man, as well as the tough persistence in pursuit of his espoused causes. He expected obedience. His courteous manners only accentuated the impact of his tall and impressive appearance. His Jewish philanthropy was avuncular rather than imaginative.[4]

Sir Moses Montefiore was the subject of two lengthy leading articles in *The Times* celebrating the opening and closing of his hundredth year.[5] He was praised for the way in which he distributed his bounty. His gifts were bestowed with a shrewd discrimination the aim of which was to raise as well as to succour. Christians and Jews both profited from his munificence. In many countries he was responsible for the alleviation of misery and the abandonment of persecution. What motivated him to do all this? Was it self-fulfilment or self-glory? This unofficial ambassador of world Jewry, in the form of the archetypal amateur, was responding to the imperatives of his religion – 'To God be the Glory'. At the end of his life he wrote, 'I hope that by divine blessing I have been of some use to my fellow creatures, both Jews and Christians, and believe I may add Moors. To God alone, who has helped and sustained me, be honour and glory.'

In the one man there were the qualities of patience, insight and fidelity. There were also the tendencies of the Jewish race towards religion, property and natural aristocracy. Benjamin Disraeli, who was born a Jew but was baptized when he was thirteen, held that Jews were naturally conservative in outlook and did not have a history of liberation and radicalism. Moses Montefiore's life did not contradict such assertions. His gifts were those of an activist – courage, conviction and determination, with more than a dash of inspiration.

No Montefiore can ignore Sir Moses, and all Montefiores revere him. But what was he to Hugh Montefiore? Giving the Eleventh Montefiore Memorial Lecture in the University of Southampton on 12 February 1979 Hugh Montefiore used the words '*pietas*' and 'sanctity' to describe his great-great-great-uncle. Christians have seized these words and used them only for their own brand of 'saint':

> In the Christian tradition we were accustomed to associate sainthood with some great renunciation, the kind of response which St Francis of Assisi made to the Gospel, or again the world-wide Buddhist movement, with its emphasis on detachment, looks back to the Gautama leaving his royal throne and sitting under the bo tree. But I think that we should recognize that the Jewish tradition is different. Certainly suffering deeply marks it; and Moses had his share of suffering and troubles . . . But . . . it is useful to remember that in the Jewish tradition prosperity is a sign of God's blessing. We have only to think about what is written in the Book of Deuteronomy or to remember the ending of the book of Job, to see the strength of this tradition. According to Jewish spirituality wealth is a sign of divine approval, and what matters is whether that wealth is used for the benefit of one's fellow men.[6]

This giving away of oneself and some of one's money in service to others affected Hugh. Here was a religion which made demands.

Shakespeare portrayed the Jew as mean, avaricious, revengeful, faithless. Moses Montefiore turned this on its head. In him we see a passion for humanity. The spirit of revenge was exchanged for that of brotherhood; the lust for gold for a genuine munificence.

For Jews he pleaded with monarchs, petitioned governments, bought land whereon he built houses, colleges, hospitals. He did everything that a resourceful mind and an inexhaustible purse could accomplish to make the lot of the Jew tolerable, if not entirely happy.

And he was considerably influenced by his wife Judith, who died in 1862. She was a woman of high idealism and intellect with literary, musical and artistic accomplishments, speaking French, German and Italian fluently, a keen student of Hebrew and even of Arabic.

Sir Moses Montefiore was childless but had a favourite nephew, Joseph Sebag, a broker of Moroccan origin, who was the son of Moses' sister Sarah. In his will Moses requested Joseph and his descendants to add the name Montefiore to that of Sebag – hence Sebag-Montefiore. Evidence has recently been found, in old rolls of bankers, of Montefiores being established in the village of Montefiore Conca before the expulsion of the Jews from Spain, making it almost certain that they went from the Holy Land to Italy and Spain. Denzil Sebag-Montefiore recalls a winter holiday in Morocco:

> When in Essuera, I asked in my rather halting French where the Mellah used to be; they indignantly told me that there never had been any Jews there. Nevertheless I found an archway that was called Bab el Sebag, the Gate of the Sebags, or to translate the Arabic fully, the Gate of the Dyers, that is, the dyers of cloths.
>
> It is a moot point where the Montefiores went on the destruction of the second Temple. They might have gone to Rome or some other Roman town, as a number of Jews did, or they might have gone first to Spain as did the majority of European Sephardi. The earliest surviving

document concerning the family is a Parochet in red silk richly embroidered by Rachel Olivetti, recording her marriage to Yehuda Montefiore in 1620. This beautiful and well-preserved embroidery now hangs in front of the Ark of the Italian Synagogue in Jerusalem . . .

The Montefiores are known to have lived in Ancona and Pesara. These were then in the Papal States, and when Pope Pius V expelled the Jews from the States of the Church, he exempted Ancona becuse of its trade with the East, which was then almost entirely in Jewish hands.

When a Medici established Livorno, also known as Leghorn, as a city where Jews could live and trade frcely, at no doubt some financial advantage to himself, the Montefiores moved there. It is possible that they took their name from, or gave it to, one of the three towns in Italy called Montefiore. I would add that there is no doubt that they gave their name to the small town of Montefiore – little more than a trading post really – which is in the State of Victoria, Australia.[7]

Sir Joseph Sebag-Montefiore (1822–1903) had a son Arthur (1853–95), who in turn had a son Charles. Charles Edward Sebag-Montefiore was born on 4 March 1884. He was in the Jewish house at Clifton College, Bristol, and later entered Joseph Sebag and Co., eventually becoming a partner and injecting vigour into a firm that had become languid. He was enormously successful and business was his preoccupation – but not to the exclusion of personal charitable work. After an exhausting day in business he would be at meetings or activities associated with his charitable work, notably an approved school, Finnart House near Weybridge, and a club for Jewish boys in East London. All his life Charles Sebag-Montefiore took his duties to the poor seriously. Many Jews did, but often by monetary delegation rather than personal involvement. He was a practitioner. As a young man he used to 'preach' in the East End of London and ran the Victoria Boys Club in Stepney. This was self-effacing work done with dignity, duty and success. This does not do justice to the character of the man. Ruth Sebag-Montefiore, formerly a Magnus and now Denzil's wife, adds a dash of relish:

Charlie [Charles] was a character. In a page of cartoons of City notables he was depicted by the *Illustrated London News* as the worst-dressed man on the London Stock Exchange. [By contrast one of the butlers, a particularly dapper dresser, was known by his cronies in the local pubs as Lord Kensington.] He was original and impulsive and not afraid to speak his mind. Family tradition had it that the OBE he was given for his innovative ideas at Finnart House would have been a knighthood but for the long, heated arguments he carried on with what he called 'those oafs in Whitehall'. He had a powerful personality and was totally unselfconscious, embarrassing his schoolboy sons by his insistence on running his account at Harrods under the name of Julius Caesar and bawling it out in front of them to the astonished assistant. [The reason he wanted to trade under the name of Julius Caesar was because Harrods repeatedly sent the bill to his wife when he had bought her birthday presents there.] He was a popular member of the Spectaclemakers Company, of which he was twice Master, but Muriel's [his wife] uncertain health and her unwillingness to play her part lay behind his decision not to become Lord Mayor, a role that was tailor-made for him.[8]

Charles married Muriel de Pass on 30 April 1913 at the Spanish and Portuguese Sephardi Synagogue at Lauderdale Road, London. The de Pass family stemmed from Jews who were expelled from Spain during the Inquisition and who reappeared in the sixteenth and seventeenth centuries in France, Holland, Italy and England. It is important to record that most Spanish and Portuguese families were forcibly converted to Roman Catholicism in the fifteen century. Many such converts, 'New Christians' or 'Marranos', believed sincerely in the Christian faith but many remained crypto-Jews and only their names were altered to suit the religious and social status of the individual.

Muriel Alice Ruth de Pass was twenty-two when she married Charles, who was twenty-nine. It is not easy to see the attraction of one for the other as they had few shared interests and very different temperaments. He was energetic, bold and practical; she was reticent and romantic. The Montefiores were clannish. The synagogue was close to but not at the centre of their lives. It did, however, affect them deeply. The de Passes were less noticeable practitioners of the Jewish religion. The family had exploded in Victorian England but had almost burnt itself out. The few de Passes that are left are non-practising Jews.

There were three children of the marriage: Denzil (1914), Oliver (1915) and Hugh William, born 12 May 1920. Hugh was named after his mother's brother, William Hugh. He was born at 35 Palace Court in Bayswater, but a few years later the family moved to 2 Palace Green, Kensington, which is now the Israeli Embassy. The house was purchased from Mrs Knight, a writer and one of the early members of the Theosophical Movement in England. But the character of the house, its furniture and decorations, reflected the Queen Anne and Georgian periods so loved by one of the house's former occupants, William Makepeace Thackeray. In fact the original house was gutted and rebuilt to Thackeray's own design. This grand house fed Muriel's romantic imagination. It was from here that Thackeray and his daughter Lady Ritchie would leave each day for a stroll in Kensington Gardens. Was it here that Thackeray penned some of his masterpieces ironically satirizing the sentiments and pretensions of the upper classes?

Charles and Muriel Sebag-Montefiore liked the house for different reasons. For Charles the palatial house represented the opulence of success and rich living. In the vast and lofty dining-room forty-five people could be and were entertained for lunch without the room appearing crowded. For Muriel it was a house of beautiful objects, exquisite décor and romantic atmosphere. In the world of the arts Charles was rather philistine. His wife had eye and ear for *objets d'art*.

Hugh was brought up in an atmosphere of detached love. There was a gap of five years between Oliver and Hugh, so at times it was rather like being an only child. In the house there was a butler, a footman, a parlour maid, two housemaids, a cook, a kitchen maid and a chauffeur. And there was Nanny Lucy Garrard, a rather sad, uneducated, kindly mother-substitute. Hugh remembers best her phrase, 'You little worritt, you!' and adds, 'Her father was a labourer in Norfolk and one of her brothers was a London policeman to whose house I was occasionally taken. She loved children but she had had a sad and lonely life with few satisfactions. Nobody really cared about her.'

Nanny Garrard had to be a mother-substitute for another reason. Hugh's mother was constantly ill and he was asked to be quiet in the house, not easy for a lively boy. Sometimes he was 'bribed' by his father with twopenny chocolate bars. His mother became a manic depressive, at times very unstable. As for the daily routine, Hugh recalls:

Breakfast was brought up, like other meals, up the back staircase by maids . . . Then my father, before he 'went to the office' at around 9.15, would come in briefly and help to teach me to read – I can remember a book *Reading Without Tears* and a large enamel plate with the alphabet on it. Then I would be taken for a walk in Kensington Gardens. Usually a gaggle of nannies got together, and the children in their charge would play with one another, by the Round Pond and the Broad Walk and the Albert Memorial. Back to lunch – it would be brought up again by one of the staff. After lunch I would go out again in Kensington Gardens, and perhaps someone would come back to tea. The circle of acquaintances tended to be restricted to cousins, or at least the children of the 'Cousinhood'. My mother might have come into the nursery around 11 a.m. to see me; and then in the evening I would go down at about 5 p.m. to be with the family, and to stay when my father returned from the office. My brothers led almost entirely separate lives, and I saw little of them. I used to wander down to the servants' hall a bit in the basement.

There were a few excursions from 2 Palace Green, including regular visits for Sunday lunch to 46 Queens Gate, the home of Hugh's maternal grandparents. His grandmother had come from New Zealand, to marry his grandfather, in a windjammer which was six weeks overdue and given up for lost – but she arrived safely. Hugh remembers her as an inoffensive, kindly woman who did her husband's bidding. As for the grandfather,

He was a funny old man. I remember he used to take me off to his study where he donned a skull cap, told me stories of Good Dog Fido and made me try to guess the numbers of banknotes, but wouldn't give me one when I got within one of the numbers.

Denzil adds,

My grandfather was Orthodox and walked to every Sabbath from his house in Queens Gate to synagogue in Maida Vale. The time came when he was too old to do this and he asked the Rabbi if he would rather have him ride to synagogue in his carriage or not attend at all. My grandfather was shocked when the Rabbi said he would rather that he did not attend so he left that synagogue and joined a Liberal one that had no such rules.

What of Judaism in the Sebag-Montefiore home? As a small boy, Hugh was taught the Shema ('Hear O Israel . . .') in Hebrew. He was also taught many of the Psalms and knew some of them by heart. He has some vivid reflections:

If we did not go to synagogue we would usually have family prayers, taken from the Sephardi Prayer Book, morning service, mostly in English, but with a little Hebrew for the more important prayers (such as the Ahlenu) and a little chanting of well-known hymns. My father was very devout, and I noticed that the shape of his bald head seemed to change at family prayers.

My father was on the Machamad of the synagogue (the equivalent of the Parochial Church Council). He later became President of the Lauderdale Road Synagogue in St John's Wood. It was a long way from where we lived and we used to take the car and leave it a discreet distance from the synagogue and walk the last four hundred yards or so, so as not to upset the really strict Jews.

The oldest Sephardi synagogue was opened in Bevis Marks in the City of London in 1702.

Above all there was Passover. The memory of the Seder

Services held at the house of his aunt is still capable of casting its hypnotic spell over Hugh. He was occasionally the youngest boy present and so would be the one who asked the questions, the Manishtanah: 'Why is this night different from other nights?' leading to, 'On all other nights we do not dip the herbs we eat even once, but on this night we dip them twice; on all other nights we may eat either leavened or unleavened bread, but on this night it must all be leavened; on all other nights we may eat all kinds of herbs, but on this night only bitter herbs; on all other nights we eat and drink either sitting or in a leaning position, but on this night we all lean.' And Hugh, the young receiver of tradition, was given his answers by the head of the household. The ceremonies date from antiquity and of course later it was not lost on Hugh that Jesus himself shared in them.

The potent atmosphere of a Jewish Passover is all-pervading. It is a combination of a family celebration with a religious motif at the centre. At the Passover season Elijah's return is hoped for. During the meal there are three large pieces of unleavened bread, one of which is called the *aphikomen*. Just before the Manishtanah, the president breaks a bit off the *aphikomen* and hides it for the children to find. Is it any wonder that symbolism has had a deep effect on Hugh, or that fifty years on he was writing an essay 'Symbols and the Eucharist' for the Church of England Doctrine Commission?

The Day of Atonement, Hugh remembers was an effort.

> We would be in synagogue for most of the day, with an orgy of confession. We would come back in the evening to an enormous meal of cold fried fish.
>
> We used to have our own *lulabs* to swing for the Feast of Tabernacles, but we did not have our own booth as some did.
>
> We used to have the lamps lit for the feast of Chanukah, but we never pretended to give one another Chanukah presents; we had Christmas presents. We also had a traditional Christmas dinner.

As a family, the Sebag-Montefiores appear to have been observant rather than strict. For example, they did not have all the complicated business of providing kosher glasses and plates.

They did not have the ritual search for leavened bread on the day before Passover. Yet they never had pork. Hugh remembers how it turned into ashes in his mouth the first time he felt free to eat it at Rugby School. On the other hand, the family had 'imitation' bacon occasionally, fried egg and fried salt beef! During Passover they would have an egg on potato instead of egg on toast. There was no question of *tephillim*.

Hugh was taught about Jewish history and the Jewish religion by a Miss Manville, a woman who acted as governess to many children of the Cousinhood. He also learnt from her enough 'liturgical Hebrew' to follow services. One of the striking aspects of worship in the synagogue was its informality. While the chanting was proceeding there might be a little conversation with a neighbour. A person might chant something different from what the others were chanting. The men sat downstairs, the women in the gallery. Attending a Jewish wedding for the first time, Hugh noticed that the bride said nothing at all. It had all been arranged in the marriage contract before the service. The spirituality, however, was very real and genuine. This was helped by the minister at Lauderdale Road, the Revd David Bueno de Mesquita, a man with full face and pointed beard, rather like a Spanish inquisitor, whom Hugh remembers with affection:

> He could not preach, but he was a very devout person, and I think that it was not much fun for him being the paid servant of the congregation, as he was cultured, every inch a gentleman, and far more religious than those who employed him. He prepared me for my Barmitzvah when I was thirteen. For one's Barmitzvah one is 'called up' to the place where the law is read by the minister, and one has to chant one's portion oneself. This was difficult for me because a) the Hebrew is written on vellum and has no points (vowels) and b) I couldn't sing. However, I got by. Then there was a great reception at home and I got lots and lots of presents. It was a kind of way of showing respect to my parents, I think.

Although the tentacles of the Cousinhood drew others into the Sebag–Montefiore family, it was still a tight, even claustrophobic community. It is interesting that the Sebag-Montefiores never mixed with the Montefiores, so Hugh never met the man who, like Moses Montefiore, influenced him at a distance. Claude Goldsmid Montefiore (1858–1938) had written much on the New Testament. He was respected and liked by Gentiles, but remained a Jew. More than that, he showed great spiritual courage in founding the Liberal Jewish Movement in England, challenging the orthodoxy of the day. Hugh remembered him in his Montefiore Lecture:

> Like Claude, I had some thoughts of being a rabbi, but like him I abandoned the idea because it seemed too narrow for me, however high the calling itself might be . . . He [adopted] a progressive view of revelation which he had found in the writings of Christian Old Testament scholars. But for him this was not just a matter of scholarship. It was a matter of practical and personal religion. The disuse of Hebrew in services, a relaxed observance of the Jewish ritual law, a liberal view of the inspiration of the Bible – these were not just ideas, they were part of his life, and part of the practical programme of the Liberal Jewish Synagogue. It created the same kind of scandal among Jews as radical Christianity can cause among traditional Christians. It incurred the hostility of the highest Jewish religious authority in the land, the Chief Rabbi. This hostility upset Claude, but it did not make him waver.

Claude Goldsmid Montefiore was a considerable figure, a great man. For him Jesus was a great teacher but in no sense God. He wanted Jews to read the New Testament. Divine revelation was to be found in it for 'all light does not shine through one window, even if one of the other windows is a Christian one'. He accepted the results of modern scholarship and could pay tribute to the teachings of Jesus at the same time as vigorously defending Judaism from Christian misconceptions, especially concerning the Torah. His liberal Judaism was there to stop the rot, to offer a religion which was not Zionist, and was not orthodox and irrational and uncritical.

In some of his writings he illustrates with great force something Christians forget in their understanding of God. 'Thou shalt love the Lord thy God with all thy heart and soul and might' means much more than the words suggest. To old Israelites the *heart* included more than a physical organ. It also implied intelligence. In the same way the *soul* also meant the life, the vital forces of man. Read in this way, the words have a fuller, richer, all-embracing meaning.

The spirit of Claude is evident in modern British Jewry. His view was that the English Jew should be taught to look on England and not on Palestine as his national home. It was here in England that his destiny was cast. This may have put him considerably at odds with other great minds in Jewry, but it is a prevailing view in this country today.

Hugh Montefiore says that what he most admired in Claude was 'his reverent search for truth wherever it may be found and a personal devotion and commitment as a Jew, despite his many contacts with Christians'.

Happy childhood memories are associated with the Sebag-Montefiores' holiday home, Tygh-na-Bruaich, Dinnet, Aberdeenshire. It represented liberation from London and the Cousinhood. There was a larger social group and female society other than cousins. There was tennis, picnic dances, reeling, and the Aboyne Games were the event of the season. The house stood in an acre of land and its rooms had pine walls and ceilings. The water would often run out and the family were wrongly credited with washing up in Malvern water. Hugh recalls that the telephone system was on a 'party line' so no conversations were private and occasionally a remark would result in a hollow laugh on the line.

Hugh's first school was Wilkinson's in Orme Square. He went to this preparatory school when he was six and, with a friend called Friedlander, formed a studious liaison.

I can remember our legs being roasted with a hot poker for not joining in ragging. It was considered important at home that I should return to school as though nothing had happened and I only realized later that this would have been a kind of inchoate anti-Semitism. Of this early period I can also remember the one and only occasion that I was beaten at home – for assaulting the cook, who had declined to vote at a General Election!

In 1929 Hugh went to Beaudesert Park School at Minchin-hampton in Gloucestershire. The purpose of this school was to prepare pupils for public school life, extending their horizons at the same time as educating them, but not cramming them with knowledge. The daughter of the headmaster in Hugh's time, Mrs Enid Keyte (née Richardson) remembers Hugh as a tall, good-looking boy, full of life and vitality, into everything, and succeeding in most things he took on. The school magazine confirms that impression. Hugh became head prefect and head boy. He was in the soccer, rugger and cricket teams, boxed and played golf. School photographs show a boy with keen eyes and a touch of flamboyance about him. There were opportunities for his flamboyance on stage and in debate.

In a one-act 'crook-comedy' *Shivering Shocks* the school magazine for 1933 records:

> H. S.-Montefiore played the part of Hughes the scientist, who had discovered a new formula for the extermination of the enemy in war, consequently he had to play the role of an extremely nervous man, who would not be at his ease until the war office recognized the value of his secret. Montefiore showed excellent judgement in the amount of nervousness to be displayed.

Hugh's first experience of appearing in print was reporting the activities of the Debating Society in the school magazine, not an easy task, as he was himself one of the most effective debaters. There were six debates each term and in 1932 he reports himself as breaking the record by speaking for fourteen minutes in a debate that 'India should be given back to the Indians'. He had a more difficult task the following year when he proposed the motion that 'The Nazi movement in Germany is mistaken' and attacked the Germans on their disgraceful treatment of the Jews. The motion was ably opposed with persuasive facts. Herr Hitler was a patriot; Germany was in a sad plight.

The school provided scholars for most of the leading public schools. Hugh was on the scholarship roll, but he went to Rugby in 1933 where he sat for and gained an entrance scholarship.

2 The Vision

Montefiore, or rather Sebag-Montefoire, for the 'Sebag' had not yet been dropped, spent a year in a 'waiting house' at Rugby before entering School House in 1934, where the headmaster was also housemaster.

Montefiore was fortunate in entering School House under Percy Hugh Beverley Lyon, headmaster from 1931 to 1948. The tradition of Olympian aloofness of the headmasters of Rugby had been broken under a previous regime, that of Albert Augustus David (1910–21) who became Bishop of Liverpool.

Lyon had been a scholar under David and, unlike David, had the personality and ability to reform without tears. Lyon was a layman, previously Rector of the Edinburgh Academy, and quickly gathered round him staff of outstanding quality. Such an appointment would have been unthinkable in an earlier time. Headmasters of Rugby were generally ordained and two of them, Archibald Campbell Tait (1842–50) and Frederick Temple (1858–69) became Archbishops of Canterbury.

The regime at Rugby was hard, but not untypical of many other public schools of the period. There was a cold bath each morning, fag calls, lots of prep (at one stage Montefiore had to learn the whole of *Lycidas*) and games. Patrick Rodger, a contemporary and later Bishop of Oxford, says: 'Rugby was certainly no place for sluggards, and the general atmosphere was one of energy and purposefulness – just right for someone of Hugh Montefiore's temperament.'

Montefiore has always plunged head-first into the activities of mind, spirit and body offered to him. Academically he gravitated towards classics which have always provided the language of theology, philosophy and ethics. This was facilitated by some knowledge of Greek learnt at his preparatory school. He particularly enjoyed the Greek political leader and orator, Demosthenes; the first of the Greek tragic poets, Aeschylus; and Plato. In another sphere Shakespeare was a favourite.

A major influence for good on the classical side was Roger Roberts. Then still in his twenties Roberts, who was later ordained, went on to be headmaster of Blundell's and then editor of the *Church Times*. For a period he had the tenure of the Mastership of Upper Bench (1934–40) which, as he recalls, 'put me in sole charge throughout the week of twenty or so brilliantly gifted boys, nearly all of whom duly got themselves elected to Open Awards at Oxford and Cambridge'. This number included four boys who were to become, and remain, close friends – Robin Barbour, later Professor of New Testament at the University of Aberdeen and a Moderator of the General Assembly of the Church of Scotland; Hubert Monroe, later a QC and expert in the law of taxation; Patrick Rodger; and Montefiore.

Patrick Rodger remembers Roger Roberts as being full of fire and enthusiasm that communicated itself to his pupils. As are most brilliant scholars and Platonists, Roberts was also a hard taskmaster and cuttingly dismissive of signs of frivolity. From him Montefiore learnt standards of intellectual and moral rigour. Roberts stopped Montefiore learning the piano, saying that together with his arts interests it was incompatible with working for an Oxford scholarship. It was not a very personal relationship, but the influence was real and lasting.

A contemporary of Montefiore at Rugby, David Ashcroft, who was later a master there before moving to Cheltenham College as headmaster, provides a picture of life at Rugby around the late 1930s, and of Montefiore:

> Rugby itself had a Spartan tradition, brain, brawn and good behaviour being the values; the Arnold religious tradition remained, but of spirituality there was, I think, very little. There was a strong emphasis on hard work, but scholars were channelled very firmly into either classics or mathematics; there were some brilliant and rather dotty

scientists on the staff, but Hugh . . . will have had precisely one term each of physics, chemistry and biology during his whole time (which perhaps may seem odd in the light of his episcopal penchant for being very *au fait* with things scientific!)

Hugh was in our eyes a very earnest and hard-working type (and that would not be a pejorative judgement), a respectable but not brilliant scholar, and not outstanding by the standard of those days, when the classical Upper Bench could be expected to produce six or seven Oxbridge scholars a year . . .

Under the liberalizing headmastership of Hugh Lyon, Rugby was shedding its philistinism, and music under Ken Stubbs, and art under Talbot Kelly, were into a golden period, symbolized by such as Marcus Dods (the conductor) – a top classical scholar, captain of the XV, concert pianist and with a marvellous bass voice.

Montefiore adds: 'I spent most of my spare time in the Art Schools, learning a lot from Talbot Kelly. I wasn't very talented, but I loved drawing. I did oil painting, water colours, etching and pottery. It is a great sadness to me that during my ministry I have never seemed to have the time to keep all this up.'

Montefiore never regarded himself as being as brilliant a scholar as his friends, but he was better at games, even if one verdict of his performance was 'splendidly eager, clumsy but gutsy'. In the record for the School XV (1938) the following appears: 'His style may look unorthodox, but in defence particularly, it is most effective, this showing in the tight and loose play. Is apt to be erratic, but he generally contrives to do more harm to his opponents than to his own side.'

These sporting characteristics spill over into traits of personality which became permanent. Roger Roberts remembers Montefiore displaying

strong and indeed passionate enthusiasm . . . which may perhaps have been both his strength and weakness . . . [In later life] there was never any doubt of his sincerity or his commitment. His wisdom and judgement were perhaps

sometimes more open to question. His popularity with his
schoolfellows (which I well remember) predicted the wide
appeal which he proved later to have in the Church. The
combination of eagerness and intellectual ability was
irresistible.

Above all there was the influence of the headmaster, Hugh
Lyon. He appeared to take a special interest in the educational
progress and welfare of Montefiore. Sometimes it was necessary to apply brakes to Montefiore's absorption with work.
There was a reason for this. One early mid-term report, 'Care-
less, slapdash and takes no pains,' made him so angry that he
has been a 'workaholic' ever since.

Hugh Lyon had civilized the regime and for Montefiore it
was a time of opening up to friendships. Peter Falk, housemaster of Tudor House (1949–64), suggests that it was Hugh Lyon
who was responsible for the 'flowering of Hugh'. He had
widened the system of education and given it a humanity which
had previously been lacking:

> This he did, partly by example, but far more by his policy
> of *laissez-faire*, relying on the ability and initiative of the
> quite exceptionally gifted set of masters, whom Vaughan
> had appointed. Music, the Art School, natural history and
> other hobbies, politics (especially the League of Nations)
> and social work occupied a boy's out-of-school life, along
> with games, which at that period in many public schools
> were the only activity officially encouraged.

> Hugh was outstanding in his ability to take advantage of
> this environment. My first clear recollection of him was in
> the scouts. My picture of Hugh is as a senior scout at a
> camp at Wray Castle on Lake Windermere: a tall, rather
> gangling figure, with his stockings fallen down to his
> ankles and altogether rather dishevelled, smiling and
> impetuous and utterly charming, and probably having lost
> one or more of the youngsters whom he was supposed to
> be looking after.

At one stage, two lessons a week of 'general culture' replaced
two classics lessons. During one term general culture was to

take the form of an introduction to biology, to be taught by Peter Falk, as the junior biologist. The class included Patrick Rodger, Robin Barbour and Montefiore. Peter Falk recollects:

> With so little time available, practical biology seemed to me out of the question and instead I prepared a course of lessons on the nature of life and on scientific method, illustrated by the work of Darwin, Pasteur and Mendel. The first lesson proceeded in deadly silence, as did the second, and so to discover if anything was getting across to my audience, I started the third with a written test. To my amazement, many of the answers, including those of Rodger and Barbour, were quite perfect and it was clear that they could have as easily won university awards in biology as they were destined to in classics, but I was still puzzled by their complete silence. Whether I liked it or not, my lessons with my professional biologists invariably developed into a discussion and they and I both seemed to gain in consequence. After the tests I asked Pat Rodger, whom I knew best of the bunch, why they listened in such perfect silence, while the professional biologists whom I taught questioned every statement that I made so that every lesson became lively. After a little thought, he replied with a slight smile: 'Well, you see, our only teacher is Mr Roberts and his teaching is so perfect that he makes every point absolutely clear and we have no need to question anything.' When I returned the question papers and congratulated the form on the result, I made a plea, if not for questions, at least for comments. It was then that Hugh comes back into the story, for from then on, it was he that took the lead in trying to start discussions. His test paper had not been quite as perfect as many of the others and he may have asked his question because he was aware of not exactly following what I was saying, but I had the impression that he was more motivated by good manners and kindness to me.

One feature of school life has so far been omitted, that of the chapel. Montefiore, being a Jew, did not attend chapel or have any 'Christian' religious education. Instead, a teacher came down from London each week to teach him and another boy, Prins, Hebrew and the Jewish faith. Occasionally Montefiore would go to London in order to keep a Jewish feast. His Jewishness fascinated his friends, without any thought being given to its implications. There was no anti-Semitism. Occasionally there were jokes, and once a group practised on him a great hoax. Montefiore was the proud possessor of an inherited half-hunter, which wouldn't go. This worried him. David Ashcroft, one of the group, recalls:

> We teased him that the God of Abraham could not answer his prayers and that he should try the Christian God; a prayer session was set up. Meanwhile the watch was filched and despatched to a watchmaker in the town, and prayer was answered; the miracle was wrought. It was widely – but perhaps not too seriously – believed that this was part of his conversion process.

In July 1976 when Robin Barbour presented Montefiore for the degree of Doctor of Divinity *honoris causa* at Aberdeen, he began an eloquent presentation speech in this way:

> Forty years ago, a Jewish boy at a school in England had a vision, rather like St Paul. Twenty years ago, people would have said that such things don't happen any longer in the Western world, or if they do, they represent the harmless eccentricities of those queer people who are religiously inclined. Today, people might rather say that these things happen all right, but that they are purely internal and personal, to be achieved by those techniques of the cultivation of the inner self which have come flooding in on the tides of the new religiosity from Asia. In this case both views would be wrong. The results of this particular vision are visible, palpable and influential, all six feet three inches of them; they are extremely practical, versatile, vigorous and down-to-earth. They are, indeed, a bishop.

That is to anticipate.

One day a sixteen-year-old Jewish boy was sitting alone in

his study, feeling rather melancholy, thinking of nothing. Suddenly he saw a distant figure in white, whom he instinctively knew to be Jesus, beckoning towards him. The figure said, 'Follow me.' He went to bed but he could not sleep. John Hoskyns, another schoolfriend who was later ordained, writes: 'He woke me up in my dormitory and said, "I have seen the Lord!" I told him to go back to bed and go to sleep.'

But Montefiore could not sleep. What he knew at the time was that:

> In the morning I was a Jew and by the evening I had become a Christian as well. I knew with absolute certitude that God had taken hold of my life; that Jesus was my Lord and that I must follow in His Way. That was almost all that I knew about my faith; and at the time it was more than enough. The next day I broke my Good News to my housemaster.[1]

Here was someone who had never read the New Testament nor taken part in Christian worship yet who was granted a vision of the person of Jesus.

Breaking the 'Good News' at Rugby was comparatively easy compared with giving this 'Bad News' (and the capials are not misplaced) to his family. They were devastated. Yet his parents continued to show their affection for him. Although they could not be expected to understand or sympathize, they ensured that relations were not extinguished. His father never withdrew his paternal hand. This was not the case with his wider family or with his two brothers. The curtain came down thick, fast and, almost, for good. This was apostasy. Hugh had besmirched the family name. The hurt to the family was deep and seemed for a long time unendurable. It is a mark of the greatness of the personalities concerned that they were able to heal the breach with the passing of the years.

Meanwhile, at school Montefiore began to read the Gospels for the first time. His approach was one of joyous enthusiasm, not unctuous earnestness. There was something else, too, caught by John Hoskyns – a kind of 'holy fear':

> He was different because he stood aside from the generally

accepted way of life and was not prepared to go along with anything which was not true or which was in any way bogus. He was prepared to stand up for that which he knew was right – but this in itself was not what frightened me. It was the *humility* he mixed with all this passion for truth and justice. He 'mucked in' totally with all we did in the House, yet he never compromised his own identity. Being totally involved, he could say, 'But John that is a nonsense,' in a quiet voice which had a determination to swim against the tide and do something to put the nonsense right. He could not bear anything which was not real or true or honest.

Conversely he was attracted to anything real and sincere. I believe that is why he was attracted to Christ. To go against one's Jewish roots, and such aristocratic Jewish roots as his, took enormous moral courage. But the God whom Hugh already knew demanded that he follow wherever truth led him, whatever the cost. But I stress that this was done with utter humility and a humour which, behind the twinkling smile and half-open mouth of astonishment and wonder, reflected an amusement which I hope and expect to see one day on the 'face' of our Creator, as all controversy is resolved in gorgeous and peaceful merriment.

When someone has such a startling conversion, it is not easy to ascertain what subliminal factors contributed to it. It is possible that the quiet pervasive Christian influence of Hugh Lyon may have been a factor, however small. Montefiore used to stay with the Lyons in the summer holidays, when on occasion they took over a prep school for their extended family. 'Public school' religion was an ambiguous influence on anyone at Rugby, although these particular years supplied a number of scholars who subsequently became bishops.[2] There were three clergy on the staff. One was Owen Fulljames, who had been a naval chaplain. He was of a sunny temperament and evangelical fervour and physical robustness took the place of intellectual or theological expertise. Another was Ernest Frederick Waddy, an amusing and rather coarse Australian, more renowned for having kept wicket for New South Wales than for what his dog collar represented. The third was Richard Broxton, a bouncy little man of the hail-fellow-well-met variety. None of these had much influence on Montefiore, although he benefited from a visit to South Wales led by Fulljames. A group of boys was taken to Pontlottyn in the Rhymney Valley. They stayed with unemployed mining families and helped them work a narrow seam which surfaced at the head of the valley. It was the beginning of the stirrings of a social conscience in Montefiore, who stayed with John Hoskyns in a very poor house. Their host was the night soil carter for all the privies in the area. They also went to the Durham coalfields. C.A. Alington gave them an interview looking every bit a 'prince' sitting in his study.

What was to be done about this new Christian? It was decided that there should be no instruction in school. Instead, Montefiore was sent to the Rector of Rugby, Richard Brook, who was also Archdeacon of Coventry. Brook instructed Montefiore, who was subsequently baptized in Rugby parish church and confirmed a year later in the school chapel. Brook was later Bishop of St Edmundsbury and Ipswich. When he died his widow sent Montefiore his pectoral cross. By that time Montefiore had himself become a bishop.

Montefiore played a fairly full part in school activities. He was a member of the OTC and on one occasion they were inspected by the memorably named Field Marshal Sir Archibald Montgomery-Massingberd, complete with white walrus moustache. It was 1937 and he assured the OTC that the next war would be won by the bayonet. David Ashcroft remembers 'standing in the front rank with Hugh behind me and, having failed to secure my bayonet for Present Arms, it sailed over my shoulder and struck Hugh in the chest! Luckily it was blunt!'

In the OTC Montefiore was placed in charge of the aeroplane section, but when an actual plane arrived he found he knew nothing about it and thereafter retreated into the Scouts. In the spring of 1938 he and Robin Barbour went on a tour of Greece in a party of about twenty from a number of public schools, under the guidance of a couple of masters from Eton. There was another holiday in Northern Ireland with Hubert Monroe. In 1937 he had spent a cycling holiday in Normandy and Brittany with his cousins Catherine and Anne Joseph, their

mother, Madge Waley Joseph, and another cousin, Esther Salaman. Catherine Joseph (now Dennis) recalls that

> Hugh kept a diary of this holiday, the only one of us who
> did. I think he must have told me one entry: 'Cousin
> Madge and the others keep asking me what I want to be
> when I grow up.' (He was then at Rugby, which had also
> been both my brothers' school.) He then wrote, and I
> think he must have shown it to me, 'I wonder what they
> would say if I told them I wanted to be a Church of
> England preacher.' At the time I thought this was a joke. I
> had no idea it was a true reflection of his true thoughts.

Montefiore never regarded himself as brilliant. He gained his
Rugby XV colours in his last year but academically he had to
work hard to achieve success. As Head of House he com-
manded respect by his energy and by balancing thought and
action. Comments in his last school report include some interesting observations:

Scripture	Interested and sensible: prone to digressions
Prose	Sometimes here he tries to be a little too clever and loses the necessary simplicity . . . but there is good evidence of all-round intellectual ability.
Verse	Enterprising and fluent – occasionally rather too much of both – but almost always interesting.

In 1938 he gained a major open scholarship at St John's
College, Oxford, and left Rugby in December, taking a one-
term post at the Dragon School, Oxford. The summer term
was spent at Lausanne University, learning French (German
was out of the question for a Jew), and he returned to England
as the war clouds were darkening over Europe.

3 War

Montefiore was lonely. He knew no one at St John's when he arrived as a freshman in September 1939. Most of his family made him feel an outcast. His conversion *had* cost something. He did not feel he had ceased to be Jewish by becoming Christian as well. Although there were Jewish Christians, there was and is a great psychological barrier which prevents many Jews from taking seriously the claims of Christ. It means 'going over to the enemy'. In the not-too-distant past, for a Jew to be baptized would have brought material advancement. He would have been allowed into university and so have the sort of career which would otherwise be denied him. Loyalty and solidarity in suffering made Jews prefer to ignore Christ, who had brought such terrible suffering to them. This same attitude, although buried in the unconscious, still operates today. In 1939 the holocaust was in the future, but there were other scars. With his particular ancestry, Montefiore could not help but feel that the emancipation of the Jews in England was recent. They were admitted to the bar in 1833, to the shrievalty in 1835 and to other municipal offices in 1845. Sir Moses Montefiore had been the first Jew to receive a baronetcy from Queen Victoria in 1847. It was not until 1858 that the House of Lords finally permitted a Jew to take his seat in Parliament. In 1939 anti-Semitism still remained in the country. The Jewishness of Montefiore could not but be sensitive to this even if he had become a Christian, although he was not personally the subject of anti-Semitism.

He was one of eight freshmen entering St John's to study classics. It was the strangest of atmospheres in which to begin one's studies. The war, to everyone's surprise, had not yet started in earnest, and at Oxford there was a mixture of normal and wartime conditions. The latter included fire-watching duties both in colleges and in departments.

Montefiore had a gorgeous room on the ground floor of the Canterbury Quad, so-called because it was Laud's benefaction. Douglas Nicoll recalls memories of that time:

The winter of 1939–40 was cold and for those like Hugh and the writer, who had rooms on the north side of the Canterbury Quad, there was a period when the large jug in our bedrooms filled with water to wash in was frozen solid for three weeks. There were hot baths, but in the far south-west corner of the Front Quad, and early morning baths were for a time not much in fashion, either.

The fact that so many of the seniors had already left to take part in the war meant that some of the normal activities of men in senior years no longer took place, and that the 1939 freshmen represented a much more significant section of the College, at least numerically, than usual . . . One evening in the summer term, one of the Freshmen discovered in his rooms the bows and arrows of the Archery Club and we all took them out and shot them down the garden. Hugh with his height immediately fancied himself as an archer and presented a splendid sight holding the six-foot bow at an angle to achieve maximum height and distance. It was he, I think, who was successful in shooting an arrow from the Garden Front clear out over the wall at the other end, into the Parks Road . . .

Hugh learned his set books by recalling the precise point on the page at which he had made an annotation or translation of a rare word – a useful trick of visual memory which has no doubt been useful to him since. Most will remember him as an undergraduate as a genial fellow with an occasional whimsical turn of phrase, and the occasional idea designed to shock.

Montefiore was reading a shortened one-year 'war' version of classics. His tutor was an extraordinary man called Meurig-Davies. The tutoring was good, since his knowledge of the classics was deep and wide. He was not one to insist on attendance at lectures, except for his own, which were on the *Orations* of Lysias. However, he became increasingly strange, lived in his garden shed and eventually 'went off his head'.

Montefiore's 'moral tutor' was Colin Roberts, the elder brother of his old Rugby master, Roger Roberts. Colin Roberts was a famous papyrologist and was engaged in cypher work during the war. Chapel life in the college was dull and the chaplain, Stanley Lawrence Greenslade (later Regius Professor of Ecclesiastical History in the University of Oxford), was too shy to have anything to offer to an exuberant and intellectual convert. However, at the University Church of St Mary the Virgin an exciting ministry had begun under Theodore Richard ('Dick') Milford. He made an immediate and lasting impression on Montefiore. Very quickly he was drawn into the Student Christian Movement, where he became an intercollegiate secretary.

The Joint (Women's) President of the Student Christian Movement for that year was Elisabeth Paton. Montefiore was immediately attracted by her brains, her beauty and her lipstick! She stood out and soon he was in love. The feeling was mutual. But all too soon they were parted by the war.

War had been declared before Montefiore went to Oxford, while he was staying with an old schoolfriend, Laurie Nicholson, on his father's farm in Oxfordshire. Nicholson's father, who used to walk nude about the house, was a bluff and kindly old man who had dividends from Nicholson's brewery and was then a gentleman farmer. Montefiore was in agony trying to make up his mind whether or not he ought to fight. The pacifist argument weighed very heavily with him, yet he could not contemplate standing to one side whilst his fellow Jews were being butchered in Hitler's Germany. So he joined up, got the King's shilling and spent his year in Oxford before being called up.

His army training began on Blubberhouses Moor, near Harrogate. This was a very different life from Oxford. The barrack room was like a school dormitory, except that the soldiers had to fold their kit in ridiculously formalized ways and do such extraordinary things as paint the coal black. There was lots of marching on the square and night guards on the bleak Yorkshire moors. The only other Oxford man there was Gunner Denis Healey, with whom Montefiore played chess and dominoes when they fell out for a smoke.

After a few months Montefiore went on to the Officer Cadet Training Unit (OCTU). It was unfortunate that the commandant of OCTU was an uncle, Colonel Thomas Henry Sebag-Montefiore DSO, MC, who was a great strong character. He ensured that there was no favouritism, to the point of giving his nephew the worst jobs and the hardest of times.

One of the instructors was (Sir) Ralph Verney, who remembers the OCTU course as being 'pretty fierce and furious':

> I had to teach these eager and intelligent young men, as officer cadets, the rudiments of gunnery and basic military discipline, which I had only learnt myself a year ago. Hugh was one of my star pupils: I think he passed out top; and as the Colonel [Sebag-Montefiore] had previously been Adjutant of the Royal Bucks Yeomanry, he and I arranged for Hugh to be posted to that regiment.

Montefiore was an exception to the general rule of recruitment, being one of the earliest officers to enter the regiment from outside Buckinghamshire. The regiment was formed as the Royal Bucks Hussars by the Marquess of Buckingham at Stowe in 1795. As a volunteer regiment it was involved with the Chartists (1848) and saw action in the Boer War under Lord Chesham. In the First World War it took part in the last cavalry charge in Palestine (in which a Rothschild was killed). In 1922 it was converted from cavalry to field artillery.

Montefiore recalls that when he joined the regiment,

> It was moved to the environs of York for training. I was at Gate Helmsley under a Colonel Vanderfelt, a London broker who knew my family. The colonel was William Whiteley, MP, a fearful man of whom we were all frightened. He was killed when his aeroplane, in which he was flying back from somewhere with General Sikorski, was shot down. The officers tended to represent beer!

(Tetley, second-in-command; Bonsor [Watneys] and Hanbury.) But there were others, like the Weatherby brothers, of the famous horseracing firm.

He was then posted to Stockton-in-the-Forest as second lieutenant in D Troop of 472 Battery under Ralph Merton, brother of the artist, who boasted he would make a fortune from seaweed after the war, and did. They lived in an enormous house with an elderly widow who had no idea until she was told that she had a priceless claret on the premises. Life was enjoyably high.

Unfortunately for them, they were put on alert to go abroad, and travelled to Tewkesbury to be kitted out. Then it was to the docks and away. Here are some of Montefiore's recollections:

> We took over a large ship. The officers were all right – they had cabins a pair – but the men seem to me to live in atrocious conditions below deck on hammocks. We thought we were going to Persia, but ended up in Bombay because of the Indian civil disobedience campaign. We went almost over to South America to avoid U boats, called in for a couple of nights at Cape Town and only had one day on shore leave; the rest of the time we seemed to run up hills in gas masks, as it was thought, quite erroneously, that the previous convoy had lost Singapore through lack of fitness. In India we went into a decent peacc-time camp at Ahmednagar to guard Nehru, imprisoned there, about seventy miles from Poona on the Western Ghats. There was a Tower of Silence (Parsee) just beyond the camp, and one used to see the vultures flying to pick over the corpses! I remember playing in the finals of five-a-side rugger in Bombay, ground brick hard. The moustaches we grew on board on the way out mercifully disappeared. We were not allowed to see much of civilian life in India, except for the occasional foray into the bazaar or trip down to Bombay, when we stayed at the Taj Mahal Hotel – very posh. But the sight of people sleeping on the pavement, and the masses of beggars, was extraordinary. By contrast, a train stopped at a station for the officer class to have a meal and when we had finished, it resumed its

journey. I was first brought up against gambling by the Colonel Whiteley betting with the Quarter Master Fenn the number of nails in his boots, etc. I found I could not keep up with mess gambling. The officer with whom I was sharing a room got infantile paralysis and died. The Colonel died on a journey home by air, and was succeeded by Mark Maunsell, a Major RA at Divisional HQ and a regular officer.

There was a plan to retake Akyab in the Arakan. The Indian Army was to take the land to Foul Point, the end of a peninsular, and 6 Brigade was to do a combined operation across the sea to Akyab. We went down to Juhu beach near Bombay and then across India, via Calcutta. In order to make tea for the troop we drew off hot water from the engine, and then had to wait until it got up steam again! The Arakan campaign was a disaster.

When we got back from this abortive expedition, I had been made Survey Officer – the person responsible for seeing that all guns were exactly on line. It was not easy in the jungle, where tin could make the local variation up to 13°. We had to use azimuths, that is to say, take readings from the sun, as on ships. I had the Survey Section to assist me. I was also responsible for the 'Meteor Telegram', that is, predicting temperature and wind at various heights, which affected the trajectory of the shell. I made my own anemometer, and used balloons filled with oxygen to find out wind speed at various heights.

When we got back we had 100 per cent malaria casualities as – typical Army – the Mepacrine ran out and the suppressed malaria broke out. We were sent to a hill resort, Mahableshwar, shut up for the war, to recover. I enjoyed myself making a survey map of the holiday resort. It was high up in the mountains. We returned to base, and did more training at Ahmednagar.

I was deeply grateful for my war service. In the first place, it enabled me to grow up. Secondly I learnt about pastoral care. We were an old-fashioned regiment – woe betide me if I did not know the names and ages of all my men's children, about their wives and homes. And we could never have our own meals until (i) the vehicles had been washed down or maintained after use and (ii) the men had had their own meals. This was excellent training for the ministry. And then thirdly, I learnt the meaning of fellowship in a big way, between all ranks.

There were times when I was frightened. I remember when I was a troop captain going along in the open in a Bren carrier [light armoured carrier] when being mortared – very unpleasant, and also feeling very unsafe when seconded to the Nepalese State Forces on one occasion. Even in the middle of a battle the mess came out, the boxes were undone and an excellent curry consumed, with firing going on all round.

Mercifully I kept very fit throughout, apart from a nasty go of dysentery in Kashmir – I was on a houseboat, and I discovered later that the houseboy used the lake both for sewage and as drinking water. 'M and B' put that right. The nearest I came to death was at Kohima, when we were pinned to the ground with sniper fire. I found my pullover nicked by a bullet, and my Commanding Officer, lying next to me, was shot in the lung and killed.

We were fed very well throughout, and in the Kohima campaign our rations and post used to float down by parachute. We tended to order luxuries from the Army and Navy to rain down upon us, and I remember having the airmail edition of *The Times*, and of all things the *Journal of Roman Studies* actually made its appearance in this way!

The Kohima campaign was an important one. General John Grover, commander of 2 Division, had been ordered to relieve Kohima, open up Imphal and to save British India from falling into the hands of the Japanese. He was opposed by the formidable General Sato under whose command were determined and brave soldiers who fought tenaciously almost to the very end, despite lack of any support or reinforcements from their rear.

Montefiore had experienced the frightful Arakan campaign but it was nothing to Kohima. As a gunner he recalls working in the most inhospitable territory –

the dense jungle so steep that in the rains one had to haul

oneself up by rope; the heat, the humidity, the altitude;
and the *khud* with *nalas* nearly a thousand feet below, the
teeming monsoon rain, the single road for all motorized
traffic, with mules or Nagas bringing supplies when you
left the road, or parachutes from the air which sometimes
overshot their target; and above all the murderous fire-
power of deep Japanese bunkers with interlocking fields of
fire, to say nothing of such minor inconveniences as jungle
leeches – there were sixty-five days of that battle as tough
as anything that the Somme had seen in the First World
War.

Victory was at the cost of 1,287 lives.

What emerges about Montefiore's wartime experiences and
how was he affected by them? By nature, temperature and
outlook he seemed somewhat out of place in a combatant unit.
Although he acquitted himself competently and with resolution
and courage when the time for action came, at first he seemed
rather vague and other-worldly and was ragged for it in the
mess. He was cultivated, sensitive and intelligent, and not
naturally suited to army life.

There were no hints pointing to his later development. He
was quiet and self-effacing, quite different from his later propensity to court publicity and 'show off'. People who knew
him during the war refer to him as courteous, likeable, a little
impractical, tolerant, long-suffering under provocation, yet
also thought to be a man of settled principles even if it was not
clear what those principles were.

Montefiore had indeed been much exercised as to what he
should do with his life. One thing was certain. He was going to
marry Elisabeth Paton if he got home (he never thought he
would). Ordination had been in his mind, but sometimes
drifted out of it. Was it really what God wanted him to do?
There was something else, too, common to many men who
were ordinands at that time. During the war the question of
whether or not they would survive was uppermost in their
minds, and thinking about, let alone planning for, the future
was an unaffordable luxury. Then came the Arakan campaign.
After that, he knew that he must be ordained, feeling a relent-
less inner pressure to proceed. Without delay he wrote to

Kenneth Riches, Director of Service Ordination Candidates and a former chaplain of Sidney Sussex College, Cambridge. This made him the laugh of the mess.

Religion in wartime had not been impressive, although there had been some moving Holy Communion services in the open air, albeit with few comminicants. The regiment's chaplains were Enoch Davies and James Schuster (later Bishop of St John's, South Africa). Montefiore was not impressed by either of them.

4 Oxford and Colloquy

Elisabeth Paton's father, William Paton (1886–1943), was a Presbyterian minister and Secretary of the International Missionary Council. He has been described as

> a singularly massive and rock-like character; firm, even exuberant, in his own clear Christian faith. He was also supremely tolerant and understanding; he could appreciate the persons and the position of Christians of all types, and he was singularly trusted by all. When he died no man in the country had his wide and profound knowledge of the Christian Church in all its branches throughout the world.[1]

William Paton was a man who devoted his life to the search for a means to Christian unity. He was an ecumenist before the word achieved popular currency and, it may be added, when there were more risks in having an ecumenical outlook. He was a personal friend of the leaders of most Churches, notably of William Temple, Archbishop of Canterbury.

His visits abroad and his deep commitment to India gave him a sage-like stature, yet he was rarely in the public eye, usually operating effectively behind the scenes. He was Joint Secretary of the World Council of Churches at its inception.

His wife Grace was the daughter of a Presbyterian minister and had at one time been secretary to Ramsay Macdonald. She became an Anglican; but ecumenism was strained to the utter-most when she later became a Roman Catholic in 1934. This saddened William Paton, deeply as he loved her. In the 1930s the Roman Catholic Church was outside ecumenical persuasion.

There were six Paton children who were all brought up in the Church of England. Two became Anglican priests: David, a well-known ecumenist neither fully nor properly used in the Church; and Michael, Archdeacon of Sheffield until his retire-ment in 1988. William was knighted and was a distinguished Professor of Pharmacology in the University of Oxford. James worked in the Ghanaian civil service before becoming warden of the International Students' Hostel in London; and Catherine became the owner of a bookshop.

Then there was Elisabeth. She was reading English at Oxford when Montefiore met her. She went on to get a first in English and then trained to become an almoner at University College Hospital. It must have been a shock to her parents when she took Hugh home. She was always glad that she did this before Hugh left for service overseas, for by the time the war was over, her father was dead.

Elisabeth and Hugh became engaged before he left England, but he said nothing to his parents about Elisabeth until he was on his ship. Elisabeth comments:

> This may seem odd, but having become a Christian was hard for his parents and for him and, given the little time we had before he went, coping with his parents would have been a bit much! As it was, they very quickly invited me to their house and both were kindness itself. They also invited my parents to lunch in the Savoy and my parents were deeply touched when they were asked if they minded their daughter marrying a Jew. After that they got on very well.

Elisabeth and Hugh were married on 1 December 1945 at St Alban's Cathedral and their friend Dick Milford of St Mary the Virgin, Oxford, officiated. Robin Barbour was best man. Mon-tefiore was married in his uniform in the style of captain.

David Paton remembers

the extraordinary generosity that Hugh's father, especially, showed to the Christian family into which his ablest son had married. I have never forgotten the way in which Charlie Montefiore behaved at the wedding reception, doing his best with great delicacy to ensure that no one felt embarrassed or out of place. To become a Christian was bad enough; intending to become a priest of the Christian Church was worse; but to 'marry out' was worst of all. When we came home from China in 1951 my wife was due to go into hospital for a hysterectomy, and in one way and another life was complicated. When we got to the house in which we were to spend the next year we found awaiting us a letter from Hugh diffidently enclosing a cheque for three months' rent, and an enormous tin of ham (!) from Hugh's parents. There could not have been a more useful gift, nor, surely, a more surprising source. And what necessity was there for distinguished Jews to bother about their son's Gentile in-laws.

Montefiore's close relations with his wife's family may have been partly a result of feeling alienated from his own brothers. Elisabeth's mother was devoted to Hugh. He was a good and generous son-in-law, making her a regular allowance and buying a house for her last years. This aspect of him combined Jewish care for the family with a naturally warm and loving nature.

Yet sensitivity was near the surface and he was easily upset. Once he broke a chair when staying with his mother-in-law and had to rush out for a long walk on his own to recover.

After their marriage the couple moved into 4 Blandford Avenue, Oxford. The house was far too large for them, but belonged to Elisabeth's godmother, who let it to them part-furnished and at a reasonable rent. They were able to take in lodgers.

The post-war St John's College, Oxford, had a very interesting mix of undergraduates, such as (Sir) Peter Strawson the philosopher, Tony Flew, philosopher and atheist (whose father was Dr Newton Flew, noted Methodist scholar and Principal of Wesley House, Cambridge) and the novelists Kingsley Amis and John Wain. These were Montefiore's contemporaries.

The array of dons and professors was impressive. Montefiore cycled three times a week down the Banbury Road to listen to Leonard Hodgson, Regius Professor of Divinity, lecture on doctrine. Hodgson had modernist tendencies but never expressed himself in strident tones. His liberalism was more thoughtful than fervent and he had a broad view of the Church of England. In some ways Montefiore's theological position approximated to Hodgson's. David Capell Simpson (Oriel Professor of Interpretation of Holy Scripture) was like an Old Testament prophet. He was always known as 'Jahweh Simpson', because he was said to have lectured for a whole term on the word Jahweh. It was essential to listen to Claude Jenkins (Regius Professor of Ecclesiastical History), who would lecture for a whole term on one Elizabethan year. Frank Leslie Cross (Lady Margaret Professor of Divinity) was shy, scholarly and amusing, whilst Robert Henry Lightfoot (Dean Ireland's Professor of Exegesis) was wholly eccentric. He was a valetudinarian, who at the least provocation would retire to bed with a shawl. As a lecturer he was brilliant.

On the fringes of academic life, but not of Oxford life, was Julian Percy Thornton-Duesbery (Principal of Wycliffe Hall). Montefiore went to Wycliffe Hall to listen to him lecturing on Colossians. No one else turned up and the lecture was given to Montefiore in Thornton-Duesbery's study. The following week Thornton-Duesbury failed to appear.

However, the two most important influences on Montefiore at Oxford were Dick (Theodore Richard) Milford of the University Church, and Geoffrey William Hugo Lampe, Chaplain and Fellow of St John's College. Of the latter Montefiore says,

He was a marvellous tutor. He took infinite pains over one, and at the same time left one with one's own integrity. He would take me for long walks . . . He was a great walker and as an undergraduate had walked to Oxford from his home in Bristol. He was delightfully vague, and wrote *The Seal of the Spirit*, his great book on baptism, on the sands at the seaside, his typewriter on his knees. He was a liberal scholar, but with tremendous knowledge.

Dick Milford was one of those priests the Church of England never knows how to use to best effect. It is not that they should be bishops, but they should be placed in positions where their influence can be felt and spread widely. Milford looked like a scarecrow with his spare figure and suits from the Co-op. Montefiore remembers him as

> an extraordinary person, very intellectual, very musical, with an astringent mind and a great power of synthesis, and great spiritual insight. He had a compelling power of expression and could and should have written some books of lasting worth. But, suffering from accidie, he wrote only one pamphlet, *Foolishness to the Greeks* (1953), even though he lived into his nineties.

His father was Humphrey Milford, university publisher. Dick Milford left Oxford to become Chancellor of Lincoln. From there he went on to the Temple but his pacifism and general shagginess did not commend him to the London lawyers. Montefiore remembers preaching for him once in the Temple church: 'You ascend a long spiral staircase to the pulpit and feel that you are speaking from the top of Cleopatra's Needle. There were about twenty in the congregation, and at 8 a.m. only us!' He retired to Dorset and developed a keen interest in ecology. Eventually he was drawn to Eastern mysticism and at the end admitted he was not an orthodox Christian any longer. However, those who knew him at Oxford sat at his feet, not least as members of the Colloquy, which Iain Davie, now a Master at Ampleforth College, remembers well:

> Hugh invited me to attend meetings of the Colloquy, a group of philosophically and theologically minded students which met regularly at the house of Dick Milford. I remember those meetings well – partly because the vicarage was unheated, and 1947 *was* the coldest winter of the century. Dick Milford would sit hunched up against the cold, with a moist nose and hands that were blue with cold beneath frayed grey mittens. His austerity, I felt, would have made St Francis wince . . . Speakers included such distinguished names as Donald MacKinnon and

Austin Farrer and members themselves included Patrick
Rodger, Ingram Cleasby [later Dean of Chester], Denys
Munby the economist, R.M. Hare, later Professor of
Moral Philosophy, Hubert Monroe, later a distinguished
QC, Richard Hare, later Bishop of Pontefract, and
Michael Paton (Montefiore's brother-in-law). The great
debate of the time concerned the 'verification principle',
purloined by A.J. Ayer from the Vienna Circle, and how
theology would circumvent its seemingly lethal
development. Perhaps equally alarming was the linguistic
behaviourism of Gilbert Ryle, and yet, when I attended
Ryle's seminars on Wittgenstein's *Tractatus*, the presence
of Michael Dummett and Elizabeth Anscombe was
enough to reassure me that belief in God was not only
compatible with the most rigorous logical analysis but was
capable of turning the tables on the logical analysts
themselves.

For Montefiore and most other members, the Colloquy was
more than just one of the undergraduate discussion groups
which abounded at the time. The meetings in the Holywell
vicarage were not only a stimulating academic argument in
congenial company, but an opening of minds and a continuous
searching for truth as an imperative for living. It was Milford
himself who made the group. He seldom spoke, but sat listening in a corner with half-shut eyes, smoking his pipe, but his
occasional interjections or brief concluding remarks showed a
distinctive cast of mind – a mixture of honesty, humility,
human and intellectual rigour which was typically Dick and
which infused the whole group. And always the discussion led
on: from economics to ethics or theology and from thence to
history or science. Milford was a good mathematician. Like
Noah's dove, members of the Colloquy were allowed no rest-
ing place as they wandered over the face of the waters.

According to Ingram Cleasby,

Hugh was already a scintillating star in that scintillating
group, but I like to think that it did much to shape his own
distinctive cast of mind, which displayed the same
qualities we admired in Dick. This was true both of his

writing and speaking, but with one marked difference. Whereas Dick's whole manner was lethargic, or even soporific (indeed, there were occasions in St Mary's when his congregation were apt to wonder if he had fallen asleep in his own sermon), Hugh had a vigour and often a fervour which could be powerfully compelling, but could also be his own undoing.

Life in this post-war period still depended on the regular issue of bread-units, and grant-aided undergraduates bought themselves cheap meals at British Restaurants. Montefiore was married. Although he had a small unearned income, money was tight. A Jewish son reading theology and intending to be a Christian priest could not ask his father for more money, and the college would not give Montefiore the full amount of his scholarship on account of his father's income. In 1947 the Montefiores' first child, Teresa, was born.

Academically the Oxford of those years was unique: returning war-veterans (the majority) mixed with youngsters who had just left school, but tutors were of the opinion that never before had academic standards been so high and the demand for knowledge so great. This was put down to the greater maturity of the immediate post-war intake, and to the incentives for making a speedy egress which were provided by war degrees.

There was still a noticeable newness to Montefiore's Christianity. This revealed itself in many ways, notably by his infectious enthusiasm for Christ. Michael Paton recalls 'Hugh's disgust at his own lack of charity after making a sharp remark about someone in his college . . . the kind of thing undergraduates are always doing in the wish to be witty. It struck me that his religion was something he was really trying to live by.'

During 1947 there was an Oxford mission, conducted by Bishop Stephen Neill, and there were evening addresses in a packed Sheldonian Theatre. The evangelical atmosphere was pervasive, but it was a graciously all-inviting atmosphere, not at all fundamentalist and exclusive. At the college meetings (each college had its allotted missioners) Montefiore was often vocal. His manner changed little over the years – a somewhat absent-minded and quizzical expression accompanied his intense concern. But he never raised his voice. His reaction to absurd interventions was, rather, to raise his eyebrows.

Montefiore had embraced Christ *and* the Church of England. The fervancy of his attachment to each took Iain Davie by surprise:

> I was entertaining thoughts of going over to Rome. It was not until 1950 that I was, in fact, 'received' into the Church of Rome, and in 1947 I was reading theology with the intention of being ordained in the Church of England. I remember the vehemence of Hugh's reaction, because its very intensity surprised me. I had hitherto thought of him as a disinterested academic – as a scholar rather than as a preacher – but now I felt the full force of his prophetic fury. As far as I can remember, the gravamen of my defection lay in my acceptance of Rome's lack of scriptural warrant for (at least some of) its dogmas, and hence Rome's usurpation of authority.
>
> I had found in the outwardly accommodating Anglican a much more radical Protestant than I had thought to be there – indeed one who could command the fervour of a minor prophet and who genuinely believed that Catholics were guilty of idolatry. But this would be to give a distorted picture, for the Hugh whom I saw in his domestic life could not have been gentler, and there is one incident that remains in my memory which is as revealing as the anti-Catholic outburst . . . Hugh had introduced me to a young man he and his wife had befriended. The young man was clearly in a very distressed state, and shortly before I met him he had tried to take his life. With the utmost tact and gentleness, Hugh and his wife had welcomed this young man into their household, and had made him feel loved. The cause of his distress, I was later to learn, was his homosexuality. I mention this because it seemed to me then, as now, that Hugh had done the Christ-like thing, and when, years later, there was much controversy over Hugh's attribution of homosexual inclinations to Jesus, I thought of this incident. For if Jesus was indeed 'tempted like us in all things' (and yet without sin), then one of the temptations he must have felt was the temptation to which the young man had succumbed. And

how else could Hugh, or anyone else, have extended Christ's compassion to the young man?

Hard work was at the centre of all Montefiore's activities, and his reward was a first in theology in 1939.

He left Oxford for Cambridge to do his theological college training at Westcott House. The principal at the time was William D.L. Greer, shortly to become Bishop of Manchester. Greer told Montefiore not to bring his wife and family to Cambridge. In those days, those whom God had joined together, theological colleges put asunder. The Montefiores made a home at 12 Chalk Grove, Cambridge, which was then the last house in Cambridge. The garden looked out on to a cornfield. It was three or four miles from the city centre and by bicycle seemed even further. Unfortunately, Montefiore had to live in Westcott House for one year, whether married or unmarried. Elisabeth was unhappy and isolated. Hugh was unhappy and frustrated. He was further troubled by a ruptured disc and laminectomy.

Their second daughter, Janet, was born in Cambridge in 1948 and baptized in the college chapel.

When Montefiore arrived, Geoffrey Styler was Vice-Principal, a lonely man who spent hours playing the piano. He soon left to be Dean of Corpus, and Alan Webster, later Dean of St Paul's, became Vice-Principal; his place as Chaplain was taken by Harry Williams, fresh from All Saints, Margaret Street, and later to become the well-known religious writer.

Greer had left to become Bishop of Manchester soon after accepting Montefiore, and into his shoes stepped Kenneth Carey, a man who had a colossal inferiority complex, despite being shrewd and a theologian of an effective and unacademic kind. Perhaps he suffered from being an old Westcott man, a product of B.K. Cunningham, who many thought *was* Westcott House. Students still heard about B.K.C. *ad nauseam.*

Montefiore remembers his student days without pleasure:

Ken was very old public school; his father had been a housemaster at Sherborne, his mother an old dragon, one brother a headmaster, and also a brother-in-law – one of those schoolmastering dynasties. Ken was unmarried, homosexual by orientation, basically frightened of women, but capable of being very charming to them, as to men, with a great love of souls, a deep caring and a wonderful pastoral gift with young men. I personally owed a very great deal to him: he introduced me to Christian spirituality and to living theology, made a friend of me. Later in his ministry, at Westcott House and at Edinburgh, he grew uphappy and drank . . . but when I knew him he was splendid, especially in Compline addresses. Westcott House had no rules, but certain norms of behaviour were expected – back to the parental syndrome . . . I was very appreciative of Ken Carey, without becoming one of 'Ken's boys' – almost his adopted children – like some. I never felt the need for intensive personal counselling and confession, as some did, with the Principal.

Montefiore was regarded as the outstanding theologian in the college. He was both loved and feared. There is a story about him driving with a friend and being held up in a traffic jam on the A1. Taking both hands off the steering wheel, Montefiore said, 'As soon as the lexicon of Patristic Greek is published the perception of absolutely everything will be changed.' The lorry in front was being driven by a man with a most enormous hairy neck, which protruded above his sweater and below his cap. Naturally the companion said, 'Do you think *his* perception will be changed?' Montefiore roared with laughter and they almost crashed into the lorry, which might have enabled them to have found out. This is the first and perhaps the tamest of the Montefiore motor-car stories.

The A1 was going to be his direction for the immediate future, as he left Cambridge for Newcastle – and ordination.

5 Ordination and Restlessness

Montefiore was glad that he was going north to serve his title as curate at St George's, Jesmond, in Newcastle. He was particularly keen to serve under John Alexander Ramsbotham, who was in the mainstream of Anglicanism. Ramsbotham's churchmanship veered towards 'high', whilst his outlook was quietly radical, not least in liturgical reforms.

Montefiore was due to be made deacon at Advent 1949. Unfortunately, the Bishop of Newcastle, Noel Baring Hudson, decided not to inform Montefiore in advance that Ramsbotham was about to leave Newcastle for Durham; he was consecrated as Bishop Suffragan of Jarrow on 2 February 1950. Fortunately the principal of Westcott House, Ken Carey, found out and Montefiore was informed a fortnight before the ordination retreat. He felt let down and wondered if he should go forward after all. It was not too late to withdraw. Moreover, he was to be paid only £200 per annum and he had a wife and two small children to support. Surprisingly and supportively, his father came to the rescue by making a covenant in Hugh and Elisabeth's favour. That solved the financial hiccup. And Montefiore's strong sense of vocation overcame the other obstacle. But it was a poor start, as he needed support and a firm guiding hand at the start of his ministry.

The population of the parish was a little under 7,000. In this part of Jesmond there were a few grand houses and a multitude of terraced and semi-detached houses. The area was going down, with flats that were deteriorating into tenements. The church itself was on a huge scale, as befitted its benefactor, a millionaire shipowner of the previous century with a guilty conscience. Unfortunately, the conscience did not extend to endowing the building. The tower was a copy of St Mark's campanile in Venice.

John Ramsbotham was leaving a rich legacy. He had driven home one main Christian concept into his people; they were the Body of Christ, nourished by the parish communion, and must regard themselves as mutually supportive, as were the different organs of the human body. The people who formed the worshipping community were keen-minded and warm-hearted. They were devoted to their parish priest and open to what he was trying to get across; so that, being prayerfully led and influenced by a surprising number of realistically praying people, they got the message, on the whole, triumphantly well.

At the ordination retreat at Riding Mill, set in beautiful countryside, what should have been a period of peace and silence was marred by the fact that the chairs in the chapel were extraordinarily uncomfortable. Not many years afterwards, Montefiore was to abandon the kneeling position for prayer. As he wrote to his brother-in-law, Michael Paton:

> As for private prayer. I have *entirely* given up the ordinary
> kneeling position. Some people I know like to pray with
> their bodies and thus like some ascetic posture. Personally
> I prefer to try to forget about mine when praying and in
> my case ordinary kneeling is out, so far as my back's
> concerned: it puts such a strain on it.
>   Usually I sit *à la* Presbyterian: I find this a good relaxing
> posture. Otherwise I kneel against the bed, which is a
> good support. I never use a prie-dieu or kneel against a
> chair. For public worship I half-kneel, half-sit in my pew.

Montefiore was made deacon by the Bishop of Newcastle in Newcastle Cathedral in December 1949. He moved with his family into 4 Woodthorne Road, Jesmond, which he describes as 'a horrible little curate's house in a terrace, but it did have three small bedrooms. Alas, the local railway was adjacent which made both noise and dirt and there was no garden.'

Montefiore was not the only person to be disappointed at Ramsbotham's departure. A parish worker was about to arrive

at St George's too. She is now an Anglican nun of the Society of
the Sacred Cross at Tymawr Convent, Lydart, Monmouth.
Sister Paula has vivid recollections of the Jesmond years, for she
and Montefiore were 'running' the parish on their own pending
the arrival of the new vicar, Henry Graham Piercy, who was a
startling contrast to Ramsbotham. Piercy was a kindly man but
lacked a sense of occasion. He had been a local Methodist, but
on becoming an Anglican moved from rather low to very high
church. Montefiore had little in common with him.

Sister Paula's first recollection of Hugh conjures up:

> the thought of him on the crowded train, speeding down
> to Durham for John Rambsbotham's consecration. I can
> hear now Hugh's far-carrying voice suggesting a suitable
> addition to the Benedicite: 'Oh, all ye deacons and
> archdeacons . . .' Despite our personal pastoral
> deprivation, it was a very joyful occasion.
>
> Hugh's sense of Church liturgy actually ran very deep
> and strong. One of the high spots of my day was saying
> Matins with him, sometimes merely as a duet, in the great
> cold barn of St George's, with the Apostles in glittering
> mosaic staring unwinkingly down at us at either side of the
> high altar as we sat together in the chancel. To hear him
> recite the psalms was effortlessly to slip into thousands of
> years of tradition and one of the stabilizing factors in our
> struggling existence.
>
> Hugh and I both felt the parish needed new blood and
> whenever we were not enmeshed in something else, tried
> to go visiting, gradually drawing in a few new young
> families that had moved out of the overcrowded city into
> the new housing area, where building, on the edge of St
> George's parish, was at last making headway. To deal
> with this fresh potential, Hugh and Elisabeth decided
> something other than the long-established Mothers'
> Union was needed, and eventually founded the Marrieds'
> Club, which remembered them long afterwards with a
> very special affection.

Sister Paula was impressed by Montefiore's rapport with the
somewhat rowdy youth elements in the parish, and the manner

in which he trained the boys for confirmation. He handled the more-than-mischievous choir boys, used to 'playing up' young curates, supremely well. There was a flourishing Anglican Young People's Association at St George's, which worked hard to support numerous parish projects. Montefiore asked Sister Paula to criticize his sermons for him, which she did.

The North likes a man who gets things done. Leadership is measured by that, often superficial, characteristic. Soon after Montefiore had reversed his collar, the church tower was declared unsafe and he had to lead an appeal: literature, a thermometer outside the church, a good laymen put in charge and a curate scurrying hither and thither persuading the mighty and not so mighty to part with their money. The money appeared. Having such jobs thrust upon him so early did Montefiore much good, but whether it was the best form of training in his first year is questionable.

Local clergy were helpful. The Archdeacon of Northumberland, Charles Henry Ritchie, lived in a house adjoining the church and was a great help to Montefiore when he had a problem or was in trouble – which was often.

The vicar of Jesmond parish church, Mansell Harry Bates, was a leading evangelical but did not mind celebrating the Eucharist wearing vestments, provided Montefiore dressed him properly in them.

The Bishop of Newcastle, Noel Hudson, usually celebrated the Eucharist once a week at St George's and stayed to breakfast afterwards. Montefiore remembers an occasion when his younger daughter upset the teapot and the bishop said, 'Now is the time to think of eternity.' Although Montefiore could be exasperated with his bishop, not least when he preached on St George's Day and informed the congregation that their patron saint never existed, he learnt to trust the bishop's judgement; and Noel Hudson came to respect Montefiore, later appointing him as one of his examining chaplains.

One of the people who had slightly overlapped with Montefiore at Westcott House was Robert Runcie, now Archbishop of Canterbury. They were going to have similar ministries for years to come. Archbishop Runcie has written:

Hugh went off to Newcastle and before he had been there

very long I had one of his letters, which we all know can be written five times as fast as a typewriter. Yet they are also legible and lucid. He had met a vicar at a bus stop. The vicar had said that he wished he could have someone from Westcott House, but he had only been at an unknown college himself, had no influence, and only a parish with a population of some 30,000 and one curate to offer. Hugh felt that this was the place for me. My principal was more doubtful, but suggested that I at least might see it in addition to the more gentle beginnings of a curacy at Hexham. I shall always be grateful that Hugh put me in touch with that vicar and that parish.

When I went for my ordination retreat, Hugh was there to become priest. It was cold and frosty and we were kept in silence in the wilds of Northumberland. Hugh confided to me that he was anxious about his first celebration of the Holy Communion. This was to be in his parish church and he would have to sing parts of it. We made an assignation in the woods some distance away from the retreat house. He brought a large altar book and paced along this woodland path singing the Preface at the top of his voice. To our amazement the bishop was taking a quiet walk in the woodland and we were suddenly confronted by him, as Hugh, looking up into the air in that astonishing way, with his spectacles slightly askew, was calling out, 'Lift up your hearts'.

Montefiore has a most pleasant voice, but cannot sing in tune. Even the prestigious (Sir) David Willcocks of King's College, Cambridge, had tried to teach him and failed.

Montefiore was ordained priest on 24 December 1950. His conversion, his marriage and his priesting were the landmarks of his life.

Piercy inadvisedly put a notice on the church door: 'Now you can call him Father.' Montefiore, who had no wish to be called Father, was more embarrassed than annoyed. It was the congregation that was annoyed.

He spent most of his time visiting and before he left St George's had knocked on every door in the parish. It may not have resulted in a rush to church, but it ensured that everyone knew that there was a church. It was never likely that Jesmond would hold him for long. In November 1951 he was invited to return to Westcott House as chaplain and tutor at a stipend of £325 plus £125 per annum for rent. This enabled the family to move into a semi-detached house (39 de Freville Avenue) with a small garden, in Chesterton, about two miles from the centre of Cambridge. Montefiore accepted with lukewarm enthusiasm, but his bishop had advised him to accept.

It was not easy to return to the college as a staff member within two years of having been a student there. But Cambridge had a magnetic pull and seemed the milieu where Montefiore would make his mark – perhaps not at Westcott House, but somewhere. He had previously been interviewed for a lectureship at Trinity College, Cambridge, but appeared to have been beaten to the post by Harry Abbott Williams, who was chaplain at Westcott House at the time. In fact Montefiore was subsequently informed by John Burnaby, who was Dean of Chapel at Trinity:[1] 'I knew you wouldn't do, but I had to have a foil for Harry.' Montefiore did not like this manipulation. He had had a previous experience which had annoyed him, of being interviewed by Lincoln College, Oxford, for the chaplaincy, when Henry Ernest William Turner had been appointed Lightfoot Professor of Divinity in the University of Durham. It was only at college hall that Montefiore was told that his rival, Vivian Hubert Howard Green was sitting opposite him. Moreover, Lincoln wanted an historican, and Green had a first in History. Green was appointed and Montefiore was not even reimbursed for his train fare from Newcastle – for an interview which he had been invited to attend. Turner himself wanted Montefiore to succeed him as fellow, chaplain and tutor.

The new line-up at Westcott House was Kenneth Carey as principal, Alan Webster as vice-principal and Montefiore as chaplain. It was not the happiest of combinations. Montefiore was too sensitive, and felt himself a *tertium quid* alongside the closeness of Carey and Webster. Then Webster got married and it was not long before he moved north to be vicar of Barnard Castle. Montefiore moved up a notch to become vice-principal and Robert Runcie came south to be chaplain.

Carey missed Webster and the relationship between principal

and vice-principal was not as close as it had been. Yet Carey was impressed with Montefiore's teaching ability. A note in Carey's private record book in Michaelmas term 1953, however, reveals anxiety that both Runcie and Montefiore were working too hard and that Montefiore was restless. There were particular tensions for Montefiore. Elisabeth attended the Sunday Eucharist in the chapel, but was not allowed to stay for breakfast. Even when they both went back to talk about marriage (when Peter Knight Walker was principal) she was asked to have her meal with the housekeeper – so the Montefiores dined at home.

Robert Runcie shares his reflections on that period:

Hugh was slightly distanced from the common life, which had a rather stifling character. When I joined the staff I felt inadequate in the face of Hugh's theological scholarship and yet was surprised to discover when his wife told me a year after my arrival how inadequate he felt because of my capacity to mix socially and make the party go.

Ken Carey attracted widespread devotion from his students and some of his contemporaries. That devotion did, in some cases, lead to dependence. Neither Hugh nor I felt that devotion which Ken Carey created, nor were we totally dependent upon him. Hugh felt the most awkward around the place. His social awkwardness and distance from college by virtue of his marriage was added to by his sense that there was a certain anti-intellectualism around as far as theology was concerned. Hugh was always very generous in sharing his scholarship with others, and unbelievably quick in putting pen to paper. He sometimes felt that his Compline addresses were inadequate. I invariably found them fascinating. He wrestled with the words of Scripture and related them to some issue of the day. Ken Carey's addresses were very devotional and, though I felt them effective at the time, I suspect I would now find them embarrassingly emotional. My own were, I believe, clever and entertaining rather than substantial. They were firmly imitative of the addresses of Harry Williams which I heard in my own time as a student at Westcott.

Hugh contributed a lot by his care of married students. He always has had a strong suit in his pastoral care of married ordinands. Ken Carey was not good with the wives, and I was rather better with students' girl-friends than with their spouses. So Hugh's pastoral instincts amongst the married added to the strength of the staff.

Hugh was an enthusiastic teacher. He was not particularly good at getting people through exams, but he was always opening up fresh horizons of thought and interest. He was not, frankly, much good with those uninterested in theology. When he discovered an ordinand who had no interest in theology he was distressed and, to some extent, surprised.

Montefiore was beginning to pursue his own theological studies. A congenial opportunity to combine pastoral work with academic theology came when he was asked to return to his old college, St John's, Oxford, as chaplain and fellow, to succeed Geoffrey William Hugo Lampe, who was moving to Birmingham University as its Professor of Theology. Carey would not release Montefiore, holding him to his three-year contract. But there were some interesting developments in Cambridge. Montefiore was beginning to review books and his first scholarly piece was published in 1949, 'The Position of the Cana Miracle and the Cleansing of the Temple in St John's Gospel'.[2] He was suggesting that the position of the miracle of turning water into wine and the cleansing of the temple may have been influenced by two passages from the Old Testament prophets.

By far the most interesting activity during the Westcott years arose out of the formation of the Church of South India, which had presented the Church of England with a challenge and a problem. First, there was the fact that a group of Churches had become one Church. The 'going-out' of four dioceses from the Anglican Communion in September 1947 to join with hitherto non-episcopal bodies in forming the Church of South India was an important event. The dioceses of Madras, Travancore, Tinnevelly and Dornakal[3] united with the Methodist Church and the South India United Church to form the Church of South India (CSI).

There was a pledge that no congregation would be asked to accept a ministry or form of worship which was against their conscience, so that an ex-Anglican congregation would always have an episcopally ordained presbyter.

The convocations of Canterbury and York had looked at their own relationships with the CSI and were going to do so again in 1955. Should the Church of England enter into full communion with the CSI? Questions were being asked at Westcott House, as elsewhere. The staff was not united; Robert Runcie took an Anglo-Catholic line on the historic episcopate in relation to South India – a stance not shared by Montefiore. The young CSI was facing all the enormous problems of presenting the Gospel to the Communists, the Nationalists and the indifferent. Could the Church of England stand aside and do little to help? Had it the right to refuse the help which full intercommunion would bring? Was there nothing to learn from the CSI about problems in England?

As always, the stone of stumbling, or rock of offence, was bishops. There was polemical warfare over South India. Was there not room for a volume of essays which would build something for the future? Kenneth Carey thought so and present and past members of Westcott House were recruited, with Montefiore as collator. The result was *The Historic Episcopate in the Fullness of the Church*[4] and contributions were made by Kenneth Carey (also editor), John A.T. Robinson, Barry Till, W.H. Vanstone, Alan Webster, Kenneth Woollcombe and Montefiore.[5]

Originally Horace Dammers, lecturer at Queen's College, Birmingham, who went out to serve in South India in 1953 and was later Dean of Bristol, was asked to write on the episcopate in the New Testament. However, he found himself forced by the evidence to take a rather negative view of the claims for the historic episcopate in that area. This was not in line with the thinking of the group and Montefiore had the difficult task of writing to Dammers to say that the essay which he had been commissioned to write should not be included.

The contributions were of a high standard and the book was widely noticed. The nub of the book's argument was that a careful study of the evidence of the New Testament and of the tradition of the Church pointed to a high doctrine of episcopacy which nevertheless fell short of making episcopacy essential to the life of the Church. If this was a true reading of the evidence, it must make a considerable difference to one's attitude to the CSI. The effect of the group's thesis was to change the emphasis in Church Order. The prevailing positions have not much changed.

While all Anglicans accept and defend episcopacy, they differ among themselves on both its theological status and the grounds which they would bring forward to support it.

Anglican Catholics maintain that episcopacy is essential to the Church's life and related in various ways to the unity, catholicity and apostolicity of the Church. A traditional view is that the historic episcopate is of the *esse* of the Church. It guarantees the Church.

Another view strongly held is that episcopacy is part of the fullness of the Church's life. It is of the *bene esse* of the Church. While admitting that in the present divided state of Christendom individual Churches can stand without it, they find it practically and theologically inconceivable that it should be lacking in some recognizable way in a reunited Church.

The two most interesting and provoking essays in the book were those by John Robinson ('Kingdom, Church, Ministry') and Montefiore ('The Historic Episcopate'). Kenneth Woollcombe's essay, 'The Ministry and the Order of the Church in the Works of the Fathers', was a trenchant piece of writing, and makes one realize that it is to the Church's loss that there have not been more works from his pen.

Robinson's principle was to subordinate the Church to the Kingdom and his conclusion set the tone for the book. 'We affirm that the episcopate is dependent on the Church, and not the Church on the episcopate. We believe its possession to be a necessary mark of the Church's fullness, rather than an indispensable qualification for being a part.'

In his own essay, *The Historic Episcopate*, Montefiore developed and justified this principle. Episcopacy is part of the well-being of the Church without assigning any more deeply theological reason for the view. In sum, episcopacy is of the *plene esse* of the Church. The historic episcopate may not be essential to the Church. The Church could exist without it, but there are sound reasons for retaining and extending it. Thus without it the Church cannot achieve its full stature.

The division and difference between *bene esse* and *plene esse* is more subtle than drastic, and the arguments not wholly convincing. Yet either ranged against the *esse* view is compelling.

The book enlarged the debate and produced some interesting responses. These ranged from a penetrating, appreciative, if critical, appraisal by the Bishop of Durham (Arthur Michael Ramsey) in *The Bishoprick*,[6] to the lashings of E.R. Fairweather, Associate Professor of Dogmatic Theology and Ethics at Trinity College, Toronto, in a booklet *Episcopacy Re-Asserted*.[7] Montefiore was particularly encouraged by the favourable attention of Norman Sykes, Dixie Professor of Ecclesiastical History in the University of Cambridge.[8]

The demands made on Montefiore by Westcott House were unreasonable and punishing. He had to bicycle in to service by 7.30 a.m. and he did not get back home until after the 10 p.m. Compline. Time off in the afternoon was a rarity. All the academic teaching for forty-five members of the college was done by Montefiore and Robert Runcie, as Carey's teaching was limited to pastoralia and prayer. The long-vacation term wrecked any August holiday and precious relaxing time with his family. Family life was beginning to suffer and his nerves were too near the surfce. It was an abominable position and, as he recalls, 'The fact that the House had no written rules made it all the worse for anyone brought up to have a tender conscience.'

He had to act. He did so by resigning with no job or future in sight. Kenneth Carey was devastated, took it personally and probably never really forgave Montefiore. Westcott House had not been a happy experience. Later, when Carey left, it was suggested that Montefiore might become principal. The answer was easy: 'No.' He could not face a return to that place.

Montefiore's announcement cannot have been a complete shock, for in Carey's private record book for the Lent Term 1954 he had noted: 'The Vac. had revealed that H.W.M. was very unsettled: physically both he and I were under the weather . . . H.W.M. has taken much more time off.'

Montefiore had no need to fear unemployment. There were many opportunities and perhaps the best for Montefiore came

when Eric William Heaton, Dean, fellow and chaplain of
Gonville and Caius College, Cambridge, moved to Salisbury as
a canon residentiary, leaving a physical and spiritual gap at
Gonville and Caius.

6   Fellow and Dean

Montefiore is sensitive to historical influences and alert to contemporary enlightenment. It is significant that his theological mind was open, tested and moulded in Cambridge, not in Oxford. The proponents and martyrs of the Reformation had been fellows of Cambridge colleges – Thomas Cranmer (Jesus), Nicholas Ridley (Clare), Hugh Latimer (Pembroke), Edmund Grindal (Pembroke), John Whitgift (Peterhouse), Thomas Cartwright (St John's). The Cambridge Platonists were philosophical divines who wrote, preached and breathed tolerance and comprehension. The word 'reasonableness' as a tenet of the Anglican way might have been 'invented' at Cambridge. By contrast, Oxford had always been more conservative and traditional in religious matters. Cambridge had more than a taint of theological radicalism in its background – and soon it was to be in the foreground once more.

Gonville and Caius College was founded in 1348 by Edmund Gonville, a priest in the diocese of Ely. In 1559 a former student, Dr John Caius, who had been a professor at Padua and was physician to Edward VI, became master of his old college and, finding it heading for paupery, richly endowed it. Caius Court, built in 1567, holds pride of place among the college buildings with its lovely Gate of Honour.

Gonville and Caius established a reputation for medicine, with some traditions in law and antiquarian and historical scholarship in various forms. It had never been an excessively clerical college, even if the majority of fellows until this century were clergy. But a theological tradition can be discerned by mentioning such names as John Cosin, Jeremy Taylor, Samuel Clarke, H.B. Swete, Charles Raven, J.M. Creed and Geoffrey Lampe.

Charles Raven had been Regius Professor of Divinity, Master of Christ's College and Vice-Chancellor of the University of Cambridge. It was he who recommended Montefiore to succeed Eric Heaton as fellow and Dean of Gonville and Caius.

The interview was rather bizarre. It took place in the master's study and those present were E.K. (Francis) Bennett, President of the Senior Common Room; Stanley R. Dennison, Senior Tutor; Patrick Hadley, Professor of Music; and the master, Sir James Chadwick OM, FRS. Chadwick was a world-famous nuclear physicist and Nobel Prize winner. He discovered the neutron, thus making possible the atom bomb. He was in charge of the British side during the making of the bomb in America. When the result of his discovery exploded he was shattered, returned to England and never entered the Cavendish Laboratory again. Chadwick had been master since 1948. The gigantic brain which had made amazing discoveries in physics was turned to the minutiae of college business. He was a depressive and when one went to see him in his study, there were smelling salts in front of him. If he was presented with a seemingly intractable problem, he would close his eyes for a time, hoping that when he opened them visitor and problem alike would have disappeared.

At the interview Chadwick could think of nothing to say to Montefiore. He asked him how many candles he liked on the altar, and sank back exhausted. Only silence followed. Fortunately one of the 'panel' asked Montefiore what he had done during the war. On hearing that he had been a gunner officer in the army, Paddy Hadley perked up and started an army conversation which continued until the interview ended.

A week later Chadwick sent for Montefiore to discuss terms – a miserable £600 per annum for being dean and £200 per annum as an official fellow. In addition there was supervising. Montefiore did not hesitate in accepting the post. A year later he became a New Testament lecturer in the Faculty of Divinity, which gave personal satisfaction, provided additional income, and significantly raised his standing with the fellowship body.

Montefiore had a set of panelled and painted rooms in Caius

Court, over the Gate of Virtue. They contained an amazing portrait of St Francis, drawn by Edward Wilson, an old Caian known to the world as Edward Wilson of the Antarctic, the doctor who was the soul of Scott's expeditions, who died a hero's death with Scott and Oates eleven miles from One Ton Camp. His drawings of birds and beasts in watercolours are well-known, but not his St Francis. Taken from one of the Della Robbia statues in Perugia, the face of the saint was entirely his own conception. Strong and full of character, the expression in the eyes was penetrating and compelling. It had a magnetic force which suggested holiness without the trappings of piety, and this appealed to Montefiore's imagination.

Montefiore's family moved into the ground floor of a large college house, Springfield, on Sidgwick Avenue. It was once occupied by the famous classical scholar, Professor Jebb, who made it the social centre of Cambridge. The Montefiores found that Lady Jebb's personality hung heavily over the house, and one of his daughters claimed to have seen a shadowy figure which resembled her. Next door lived a colleague of Montefiore, an explosives expert who organized set-piece maritime battles each 5 November.

By the time Montefiore was appointed New Testament lecturer, he had had a third daughter, Catherine. The three children were at the Perse School for Girls and he was able to spend more time with the family. They bought an old vicarage at Abergwesyn, a hamlet in mid-Wales ten miles or more from Tregaron, where they were able to relax in remote and peaceful surroundings. Montefiore particularly remembers one blissful long vacation there, which he spent preparing his lectures while the family walked, roamed and swam, with kites and peregrines hovering overhead.

Montefiore remembers the college personalities with affection. Francis Bennett, who had contributed little at Montefiore's interview, had been a fellow all his academic life. Of German–Jewish extraction, unmarried, a great friend of E.M. Forster of King's College, he was the epitome of a cultured Englishman. He was faithful in his attendance at all college occasions and was both respected and loved. When Montefiore attended Institutions in connection with college livings, Bennett went too. On one occasion he courteously removed his hat and bowed as Montefiore and he drove past a man in the street. On being asked what he was doing he replied, 'He is a sweep,' thus revealing a very superstitious nature.

Stanley Dennison, the senior tutor, serious and good, was a weekly communicant and supported Montefiore in many ways.

The master was also a great supporter of Montefiore and attended Sunday chapel on a regular basis. Although he did this out of duty, there was a suspicion of something more: not quite commitment, but certainly a strong feeling for religion. Montefiore remembers his first Sunday:

> I had to preach and the preacher always sat next to the master at dinner. I felt incompetent to make conversation with such a great man. We sat in silence through the soup and entrée, and at the main course he ventured the remark, 'I've had these boots for twenty-five years.' I also remember when I changed the Bible readings from the Authorized Version to the Revised Standard Version. 'What on earth was that reading we had tonight?' he demanded. I explained the need for Scripture readings to be intelligible. 'I don't give a damn what it means, but what it sounds like,' reposted the master.

Above all, there was Professor Patrick Hadley, who was also precentor for thirty-three years. Hadley had a very good reputation for the high quality of music at Gonville and Caius. He was one of those musicians who had a genius for extracting beautiful sounds from sometimes indifferent voices. The choir came because Hadley enhanced their lives. He loved folk tunes and understood why non-professionals loved music. His composition of the Sanctus for chapel worship revealed spiritual perception as well as musical insights. Montefiore says of him:

> He was an inspired choir conductor, and understood the need to keep the singing congregational. The chapel choir was, in its secular form, the college chorus. I had eight choral exhibitioners and altogether at one point there were fifty-three members of the choir. (The power of the Caius choir was well known in the university – it was alleged at one time to have swung a Union election!) Paddy had a

wooden leg, as a result of a First World War amputation. I remember a glazed look coming over someone being interviewed for an organ scholarship – he had suddenly noticed that one of Paddy's socks was kept suspended by a drawing pin. Unfortunately Paddy used to have outbursts of drinking – one always knew when the college butler was seen going to his room with a basket of port bottles. I remember him once in chapel after such a bout, trying to stop undergraduates coming into chapel because it meant the swing doors opening – 'It makes a draught,' he complained. Paddy loathed sermons. I had to warn visiting preachers that after their Invocation at the beginning of the sermon they would hear a loud click – it was Paddy ostentatiously starting his stop watch. After ten minutes Paddy got very restless, sighing loudly and groaning. Paddy had an estate in Norfolk and was convinced that as his father had died at sixty, so would he. When his sixtieth birthday was coming up, he took a room at The Evelyn, a well-known Cambridge nursing home, to await his demise – which didn't come!

The fellows of Gonville and Caius were distinguished men and it was said that their corporate IQ was the highest to be found at any high table in Cambridge. The scientists, who impressed Montefiore most, ranged from lukewarm Christian to militant unbeliever. Conversations with these men gave Montefiore a new confidence. Occasionally he could be irritated by the high table vapourings, as when Sir Edward Bullard, the great geophysicist, said triumphantly that the Russian sputnik had disproved the existence of God. There was the usual Cambridge high-table clever talk and cynical gibe – but also much wisdom and wit. One Cambridge don asked Montefiore if he could decline *uno*. 'Of course,' he replied. 'It goes quite differently from *amo*, *amas*, *amat*,' retorted the don. 'It's an irregular verb – *uno*, *Unesco*, *unite*, *unanimous*! You want to. You can't.'

It was not long before Montefiore was elected to the College Council, a group consisting of the master and twelve dons who ran the college. This was time-absorbing but worthwhile and much enjoyed by Montefiore. His only irritation was the attitude of the bursar, who thought money was to save not to spend – and this in a very wealthy college. Yet there were real difficulties in the college resulting from disturbances in the recent past. Squabbles in colleges are recorded in history and fiction, and C.P. Snow's *The Masters* could as well have been set in Gonville and Caius as in any other Cambridge college. Christopher Brooke, the college's historian, refers to the 'Peasants' Revolt':

> an episode now deeply entrenched in the mythology and folklore of the College. At a hastily summoned gathering two days before the General Meeting in October 1950, a group of Fellows, mostly, but not all, natural scientists, and mostly, but far from all, under forty, made a plan to change the composition of the Council and support two of their number for election to it. The Peasants' Revolt came in on a tide of genuine academic idealism which was to generate an admirable enthusiasm for lofty aims; it also generated hard feelings, personal misunderstandings, misery and faction which were only finally laid to rest under the Mastership of Needham.[1]

As Montefiore soon learnt, the Peasants' Revolt had been a successful attempt to unseat the 'establishment' – the master and the tutors – who had been running the college in a way which frustrated the statutes. Sir Edward Parkes, a former fellow and now Vice-Chancellor of Leeds University, notes that:

> affairs in Caius in that period were much influenced by a group of young arts dons who mostly held college appointments, but not university ones, and whose principal interest was in preventing change. Hugh was not well regarded by them, but he was much more integrated with an older group of dons who were forward-looking and who wanted various measures of reform.

Dissension was rife and undercurrents of mistrust were fast-moving. Although Chadwick was warm in his personal approach to young fellows, he was by temperament out of sympathy with the thinking and behaviour of some of these 'new men'. Master Chadwick in his old age became very conservative and in the end was forced out, resigning on a matter of principle in 1958.

Montefiore reflects on the ensuing mastership election:

there were two factions, both blocked. In desperation one faction tried to get their greatest enemy, the bursar, to stand, realizing that he would only have a few years, and then they hoped to get in their candidate. The bursar was warned! An Oxford candidate of great distinction was blackballed on the grounds that he was living with his secretary; and I was despatched to find out. The president of the SCR, by this time Sir Ronald Fisher, was in charge of the election. Fisher is the most intelligent man I have ever known. Doing a crossword, he never filled in the interstices of words on the grounds that it was a waste of time. He attended chapel regularly, and preached. He was said to wear the hood of a different honorary degree each Sunday of term. He lived in his laboratory, so escaping a reduction in salary for living in college. He was a professor of genetics who suitably had some six daughters; but he lived separately from his wife. I should think he would be intolerable to live with. He loved his pipe, and he was retained by the Tobacco Association to make their case – he claimed that those who got lung cancer were going to get it anyway and so why shouldn't the poor devils have the pleasure of smoking . . . I persuaded Sir Nevill Mott (Cavendish Professor of Physics and a fellow) to stand, and he got it. He was not a success . . . he did not make his wishes clear enough but was upset when they were not acted on.

Sir Nevill Mott would not dissent from this view. He admits inheriting a very divided college. 'It was Hugh with all his charisma who persuaded me to stand, telling me that my wife and I could "heal" the college, but after seven years it went sour on me and I got out.' The two characteristics of Montefiore that stick in Sir Nevill's mind are 'energy' and 'unpredictability': 'One did not know what line he would take on any issue.'

As much as Montefiore enjoyed the privileges surrounding high table, his new work gave him opportunities for a pastoral ministry and a teaching one. He was also hoping to embark on some theological research.

As dean of the college, he had general duties and had to interview all freshmen when they arrived. This was not sufficient if he was going to establish any relationship of trust with them. So he invited some to lunch and others to breakfast, until a college concert had a skit on 'How many freshmen did the dean have for breakfast this morning?' There were about 125 freshmen each year and with research students the total was over 400. Montefiore recalls one year when he was laid up with gastric flu at Springfield:

> I knew that if I didn't see the freshman when they first arrived, I never would. I heard that bubbly was very good for you on these occasions, because the sugar gave energy, the alcohol helped you to sweat, and the fizz eased the tummy. I well remember the look on the frightened freshmen's faces when they were in turn ushered into my bedroom, and saw the dean lying in bed in pyjamas with a magnum beside him! They realized then that they had indeed left school.

The college was generous with entertainment allowances and food in plenty was sent to Montefiore's rooms. He reckoned to put on a stone in the Michaelmas term because freshmen were shy and would not eat unless he did. He regarded it as a good ploy to get over their shyness, for if they had a knife and fork, at least they knew what to do with their hands.

Montefiore learnt quickly to distinguish between the natural diffidence of freshmen reduced to a stutter and silence, and those self-assured men who had the patter and vocabulary to match their egos. Montefiore himself has never been as self-assured as he often appears. But to freshmen he could be a formidable and intimidating figure. He gained a reputation for deflecting self-important or self-absorbed young men. He would egg a man on to assert his opinions with a crescendo of interest – 'Really? Really? Really!' – and then there would come, 'Oh. Really . . .' with leaden finality.

Eric Heaton had left a goodly and godly inheritance which Montefiore expanded and developed in his own way. Professor

Ian McFarlane, senior tutor from 1956 to 1961, contrasts the two deans:

> The deanship is, in my view, a temporary post and deans of calibre – unless they go on to a senior theological appointment, should move back into pastoral work. A good dean is essential, as he is in a post of responsiblity but without the normal tutorial authority. Both deans kept chapel as a centre of valuable activity. Whereas Heaton belonged more, as I saw matters, to the Fisher wing of the Church, Hugh had a more evident spiritual quality; no doubt as a convert he saw things afresh.

Montefiore was at Gonville and Caius from 1954 to 1963. These were years when there was a revival of the thought and practice of religion in Cambridge. Gonville and Caius, like most colleges, benefited by chapel attendances. Montefiore wanted to harness this interest through worship and preaching. He created 'The Church in Caius', a loosely linked but dynamic fellowship of men who worshipped together and who in the Lent term undertook a course of study following notes put together by Montefiore. Eric Heaton had been able to make progress without altering the times and pattern of worship: Montefiore changed that against much opposition. He introduced Sung Eucharist at 8.30 a.m. getting choral exhibitioners, the organ scholar and precentor out of bed to sing before their voices had properly woken up. The time of breakfast was changed to accommodate all those Christians who wanted to worship at this early hour, and Matins was abandoned. It was not unusual to have a quarter of the college (100) communicating. Paddy Hadley wrote some special settings for the Gloria and the Angus Dei. Montefiore's aim, for which he fought long and hard, was to make worship in chapel a congregational occasion and not an esoteric musical concert, though he allowed the exhibitioners their head at Evensong on Mondays (plainsong) and Wednesdays (special anthems). These were services of musical excellence and spiritual beauty.

With the worship went preaching. At the Eucharist Montefiore would preach for three or four minutes on the Epistle or Gospel, giving a reflective comment on the passage of scripture. At Evensong the emphasis was on preaching, and the chapel was full. Montefiore preached with clarity, humour, depth of commitment, memorable turn of phrase and absolute honesty. His sermons were not meant to be entertaining. Their purpose was to nourish faith.

Aspects of Montefiore the priest, evident at Gonville and Caius, did not change much with the passing of the years. To see him conducting public worship was to witness an interesting mixture characteristic of the man. He never looked tidy: neither in surplice and stole, which was the college vesture for Holy Communion, nor in the eucharistic vestments which were worn in Great St Mary's. For someone who was meticulous about the ordering and dignity of public worship, he was casual about his dress. The college chaplain had to ensure that his surplice was down at the back and the stole of equal length on both sides. What did this matter to him? He once told the chaplain that the main function of a priest was to lead people in prayer.

Once, when returning to preach at Gonville and Caius, he pondered aloud on some of the texts he might have chosen for the sermon. One was 'How shall I sing the Lord's song in a strange land?' 'But,' he commented, 'the choral exhibitioners will remember that I wasn't very good at singing the Lord's song on home ground.' Yet to hear Montefiore lead the intercessions at Evensong, or to see him at the altar, was to know that here was a man of God and a man of prayer to whom his faith was the single most important thing in his life.

Montefiore tried to unite all Christians in the college. That was behind his idea of The Church in Caius. All baptized persons were members of it and invited to take up full membership by accepting a simple rule of life which included some worship in the college chapel. Most Free Churchmen supported Montefiore. Anglo-Catholics tended to be suspicious of his theological views. But it was the evangelical undergraduates of the Cambridge Inter-Collegiate Christian Union (CICCU) who distracted him most. Christopher Mayfield, now Bishop of Wolverhampton, was one of them. He recalls:

> During my fourth term in Cambridge, Michaelmas 1955,
> Billy Graham led a mission organized by the Christian

Union . . . I personally was much helped by Billy Graham's visit; indeed my faith 'took off' in a way that I had not hitherto expected. I was just short of my 20th birthday then. Like many young converts, I was not only full of zeal; I was also dismissive of others who did not appear to 'see the light' as I now did. So, one day later, meeting Hugh in one of the courts at Caius, I said to him . . . 'Of course the trouble with you is that you are not converted!' In my blindness and ignorance I did not know that Hugh was a member of a distinguished Jewish family and also a Christian! In spite of my stupidity (or perhaps because of it) Hugh kept in touch with me over the years as I tested my call to ordination and was ordained in 1963. When I arrived in Wolverhampton as the bishop I found that I was a member of a group of West Midlands bishops that included Hugh, then Bishop of Birmingham. When I went to my first meeting . . . Hugh introduced me to the other bishops . . . 'You will know Christopher. A long time ago he told me that I needed to be converted. And he was probably quite right!' It was beautifully and graciously said, so everyone was able to laugh quite easily.

Montefiore managed to hold many CICCU undergraduates. They recognized his sincerity even when questioning his theology. Perhaps they knew of individuals, not of their persuasion, who owed their faith and their vocations to Montefiore. There were many, just as there were those who had to be discouraged from choosing a path that would turn out to be a cul-de-sac. Two 'testimonies' are interesting.

Dr Anthony Marks is now priest-in-charge of Grosvenor Chapel and warden of Liddon House.

My own greatest debt to Hugh is my vocation. Not that he ever spoke to me about the possibility of ordination, or that I ever discussed it with him. I arrived there rather later and by a rather different route. But he sowed the seeds in two ways. In the course of my third year of reading the Modern and Medieval Languages Tripos he invited me to breakfast and suggested that I should spend the following year reading Part IA of the Theology Tripos. His reasoning was (or he claimed it to be!) that if I did well enough I was hoping to do research into the German literature of the sixteenth and seventeenth centuries and the theology and church history would provide a useful background. Or, alternatively, if I ended up as a teacher, I could offer divinity as a second subject, which might be a help in getting jobs. Whether he thought that it might lead in another direction, too, I have never found out. But he was no fool, and I'm sure he had his suspicions. In the event I thoroughly enjoyed it, and I was lucky enough to have Hugh as supervisor for the New Testament, going once a fortnight to his study in the tower of Great St Mary's. The other thing he did was more indirect, but I think of even more lasting significance. When we arrived for the Michaelmas term of 1961 we discovered that the mangled version of Morning Prayer which had been on offer in the previous year had been replaced by a daily Eucharist. Previously I think there had been a Eucharist on Wednesdays and saints' days. This seemed strange to many, as there was never more than a tiny congregation, but the explanation given was that the clergy wished to celebrate more frequently than once a week. But in the course of the next five years or so I came to value the daily Mass more and more, and since then it has remained as a constant feature of my life, first as a layman, and now as a priest. And in the end I think it was really through this that I discovered my vocation.

Denys de la Hoyde returned to Caius as chaplain. He is now vicar of Pool-in-Wharfedale:

I owe my Christian faith to Hugh. He and I arrived at Caius together, he as dean and me as his only freshman theological student, in 1954. I thought when I arrived that I wanted to be ordained though for not very clear reasons, having grown up in a vicarage as a conventional Christian with a very unformed faith, and now at Cambridge straight from national service, which had been fun. Hugh taught me what it meant to be a Christian.

There were two things in particular . . . his teaching and

his preaching. I don't know what I got from my supervisions with him except a love of wanting to think and do theology. He taught me New Testament and Doctrine and . . . I saw a beauty in scholarship as, with logical coherence, the foundations of Christian faith were laid open. It was reasonable and rational to believe, because there was Hugh doing it and leading you on step by step into a richness of faith. I began to love God with my mind and to delight in doing it.

Some things which I still remember Hugh saying have been benchmarks through my life, e.g. 'Personhood is the highest category which we know as human beings; God must be at least the very highest category we know; he is more, but he is at least person, personality.' So I learnt from Hugh to begin to worship God in the person of Jesus Christ. And in his teaching and preaching Jesus came alive as a real person. Another one of those benchmarks: the quality of life that Jesus lived. If I want to know what God is like, I look to that quality of living in Jesus, so much so that as I look at him I see God and can say that he is God's son – i.e. the reality and quality lead to the doctrinal affirmations, rather than the affirmation of doctrine leading to the quality of living. Christian faith is pragmatic.

The Church in Caius was meant to be ecumenical and Montefiore was quick to emphasize the comparative legal freedom of the college chapel as 'peculiar'. Free Churchmen of good standing could take communion. Yet although he was a committed ecumenist, Montefiore was not without emphatic confessional views. These diary entries outline some of the problems:

J. came to see me tonight. He has drifted out of Methodism and become Anglicanized through the chapel, and he wants to be confirmed. It would be, he said, his contribution to Church unity. I started to be damping and pointed out that he could effect more, in the end, for Christian unity by remaining a Methodist and by working as a layman for the reunion of Anglicanism and

Methodism. But he's gone too far, as I had to admit. He
regards the reasons for Methodism, good at the time, as
non-existent now; he dislikes the subjectiveness of its
worship, its low sacramentalism, its concept of a small
gathered church. Of course he's right and I'm glad he
thinks this. But where will be a chance for reunion if men
who think like him become Anglicans? We shall have to
negotiate with a rump of die-hard Methodist
conservatives. And Methodism does have something we
neglect in the C of E. [29 November 1959]

Received a note from C. that he and his fiancée will be
received into the Roman Church at 12.15 p.m. tomorrow
and inviting me to attend. I am rather relieved that I shall
be holding a supervision then. This is the first time this has
happened in the five and a half years I've been here,
although I have received more than one *from* Rome. I feel
rather like a father whose son is marrying a girl of whom
he does *not* approve but who nevertheless sincerely wishes
the couple what happiness and success they can get.

The Roman Catholic chaplain in Cambridge was Monsignor
Gilbey, reputedly the only Roman Catholic priest living on his
own patrimony. Gilbey went to see Montefiore on one occasion
when a Roman Catholic committed suicide. Gilbey arrived
wearing a cassock and cloak, accompanied by an undergraduate
acolyte. Once Montefiore dined at Fisher House, where Gilbey
lived and held court. There was a muffled ring from inside a
commode. Gilbey opened it and took out a telephone, explaining that he could not bear to have these new-fangled things
openly in the room. In the end there was a rumpus with the
students because Gilbey refused to have the Newman Society
tainted by female members. He resigned, and Montefiore
invited him to a farewell dinner in Caius with some chosen
friends of his. It was a tribute to a fine pastor. Gilbey's successor
was 'new' rather than old-fashioned. He did not last long.
    What qualities and deficiences did undergraduates find in
Montefiore? There was moral conviction, courage and fervour
– a characteristic one often notices in Jews. He was a man of
passion and his courage was matched by sensitivity to criticism.

Ian Brockington was an undergraduate at Caius and a member of CICCU, and he later renewed contact with Montefiore at Birmingham. He is now Professor of Psychiatry at the University of Birmingham. He says of Montefiore:

> His manner of relating to people betrays the mixture of courage and determination to break down barriers of reserve with a lack of care. I don't think he ever feels one of us – a simple human being like any other. He feels intrinsically (and of course is) a very special person, not only as an individual but as a type almost unique. Nevertheless I feel some regret that he has never become what I would like – a friend . . . but I have a great affection for him.
>
> The breadth of his outlook and sympathies is tempered with intolerance. He was very stiff with a fellow medical student who was forced into marriage by pregnancy, and was intolerant of the evangelicals who knew they were saved, not just trying their best to be Christian. Later, when I drifted away (temporarily) he found this difficult to accept. For him the Resurrection was a solid historical fact and the question was always whether or not I had returned to the fold. A great public personality, but chiefly, for me, a man of exemplary moral passion.

Montefiore cared for and about undergraduates. They were his pastoral care and responsibility. At the end of term he would be exhausted to the point of collapse. The entry in his diary for 11 January 1960 read:

> The whole racket is about to begin again. I feel very remote from it all after a vacation; and then I see the undergraduates again and they melt my heart and I find myself loving them deeply and caring for them; and after a day or so the stimulus begins to work and my tempo of living and ratiocination increases. But just at the moment I'm a little flat, a little self-pitying as I contemplate the end of a delightful 'leave' with my adorable family.

Once back at Caius he put the undergraduates and teaching

first and always he offered to help anyone, whatever the problem. Once a Bulgarian, at Cambridge on a British Council scholarship, told Montefiore that he was a Bulgarian spy, and wished to change allegiance and spy for Britain. Would Montefiore help him? This resulted in a *crise de conscience*. Should Montefiore take up the case? He decided to do so, had an interview with the chief constable, who informed MI5. Montefiore recalls how MI5 came down to Cambridge to interview the Bulgarian after some ridiculous manoeuvres to shake off non-existent shadowers. They took a dismal view of the Bulgarian, especially when he took a group of friends to Russia during the long vacation and they thought they had lost him. But he returned to Cambridge. His object was to get more money. The Bulgarian embassy paid all his college bills but would not give him a personal allowance. He hit on the happy scheme of ordering crates of whisky from the buttery and selling them cheaply to his fellow students. The embassy paid his bill and no questions were asked.

There were the usual student capers, japes and wheezes. On one occasion two of his pupils had been discovered in the hours before daybreak near Senate House with M1 motorway signs which they intended erecting over Trinity Street. The case came to court but was dismissed after Montefiore had recruited a very able solicitor who was able to show that no larceny had been committed as there was no intention permanently to deprive the Minister of his M1 signs.

On another occasion Montefiore was cycling in to celebrate the Eucharist one Sunday morning when he spotted on the roof of the Senate House an object which could only be described as a motor car! A senior engineering scholar had masterminded the astonishing feat of getting it there, as a result of a bet in a pub. All Cambridge seemed to gather to watch the fire brigade get it down – they had to dismantle it in order to do so. The mastermind was never brought to book although he had almost given himself up when he thought the firemen were in danger themselves.

Montefiore was always willing to speak on behalf of his undergraduates. One brilliant student appeared in court in London following a political demonstration. Montefiore's testimony as to his good character was sufficient to save the student.

There were the usual range of religious and moral dilemmas requiring counsel. The chief problem was the pressure and expectations of parents, their lack of understanding and tendency to cling. Montefiore was determined to cut parental umbilical cords where they were hampering adult relationships. Yet he was careful not to have students exchanging one dependent relationship for a lean-to one. He did not push himself on students, having made up his mind that as dean he would not enter a student's room unless invited. Moreover, he never drove a wedge between the college and the chapel: all must be treated equally. Thus Montefiore's method of being available meant that any student, not only those with 'chapel' allegiance, with any problem, found him approachable. David Kunzle, now at the University of California, found Montefiore was warm, soft and vital and, when necessary, challenging: 'He was a man with whom you could be immediately intimate; he asked me to call him Hugh, which surprised me. He revealed himself and this was unusual. Dons were dons: and chaplains and clerics were fussy and buttoned-up people. Hugh was an exception.'

There was a strong feeling that Montefiore was on the undergraduates' side. They knew he was not always liked by other fellows. His strong convictions and opinions about how the college should be run did not meet with great approval. He detested the rigging of Faculty Board elections. In exasperation, he noted: 'We keep the trappings of democracy; the system is run by meritocrats. Who, I wonder, is deceived?' The governing body may have been annoyed with Montefiore, and soon realized that if he thought he was right, he could not in conscience let go until he had got his way.

The governing body could afford to bide their time and they were going to make sure that the new dean would not be anything like Montefiore. They temporized after his departure, leaving a chaplain holding the fort. It is not without significance that Nevill Mott, the master, failed to have his nomination for bursar, senior tutor or for Montefiore's successor appointed. Caius was not a happy fellowship body. While Montefiore was there he was strong enough to blunt some of the knives, but when he left they were resharpened.

Whether the fellows were united or not, there was a real *universitas* of learning, in which Montefiore revelled. Subjects ranged from astrophysics to Tibetan. The latter attracted no pupils until eventually a girl enrolled – much to the fellow's annoyance!

Whilst Montefiore was a fellow, Caius built Harvey Court on the far side of the Backs, where the college owned much land. This was an interesting venture. The fellow in astrophysics worked out how many hours of sunlight there would be in the centre of the court in June and in January.

Montefiore was made to feel responsible for one bye-fellow in particular, Emmanuel Alexandre Amand de Mendieta, a Belgian who had been a Benedictine monk. He was well known among scholars for his work on St Basil the Great. He had walked out of his monastery before it was fashionable to do so, married a young Belgian girl, and was received into the Church of England by the Archbishop of Canterbury in 1957. His first celebration of the Holy Communion, as an Anglican, was unfortunately widely publicized. Montefiore was determined that the press should be excluded. It took place on a weekday morning before breakfast. The college gates were closed and only invited guests were allowed in the chapel. The precaution was taken of stationing a boxing blue outside the chapel, which was both fortunate and necessary as one tabloid newspaper had sent down an old Caian who had gained access through the kitchens.

De Mendieta felt isolated and once went to Montefiore in tears: 'No one made a communication to me during dinner,' he said. 'I had to sit in silence.' 'Did you speak to anyone?' Montefiore asked. 'Of course not,' he replied. He was almost entirely dependent on Montefiore. He could only speak 'francophile English' with a strong accent. He was sometimes almost unintelligible. Montefiore had tried speech therapy, but was told de Mendieta's tongue was too short.

Montefiore was concerned as to what would happen to de Mendieta after the three-year fellowship ended in 1960. Nothing transpired. Dr Joseph Needham, a fellow and the famous sinologist, came to the rescue. The college statutes permitted the election of a fellow of outstanding distinction. Needham decided that this was appropriate. All de Mendieta's voluminous writings were put into a tin trunk and carried round by the college porters to the rooms of members of the

College Council. Needless to say, there was no election.

The Archbishop of Canterbury (Geoffrey Fisher) acted as if Montefiore were responsible for de Mendieta's future and did but little after having received him into the Church of England. Montefiore took note whenever a residentiary canonry became vacant, and wrote forthwith to the bishop concerned, but to no avail. It was always 'bespoke'. Then in 1962 at Winchester two fell vacant at the same time, and the kind heart of Falkner Allison, then Bishop of Winchester, melted. At Winchester de Mendieta lived happily – though still unintelligible in the pulpit.

As the undergraduates' don, Montefiore is remembered in various ways. On social occasions, at college dinners and especially at those functions when undergraduates were present, Montefiore was in his element, exuding fun and laughter, *bonhomie* and wit. The Shaker Dinner and the Shaker Breakfast were especially memorable events, when he was the centre of the jollity. Yet there were times when he was the absent-minded professor who could cut people dead in the street or the court: but for these lapses people were very ready to forgive him.

Whatever his other duties, Montefiore never lost sight of his primary function, that of a priest presenting the Christian faith as a live option, worth considering seriously because it made sense – the *reasonableness* of Christianity. He had the unusual ability to preach to both mind and heart. What of the teacher and scholar?

7   'Everything I've Got'

Nature has its own way of stilling human tornados. The pace at which Montefiore worked was physically exhausting, mentally excessive and morally wrong. It has become fashionable to refer to people as workaholics, which often means an excess of dedication or an insatiable lust for work. H. Hensley Henson was an example of this excess and the words he used of someone else also apply to himself: 'Like most young clergymen who are worth anything, he started with gross mismanagement of himself, assuming that excellence of purpose can atone for neglect of the laws of health.'[1] It is a fault for it means that there are areas of neglect – perhaps family, friends, or other interests, but chiefly one's own stability.

Montefiore paid little heed to the hectic life he lived: lecturing, writing, preaching, thinking, reading, endless pastoral calls on his time, much travelling (for he was in demand), and a family still growing up. There were times when he was in danger of burning himself out physically and mentally, which showed in his Achilles' heel – his back. Sustained strain and stress put him physically 'on his back'. He suffered great pain and had to abandon everything he was doing, as a note in his diary for the Easter vacation, 1960, records.

It included the end-of-term examination of choral exhibitioners, the preparation of a course of lectures for Part II (The New Testament Doctrine of Man), the preparation and delivery of a course of lectures at Wells Theological College during Holy Week, the delivery of addresses at S. Margaret's, Westminster, on Good Friday, the opening of a discussion at 'Dons and Beaks' on the implications of the ending of national service, etc. As a result of all this I regret to say I broke under the strain during the last week of term and simply cleared out for a month leaving everything in the air. Appalling feeling of 'angst' over lecturing, inability to sleep, stress and strain.

Elisabeth also suffered from strain and her back, too, cracked under it. Montefiore was still feeling far from well, wondering when or if he would be fit again, when he heard that his father was very ill.

Saturday 7 May 1960
Drove to London . . . Dad v. bad and unconscious . . . By 5 p.m. Dad v. weak indeed, doctor re-called and he was there when Dad died at 5.42 p.m. Thank goodness he is at last released from the burden of flesh . . . How quickly death changes the body! One minute the flesh is alive with instinct and personality. Within a quarter of an hour the body is a piece of marble. It is ridiculous to associate such flesh any further with personality. But it does look peaceful, compared with the losing fight with life a few minutes earlier. Watching my father's death confirmed me v. strongly in two beliefs: (i) death is *but* an incident, for all its awfulness and solemnity. On what grounds *dare* one say that death is the decisive moment? (ii) belief in the saving work of Jesus is not essential before death. (What is necessary after death we have no means of knowing.) My father lived and died as a good and virtuous Jew. I am sure that God will take him lovingly to Himself in ways known only to Him. Of course I wish that he had known the truth in Christ (and did he perhaps half-believe it?) but I do not hold for a moment that such a conviction makes any difference to his eternal destiny – such a conviction, that is, held during his lifetime . . . Difficulty over funeral arrangements, as orthodox Jews do not answer the telephone until the Sabbath is out! The body is laid out by the Lavadores, the highest honour the synagogue can give! No trouble about undertakers – all done through the

secretary of the synagogue. Everyone has a simple black coffin.

Monday 9 May
Bought a black hat & black tie and had my hair cut for tomorrow's funeral.

Tuesday 10 May
Travelled down to Ramsgate for the funeral. The funeral service began in a scruffy little mortuary which had not been used for six years, with Dad's coffin (a black box) being on a bier covered by a tatty pall. Pereira & Abinnu walked seven times round the bier leading the chanting of the Supplications. Then the coffin was taken to the grave and as it was lowered in Psalm 91 (in Hebrew – as the whole service) was recited. First we three sons, then the rest of those present, threw in three handfuls of earth. Next we had to 'wash our hands with pure water' – Denzil reminded me. Then back to the scruffy mortuary. The chief mourners say Mourners' Kaddesh – but I did not join in. At the end all present came and shook Denzil, Oliver and myself by the hand . . . Then we went to the minister's house and the chief mourners were given hard-boiled eggs – a curious custom. The minister later told me that originally the neighbour offered food as the mourners were supposed to be too busy and eggs were the easiest, but that later the symbolism of resurrection was attached to the eggs. It was some comfort at any rate not having greasy undertakers and smooth black cars. The whole thing was informal and ritualistic and reminded me faintly of the R.C.'s, and utterly un-Anglican in ethos. Flowers were permitted but care had to be exercised to see that they were not in the form of a cross. I was strangely moved by the coffin being lowered. The death of a parent is, if nothing more, the end of an epoch: but it was much more than that. I felt much more emotion than I had thought possible.

After the death of her husband, Montefiore's mother went to live at Burrswood, near Tunbridge Wells. Burrswood was a centre for divine healing and medical care in which orthodox religion and medicine worked hand in hand. It had been established by Dorothy Kerin. Montefiore's mother had often spent time there previously and had got to know Dorothy Kerin. His mother had had a troubled life. Her upbringing had been very different from that of her husband. She was brought up in the Jewish faith but she was free to attend church, which she did from time to time. She had hesitated before marrying Charles Sebag-Montefiore for, although she was fond of him, he seemed much older than she in spite of his being only twenty-nine when she was twenty-two, and his drive and ambition frightened her. By the time Montefiore was born she had become quite ill and his childhood memory of her is one of a long series of illnesses. She was generous and romantic and was the least affected by Hugh's conversion to Christianity of all his family. At the time he did not know why. When he started to study theology at Oxford after the war, she persuaded him to change his hyphenated name from Sebag-Montefiore to Montefiore.

Montefiore gradually realized that the illness from which his mother suffered was mental in origin and that she had been diagnosed as 'manic depressive'.

Towards the end of her life she herself was baptized and became a believing and practising Christian, although this was not known in Jewish circles as she was rarely seen. Montefiore visited her at Burrswood and was with her when she died, peacefully, in July 1977 in her eighties. She had a powerful influence on him, as Jewish matriarchs do, and yet while she lived he suffered from a feeling of nameless guilt. None the less he was fond of her, yet he had not found it possible to share his faith with her and, once a Christian, he was not able to share his Jewishness with anyone.

Montefiore's feeling of Jewishness often surprised. At a dinner given by the Master of Caius in June 1960, Montefiore met two other Jews – Professor Nabarro and Miss Leshke – and noted in his diary: 'It is strange how Jews manage to combine intelligence and vivacity. What a very remarkable race we are. I am sure that there is more to Judaism than Christian theology seems to allow.'

There has always been a mental restlessness about Hugh

Montefiore. That is why he would not have been satisfied with pursuing a purely academic career. A lifetime of learned footnotes did not appeal. Moreover, he had not been ordained to remain for ever in the college milieu, much as he enjoyed it. To date, Caius had been the most satisfying period of his life. But he needed a new challenge. What should it be? In 1961 he had been approached about the University Church of St Mary the Virgin, Oxford. He was tempted by the pastoral work, but Oxford was not as vital as Cambridge at the time.

Meanwhile he was writing his commentary on Hebrews and there was also the opportunity of travel, a sufficient distraction from the cares of Cambridge. He did not grumble when he was asked to give some talks or lectures during his journey.

In March 1963 Montefiore left for Rome. He was unimpressed with the Roman remains except for the unbroken columns. Much more appealing was living history, which he found in a place like San Clemente – 'Wonderfully simple and peaceful – I loved it.' In the immensely impressive basilica, run by some hearty Irish Dominicans, he could *feel* the history. Jerome had known the church in 393 and Gregory had delivered two homilies there. Said to be built on Clement's house, the crypt is the original church, but the upper floor houses a church built on the original design with the choir moved upstairs.

On 6 March he attended a general audience of Pope John XXIII. The Secretariat for Unity had provided the ticket, and although one of 3,000, he found himself with a front-row seat.

> The old man was due at noon, arrived at 12.30 p.m. amid tumultuous clapping, seated on a sedan chair, attended by a large suite . . . The pope looked white and anaemic and very old, but livened up when he began to speak, which he did for over twenty-five mins., all about S. Joseph (*not* BVM), patron of universal church. He paid little attention to his chamberlain, insisting on presentations before he spoke, and bursting into French for five minutes just when it was announced that he would pronounce the Benediction. He had all (except his suite) with smiles on their faces and laughter on their lips: he must be the terror of his bureaucrats. These court officials had suave voices, wore beautiful clothes, elegant, etc. Somehow one

understands Roman Catholicism better here. It has taken over and baptized the Imperial Ideal. The obelisks have crosses, the Phantheon is a Christian Church, etc. The evidences for Roman Catholicism are so *solid* and so impressive that it's obvious why (psychologically) tradition counts for more than truth. Reform could never begin naturally from Rome – but then the pope is plainly a man of God.[2]

On 9 March he left Rome for the Lebanon. Place and people were unappealing.

On 11 March Montefiore flew to Jerusalem (Jordan) and noticed that Israel was called on the maps 'Occupied Country of Palestine'. He was staying at St George's College as a guest of the principal, Canon F.V.A. Boyse, who was pro-Arab. Montefiore had to 'sing for his supper' by giving some lectures. He was a little scared once he knew that they would be attended by most of the Roman Catholic Dominicans in Jerusalem. Nervous shivers ran down his spine when the head of the École Biblique said to him, 'We are putting our Coptic scholars in the front.' Montefiore was to lecture on St Thomas' Gospel, which was originally written in Coptic. The language was not completely unrecognizable because it had many 'loan words' in Greek script. Moreover, he had studied the subject and had written a paper on 'A Comparison of the Parables of the Gospel according to Thomas and of the Synoptic Gospels'.[3] The article also appeared in *Thomas and the Evangelists*, a joint work with H.E.W. Turner,[4] Van Mildert Professor of Divinity in the University of Durham, who had

delivered two lectures on the Gospel of Thomas at Codrington, Barbados, and subsequently as public lectures in Durham . . . We took different views of the relation between Thomas and the canonical Gospels. I still believe that Thomas was acquainted with and basing himself on the Synoptic tradition, Hugh regarding him as independent. I was entirely happy to share a volume with him.

They later met as members of the Doctrine Commission.

Professor Turner says, 'Hugh stood definitely to the left of centre theologically while I was moderately but determinedly right. Yet although some of the radicals seemed distinctly impatient about those who were not in agreement with them, Hugh was always conciliatory and friendly.'

Montefiore's lectures in Jerusalem were well received, as was Montefiore himself. Naturally there was especial interest in his Jewish roots, even if he did forget who and where he was when he walked to the Hot Spring Baths at Tiberias – on the Sabbath! This was noted in the Jewish press. But there was thrill and pride in following in Sir Moses Montefiore's footsteps – although 'footsteps' is not the right word to use. Sir Moses had to be carried into the Temple Area by Arab porters, as Jews feared to enter lest they trod unawares on the Holy of Holies. Visiting the Montefiore quarter in Jerusalem was a moving experience, as was the sight of the Montefiore windmill, which was there to encourage Jews to grind their own grain.

It was even more important to be in the land of Jesus Christ. Montefiore was fortunate in having as his guides two members of the staff from St George's College: John Wilkinson, who was later head of the British School of Archaeology in Jerusalem, and Canon Edward Every, the chaplain. John Wilkinson showed him the ancient sites. A visit to Petra left Montefiore breathless.

Everywhere the Bible and history crowded in on Montefiore. When he made his way to Chorazin he reflected how that prophecy (Luke 10:13) had been fulfilled. When the Fathers of the Assumption were excavating to build the Church of St Peter Gallicante they found a Jewish street, baths, houses, etc., of the period before AD 70 and even a house with servants' quarters, dungeons, weights and measures. Montefiore noted in his diary: 'Evidence for the House of Caiaphas very strong I think, and one could see where Jesus was interrogated – court-yard where he looked *on* Peter. Tradition says Jesus was flayed here.'

Bethlehem, Bethphage, the Mount of Olives with the Church of the Ascension (shared with a Mosque), the Dead Sea, Mountains of Moab, the wilderness of Judaea, Jericho, Qumran – all had double significance for Montefiore. Some of the Christian sites were too commercialized, even then, for authenticity and comfort, yet his historical imagination helped him to distinguish between the possible and improbable. It was otherwise with some Jewish sites. He could not bear to see David's 'tomb', because it was bogus.

Other divisions pressed themselves upon Montefiore – as when he nearly became lost in the Muslim part of the Holy City by the Wailing Wall. He took a wrong turn towards the chief mosque and a large stone fell just behind him. Thenceforward he was careful. He made this observation in his diary on 19 March:

> Most people I've met sympathize with Arabs against the Jews, reckon that the Jews arrange 'incidents', admire the King [of Jordan] greatly, reckon he is v. brave and insecure on his throne, because of Cairo promises to get back Israeli territory. This country is certainly a land of sorrow and distress and the fate of refugees is shocking, with deficiency diseases, apathy and hatred on their faces. The Arabs are certainly a very lovable people, rather like sweet children, valuing friendship v. highly, but volatile and changeable.

Montefiore was on the top of Mount Carmel when a telegram arrived offering him the living of Great St Mary's, Cambridge. Of course he knew it was vacant, for his good friend Joe Fison had been nominated Bishop of Salisbury. But it had not crossed his mind that he would be considered for the place, or even that he might be interested in such an appointment.

He returned to England at the beginning of April 1963. He sought the advice of the Archbishop of Canterbury (Michael Ramsey), the Bishop of Edinburgh (Kenneth Carey) and Alec Vidler of King's College. The advice was conflicting. Great St Mary's had been 'put on the map' by the dynamism and imagination of Mervyn Stockwood, who was followed by the vivid and unconventional personality of Joe Fison. Was Montefiore the right man to follow them? Was it not a job – to use a dramatic analogy – for a producer rather than a playwright or actor? Surely Montefiore was not a producer but rather a playwright who had hardly begun. He was dedicated to theological thought and accepting Great St Mary's would thin out those who were qualified and capable of responding to the recent storm arising out of *Soundings, Honest to God* and similar works. Yet Great St Mary's was the centre of Church life in Cambridge, and well-known throughout the land. All the more reason to have in that place someone who could speak with authority about the 'new theology', someone who could see the value of the new ideas and answer them effectively.

What should he do? It was a turning point in his ministry. Either he continued in a college and became an academic, or he brought his academic learning to the service of a pastoral ministry. Montefiore knew he was not of the very highest calibre for professional work and, more important, he had not been ordained to bury himself in university libraries. Moreover, he knew from the experience of other people that God often uses a sabbatical for preparing someone for a new job as much as for 'refurbishing' one to do the old job better.

The Archbishop of Canterbury wrote to him in 10 April 1963:

> I don't think it only a question of weighing . . . the cause of the University Church and the cause of Caius and the opportunities which go with it: it is also a question of weighing them in the light of the fact that you have already been doing the latter for some years. That being so, I think it is relevant to consider these points:
>
> 1 It is a very distinctive and important work that is offered to you, and you have been judged to have the gifts for it. Not many others can have the combination of gifts, together with an understanding of Cambridge. But quite a few may have the gifts for the work at Caius.
> 2 It would be for you, while there is yet time, a considerable widening of pastoral and other experience: all your long-term powers of service would benefit greatly from this.
> 3 I expect it would mean a sacrifice in the leisure to read and write. This would have to be faced – no long vacations. But it would be *very far* from a total loss in respect of this: it would be reading and writing at a *slower pace*, and with the art of using odd hours and half hours! But – *experto crede*, if I may very humbly say so – there really is a sort of mental quickening which comes from a more varied

pastoral activity, and something deeply joyful in it.

Those are the things about it which occur to me most clearly. These decisions are never easy, but I believe that when one has struggled to weigh out 'pros' and 'cons' there comes a sort of 'hunch' which leaves one in no doubt.

In a way Montefiore had no choice. He has a strong sense of vocation, of being led, ever aware that vocation has two sides: God calls through his Church – that is the exterior call. The response comes from the individual, via the interior call. Acceptance brings its own peace.

Once the announcement was made, Montefiore made it clear that he was going to Great St Mary's not as a don, but as a parish priest; he resigned his university lectureship and his fellowship at Caius would lapse; 'I'm all set to give everything I've got to the parish of Great St Mary's.'

A number of factors made Montefiore's departure from Caius an especially painful wrench. The master, Nevill Mott, wrote: 'I shall miss the warmth – and the belief that the college matters – that you bring into college life.' After Montefiore left there was little warmth left in the college for Mott. He resigned in 1966 but rose to still greater heights of scientific discovery – from wave mechanics and atomic structure to solid-state physics. He received the Nobel Prize in 1977.

Geoffrey Lampe was appointed acting dean until Montefiore's successor, J.V.M. Sturdy, was appointed in 1965; he remains chaplain and dean to this day.

There were two further difficult legacies. One concerned St Michael's, Cambridge, which was part of the united benefice with Great St Mary's. St Michael's, whose history could be traced back to 1211, had long been out of regular use. Many abortive suggestions had been made about its future. Architecturally the church was a complete specimen of the Decorated style. It was directly opposite Caius' main buildings and the churchyard already belonged to Caius who wanted the church for a library. Negotiations were already taking place when Montefiore changed from don to vicar. Surely this would accelerate negotiations. It did, but not in the way Caius intended. As soon as he moved to Great St Mary's, Montefiore broke off negotiations and brought in the architect George Pace, who quickly prepared imaginative plans to transform St Michael's, preserving the unique features of the church and yet creating a valuable hall and rooms in the centre of Cambridge from which city and university alike could benefit. An appeal was launched, supported by the mayor (J.B. Collins), who was a member of Great St Mary's congregation, the vice-chancellor (J.S. Boys Smith) and others.

Montefiore and his Parochial Church Council believed that since the Church of God should serve the whole community, a church building should, when appropriate, have a similar function. Uniting town and gown was a large plank in his ministerial platform.

The second bone of contention concerned a college musical which included sketches about the 'wicked dean', which were hurtful and uncharitable rather than satirical – and Montefiore *was* hurt.

Yet the machinations of academic life are such that there were lengthy discussions preceding his departure as to whether or not to make him an honorary fellow. Eventually Caius decided not to do so since this was an honour given rarely, to really distinguished scholars, but he was made a member of the Room and remained director of studies for just over a year, with a room in college for his use.

And so to Great St Mary's, the university church. Originally called St Mary's by the Market, the church is not a building of exceptional beauty. The handsome roof is of interest. Galleries had been put in in 1739 to accommodate the numbers of people who thronged to the church to hear famous men preach the university sermons. The one reserved for doctors and heads of houses was known as Golgotha, the place of the skull. After long years of neglect Mervyn Stockwood had packed the galleries with people Sunday by Sunday.

Of course, the Montefiores were no strangers to Great St Mary's. Their children, Teresa, Janet and Catherine, were confirmed there and Joe Fison often called on Montefiore's help at the parish communion during vacations.

Change of job did not involve a change of residence. With the permission of Gonville and Caius, Montefiore stayed at Springfield. It was thrown open to the parish of Great St Mary's. The vicarage, which was further from the church than Springfield, had to be let unfurnished on short leases. This was something of a burden but the choice was Montefiore's.

There were conspicuous differences between Montefiore and the former vicar. People drew attention to what they regarded as Montefiore's main weakness – an inability to spend time with people. They felt that all the while he had to get on with the next task in hand. Time pressed. In contrast Joe Fison had managed to make one feel that one was the only person in the world who mattered to him. At first the congregation missed that feeling, and often found Montefiore brusque, rude and uninterested. Yet he was deeply concerned with individuals and was a caring pastor. One member of the congregation had been particularly upset by Montefiore walking past her in King's Parade and completely ignoring her. At Evensong one of the curates mentioned this and Montefiore tore off at great speed in his red Mini to see the lady. He charmed her completely, as he could, and all was forgiven. She was impressed that he had bothered about it. She did not realize that her vicar was vulnerable and needed to be loved.

This reveals something important about Montefiore./On the surface he is self-possessed and can seem the extrovert, a dominating and domineering personality, yet he can be very easily hurt by an unkind review or by a personal attack in a magazine or newspaper. Despite impressions to the contrary, he was and is a deeply caring person. He remains a strange mixture of immense compassion and academic detachment.

Joe Fison had left few records, and his administrative abilities were nigh-on non-existent. Montefiore rectified this and galvanized his staff into action. There were two curates, a full-time secretary and verger – the latter paid by the university. There was an office and study in the church.

Montefiore took the training of curates very seriously and few would argue with Ian Ogilvie: 'The most stimulating, enthusiastic, hard-working, demanding, brilliant, infuriating, dynamic person I have ever worked for!'

The staff were expected to say the Daily Offices together, and only if Montefiore was away would he miss them himself, though with his hectic schedule he often used to arrive all of a heap just as the church clock stuck five and 'O Lord open thou our lips' was being said. He insisted on a period of meditation every morning after Matins and before the Eucharist. He believed in a discipline of prayer and led by example.

Barney Hopkinson, now Archdeacon of Sarum, was a curate:

Sermons to be preached on Sunday had to be handed in by Thursday, and were returned on the Friday or Saturday with detailed comments and suggestions. Some comments seemed to be trivial 'niggles'; others went right to the root of the role of the preacher: 'What are you actually asking them to *do* – if they take you seriously?' 'Are you wanting to encourage, or just criticize?' I can honestly say I learned more about the preacher's art from Hugh than from my theological college. He was also meticulous about liturgy. 'You must become a liturgical animal,' he would say, and for the first few months I received a detailed list of my shortcomings after almost any service I conducted. Again, the comments ranged from the apparently trivial to the vitally important, often in random order. An odd mannerism might be followed by a failure in voice production or a theological misdemeanour in the intercessions. 'You cannot treat the Almighty as a weather-clerk. Even if there is desperate flooding in Kent, you may not pray for fine weather there.'

Hugh went to immense efforts to make sure that everything went right in our worship. Unfortunately his very concern sometimes had the reverse effect. His nerves were stretched to the limit just before a major special service, and often he would prowl around double-checking on everyone and everything, which meant that verger, curates, organist and choir were not always at their best when the service started. The first time that Hugh had to miss an important service the anxiety level reached a new pitch. Trevor Huddleston was to preach and we expected a packed church at the 8.30 p.m. service. But Hugh was committed to a course of lectures in Belfast, and could not possibly be back in time. Very reluctantly he agreed that the curates would have to conduct the simple service which introduced the sermon. I was given detailed instructions about the style of introduction that I should give and about the notices. I prepared myself very carefully. When I arrived at church that evening George, the verger, met me. 'He's decided to do the notices himself – they're all here on tape.' So I had to stand in the central pulpit in front of some two thousand people to introduce the recorded voice of the vicar giving the welcome and notices.

Another former curate, Canon Richard Garrard, adds:

Hugh's speed and attention to detail was immense. It also became a menace from time to time . . . On one occasion he became greatly concerned because we had no more ink for the Roneo machine which produced the weekly notice sheets handed to the congregation as they arrived at church. Hugh dashed over to Caius College . . . and begged a bottle of duplicating ink from the office there. He returned to the office carrying a bottle of Gestetner ink, which he proceeded to pour into the Roneo. George Clarke, the verger, mentioned the discrepancy but Hugh was intent on the job. He turned on the machine and in a moment the Gestetner water-based ink filled the air and reduced me to helpless and scarcely concealed laughter.

But Hugh could admit he was wrong, he could apologize handsomely when it was necessary. This I found to be one of his most endearing traits. On one occasion I had to organize police, ambulance and fire brigade to remove a frenzied mental patient from the top of Great St Mary's tower, where he had gone to commit suicide. Matters were not made easier because the media people also turned up, hoping, presumably, for a dramatic picture of a suicide leap. An undergraduate who had found the man on the tower-top was very distressed, and in need of coffee and a good listening to. The whole event blew up about forty-five minutes before Evening Prayer. I was less than pleased when high-speed Hugh gave me a ticking off for missing Evening Prayer that day but the next morning his apology was complete and handsome. I often recall that incident whenever I am tempted to intervention and hasty correction.

The church's worship was at the front of Montefiore's concern. He was particularly pleased when one curate gave the church a beautifully made oak communion table for the nave altar as a thanksgiving/leaving present. The Eucharist was at the heart of daily and Sunday worship; Montefiore did not like the distant sanctuary altar and the nave altar gift was like manna from above. Confronted with such a gift, the Parochial Church Council had to accept it, but Montefiore still remembers the consternation which its introduction caused to some. A normally peaceful and kindly single lady came out of church shaking her fist at the vicar saying, 'You have taken away my long walk to God.' A prominent layman, the Cambridge city architect, left in protest, but as he returned when Montefiore left, it is possible that the vicar rather than the altar was the problem.

Of course, Montefiore was expected to do two jobs: one for 'gown' and one for 'town' and the town took up far more time than the university. He understood better than his precedessor every nuance of college and university life. He knew the value of using undergraduates yet never relying too much on them. From the start he determined never to counsel a student unless approached specifically for that purpose.

At Great St Mary's Sunday was an exhilarating beginning for the congregation but an exhausting conclusion for the clergy. There was a said Holy Communion at 8 a.m. followed by the chief morning service, Sung Eucharist, at 9.45 a.m. This was the heart of the fellowship. As there was Matins and a sermon at 11 a.m., Montefiore tried to introduce a four-minute sermon at the Sung Eucharist, with an egg timer in the pulpit. The curates tended to turn it upside down when it had run out and went on with their preaching. Evensong, with a sermon, was held at 6.30 p.m. and two hours later, in term time, there was the university service.

Inviting and entertaining preachers was a major occupation. Courses of sermons and the preachers were planned at least one year ahead. World-famous men and women in various fields, bishops and archbishops, came to Great St Mary's. Montefiore's manner with them was easy and polite. Yet he always told them what was expected of them. On one occasion a speaker at the university service talked too long. Montefiore, seizing a suitable moment as the speaker paused, announced the final hymn.

I used to invite Christian politicians because I thought they ought to be heard. Some were disappointing . . . but some first rate . . . Enoch Powell I approached when he was Minister of Health. I invited him to preach on a subject related to health and caring: he said he would only preach on the Athanasian Creed. I told him it would not fit in the course. The following year I approached him again, and his response was similar; and so I had him to preach on the Creed. The church was packed with undergraduates who listened open mouthed to his belief that God only called a few to salvation, and without doubt there would be a large wastage – this from a Minister of Health! His sermon was delivered with sweet reasonableness. I also had George Brown to preach. He was very rude to some students who came to meet him earlier. His sermon passed off without incident, but so as to get my car out of Great St Mary's, he evidently enjoyed playing the policeman and holding up all traffic in the main road of Cambridge – something picked up later in the papers.

Malcolm Muggeridge, before he committed himself to Christianity, and was wondering about it, was a fine preacher. Billy Graham was invited, and I discovered that it was the Sunday before Tripos began. I told him that I wanted the undergraduates to be Christians but not to fail their exams, and asked if he would cool it; and he did. He preached a fine Whitsuntide sermon without any emotionalism. Tony Bridge, the former Dean of Guildford, was a fine preacher. He used the worst language I have heard in the pulpit, but with great effect. His forthright manner brought home the truth of Christianity to many. Fr Corbishley preached the first RC ecumenical sermon in a C of E parish church.

The best preacher of all at the evening services was without doubt Archbishop Michael Ramsey. He obviously greatly enjoyed these occasions. He had a wonderful combination of seriousness, lightness of touch and humility. The undergraduates loved him. He was excellent at answering questions afterwards. I remember one student asking him how he could be driven about in a huge Rolls with so much poverty in the world. He answered: 'Well, in the first place it is not a Rolls but a Ford; and in the second place I have to be driven so that I can write my sermons on the way.'

I tried to do something about the arts and the law. Denning preached, and W.H. Auden gave a poetry reading . . . the church was dangerously over-full with people standing in the aisles and no movement possible around the doors . . . we had to rearrange people so that in the event of an accident it would be possible to get out. It was a very memorable occasion . . .

Another interesting occasion was when Kaunda was over for the Commonwealth Conference . . . the only preacher I have known where the undergraduates, at the end of the sermon, spontaneously stood on their pews and gave him an ovation. I was alarmed when the police only sent two men to the church. I expostulated: 'But he's a head of state; you must give him proper protection when he comes.' They replied that if he had been a European head of state they would have sent dozens, but since he was an African, he would be bound to be popular with the students and they need not bother. They were right!

Other notable preachers at this time included Trevor Huddleston, Colin Morris and Martin Niemöller. It was a particularly notable achievement to bring Niemöller to Great St Mary's. There was a quiet nobility about his bearing which is often the mark of those who have stood out and suffered for their faith. When he arrived at Springfield he had a terrible cold and Elisabeth asked him what she could give him. He said, 'Madam, there is an old German naval remedy, rum and tea,' and proceeded to pour them into his cup in equal quantities.

And there was Duke Ellington. Unlike Pastor Niemöller, he did not mount the pulpit steps, yet did 'the most important thing I have ever done'. He continued:

It has been said that there was once a man who accompanied his worship by juggling. He was not the world's greatest juggler, but it was the thing he did best. And so it was accepted by God. I believe that no matter what the skill of a drummer or saxophonist, if this is the thing he does best, and he offers it sincerely from the heart in – or as an accompaniment to – his worship, then it will not be unacceptable because of the instrument upon which he makes his demonstration.

Duke Ellington and his Orchestra had first given a concert of sacred music in Grace Cathedral, San Francisco, in 1965, which was repeated that year at the Fifth Avenue Presbyterian Church in New York. Two months later it was performed before the High Altar of Coventry Cathedral.

Montefiore invited Duke Ellington to come to Great St Mary's in 1967. The result was one of the highlights of Montefiore's ministry in that place. There was a packed church and 500 more people were in the Senate House where the concert was relayed. The atmosphere was electric with style, mood, contrast and musical excellence offered to the glory of God.

On the afternoon before the concert, the 'Duke' relaxed on a camp bed in Montefiore's study. They talked, and it seemed that they had formed some affinity. When Montefiore formally welcomed the Duke before the crowd, there was a warmth of regard in their faces – the fabulous American jazz-band composer and leader and the university church vicar – both believers, both perfectionists, both showmen.

To some extent, any successful vicar of a major university church has to be something of showman, an impresario. Montefiore knew exactly how to stir controversy when controversy might help a cause. He saw the story angle for the press in whatever project he was pursuing.

Yet there has to be substance. For Montefiore it was a combination of worship and pulpit teaching. He really believed in church worship at a time when the received wisdom, even in theological colleges, was that it was rather a bore really: and the sooner you got your old clothes on and went out and 'loved' somebody, the sooner you were really following your faith. William Loveless, who became a curate at Great St Mary's at the age of forty-three, writes:

> Hugh showed in the deepest sense to those close to him
> that that was not true: that each of us needs to worship
> from the depths of our hearts – and how I remember, in
> this respect, the very early morning services of just the
> tiny group of us each day at Great St Mary's. What he also
> showed me particularly was that – with the right technique
> and effort – you could make any church service that you
> led really take hold of people and help people. That was
> one of his most precious gifts to me for my later career as a
> vicar.

I use the words 'pulpit teaching' rather than preaching. Montefiore was a teacher rather than a preacher. The physical
presence in the pulpit and the mannerisms were of a teacher –
expressive face and hands. He took immense pains with his
sermons, which never failed to interest, excite and inform, and
usually they had an attractive, amusing edge to them. He
showed an enormous capacity for assimilating and assembling
facts on the most complex issues. He could be relied upon to
clarify topics for those who heard his sermons. But did he delve
as deeply into his own convictions and judgements as might
have been wished? Did his superb presentation and faultless
fluency sometimes conceal rather than reveal him? His convictions on some issues were, for example, by no means radical,
but when it suited him he could certainly make it seem that they
were.

People felt the reviving sting of his healthy impatience with
everything that was sophisticated, pretentious, vague, unsure.
He taught by his example that the finest triumph of the intellect,
its supreme moral function, is achieved only when it simplifies
and elucidates. Here again is the teacher.

He was also a controversialist. Sometimes he stumbled into
controversy through an ill-chosen phrase. There were times
when he courted controversy, knowing full well the consequences of his actions. He saw this as stirring slumbering
Anglicans. He preached against moral confusion and against
spiritual emptiness in city and university.

In 1967 a conference of the World Congress of Faiths was

held at Christ's College, Cambridge. It was attended by Christians, Buddhists, Hindus, Jews, Moslems and Sikhs. A service was arranged at Great St Mary's at which Montefiore would preach. There were attempts to persuade the Bishop of Ely (E.J.K. Roberts) and the Archbishop of Canterbury (Michael Ramsey) to intervene and 'ban' the service. There was disquiet about having a 'service for people of all faiths': in October 1966 the Lower House of the convocation of Canterbury had passed by an overwhelming majority a resolution deploring such services. In May 1967 the Archbishop of Canterbury refused to approve a multi-faith service arranged for Commonwealth Sunday at St Martin-in-the-Fields, London. As a result, that service was cancelled.

But the order of service which had been drawn up for the Cambridge service did not at any point conflict with the Christian doctrine of the uniqueness of Christ. Moreover it was supported by Francis Palmer, the evangelical vicar of Holy Trinity, Cambridge.

The service went ahead on 24 September 1967. In his sermon Montefiore said that people who believed in the goodness of God could not possibly believe that he had disclosed himself within one religious tradition alone. Nor could they believe that eternal salvation for all men lay within the confines of only one religious institution. He added, 'As a Christian, I may clarify my position by saying that, according to the tradition that I have received, Christ died not for members of the Church but for the salvation of the whole wide world.' Canon J.C. Wansey, Rector of Woodford, Essex, and well-known Church Assembly figure, organized an 'anti-service' on the pavement outside Great St Mary's, but fortunately the Lord frustrated it with heavy rain!

In 1968 King's College Chapel, Cambridge, was re-opened following cleaning and restoration. A few remarks in the Great St Mary's newsletter of December 1968 caught the headlines. Montefiore wrote:

Astronomical sums of money have been spent to good effect and, if there is a certain loss of the numinous, there is certainly aesthetic gain. At the same time certain questions must be asked, because King's College Chapel is not just a

private place of worship: it is a national institution, . . .
The lowering of the floor has been undertaken to provide a
proper setting for Ruben's *Adoration of the Magi* under the
East Window – at the expense of the Holy Table. This
painting now takes the place of the Empty Cross. Is this a
symbol of secularization? . . . What Christian symbols
will the Chapel contain? Is it right to subordinate liturgical
function to aesthetic effect? These questions should be
asked – and answered.

The dean of King's College was David L. Edwards, now
Provost of Southwark. Agreement on the re-ordering had been
agreed before he was appointed. The new scheme made it
possible for the priest to move all round the altar. And, once
Montefiore had drawn attention to it, the centrality of the Cross
in its physical aspect could not be ignored. A beautifully
designed and simple cross now stands on the altar.

These are two examples, plucked from a continuous flow of
issues. On most issues Montefiore tackled he did his research
and homework at enormous speed, verifying his facts in a way
which most people do not attempt. His capacity for work has
always been as amazing as his energy. He proved himself to be
an unusual kind of all-rounder, one from whom the pastoral
imperative and the sense of mission have sounded out in a
distinctive way. Professor Robin Barbour, who has known him
from schooldays, comments:

He has suffered, of course, because he is supposed to be
indiscreet in some ways and to say things which will shock
just because they do shock. Both charges are unjust. He
has a very real understanding of human situations; he
knows how power operates in ecclesiastical as in other
situations, and while he may very occasionally have
allowed his name to be linked with projects or research or
opinions which have proved to be less than well-founded,
he has never allowed considerations of prudence or self-
preferment, policy or a false peace, to interfere with the
truth as he sees it.

Great St Mary's was a splendid forum for Montefiore.

Powerful memories from one of his curates, Ian Ogilvie, seem appropriate to bring this chapter to its conclusion:

> The 1960s was the time when the Church was experimenting in different ways with liturgies and also with the use of pop music in church. I had become interested in this in my first parish in Clapham and suggested to Hugh we ought to do something of this kind, not for the students but for teenagers in the city, who were often quite unconnected with any church. We were the city as well as the university church. Hugh was initially dubious, but agreed, and I was put in charge. The first time he flapped around, interfering, changing things and driving us all mad. When over 1,000 youngsters rolled in, wearing jeans and sweatshirts and long hair, he looked worried, but I think really quite pleased. We had stewards to keep an eye on everything and Hugh was here, there and everywhere. He surprised three boys in the loo during the service, all smoking, 'Just having a fag, Gov,' they said, 'during the sermon!' Although it was not really his scene, Hugh allowed these 'beat services' as we called them, to go on every quarter and once he saw the curates could cope he left us to it, taking his share in leading them.
>
> Great St Mary's was a preaching box for students, as refounded by Mervyn Stockwood, and the 8.30 p.m. Sunday services were the showcase . . . Hugh once described being vicar of Great St Mary's as being ringmaster of a circus. It was certainly true of his own style. He did not have the easy wit of Mervyn or the childlike delight and sense of humour of Joe Fison, but he held his audience and his humour and profundity came out in his always thoughtful choice of readings and music, which went with the famous preachers. When he preached at 8.30 he never drew a huge crowd, but his sermons were always thoughtful, logically and clearly presented and of a high quality. Although sometimes known by the students as 'Montefiasco', a nickname that was really very affectionate, he was much respected in the university among the younger generation, though sadly his relations with some senior members were not always too happy.

We turn now to his theological development at Cambridge.

8 Squalls and Tempests

Montefiore was in the thick but not at the centre of the theological and ecclesiastical ferment of the late 1950s and 1960s. Somehow he escaped the total radicalism of many of his contemporaries who seemed eager to introduce brand-new and brand-named theological thinking at the same time as seeking to democratize the ecclesiastical structures and modify or overturn the Church-State relationship.

Montefiore has always resisted the slightest hint of disestablishment. He holds that disestablishment would generally be regarded as the repudiation of Christianity by the State. Establishme t symbolizes the wistful religious aspirations of English people and prevents the Church's natural tendency to degenerate into a sect within a pluralist society.

Montefiore's individual brand of theological radicalism has not taken him into the same camp as John Robinson and his ilk. He was never part of what became known as the 'Southwark-Cambridge axis' despite his ministry in both places.

Moreover, Montefiore has marvellously managed to escape what he eschews – ecclesiastical labelling. Many is the time when friendly critics and uncritical foes have both attempted to pin a label on his restless person. The labels have not stuck.

No party could claim him. He supported some reforming movements but was never a full-hearted member. Such movements bypassed the deep malaise affecting the Church, which was mainly spiritual. The new age of science, technology, sociological and psychological insights, secondary and university education were areas more likely to interest and captivate his time and mind.

Montefiore's position in the Church of England has always been in the centre. The central position makes demands on conviction, conscience and courage. It has become fashionable to deride the central position and declaim its advocates. Yet this is where history has drawn some of the most powerful and persuasive exponents of Anglicanism.

The centre needs to be distinguished from the middle. In the *middle* one can find jelly-wobbling indecision, lukewarm commitment, theological apathy and ecclesiastical ignorance; in short, a religion which seems to have had most of its Christ-like life drained from it, an organization rather than a living organism. In the *centre* is the spring which sustains and surprises those who drink its energizing water, refreshing, renewing and challenging movements and prophets. The centre has also absorbed the best of the vastly different influences which have periodically strengthened the Church. The Evangelical Movement brought into the Church a strongly positive wave of evangelical enthusiasm, tinged with Lutheran pietism. The Tractarian Movement, which came later, contributed a revived sacramentalism, a sense of liturgy, an emphasis upon personal discipline of life on the lines of strict churchmanship. The Broad Church Movement, as much intellectual as religious, tended to stick relatively loosely both to dogma and to ecclesiasticism. At its best it has stood for the spirit of intellectual freedom, for candour of mind and devotion to truth for truth's sake, and the dedication of the intellect to God.

All three of these movements at times have been troublesome, and the more extravagant of their respective adherents have often exhibited but scanty regard for the central mind of the Church to which their allegiance and loyalty were pledged – they have looked outside Anglicanism for their inspiration. But they have all contributed something and the central mind of the Church of England has been deeply influenced by each of the three.

The evangelicals have kept alive in it a burning love for the conversion of souls and for the winning of the world to Christ. The liberals, in the steps of the Broad Church Movement, have witnessed to the necessity of bringing all modern thought into the service of the Master, and of using the intellect in the presentation of Christian truth. How important this is for a Church which has an appeal to sound learning. The Anglo-Catholics have given to it rich ideals of worship and of church-manship and restored to it a deeper sense of the sacramental life. The central mind of the Church has absorbed all that is best in these movements and they have found a focus in the life, work and thought of Montefiore.

The Cambridge Theological Faculty was an important influence on Montefiore's theological development. He was invited on the strength of his first from Oxford to the New Testament Seminar presided over by Professor C.H. Dodd.[1] Dodd was kind and helpful to the young aspiring Montefiore and complimented him on his paper, 'The Position of the Cana Miracle and the Cleansing of the Temple in St John's Gospel', to which reference was made in Dodd's great work on the fourth Gospel.[2]

Dodd was the doyen of English New Testament scholarship and General Director of the New English Bible. Energetic in mind, rapid in speech and neat in appearance, Dodd was an attractive as well as a profound thinker, and Montefiore considers that it was Dodd's encouragement that made him want to be a New Testament scholar.

After Dodd retired, the New Testament Seminar was led by Charlie Moule, Lady Margaret Professor of Divinity.[3] His was always essentially an orthodox mind whose keen evangelical convictions never interfered with his scholarship. Montefiore thought him a 'marvellous person . . . generations of young scholars and students owe him a vast amount.'

Montefiore has memories of other seminar people. W.L. Knox of Pembroke[4] seemed to live Greek literature. 'Just a minute,' he would say, ascend a ladder in the Divinity School Library where the seminar was held, and read out an obscure passage from Philo which wonderfully illuminated the point under discussion. He was distinctly Catholic yet refreshingly modernist in his outlook:

the Christian should have sufficient confidence in the inherent strength of the Catholic system to view with equanimity the exploration of every possible avenue of enquiry. If a particular line of thought is really, as it seems to him at the moment, fatal to the whole content of Christian devotion, it will certainly come to nought. If his fears are unfounded, it can only lead to a fresh apprehension of the truth and the enrichment of Christian devotion.[5]

Such thinking was interesting to Montefiore. People like Knox, who was also a member of the Oratory of the Good Shepherd, were fearless because they were spiritually earthed, unlike some modernist theologians whose explorations caused them to fly away with the idea they were pursuing, losing bearings and root.

Remarkable contributions to the seminar were made by David Daube,[6] who had been at Caius but went on to be Regius Professor of Civil Law at Oxford. He was a rabbinic scholar of repute. Henry Chadwick,[7] who flitted between regius professorships at Oxford and Cambridge, always seemed to have encyclopaedic knowledge and always just saved himself from portentousness by a nice touch of wit.

Henry Chadwick's brother, Owen,[8] was Master of Selwyn College for most of the time Montefiore was in Cambridge. As Professor of Ecclesiastical History he had many admirers. It was noticed that he did not commit himself to popular theological causes, but his spirituality and the modesty with which he carried his learning made a deep impression. Montefiore notes: 'He had a beautiful command of English as well as great knowledge and learning.' Owen Chadwick was one of the liveliest sages of the Church of England and not only of the Church. He went on to be Regius Professor of Modern History and Vice-Chancellor, in which capacity he coped wonderfully with revolting students in turbulent times.

Owen Chadwick's predecessor as Master of Selwyn was William Telfer.[9] Montefiore remembers him as 'a strange, old-fashioned theologian':

He gave a Compline address [at Westcott House] on the 'process of nidification'. His sister's dog seemed to play a large part in his life. He asked if he could give a lecture to the students of Westcott House about the Virgin Birth, about which he felt strongly. He recalled his earlier days as a chaplain to the Youth Club, ascending a Welsh mountain stream to find at the top a dead ewe – his analogy for lack of belief in the Virgin Birth!

From Sidney Sussex came two opposites. First there was B.T.D. Smith, who had been dean and much later vice-master. His religious belief diminished with his advancing years and by the time Montefiore heard him lecture on the parables he did not appear to believe anything at all. From 1951 the dean was Robert Pierce Casey. A mature scholar but not long in priest's orders, he practised psychoanalysis. A man of strange habits, he was in the long tradition of batty high churchman at Sidney. He preached what was said to be the 'highest' university sermon on the Blessed Virgin Mary since the Reformation.

An older theologian was Percy Gardner-Smith who, with his sepulchral voice, was well known as ending the creed long after others had finished. He was a considerable scholar, spanning the heady days of Jesus College in the time of J.F. Bethune-Baker[10] but seemingly left over from a previous generation.

Of Donald MacKenzie MacKinnon, Norris-Hulse Professor of Divinity, Montefiore writes:

He is the only person I know about whom all the apocryphal stories are true. He was a popular lecturer with undergraduates: he had a course named just 'Evil', illustrated by the Brides in the Bath, etc. He had a heart of gold, a brilliant mind, and the capability for quoting from the most abstruse articles in the most abstruse journals. He would visit one in college and talk in a fascinating way until he suddenly realized the time and then abruptly say, 'Well, I must go,' and depart without a word more . . .

A major influence on me was Charles Raven – theologian, prophet, botanist, scientist – Master of Christ's College and Vice-Chancellor of the University. He combined profundity and showmanship. When I was a student at Westcott House I will always remember his oratory in the pulpit. 'I need to be broken.' He later told me that he had to give up taking missions as he mesmerized hearers and took away their freedom of choice. When he died in 1964 I officiated at his funeral service.

We shall hear more later of other names, but for the moment Montefiore's crisp comments on them will suffice as an introduction: John Burnaby, Regius Professor of Divinity, 'gloomy, learned, clear'; E.C. Ratcliffe, Ely Professor of Divinity, 'urbane, leisured, liturgically encyclopaedic'.[11] The younger theologians included Maurice Wiles,[12] 'no one would have known in those days that he would turn into the great heresiarch'; John Bowker,[13] 'very versatile'; Peter Baelz,[14] 'always sage and sensible'; Don Cupitt,[15] 'in his godly phase'; Roland Walls,[16] 'a great eccentric, brilliant, but his ideas were on the back of an envelope and he never wrote them up. I was a devotee but wrecked his academic career by getting the lectureship he didn't. He was a superb pastor.'

Montefiore attended Dodd's last course of lectures and was struck by his knack of opening his New Testament at exactly the right page. Dodd's theological mantle appeared to pass to the comparatively young John Robinson, Fellow and Dean of Clare College, until Mervyn Stockwood whisked his former curate away to Woolwich. John Robinson's lectures on Romans and on the Theology of the New Testament were always crowded. Montefiore says, 'John was a brilliant scholar and he always had to produce a novel thesis. In his youth this was usually mind-blowingly radical; and in his later years mind-blowingly orthodox. I got to know him very well, and loved him dearly.'

A great many people fell under John Robinson's spell. Yet there was a stifling feel about theology in Cambridge. Montefiore admits, 'We were all in the grip of John Robinson's "biblical theology", which came near to fundamentalism, and certainly allowed you to choose the parts of the Bible you preferred.'

Although Montefiore was developing his own brand of radicalism, he was increasingly dissatisfied with Robinson's. Talking with Howard Root, Dean of Emmanuel College,[17] he wondered what could be done to counter Robinson's theological views. There was at hand in Cambridge a theological midwife. After the suicide of the Dean of King's College, who threw himself to death from the chapel roof in 1956, it was evident a strong man was needed there. Montefiore suggested Alexander Roper Vidler, Canon of Windsor and editor of *Theology*. Vidler had been a fiery priest in Birmingham – banned by Bishop E.W. Barnes. At St Aidan's, Small Heath, he was known to have preached on the text, 'Ye generation of vipers, who has taught you to flee from the wrath to come?' He was Catholic in religion and a member of the Oratory of the Good Shepherd. He also embraced 'the new theology'.[18] Montefiore saw much of Vidler when he was appointed at King's. The fire gave place to urbanity. Vidler used to lunch with the Montefiores on major feast days. When asked to provide a reference in connection with an educational endowment policy for one of Montefiore's children, Vidler said he would when he got to know her better, so he took eight-year-old Catherine out to dine at the Arts Theatre Restaurant, with great courtesy.

Howard Root and Montefiore went to see Vidler. Did he agree with them? Yes! What should, and could, be done? First, a small group was invited to meet in Vidler's rooms. They would read papers to each other. The original group included George Frederick Woods of Downing College;[19] Harry Williams of Trinity College; Joseph Sanders of Peterhouse; John Burnaby of Trinity College; Howard Root; Alec Vidler and Montefiore. Although Geoffrey Lampe, Ely Professor of Divinity, was not at the first meeting, he was an interested party.

After a short time, Vidler said, 'I think that there's a book here,' and 'summoned' everyone to a conference at Launde Abbey in Leicestershire. There were two areas of weakness in the group – science and comparative religion. They plugged the gap by inviting John Habgood, then Vice-Principal of Westcott House and a trained scientist, and Ninian Smart, H.G. Wood Professor of Theology at Birmingham, who was knowledgeable about other religions, to join them. Also invited were Henry Chadwick and A.H. Dammers. Chadwick decided not to participate and at the time seemed more interested in the history of dogma than in dogma itself. Dammers was a parish priest in Sheffield. Montefiore's diary continues the story:

1 January 1960
Left for Launde Abbey at 3 p.m. feeling a terrible

responsibility for driving the car, as I felt I had the brains of the C of E within – Joe Sanders, John Burnaby, Howard Root and Harry Williams . . . This conference is more like an hilarious house party than anything else. Launde Abbey is a wonderful stately mansion. Thomas Cromwell dissolved the monastery, built the house and wrote in his journal, 'Memo: I for Launde.' But Henry VIII cut off his head first. And now at last it has come back into the Church as a diocesan retreat and conference centre.

2 January 1960

'Conference' gets really under way. This is a high-powered group of 'top theologians' (except for myself) who are revolted at the reactionary orthodoxies of today and who want to admit that we don't know many of the answers. It is more like a Confession of Doubts than a Confession of Sins. Dammers this morning introduced the 'Christian Mission' and Habgood this afternoon 'Science and Christianity' and Heaton this evening on 'Revelation and the Bible' . . .

3 January 1960

Conference continued. We decide not to decide now about producing a new volume of essays and reviews, but to meet again in a year's time with the draft of our essays. We allocate subjects to ourselves and I get Christology – thrilled at the subject and downcast at my incapacity to cope.

Plough Service at Launde Abbey in the evening. I went to mock and stayed to pray. All very moving – a service which meant a lot in that remote farming community: and so much of it consisted of versicles spoken by the farm hands and farmers themselves.

Session with the Bishop of Leicester (R.R. Williams) in the evening. I came away feeling we had misjudged him. We felt that 'they' were responsible for all the tightening up going on in the Church of England, but obviously much of Leicester's job consists in protecting his layfolk from a reactionary clergy and trying to get sense out of a stuffy convocation. He gave a brilliant sketch of the Archbishop of Canterbury: really a liberal-minded man and convinced of the inevitability of agreement between opposed parties: but when he is convinced of the one and only solution to other people's differences he becomes absurdly authoritarian in imposing it. *Domine defende nos.*

Eventually a volume of essays was agreed, under the expert guidance of A.R. Vidler.[20] He wanted the volume to be in the tradition (if on a more modest scale) of *Essays and Reviews* (1860); *Lux Mundi* (1889); *Foundations* (1912) and *Essays Catholic and Critical* (1926). The composite title, *Soundings*, was justified in Vidler's Introduction in this way:

> It is a time for ploughing, not reaping; or, to use the metaphor we have chosen for our title, it is a time for making soundings, not charts or maps. If this be so, we do not have to apologize for our inability to do what we hope will be possible in the future generation. We can best serve the cause of truth and of the Church by candidly confessing where our perplexities lie, and not by making claims which, so far as we can see, theologians are not at present in a position to justify.

The essayists were Howard Root, John Habgood, George Woods (two essays), Harry Williams, Ninian Smart, Joseph Sanders, Geoffrey Lampe, John Burnaby and Montefiore. Montefiore's essay was 'Towards a Christology for Today'. At the time he was particularly attracted to the thinking of W.R. Matthews, Dean of St Paul's Cathedral. In his Synopsis Montefiore asserts:

> The divine activity is always and only revealed as self-effacing love. Atonement is God's loving activity in Christ enabling a man to come to terms with himself and so with the love that surrounds him. Man can only relearn to love by acceptance that he is loved as he is. This is made possible by God's identification with man in Jesus and by Jesus' loving acceptance of the worst that men can do to him. Jesus may be called divine because in him God acted

to enable men to find loving relations with God and their fellow men. Jesus' life and thought were fully human, and the divine activity was fully present in him so far as is possible in a man. The paradox of grace provides the best analogy whereby we may conceive of the union of divine and human in Jesus.

Montefiore's argument was sound and interesting rather than new and radical, although that was not the view of theologian E.L. Mascall, who lambasted Montefiore with most of the other contributors in *Up and Down in Adria*.[21]

Soundings received the widest notice. Little if any of this kind of thinking had come from the Church for a very long time. There was a freshness about the book and some, but not all, of the essayists would not have dissented from A.H. Clough's verse:

Where lies the land to which the ship would go?
Far, far ahead, is all her seamen know.

Theological thinking and ecclesiastical activity had been timid, defensive, frightened. 'Let go', 'explore', 'be not afraid' were the stimuli that brought *Soundings* to fruition. It was time that Christians began to think again. Opponents of *Soundings* and what followed said that in order to encourage people to swim and to be self-reliant, they were pushing thousands off the raft of faith into the stormy seas of doubt.

Most thoughtful reviewers, including Henry Chadwick in *Theology*[22] and John Robinson in *Prism*,[23] alighted on the contributions of Alec Vidler,[24] Howard Root[25] and Harry Williams[26] as the most stimulating and provoking, although individual reviewers were helped by some of the others, for example John Burnaby on 'Christian Prayer' and John Habgood on 'The Uneasy Truce between Science and Religion'. It was obvious that Harry Williams would get the limelight, with his challenge to the Church to take account of the discoveries of Freud.

Freud's genius consisted in his discovery of a completely new system of explanation which was able to make sense of subjective feelings so far unexplained . . . For

Augustine the reality was God: for Freud, the unknown self.

Harry Williams was to spend the next years freeing himself from himself by a degree of self-exposure that was rare and uncomfortable. For him the ultimate test of love is when one is as naked as a raw nerve to another person. The pulpit became a theological couch where he would tell almost all. In the end he joined the Community of the Resurrection, Mirfield, from where he has produced a succession of books, beautifully written and theologically helpful.

Montefiore's relationship with Harry Williams at Cambridge was mixed. Both were men of honesty and passion, but they crossed swords often in private, and sometimes in public, on many issues. Harry Williams joined the unbeliever in the jungle where the writ of Christ was not recognized. It was a land of guilt complexes – something of an obsession with him. Montefiore was more theologically earthed than Williams. This is a point of great importance.

One of Montefiore's books of this period was *Beyond Reasonable Doubt* (1963). Bishop William Wand, one time Bishop of London, called this 'a golden little book, completely honest and full of faith. It would be difficult to pack more wisdom into less than fifty short pages.'[27] On the cover was the arresting sentence, 'If you are looking for a faith by which to live, what is truth for me may be life for you.' The book contained a course of four sermons preached in the chapel of Gonville and Caius during the Lent term 1962 under the title 'What I really believe'. Montefiore was able to show that the Christian faith could stand up to the most rigorous scrutiny (that was the theologian); that it could be vigorously portrayed (that was the preacher); and that it must be related by love to individuals (that was the pastor). The pastor earthed Montefiore. That is why he was unhappy with John Robinson's *Honest to God*, which appeared in 1963. John Robinson's biography[28] describes how the book came to be published:

John decided to send a copy of the manuscript of what he had written to several to his friends, and to ask them to come to supper, bringing with them their answers to three questions. First, should what he had written be published? Secondly, if it should be published, what amendments did they suggest? Thirdly, what should the book be called? . . .

The supper was held on the evening of Friday, June 29, 1962. The new Archbishop of Canterbury [Michael Ramsey] was invited and was sent a copy of the manuscript. Understandably he was too busy to accept and had not got the time to read the manuscript, but he sent warm good wishes. The others invited were Timothy Beaumont, editor of the radical Anglican monthly, *Prism*; David Edwards, editor of SCM Press; Eric James; Dennis Nineham, Professor of Divinity, University of London; Al Shands; and Canon Max Warren, General Secretary of the Church Missionary Society since 1942. David Edwards was invited as prospective publisher . . .

After a great deal of talk over supper everyone agreed that what John had written should be published without drastic amendment . . . It was in fact Ruth [Robinson's wife] who suggested the title *Honest to God*. John at first thought it too flippant, but David Edwards pounced on it and said: 'No. That's it!' Al Shands well remembers John's last remark of the evening: 'When it's published, I hope you will come to visit me on some theological Devil's Island!'

This account needs supplementing: Montefiore, too, was invited to the supper party. He found it an 'odd' meeting. Robinson was no longer the Cambridge don. He had been talked into being a bishop by Mervyn Stockwood, when he was by nature a don, married to a Christian humanist, although that assessment does not exhaust the depths of John Robinson's theology nor the inwardness of Ruth Robinson's psychology. Whilst Montefiore approved of *Honest to God* being published, he thought that certain passages should be substantially changed, as they were likely to be misunderstood. He wrote to Robinson, who replied, 'What I have written, I have written.'

The impact of *Honest to God* is too well-known for repetition. It was linked with *Soundings* and *Objections to Christian Belief*,[29] which changed the climate, even the direction, of theological thinking. *Soundings*, as did the other volumes, set out to 'establish or re-establish some kind of vital contact with that enormous majority for whom Christian faith is not so much unlikely as irrelevant and uninteresting'. How far the books were successful in appealing to the unthinking masses is open to question. But within the Church and on its periphery they, and particularly *Honest to God*, were seminal works.

I have said that Montefiore eschews and escapes labelling. But let me provoke him into defining himself. In theology Montefiore is very typical of the moderate liberal Anglicanism of his generation. He is not quite so forceful and idiosyncratic as his contemporaries John Robinson and Harry Williams but, however loosely, he belongs with such figures. Their point of departure was the personalism of someone like Charles Gore. They were not metaphysicists, nor highly trained philosophically, but they were psychological theists who instinctively felt that the personal is somehow highest in the universe, and who believed that in prayer and religious experience they could intuitively cognize God's personal presence. People in this tradition in the early part of the century were 'personal idealists'. Later they were influenced by Martin Buber, John Macmurray and other philosophers of the personal. Finally, in the twenty years after the Second World War many of them moved into the rapidly expanding caring professions. Perhaps the most influential books reflecting their kind of Christianity were D.M. Baillie's *God was in Christ* and Robinson's *Honest to God*. In his essay in *Soundings* Montefiore endorsed Baillie's approach, but Montefiore's theism is basically realistic, and he never went as far as Robinson. Nor was Montefiore radicalized by the influence of depth-psychology, as Harry Williams was.

Montefiore reacts to this theological appraisal in this way:

I was greatly influenced by William Temple's writings as a young man – hence my interest in evolution. I was also influenced at Oxford by Eric Mascall and neo-Thomism – hence my grappling with natural theology. Charles Raven influenced me at Cambridge – hence my emphasis on Christian experience. I had a love/hate relationship with Harry Williams – I welcomed his psychological insights, but I abhorred his 'sitting light' to the Gospels.[30] In historical criticism I found myself in the tradition of C.H. Dodd, believing that there is real historical knowledge about Jesus; and for this reason I found Dennis Nineham very tiresome. As for John Robinson, he was a personal friend and I suppose he greatly influenced me; but I couldn't take his early 'biblical theology' and I found the way he always had to argue an extreme case rather provoking. You mustn't forget that Geoffrey Lampe was my tutor and C.F.D. Moule my New Testament professor when I was New Testament lecturer – they both influenced me considerably.

If I must have a label, I'd rather be a liberal Catholic than a liberal evangelical. Charles Gore, strangely enough, was never a hero, although I share with him the belief that historical criticism will lead to 'mainstream' (or 'Orthodox') conclusions. Martin Buber was certainly an influence – I'll always remember the first time I read *I and Thou* at Westcott House; but I recall reading only one book by John Macmurray, *Reason and Emotion*, which certainly had a powerful effect on me. Also John Baillie and D.M. Baillie had a vast influence on me. Is this all a great muddle? Perhaps it is and perhaps it is typical of me. I have never been a lover of the systematic and (while I avidly read Brunner) I cannot stand Barth!

The aim of Montefiore's theological exploration was rarely to reach academic goals alone. That is why he subjected his journey and his findings to spiritual scrutiny and pastoral sensitivity. Moreover, his own personality intruded – energy, zest and *chutzpah*, marks of the stormy petrel. Yet if there was a lack of total detachment there was a healthy dose of courage and fearlessness noted by Professor Maurice Wiles:

What I have admired about Hugh has been his readiness to tackle important new topics and to take the trouble to learn the facts of the case so as to bring his spiritual insights to bear properly upon them. That pioneering spirit involved a kind of courage that is not all that common amongst people with his measure of academic training and skill.

Roland Walls catches the excitement engendered by Monte-fiore's theological stance.

He comes in therapeutically, obliquely to one's questions. He can change the pattern by a remark which is like a touch or tap on a kaleidoscope. He did this especially in theological debate, making what can always fall away into clichéd boredom into something exciting. That's the word – 'exciting'. He could and can get you going again.

There is danger in underestimating Montefiore's nimble theological mind. Often he sees the kernel of an argument quickly and accurately. A number of misses are worth the occasional hit. Patience can be a refuge for lethargic minds. Healthy impatience provokes the timid and rebukes the lazy thinker.

Don Cupitt, who had been a undergraduate studying theo-logy at Trinity Hall when Montefiore was Dean of Caius, adds:

During the late 1950s and 1960s I saw Hugh fairly often. After he left Cambridge in 1970 I saw him only at those times when he had conscripted me into joining him in pursuit of one of his enthusiasms. The chief of these was the environmental group which eventually published *Man and Nature* (1975). In 1984 we disputed on a television programme, Hugh taking the customary liberal-Anglican realistic view of God as an empirical hypothesis, which he develops in *The Probability of God* (1985). By this time things had changed. Up to the mid-1970s or even the late 1970s we were fairly close in outlook, but now a chasm separates us.

To my mind, Hugh's most outstanding qualities are personal rather than intellectual. Many or most churchpeople are in varying degrees somewhat driven, anxious, grey and inhibited. Hugh has always been a whirlwind, ebullient, courageous and full of new enthusiasms. Sometimes they have been eccentric or even (I think) deplorable, recalling F.D. Maurice's 'I have laid a good few addled eggs in my time.' They have given rise to jokes at Hugh's expense. People would comment on the

Montefiore method of arriving at the truth – keep on talking until you find that by accident you have said something sensible. But personally I envy Hugh his uninhibited vigour and resilience: his personality type is as rare among churchmen as it is admirable . . .

In general Hugh appears untouched by German idealist philosophy and all that it has led to. His religion is of a designer-God and the historical Jesus is highly Anglo-Saxon. Perhaps, too, it moves in a region where English liberal Christianity and liberal Judaism have long sensed a mutual affinity.

For Professor Dennis Nineham, Montefiore comes across as

a man of great integrity. He would never, I think, temporize, and if he feels something is true, or needs to be done, he feels the need to speak out, or initiate action. One of the most marked – and admirable – qualities is his always being prepared to put his money – and his personal energy and activity – where his mouth is, as they say.

Where I suppose I have felt least happy about Hugh, ever since I knew him as an undergraduate, is over his judgement. He seems to me to allow his heart to run away with his head on occasion and to take a one-sided view of issues, from which it is almost impossible to dislodge him . . . It is not so much that he is stubborn as that he seems simply unable to hear other considerations than the ones that move him. He is a tremendous black and white chap, and on certain issues there seems to me to be no grey area at all. This, of course, can be a strength when it comes to taking vigorous action or rooting for a cause, but it is a less happy thing where scholarship is concerned.

Montefiore detests Anglican humbug and hypocrisy and demonstrated the 'integrity' mentioned by Dennis Nineham in his attitude to the Thirty-Nine Articles of Religion. It has never been easy to discover a fully authoritative statement of Anglican theological belief, but the Thirty-Nine Articles have constituted the nearest thing to one. They have been fixed in time as a succinct summary of Reformed faith. The articles were drawn up with a fourfold purpose:

> first, to ensure that the Church of England should henceforth be, and be seen to be . . . 'a true and Apostolical Church, teaching and maintaining the doctrine of the Apostles'; second, to ensure that the clergy should be of sound faith, so that the laity would not be exposed to unorthodox teaching . . . third, to advance the Church's inward unity and well-being by 'the establishing of consent touching true religion' . . . fourth, to set due limits to the Church's doctrinal comprehensiveness. While the wish for a solid front against Rome was undoubtedly the dominant motive in seeking as wide a comprehensiveness as possible, so that the doctrinal demands of the Articles were (in terms of their period) minimal, nevertheless limits had to be set.[31]

Over a long period since the articles of 1571 were imposed, dissent to some of them has been a feature of Church life. Under the provisions of the Clerical Subscription Act, every person about to be ordained priest or deacon had to make and subscribe a declaration of assent. Similarly every priest instituted to a cure of souls had to assent and, more significantly, read the Articles before the assembled congregation on the Sunday following his institution. After the Second World War this practice was increasingly kept in silence. Occasionally a newly instituted incumbent would use the Articles to expound on the doctrine of the Church. Montefiore's particular aversion was Article Thirteen:

> *Of Works before Justification.* Works done before the grace of Christ, and the Inspiration of his Spirit, are not pleasant to God, forasmuch as they spring not of faith in Jesus Christ, neither do they make men meet to receive grace, or (as the School-authors say) deserve grace of congruity: yea rather, for that they are not done as God hath willed and commanded them to be done, we doubt not but they have the nature of sin.

Montefiore, with his antecedents, could not believe that

every single action of every member of the Jewish faith had the nature of sin. How could he subscribe to such an article?

On his first Sunday at Great St Mary's, 19 September 1963, he took the unprecedented step of making a supplementary Declaration of Assent in these words:

> By declaring my assent to the Thirty-Nine articles of Religion I am gladly assenting to the general position taken in these articles in relation to the unreformed Catholic faith and to the faiths of the reformed Protestant faiths. I am therefore not declaring *ex-animo* acceptance of each individual article.
>
> In asserting my belief in the articles, the Book of Common Prayer and the Ordinal, I take account of the period in which they were written, and I accept them as agreeable to the word of God as this was then understood and expressed.
>
> By declaring that I will use the form in the said book and none other, except so far as shall be ordered by lawful authority, I am declaring my loyalty to the Book of Common Prayer and my belief that the excepted clause in this declaration allows me to continue the liturgical traditions of this parish in accordance with the spirit of the said book, subject to the good will of those set over me in the Lord.

There was a great fuss about this, but an unexpected and satisfactory outcome. It was one of the factors that, together with his theological expertise and his position as vicar of Great St Mary's, led to an invitation to join the new Archbishops' Commission on Christian Doctrine, announced on 22 March 1967.[32] The chairman was the Bishop of Durham (Ian Ramsey) and the membership included Jim Packer, Warden of Latimer House, Oxford; Michael Green, Registrar of the London College of Divinity, both leading evangelicals; the Anglo-Catholic Cheslyn Jones, Principal of Chichester Theological College, A.M. Allchin of Pusey House, Oxford; Professors Henry Chadwick, C.F. Evans, Dennis Nineham, H.E. Root, E.J. Tinsley, H.E.W. Turner and Maurice Wiles, who became chairman on the death of Ian Ramsey. Two members were to

become influential and controversial bishops – David Jenkins
(then Chaplain of Queen's College, Oxford) and John Baker
(Chaplain of Corpus Christi, Oxford). Ninian Smart, Professor
of Religious Studies, University of Lancaster, was joined by
another layman – and regrettably the only philosopher on the
commission – J.R. Lucas, Fellow of Merton College, Oxford.
Montefiore was the only parish priest and he was from no
ordinary parish.

The first task laid upon the commission was: 'to consider the
place of the Thirty-Nine Articles in the Anglican tradition and
the question of Subscription and Assent to them.' The commission considered various possiblities. Should the articles be
revised, re-written or scrapped? Was there a radical way forward? Naturally care had been taken to set up the commission
in such a way that all aspects of the Church of England were
represented. This supposed democratic strength proved to be a
stone of stumbling, as the members of the commission were
unable to agree on anything theological. Agreement depended
on finding an acceptable formula, which is quite a different
matter. Their first report *Subscription and Assent to the Thirty-
Nine Articles* (1968) only emerged after John Baker produced a
form of words to which all members could agree.

A new declaration and Form of Assent was recommended
and, as Montefiore admits, 'Probably it provides the only
occasion when a layman hears about the sources of authority for
the Church of England.'

> *Preface.* The Church of England is part of the Church of
> God, having faith in God the Father, who through Jesus
> Christ our only Lord and Saviour calls us into the
> fellowship of the Holy Spirit. This faith, uniquely shown
> forth in the holy Scriptures, and proclaimed in the catholic
> Creeds, she shares with other Christians throughout the
> world. She has been led by the Holy Spirit to bear a
> witness of her own to Christian truth in her historic
> formularies – the Thirty-Nine Articles of Religion, and the
> Book of Common Prayer, and the Ordering of Bishops,
> Priests, and Deacons. Now, as before, she has a
> responsibility to maintain this witness through her
> preaching and worship, the writings of her scholars and

teachers, the lives of her saints and confessors, and the utterances of her councils.

In the profession you are about to make, you will affirm your loyalty to this inheritance of faith as your inspiration and direction, under God, for bringing to light the truth of Christ and making him known to this generation.

Form of Assent. I, A.B., profess my firm and sincere belief in the faith set forth in the Scriptures and in the catholic Creeds, and my allegiance to the doctrine of the Church of England.

But the formula was flawed. There was ambiguity in the words, as Professor Stephen Sykes noted in *The Integrity of Anglicanism.* The faith is said to be uniquely revealed in the Holy Scriptures and set forth in the catholic Creeds, but this does not affirm that everything in the Creeds must therefore be declared to be true. The statement requires, so far as the Thirty-Nine Articles, Book of Common Prayer and Ordinal are concerned, 'loyalty to this inheritance of faith as your inspiration and direction under God in bringing the grace and truth of Christ to this generation'. 'Inspiration' and 'direction' (subsequently the word 'direction' was replaced by 'guidance') is not the same as affirming the theology in these documents. It is compatible with such affirmations but it does not include it.

Although the work of the Doctrine Commission grew out of particular needs of the Church, it did not fulfil these needs. An example came in the report *Prayer and the Departed.* Members of the commission were, or appeared to be, irreconcilably divided. The evangelicals were determined that the Church should not pray for the dead while the Catholics were determined that the Church should so do. Montefiore notes:

Ian Ramsey (chairman) was brilliant in keeping all sides together, but his trouble was that he had such a sophisticated mind that his qualifications almost meant that black became white. The report is useful because of its appendices on the evidence of psychic research[33] and what the Anglican Fathers said, but its actual conclusions were an evident non-starter: 'May God in His infinite mercy bring the whole Church, living and departed in the Lord

Jesus, to a joyful resurrection and the fulfilment of His eternal kingdom.' It was too long-winded, and did not apparently pray for the dead, but the evangelicals would not, although they were forced to concede that one could pray for the Church which includes the dead! We were allowed to commend individuals to God, including, incidentally, non-Christians; but that is hardly praying for them.

Montefiore was frustrated and disappointed with the commission and saw most of its work as a series of missed opportunities. It was too donnish. Its members may have represented different theological positions within the Church, but they were outside the mainstream ministry of the Church. Only the chairman, as Bishop of Durham, and Montefiore could be said to be in the mainstream. Montefiore felt the lack of theologians in religious orders such as the Roman Catholics would have had. The Church of England's donnish tradition was, by contrast, a rather arid and secular tradition.

When the Series III Holy Communion Service had been issued it was discovered that there was no provision for 'reconsecrating' if the bread and wine ran out. What should happen? Should a prayer be offered? Or should wine be added and more bread set apart in silence? In the end, the Doctrine Commission decided on the latter course, and then found that, as in Rites A and B, their advice had not been followed. Discussion of this point meant that the whole of Eucharistic theology had to be considered. The result was a symposium on different aspects of it, resulting in a set of individual papers being published as *Thinking about the Eucharist* (1972). Montefiore's contribution, 'Symbols and the Eucharist',[34] was written 'because I believe that for most people the symbolism of what is done is more important than the theological correctness of what is said'. In his essay two statements were made:

To worship in the eucharist is to pay attention to God through the rite, and so to find oneself in a relationship of grace. It is not primarily to pay attention to the logic of the words but to use the images conveyed by the words and the symbolism of the ritual actions as means of paying attention to God . . .

the spoken images and enacted symbols of the rite, which
form the jumping-off point for day dreaming, can be
controlled by the will so that they, together with all the
rich devotional associations – conscious or unconscious –
which they evoke, become the vehicle for an act of
profound attention to God through Christ.

This tells us something about Montefiore's own liturgical
position. He appreciated the richness of image and symbol
contained in and evoked by Cranmer in the Book of Common
Prayer. He did not like the 'brevity and terseness' of Series II.
The action did not flow. But he appreciated some of the later
Alternative Services. Structure is important to him. As a celebrant, he keeps to liturgical rules, feeling uncomfortable with
unconventional experiments.

There are some people who can create dynamic, vibrant
liturgy. Montefiore is not one of them and is wary of *ad-hoc*
arrangements which are a feature of some Anglican parishes.
Everything is already there, in word and symbol, in the Anglican liturgy, for the celebrant to lead worship in a dignified and
relaxed way so that the focus is on God, not the priest, and so
that the people may participate in a completely natural way.
None the less there were occasions when Montefiore made
instant liturgy come alive. H.E.W. Turner recalls an incident at
the Doctrine Commission meeting at Pusey House:

We had met in the Chapel which was arranged in pews.
Hugh, who was to celebrate, invited us to 'gather round'
and he celebrated making us stand round in a semi-circle.
This was the first time I had come across this particular
way of celebrating and receiving, but he made it seem so
natural and right.

Elisabeth Montefiore was for fourteen years a member of the
Liturgical Commission. She and Hugh would compare notes
from their different positions and perspectives and interests.
They had much to do with the new Marriage Service, part of
which is modelled on the Jewish service.

The major report from the Doctrine Commission to emerge during Montefiore's membership was *Christian Believing*, which is considered in a subsequent chapter.

Montefiore was frequently 'in the news' for his utterances from the pulpit of Great St Mary's and elsewhere. He was a well-known figure in the Church at large and there was no reason to think that he would take a different direction from his immediate predecessors at Great St Mary's, who had become diocesan bishops. Any plans the Church might have had came to an abrupt halt in 1967.

Montefiore was asked to read a paper at the Fiftieth Annual Conference of Modern Churchmen, held at Somerville College, Oxford, 24–28 July 1967.[35] Montefiore's paper was entitled 'Jesus, the Revelation of God', and his purpose was to investigate in what ways the human character of Jesus discloses the nature of God. In view of the ensuing controversy, it is important to note that Montefiore was not himself a member of the Modern Churchmen's Union, and neither were some of the other speakers.[36] As it was the Jubilee Conference, numbers attending were high – between 250 and 300 – and the opening sermon was preached by the Archbishop of Canterbury (Michael Ramsey). It was inevitable that there would be some publicity for the conference.

Let Montefiore explain how he set about his task:

First, I asked myself how God could disclose himself to men at all. Next I tried to consider how God discloses himself in general in nature and more particularly through human personality. I then proceeded to the question how God's self-disclosure through Jesus is unique. I dismissed the idea that it was simply the teaching of Jesus that is unique, and I dismissed also the idea that it is only the death and resurrection of Christ that is important. I came to the conclusion that if Jesus was to disclose adequately the Transcendent God, he must be fully human, and that the divine could only be mediated through his full and complete humanity. From that point I went on to consider the human personality of Jesus from the evidence of the Gospels. I tried to separate those characteristics of Jesus which were common to all men, those which he shared with people of his time, and those which were peculiar to himself. I looked at those peculiar to himself in some detail, because for me the human character of Jesus is a lens through which we can see straight to God.

I noted several characteristics of Jesus that were special to himself; for example, the change in his way of life from his baptism onwards, his passionate love of God, his utter obedience to his Heavenly Father, his destiny to suffer and so on. I stressed that the perfection of Jesus was real, that it was a moral and spiritual perfection and consisted in his utter and complete obedience to his Father's will. I noted that before his baptism for thirty or more years he lived a humble and obscure life in which, he seemed to me, speaking as a New Testament scholar, to have as yet no real consciousness of his messianic vocation. This is to me the human characteristic of Jesus which portrays most powerfully the self-effacingness of God.

I noted also in passing that Jesus, during the period of these thirty years, seems to have remained unmarried. This was most unusual, since it was the duty of a Jewish male to marry and produce an heir.

Montefiore then quotes from his paper:

Men usually remain unmarried for three reasons: either because they cannot afford to marry or because there are no girls (neither of these factors need have deterred Jesus); or because it is inexpedient for them to marry in the light of their vocation (we have already ruled this out in the case of Jesus during the 'hidden years' of his life) or because they are homosexual in nature, in as much as women hold no attraction for them.

On the day Montefiore delivered the paper, he drove over to Oxford from Cambridge in the company of Dr W.H.C. Frend, a longtime member of the Modern Churchmen's Union (fellow of Gonville and Caius, lecturer in Divinity at Cambridge and later Professor of Ecclesiastical History, University of Glasgow). By the time they reached Potton the car faltered and a cracked cylinder block was diagnosed. They limped back to

Cambridge, got another car and raced to Oxford, arriving shortly before Montefiore was due to speak. He did not enquire if a reporter would be present, although he knew the papers were to be published. However, a reporter was present, and he seized on the short passage on the sexuality of Jesus, notably the word 'homosexual', and blew it up to headline proportions – offering Fleet Street a tasty morsel.

By midnight of the day of the lecture (25 July) the national press were in hot pursuit. By lunchtime the following day, when Montefiore arrived home, the Archbishop of Canterbury had made a statement: 'There is no evidence whatever to support Canon Montefiore's reported views. Christians believe that Christ's dealings with both men and women were those of a perfect man.'

There was some criticism of Montefiore at the Modern Churchmen's Conference itself. One participant said the remarks were 'a smear on our Lord', giving pain to some and ammunition to others.

Suddenly the name of Montefiore was on everyone's lips, and newspapers throughout the country, and soon from all over the world, gave the remarks headline treatment. Within days over one thousand letters reached Montefiore and there were incessant demands for his resignation. The stench of anger was everywhere and Ian Paisley was not untypical in the language he used in a telegram: 'Bible Protestants of Ulster abhor your smear on Christ and charge you with diabolical blasphemy.' There were even graffiti in London.

Meanwhile the Archbishop of Canterbury had read Montefiore's paper, which had been sent to him by Norman Pittenger of King's College, Cambridge.[37] The Archbishop wrote to Montefiore on 28 July 1967:

I know that the old-fashioned liberal treatment of the Gospels supposed that they could yield information sufficient for speculation about Christ's psychology and emotional relationships. But I had supposed that methods of criticism and exegesis more recently in vogue discouraged us from thinking that the Evangelists offered any information of this kind and that there was little point in our speculating about matters on which they are silent. I

doubt the validity of the inference that it was men whom
Jesus loved, because the accounts of the love of Jesus for
the disciples and the role of a 'beloved disciple' come in
chapters of the Fourth Gospel, which are highly
theological and I should have thought yielded no data
of a psychologizing kind whatever. But I am sorry you
have been involved in a turmoil which I hope will die
down.

It did not die down. Montefiore was completely unprepared
for the backlash of hate. It was emotionally and physically
draining. And he was not a university don with a cosy Cambridge court to walk round but a busy parish priest fully
exposed to his own parishioners, many of whom were bewil-
dered and disturbed by his words. One of his curates, William
Loveless, notes: 'He resolved immediately to preach a sermon
on his total faith in and commitment to Jesus Christ: it was a
marvellous sermon, and helped enormously to steady at least
the local situation.'

This sermon was preached on the Feast of the Transfiguration, 6 August 1967, and was entitled 'Our Lord Jesus
Christ'.[38] It was both moving and encouraging for Montefiore
to see, sitting beneath the pulpit, his own bishop, the Bishop of
Ely (E.J.K. Roberts). In more ways than this the Bishop of Ely
was a strength and support, as Montefiore publicly acknowledged in his September 1967 newsletter:

I would like to thank publicly our Bishop for all that he did
to help so generously with his counsel and support. I have
been among the first to beef about episcopacy when it
seems to go wrong; but I wish that more people would
realize that when there is a loving, wise and sympathetic
bishop, it is the most marvellous system of church order in
the world.

In his sermon, Montefiore referred to the 'sensation' in these
words:

It is precisely my concern to show Christ's complete
identification with mankind that raises for me a question

about our Lord's celibacy. I raise it with reference to those thirty 'Hidden Years' at Nazareth, when it seems that as yet he did not know either his vocation to be Messiah or his status as Son of God. Why did he not marry? After all, he was fully a man. Of course there is no evidence, and we can only speculate, and speculation must be done with reverence. But having raised the question we must look it in the face – why did he not marry? Could the answer be that Jesus was not by nature the marrying sort? I want to make it crystal clear that when I suggest this possible answer, no question of Jesus being less than perfect was or is involved or implied. It is of course important not to confuse temptation with sin. Jesus was tempted as we all are in every possible way; yet without sin.

I would wish to claim that this kind of speculation about the nature of our Lord can be valuable if it underlines, as I believe it does here in a particularly vivid way, how God in Christ identifies himself with the outsider and the outcast from society. It gives real point to two texts from St Paul in which the Apostle was referring to our Lord's death. He wrote to the Galatians that 'Christ has redeemed us from the curse of the law, having become a curse for us' – an astounding phrase – and to the Corinthians that 'Him who knew no sin he made to be sin for us' – an equally amazing thought. We have forgotten with what horror the Jews of Jesus' day regarded the claim that the Son of God had been killed on a Roman crucifix. The symbol of the Cross is something we have grown so used to that we don't realize how it filled them with disgust.

And so, if at first you have been filled with repugnance at all this, then it might be worth reflecting that you are probably reacting with the same feelings as the Jews then reacted to the scandal of the Cross. Perhaps this is one of the few ways in which we people of today can be shocked into realizing what a scandal Christianity really is according to the beliefs of this world: this really is the first being last and the last being first. Perhaps only this kind of shock can make us realize the amazing nature of God's love and care, and the overflowing compassion which lay behind Jesus' identification with the outcast.

Reflecting later on the controversy, the stigma of which did not leave him until he was Bishop of Birmingham, Montefiore realized he should not have used the word 'homosexual', but rather a phrase such as 'not of the marrying kind' and that he should have given the possibility of a reporter being present more than a passing thought:

> I now regard this as a culpable omission on my part, and I greatly regret it. In fact I used the word *homosexual* because it is the technical word to use in this connection. I did not describe Jesus as a homosexual: I was speculating about whether Jesus was homosexual in nature. I used the phrase, I think, because shortly beforehand I had been editing for publication a lecture given in Great St Mary's by V.A. Demant, the Professor of Moral and Pastoral Theology at Oxford.[39] Professor Demant said: 'The homosexual disposition is no form of unchastity at all, and some people with that disposition are very useful and devoted members of society.' Let me repeat. A homosexual is sensitive to people of his sex, and delights in their friendship: but this does not for one moment imply that he is necessarily involved in an improper relationship. Moreover we are told in the Old Testament that David, who had many wives, had a love of Jonathan which surpassed other emotional experiences in his personal relationships.

Following the controversy, Montefiore was cast down in spirit. The future seemed suddenly black. Was there a future at all outside Great St Mary's? For more than a moment he wondered if there was even a future at Great St Mary's. A Christian is to expect tribulation. This was the beginning of a long dark night. He knew that the Beatitudes say one should be exceedingly glad when one is misrepresented and spoken against. He could not feel glad. Knowing that he had been misrepresented and was now mistrusted was a living agony and led to a breakdown in health. None the less he continued to proclaim the living Gospel of Jesus Christ from pulpit and platform and he did not avoid controversial subjects. In some way they appeared to accelerate as he was 'good copy'.

Professor Dennis Nineham, who had spoken at the Modern Churchmen's Union Conference on 'Jesus in the Gospel', thinks Montefiore's words were 'a rather characteristic episode' of impulsiveness and hasty judgement.

> When I added a note to my own contribution (in *Christ for us Today*) explaining why I thought that the Gospels do not provide the sort of evidence that would enable us to decide the matter either way, he took it as a direct personal attack. Far from it – I should have no hesitation about ascribing homosexuality to Jesus if I thought there was any evidence to warrant doing so. Characteristically, Hugh's wrath endured but the twinkling of an eye.

Wrath elsewhere lodged and lasted for a very long time – not least in the mind and file of John Hewitt, the Prime Minister's Appointments Secretary. We now know[40] of the determination of John Hewitt to ensure that Montefiore did not become an English diocesan bishop. It was only when Hewitt had left Downing Street that he became Bishop of Birmingham.

In 1967 Montefiore was about half way through his ministry at Great St Mary's. He did not know that. The future looked bleak and he knew he could not keep up the gruelling pace he had set himself. Yet he was incapable of slowing down.

9 Constraining the Waters

Montefiore sat light to the organized reform movements of the Church of England, notably the Parish and People Movement, which, in its various guises, was the vehicle carrying most of the radicals of the 1950s and 1960s. At the same time, he was wanting to form and lead a new movement called, perhaps, the Faith and Freedom Movement.

He shared some of his thinking with Nicolas Stacey, Rector of Woolwich, who goaded him into inviting hand-picked people to attend an informal conference in 1966 over two days at Cambridge. Although a cross section of the religious scene was invited, no one save Nicolas Stacey was tarred with the brush of *Prism* or Parish and People, South Bank or academic remoteness. The emphasis in almost every case was on pastoral responsibility. Those invited were a country priest, two priests from housing estates, one lately in a middle-class north-country living, the vicar of a South London parish, a lay woman, the principal of a theological college, a Cambridge dean lately in a working-class parish, a New Testament professor, a representative of a non-Anglican Church and a lawyer.[1]

In a working paper prepared for the conference, Montefiore made it clear where his convictions lay:

The malaise affecting the Church of England is mainly spiritual. She has not yet come to grips with the new age of science, technology, sociological and psychological insights, secondary and university education. She has not yet spoken with real conviction a clear, comprehensible and credible Gospel Message to the distracted and uncertain world of the mid-twentieth century. Always conservative in nature (for after all her main task is to conserve the Gospel), she has been overtaken by the speed of change. Man is changing his ecology with unprecedented speed: the Church of England is advancing at her usual sedate and ceremonial pace.

If the Church of England is to shake herself and to rise to her present pastoral opportunity, she must find a tremendous release of energy and enthusiasm. She will be required to live dangerously, experiment widely and to co-operate fully.

Montefiore wanted to launch a popular movement, to initiate massive reforms on a national scale, freeing the English Churches from the legal requirements of a past age and enabling them to become a united, but not uniform, community in Christ. He wanted to recapture the spirit of William Temple's Life and Liberty Movement. He did not see clearly that once the ideals of Life and Liberty had been institutionalized, the spirit of the movement vaporized and its bright light dimmed. The National Assembly of the Church of England became the forum for debate in which bishops, priests and laity mingled, but did it sufficiently, or at all, break down the barriers between these groups of people? Montefiore is a man of the Reformation. Whilst admitting that the Reformation was disgraced by violence, stained by corruption and bent to the service of much wickedness, he maintains it secured for mankind a twofold enfranchisement. On the one hand it broke down the medieval distinction between clergy and laity: on the other hand, it dissipated the old delusion of asceticism which had filled the cloisters, and restored to Christians their natural liberty as well as their spiritual priesthood.

Perhaps the Reformation went too far in vindicating the rights of individual conscience against the claims of external authority. Yet the Church Assembly seemed unable to unite the warring forces, and there was a class distinction between bishops and clergy and laity which did not disappear with the advent of the General Synod.

Montefiore was not sure how a new Faith and Freedom

Movement could be formed, but that such a movement was necessary, freed from all partisan tags, remained his conviction.

Nothing of a practical nature came of Montefiore's initiative. However, in 1966 Montefiore was elected a proctor in convocation for the diocese of Ely, which meant that he would sit in the lower house of the convocation of Canterbury and be a member of Church Assembly. He was already widely known in the Church and was the confidant of a number of bishops, yet he was always independent in his thinking. In 1959 he had been appointed a canon theologian of Coventry Cathedral and was examining chaplain to the bishops of Newcastle (H.E. Ashdown), Coventry (C.K.N. Bardsley) and Blackburn (C.R. Claxton).

Montefiore was a vocal supporter of the Anglican-Methodist union scheme. When it was not accepted by the convocations in 1969 he was convinced that the credibility of the Church of England was damaged, leaving supporters of the scheme in deep frustration. To take the scheme back to the convocations would be to run the risk of a setback, which would be disastrous and give a handle to those in the House of Laity who wanted to make it a laity-versus-clergy issue by alleging that the views of the House of Laity were again being by-passed. The scheme was not re-presented to convocations but to the new General Synod in 1972 – and it fell again. By this time Montefiore was out of the Church's 'government' and was beginning to learn how difficult it is to reform a Church that is episcopally led and synodically governed.

As a speaker in Church Assembly he did not find an immediately enthusiastic audience. He liked the cut-and-thrust of debate and had a style to match it. Church Assembly was not like that. There were too many prepared speeches and a chairman (the Archbishop of Canterbury) who was too kind to those speakers who were determined to make *their* points, unconcerned that they had been made more effectively and succinctly by previous speakers.

However, on 5 February 1970 Montefiore made his mark by speaking on a subject on which he had become an acknowledged expert. The occasion was a debate on the report *Man in His Living Environment*. Environment and ecology have become such commonplace words that it is important to appreciate that Montefiore was a pioneer. His interest in the subject began with a book. Montefiore was a curate in Newcastle in 1951 when he read Michael Roberts' remarkable *The Estate of Man*.[2] Michael Roberts was richly versatile as a poet, mathematician, philosopher and teacher. His books included *The Modern Mind* and *T.E. Hulme* and he edited *The Faber Book of Modern Verse* and *The Faber Book of Comic Verse*. He had taught in Newcastle before travelling south as principal of the College of St Mark and St John in Chelsea. What appealed to Montefiore was the unity of Roberts' thinking, the clarity of his exposition and the compelling force of his argument, substantiated by verifiable statistics. In his Introduction, Roberts posed the prophetic question:

> in spite of recent hardships, we often talk as if we had an inexhaustible reservoir of material and skill: we overlook the limitations of our resources – moral and intellectual as well as material – and we sometimes fail to recognize the limits of man's capacity to adapt himself to the conditions which he has helped to create. The object of this book is to inquire into such limitations . . .
>
> The main questions are these: what are our total available resources in terms of material population and skill; to what extent are these resources likely to increase or decrease in the near future; what limits are there to the natural productivity of the soil; and what limits are there to the adaptability of man?

From the moment of reading this stimulating volume Montefiore's preoccupation with the Christian concern for the environment began. Forecasts of environmental doom are sometimes said to be symptomatic of a culture that has lost its nerve and that their popularity today betrays a mass neurosis: 'Life is for living', it is better to enjoy the present than to feed one's imagination on possible future disasters. Some environmentalists seem to take pleasure in making the flesh creep with clairvoyant disclosures of terrible catastrophes to come. This was not Michael Roberts' way and it was not to be Montefiore's way. A prophet sees things as they really are.

But what could be done about the whole complex of environmental issues, combining questions of resources, population and pollution? What was the Christian imperative? On this major issue Montefiore read and researched in depth and detail before he opened his mouth. He appreciated that the task before him – lightening the darkness of the Church of England on the environment – was difficult. A deep strain of Protestantism remained in the psyche of church-going Christians, despite outward ceremonial. Montefiore saw Protestantism as tending to make Christianity simply an inward experience, whereas it is about the Word made Flesh and the whole wide world which God has given people to enjoy and to use aright. On one occasion he went into the evangelical stronghold of St Aldate's, Oxford, and said plainly:

> God has a cosmic plan of salvation, a plan for the whole planet and a plan for all men, and not just for individuals. Protestants have rightly emphasized the transcendence of God, for so he is. But if you overemphasize this, you put such a distance between God and the world that the world seems bereft of God; it becomes secularized, and so it doesn't matter what you do with it. And it is I think this which has underlain much of the Protestant get-rich-quick philosophy, and raping the world's resources and somehow combining this with an inward piety quite remote from the world of commerce and business.

Montefiore felt society needed a kind of baptism, a reorientation. At baptism we renounce the world, not so as to escape from it, but so as to embrace it. To enjoy the world is the opposite of possessing it.

Was man capable of this kind of re-orientation, of repentance? It was by no means clear, as Montefiore discovered when he read another book which had an impact on him. *Dance with the Devil* by Gunther Schwab[3] is a dramatic encounter between a poet, an engineer and a woman doctor; unable to find what they want from God, they are invited by a journalist to see what the devil has to offer. One exchange between two of the people concerns the meaning of progress which enables man to adjust himself to changing circumstances:

Mondo: That is precisely the meaning of the idea of progress, which is my own invention. It means that man continues to change his environment at a mounting pace and with pathological haste. Man is quite incapable of bringing about any change in himself at a comparable speed.

Sten: Then man will return to nature?

Mondo: Man has neglected and lost his capacity to do so. Faced with the powers of nature, he is no longer capable of life. Every beast, every tree is more efficient than he. Take away from man his money, his house, his food; take his clothes and his car, and all the aids with which he supports his decadent existence, and place him naked and helpless in the world of natural forces before which every bird, every blade of grass must justify itself. You will find within the realm of nature no more pathetic figure than Man.

It is I who invented the slogan that salvation can only come from progress; it is I who tossed that nonsense into the midst of mankind. I taught them to value progress above everything; it is I who planted that hysterical haste in the human heart that eternally seeks the new; it is I who taught them to despise the eternal and unchanging, and all slow and healthy growths, made them bring 'Progress' to the unspoiled races and so poison them in body and mind.

Montefiore became obsessed with his passion, but never at the cost of sacrificing proper research. He began to speak and preach on the subject. He was likened to an Old Testament prophet, sometimes in a favourable light (then he was Isaiah), more often in a gloomy manner (then he was Jeremiah). That did not worry Montefiore, who regarded Jeremiah as the most sensitive of the canonical prophets, torn by inner conflict: 'So black was his message that he cursed the day of his birth.' Like Jeremiah, Montefiore contained within himself a logical paradox concerning this doomed world-order. There was both a call to repentance and a certainty of coming doom. So passionately did he feel that once when he was laid up with a muscular spasm in his back, he put on his cassock over his pyjamas in order to fulfil a preaching engagement in the university pulpit on this theme.[4]

Montefiore collected his own statistics from newspapers and other sources about the changes which were taking place in the environment. Presenting his case with passion and knowledge was to lead him into prominence in this field. His challenge to Christians as well as to non-Christians was making him an uncomfortable figure. The late Bishop of Leicester, R.R. Williams, introduced an early piece by Montefiore in a short composite work, *The Responsible Church*:[5]

> In 'Man's Dominion' Canon Hugh Montefiore presents us with an apocalypse, an unveiling of things that are coming to pass on the earth almost without our knowing, which are going to affect the lives of generations yet unborn in every part of the globe. Here, indeed, is a prophetic word, compelling us to say, not 'Am I my brother's keeper?' but 'Am I my grandchild's keeper, or the keeper of my great-great grandchild?'

'Man's Dominion' was also the general title of three lectures delivered by Montefiore at the Queen's University of Belfast in January 1969. These were subsequently published as *The Question Mark: The End of Homo Sapiens*[6] with a Foreword by Dr Joseph Needham, Master of Gonville and Caius, who endorsed the author's general argument supported by a formidable array of facts about the terrible results of man's obsession with a rapid and easily acquired material prosperity. Dr Needham felt proud 'that a priest of the Church of England should thus lead the way in demonstrating so clearly one of the greatest tasks before contemporary society'. Such a view was underlined by Dr Bernard Dixon, editor of *New Scientist*, who thought it 'an uncommonly good book about Man, about science, and about society . . . which is quite unique in being so well informed'.[7] Brian Wicker in the *Guardian* praised the book's clarity of outline whilst noting that the thesis needed more filling out to satisfy the sceptic.[8] But he caught the spirit of the book:

without some vision of the world as open to transformation in an eternal perspective, man is unlikely to recognise any such responsibility. Priorities will remain wrong as long as men think of this familiar world as definitive of human possibilities. An eschatological vision is an imperative antidote to the cosmic *laissez-faire* of contemporary trends.

The Question Mark was both landmark and beacon. Jeremiah had become Amos dealing with man's corporate evil as seen around us. Only by listening to the prophets (and Montefiore) and returning to the fear of the Lord can man 'turn back and forswear his foolish ways . . . Theistic religion far from being outmoded in these days of science and technology, appears to be the only hope of a world endangered by science and technology.'

Montefiore showed himself to be wary of Teilhard de Chardin, whose writings were very widely read. In *Le Milieu Divin* de Chardin wrote: 'The greatest mystery of Christianity is not the appearance but the transparence of God in the universe.' Montefiore suggests that de Chardin wrote out of speculative faith rather than reasoned calculation, which is why their respective views of God and His activity in the universe differ. De Chardin is more optimistic with regard to the Kingdom of God. He believes transfiguration is all important, as it lights up a new dimension of life *now*. Montefiore scoffs at this sane eschatology, preferring an Old Testament approach or a Revivalist perspective of eternity with a judgement.

The book was very widely noticed, read and praised, as well as being constructively criticized. U Thant, Secretary-General of the United Nations, thought it 'timely', Arthur Koestler thought it 'impressive' and Gordon Rattray Taylor, whose work *The Doomsday Book* was to appear a year later, realized Montefiore had beaten him to publication on a similar theme. (His book was at page-proof stage when Montefiore's was published.) Taylor had broken off another project to write his book after reading advance copies of papers delivered in the United States on the global implications of pollution. He, too, had reached the Montefiore conclusion that the basic issue in conservation was a religious or spiritual one. Without realizing it, their last sentences were almost identical: 'It is the future of the human race that we have been talking about.' (Rattray Taylor); 'Nothing less than the future of the whole of mankind is at stake.' (Montefiore).

It was not Montefiore's style merely to leave the printed words on the page. He wanted action, and urged the Archbishop of Canterbury, in the spirit of the resolutions of the 1968 Lambeth Conference, to begin consultations with the spiritual and moral leaders of mankind, for a conference complementary to that of the United Nations.

Prompted by the new enlightenment, the Church of England Board for Social Responsibility had been examining the ethical basis of man's use of natural resources, particularly those associated with the living environment. It had set up an ecumenical group[9] which produced its first report *Man in His Living Environment: An Ethical Assessment* in 1970, as an offering for European Conservation Year. The report was debated in Church Assembly, Spring 1970. Before the debate Montefiore had an interview with Anthony Crosland, Secretary of State for the Environment. Did he approve of the initiative of the Church in this area? The reply was an unqualified 'yes'.

The debate was the first of its kind. The Bishop of Norwich (Launcelot Fleming), one of the few bishops who understood the issues before they were thrust at him, made an important contribution. Thanks to *The Question Mark*, Montefiore was a conspicuous speaker in the debate. Montefiore spoke with urgency and impatience. The Church must act *now* 'in conjunction with anyone else who would help, in promoting the survival of man, and so thereby, surely, furthering the purposes of God, who created and redeemed man, and, if we are willing, will sanctify him.'

Bishop John Robinson, formerly of Woolwich and then Dean of Trinity College, Cambridge, but who still represented Southwark in Church Assembly, criticized the theological dimension of the report: 'This is not good enough for the Church's distinctive contribution and indeed as the sole rationale for our being in this field at all.' He preferred *The Question Mark*.

At least *Man in His Living Environment* was a start, if a poor one. Montefiore was only too aware that the Christian faith does not give its adherents special sources of knowledge, nor does it provide heaven-sent answers to difficult and complex problems. In the future Montefiore was to be in the dense jungle, asking what contribution Christians can offer in these matters. We shall see how he has tried to lead people out of the jungle by finding insights from the biblical record, from the traditions of the Church and from the deliverances of the human mind.

Dr Joseph Needham, who wrote the Foreword to *The Question Mark*, became Master of Gonville and Caius in 1966 when Montefiore was at Great St Mary's. Needham was a Christian socialist and attended the famous church of St John the Baptist, Thaxted, where the red flag flew and the Magnificat was a manifesto. When he was first elected a fellow of Caius in 1924, nobody would speak to him at dinner. He did not endear himself to his conservative colleagues when he said that the United States of America had dropped infected flies on the Chinese. Needham, a bio-chemist, was in China with UNESCO during the Second World War and decided to devote the rest of his life to a work of reconciliation between China and the West by writing a history of Chinese Science – one of several projects which he still carries on at the Needham Institute in Cambridge. Montefiore regards him with considerable affection and respect. Their personalities are quite different. It is not always easy to discover Montefiore's 'still centre'. As is often the case with the children of manic depressives, he suffers from mood swings and the obverse of his imaginative, innovative, energetic and creative ways were his depressive periods when he could easily imagine slights. The turbulence of some aspects of college life in Cambridge, and at Great St Mary's, was painful. In contrast Dr Needham could write to Montefiore:

> Funnily enough, I don't fear the 'turbulence', partly because I don't seek, and never could, to constrain the waters – you know the phrase in the *Tao Tê Ching* I should like to live up to: 'the sage has no personal wishes, therefore all his desires are fulfilled'.

That exemplifies the difference between the two men. It is

also a difference between sage and prophet, whilst not excluding the possibility that the one does not preclude the other!

'Getting things done' has always been one of Montefiore's attractive characteristics. He has been quick to see gaps or needs, immediately offering to fill them. New Hall, Cambridge, was founded in 1954 to provide more places for women in the university. On the original site there was no adjacent chapel, and the undergraduates were invited to Queen's Chapel, where a number of them regularly attended services. Montefiore, when at Gonville and Caius, acted informally as chaplain to New Hall, and was formally appointed chaplain in 1960. He continued as such for some time after he had moved to Great St Mary's. Dame Rosemary Murray[10] writes:

> The very fact that he was someone whom I felt I could ask and who agreed to act as chaplain of this new college for women says something about him.
>
> Not only did I feel that New Hall should make provision for the 'religion' of its undergraduates, but I have always felt that there should be several people as well as her tutor to whom an undergraduate could go in times of crisis or difficulty. The chaplain is one of these and is therefore concerned with undergraduates of all faiths (or none) and not only with those who are Anglican in name. The role of the chaplain for New Hall was therefore very largely pastoral.

Women undergraduates were no new experience for Montefiore. When he was on the staff of Westcott House he had acted as pastoral chaplain for Girton College, spending one afternoon a week there. Montefiore had the indefinable capacity to appeal to undergraduates and it showed no less at New Hall than at Caius and Great St Mary's. Professor Barnabas Lindars thinks this attraction was a combination of personal magnetism, enjoyment of being with young people and an intuitive capacity to be on their wavelength: 'Hugh is an all-round person, not the sort of man to be "all for youth", but from the young people's point of view he is someone to whom they respond.' Both male and female undergraduates continued to seek him out for counsel. They knew they could expect an answer, even if it was an unpalatable one.

Montefiore had links with Newnham College too. He was Director of Studies at a time when Newnham did not have a tutor or lecturer in theology. Mrs Margaret Barker remembers him as 'conspicuously the best teacher in Cambridge', whom she 'liked enormously as a person' – the two did not always cohere.

My most vivid recollection is of the study in the tower of Great St Mary's, where I had my supervisions every Monday morning at nine o'clock. Hugh had no time for the late-rising, leisured undergraduate, as I remember, and expected everyone to work hard. On one occasion I arrived with an unfinished essay, because I always tried to keep Sunday free of work (a relic of my very strict Church upbringing). I explained that the essay was unfinished for that reason and was told, 'Six days shalt thou labour and do *all* that thou hast to do.' I never missed an essay time again! He taught through thick and thin; in those days he suffered from a bad back, and I remember several supervisions when HWM was lying full length on the floor of the study with a pillow under his back, whilst I read my essay to his head end. He was a terrifying teacher, but I respected him for it. He knew *everything*, and scrutinized essays with the eye of the Last Judgement. Nothing escaped. It was the best training I had in Cambridge, and doubtless how I got my firsts. When, in later years, I have seen him on TV demolishing some poor opponent, I have often felt a sneaking sympathy for his victim. He was very hard work, and had the great gift of being able to isolate a problem and summarize evidence with the speed of light. I am sure we did more in an hour than most people did in a term. The reading lists he gave were horrendous, but he knew them all himself, and there was no flannelling in supervision. People whom I have met subsequently have been amazed that it was possible to survive the HWM experience and a) still be a Christian, and b) still be his friend. This shows, I fear, how badly he has been depicted by some groups within the Church. The evangelicals do not like him, and the high churchmen certainly do not. They both fear his learning but seem to have ignored the deep spirituality of the man who has embodied what it means to love God with heart and soul and *mind* and strength.

He was also a fascinating person to listen to; doing St Paul with Hugh was a revelation, since he had the Jewish background himself, and there is no substitute for the real thing. He was, I suspect, both too clever for the Cambridge of the mid-sixties and too sincere; too committed to the faith as faith, rather than as an academic discipline, or the key to a cosy tenured life . . . For many years, if the TV wanted a comment with a theological basis on something of current concern it was to [Montefiore] that they turned. Why? Because there was nobody else who married the two disciplines.

Montefiore was also director of studies at Sidney Sussex and St Catherine's College, until they had too many people reading theology for him to cope.

When the original advertisement about the intention to open subscriptions for Churchill College appeared in the *Cambridge University Reporter*, there was no mention of a chapel nor of a dean or chaplain. Montefiore wrote a joint letter with his friend Barry Till (Fellow and Dean of Jesus College) to the *Cambridge Review* asking for clarification of the trustees' intentions with regard to providing for the religious life of the new college. This was answered by Noël Annan (Provost of King's), one of the trustees, who made it clear that no money would be set aside for a chapel or for the official acknowledgement of religion in the shape of a chaplain, but if money was given for this specific purpose it would be so used.

Montefiore immediately sent a cheque for a small sum which opened the Churchill College Chapel Fund. His view was that if his cheque was accepted that was a sign, even a commitment, that there should, or would, be a chapel; otherwise the cheque would have to be returned. The cheque was banked. Montefiore persuaded some fellow deans to act in like manner, and a few did so.

Noël Annan made it clear to Montefiore that unless a substantial donation was made there would be no chapel. This was a matter of public concern, for it had been stated that the college would be on the traditional Cambridge model. With most Cambridge colleges the statutes mention religion as one of the aims of the college. No such clause appeared in the original draft statutes for Churchill College. However, these were improved following pressure, and provision was made for the appointment of a college chaplain and a space for a free-standing chapel had to be included in the approved plans for the new foundation. A large room in one of the college buildings was to be set aside for a chapel until such time as money was given for a proper chapel.

The trustees were unwilling to launch an appeal for a free-standing chapel, so their genuflection to religion was rather an empty gesture. Montefiore wrote to Timothy Beaumont,[11] who had been one of his students at Westcott House, and whose father had been in Montefiore's regiment during the war. Timothy Beaumont had inherited his father's fortune and was very generous indeed in giving money for good causes. Montefiore knew plenty of wealthy Jews, but Timothy was the only rich Christian he knew. Would he support *this* very good cause?

University 'politics' are unstable, unseemly and unsatisfactory. They played a part in Churchill College Chapel. During 1961 the Master of Caius (Nevill Mott) informed Montefiore that Francis Crick[12] had resigned his fellowship at Churchill because it was to have its own chapel. Montefiore knew Crick because he had dining rights at Caius. He was a brilliant scientist who had discovered how genetical inheritances are coded on chromosomes. As he worked for the Medical Research Council, he was technically not a university officer. Crick was strongly atheist and anti-religion. Sir John Cockroft,[13] the Master of Churchill, was in an unenviable position. He was an Anglican, a communicant, but he did not display or openly witness to his faith.

John Morrison,[14] the senior tutor of Churchill, went to see Montefiore. Morrison was a loyal Anglican and was increasingly concerned by developments. Montefiore also heard from Anthony Hewish,[15] who, had been a fellow of Caius until October 1961 and had left for Churchill. Hewish was an Anglican and a sidesman at St Edward King and Martyr in Cambridge. It became clear that the Christians among the fellows did not want to be thought intolerant, saw good in other religions and, through a typically donnish desire for impartiality, thought they were being liberal-minded in agreeing to three resolutions: resolutions which were supported by some genuine agnostics and some rather pugnacious atheists: 1 that the college chapel could be used, with the approval of the Council, for religious services of any religion; 2 that the college chapel should not normally contain any religious emblems that could cause offence to members of any other religion; 3 that the college chapel should be open at all times for meditation.

Montefiore was incensed. He agreed with Morrison that the three resolutions, although liberal in form, were really an attack on Christianity. Indeed, Morrison wrote to the master with his resignation as from September 1963 when he thought the battle lost. None of the movers of the resolutions would themselves have wished to use the chapel for a religious service, Christian or otherwise. No non-Christian bodies had been asked whether they would like to use the chapel for services. The Jews attended the synagogue in Cambridge; Hindus were happy to worship in a Christian chapel; Buddhists and Confucians could be dismissed as non-existent at that time.

Montefiore went back to Timothy Beaumont. The easy answer was for Beaumont to withdraw his benefaction – but this would be what the anti-Christian lobby wanted. Neither Montefiore nor Beaumont wanted anti-Christ to win. A careful letter was drafted and sent to Sir John Cockroft at the beginning of January 1962. The starting point was one of the statutes of Churchill College:

> Services in the chapel shall normally be held in accordance with the usage of the Church of England. The Council shall make such regulations in regard to holding of services in the chapel as it may think fit.

Beaumont had signed the covenant for the benefaction, based on the statute. Now he was being put into a false position. It had become common knowledge that he was the benefactor, and to withdraw his favour would lead to misunderstanding. On the other hand, if his covenant stood alongside the resolutions it would generally be assumed that he had given money for a purpose which he had never intended. As a Christian priest, he would not wish to give large sums for a religiously neutral building. He understood that occasions might arise when adherents of some religion other than Christianity would wish to hold services in the college chapel, and that the College Council might very properly wish to give them permission. Beaumont suggested that if the chapel were built and furnished for its normal use, on the occasions when a religious service other than a Christian one was held, the Christian furnishings could be temporarily removed.

Sir John Cockroft agreed and then consulted his colleagues. Following these consultations Sir John met Timothy Beaumont and the news he carried was not good. The governing body remained adamant that the chapel should be open for medi-tation to members of all religions and that therefore there should be no permanent cross. Beaumont felt this was

> a moment when one should take the scandal of the Cross perhaps even more literally than St Paul meant it, and dig our toes in. The only compromise I can think of might be the inclusion of a separate Chapel of Unity for meditation in the main chapel, but this is probably going to complicate the architect's task . . .

Montefiore absolutely agreed with what Beaumont said about the *skandalon* of the Cross.

Montefiore was determined the proposal would not fall, and equally that the chapel should be conspicuously Christian. At a meeting with John Morrison on 22 February 1962 a brilliant scheme was hatched which would obviate difficulties. Churchill College did not yet own its own money and its own estates, although it was self-governing. The money and the estates still remained in the hands of the trustees. The suggestion was that the Churchill College Chapel Trust should be set up, quite a distinct entity from Churchill College itself. The master and other Christian fellows of the college would form the chapel trustees. Churchill College trustees would be asked to make over to the Chapel Trust a plot of land on the college campus. Beaumont would be asked to revoke his covenant to the college and to make it instead in favour of the chapel trust. The chapel would be built on the chapel trust plot of land. Thus the chapel would not belong to the college, and the anti-Christian dons of Churchill would have no grounds for complaint. On the other hand, the chapel would be on the college campus;[16] it would be used as the college chapel and no one would know that it was not an ordinary college chapel. Was this a brilliant way out of the impasse? The bursar backed the scheme and within days the master, too, had supported it. On 28 February 1962, at a college meeting, the matter was voted upon. The result is there for all to see. Churchill College Chapel, but for Montefiore's initiative and Beaumont's money, would never have existed. Unfortunately there is an unsatisfactory tailpiece to the story. There is no chaplain at the college at the moment. Instead, there is a secular counsellor, and a non-parochial clergyman attends on Sunday to take chapel services.

Throughout the Cambridge years, Montefiore's vocal and literary output was vast. Although impatient to reach a wide audience, he did not neglect theological research, and articles by him appeared in theological journals such as *Novum Testamentum*,[17] *New Testament Studies*,[18] *Expository Times*,[19] *Journal of Theological Studies*,[20] *Historia*[21] and *Theology*.[22]

In many of these articles Montefiore is exploring faith as much as explaining doubt. It is in keeping with his character and the powerful nature of his conversion. He was not constantly taking his own spiritual temperature. He concentrated on Him to whom the darkness and light are both alike. At times when he felt little or nothing he pinched himself, remembering that convictions are deeper than feelings. He saw nothing wrong in containing doubts, for they reminded him of the infinite majesty and glory of God, beyond his full comprehension. After all, theology is more concerned with the proper posing of questions than with their neat and tidy solutions. It was possible to maintain one's intellectual integrity whilst recognizing that in this world knowledge of God will be incomplete. *Exit in Mysterium* – it vanishes into mystery. Perhaps that is why Montefiore leaps off the theological treadmill, content with Daniel, who said, 'Verily, thou art a God that hidest thyself.'

Accordingly, when considering the paucity of references to

Gospel events in contemporary or near-contemporary non-Christian literature, he scratched around for brief allusions in the writings of Tacitus, Suetonius and Josephus. There was adequate testimony to the death of Jesus, but why did not the other Gospel events arouse general, if not widespread, interest? In 'Josephus and the New Testament' he sought mention of or corrobative evidence for the star at Jesus' birth; the rending of the temple veil; the cleansing of the temple; the resurrection of Jesus; the ascension of Jesus, and the descent of the Spirit of Pentecost. Montefiore's exploring led to the discovery of some slim similarities and some gaping differences in the Gospel narratives compared with Josephus' *Jewish War*. But nothing disturbed his faith, which is why twenty-five years on he was so incensed with the statements of David Jenkins, Bishop of Durham. Anything tinged with heresy revolted Montefiore. Reviewing two books in *Theology* in 1955 he concluded:

> The task of theology in any age may well be thought to lie, not in the provision of answers, but in the correct formulation of problems which must ultimately be solved not by thought but by life.
>
> The Church of England today indulgently tolerates heresy and regards it as less important than charity. The early Church was not so sure.[23]

Most of Montefiore's published works were for a wider readership, and the major premiss from which he moved was in the background of his work. His concern was for enlightened, if partial, discovery, more than for never-ending exploration. Questions must be faced, not dodged, and the lust for unambiguous answers should be resisted, for that may extinguish rather than light up faith. In his book *Awkward Questions on Christian Love*[24] Montefiore writes:

> I cannot commit myself to a belief in God until I know roughly what I mean by that three-letter word. To a large extent the matter turns on what is meant by God. The inmost nature of the Divine Being is bound to be mysterious to mortal men; but if we can give *no meaning at all* to the word God, then we have no further need of the

hypothesis. Many people have their own private notion of God. For myself, I am content to understand the word God approximately in the sense of traditional Christian theism.

Why do I believe in him? I can offer no proof, only the grounds of my faith. I am not of course conscious of these grounds when I commit myself to God: an act of faith looks forward to its object, not backward to its roots. Yet the grounds of my belief are none the less real for that.

Montefiore's excellent method was to expound the doctrines of the faith by showing how he had made them his own. He sought the truth while teaching it, and he took the enquirer along with him. Is he not what the New English Bible calls 'a teacher of the law who has become a learner in the Kingdom of Heaven'?

This approach is evident in *Beyond Reasonable Doubt*[25] and *Truth to Tell: A Radical Restatement of Christian Faith.*[26] The latter was a collection of Montefiore's sermons preached in Great St Mary's, in which he successfully sought to show that radical Christianity could be not only true and positive but also relevant and redemptive. Some of his other sermons appeared in the two volumes he edited which brought together sermons preached by distinguished visitors to Great St Mary's.[27]

The vast subject of personal relations – including marriage, divorce and re-marriage – occupied a sizeable chunk of Montefiore's thinking, and he was to be a great reformer in these matters. During the Cambridge period he gave a lecture on 'Personal Relations before Marriage'[28] in the Easter term of 1962 under the auspices of the Faculty Board of Divinity and the Keene Lectures.[29]

Reviewing *God, Sex and War*,[30] David Jenkins (then chaplain of The Queen's College, Oxford) noted Montefiore's facility for theological speaking without speaking theologically – a gift, once again, of the academic and the pastor:

Canon Montefiore's 'Personal Relations before Marriage' is quite first class. It is practical and down to earth while quite clearly based on theology without appearing to cite theology. It is to be studied both for itself (there is actually

specific advice on 'how far should I go?') and as a model
for gaining a hearing from the anti-authoritarians of today
who yet really do need and feel a need for guidance. This
lecture itself is easily worth the cost of the book.

Two books which attracted much attention were addressed
to different constituencies. First, there was Montefiore's *Commentary on The Epistle to the Hebrews*[31] which he regarded as the
most original writing in the New Testament and possibly the
earliest: the only document written throughout in first-class
Greek, it is the product of a first-class mind – a powerful
personality of the primitive Church who was precise, creative,
rigorous both in mind and in heart, equally at home with his
Jewish heritage, the Septuagint Scriptures and the Alexandrian
writings of Philo Judaeus. Who was the genius? In his Introduction Montefiore presents a well-constructed thesis arguing for
the authorship of Apollos. However, his lucid and balanced
exegesis is largely independent of the introductory material. It
is a commentary well in the tradition of Westcott, Moffatt,
Robinson and Bruce.

The second book arose directly from his pastoral ministry
with the students at New Hall. *My Confirmation Notebook*[32] was
especially produced for the preparation of adult and older adolescent candidates. Montefiore used these 'notes' during his
years at Great St Mary's. They were an attempt 'to give a
constructive outline of the fullness of the Christian way of life
as it may be understood by an intelligent Christian of the mid-
twentieth century'. Present-day parish priests should note that
the 'syllabus' is set out under twenty-one headings intended to
cover a period of preparation lasting about six months, with
some holiday breaks. Confirmation preparation at Great St
Mary's was rigorous. Candidates knew their faith and what it
demanded of them well before the bishop came to lay hands on
them. The principal of Bishop's College, Cheshunt, Philip H.
Cecil, was not alone in admiring and commending the volume:

> The authoritative guidance for which most laypeople still
> look to their clergy is provided in clear and unequivocal
> form . . . Your reviewer looked with particular interest at
> the section on 'The Death of Jesus' where he found

Atonement teaching of a kind at once completely orthodox and completely understandable to today's enquirers; the section on 'The Sacraments' provides one of the best brief summaries of the subject to be found anywhere; that on 'Guilt and Forgiveness' goes right to the heart of the matter. The sections on 'Holiness' and on 'Basic Christian Attitudes' give ascetical teaching of several kinds, not omitting a note on spiritual reading, with a booklist; that on 'Money, Service and Witness' could not be more practical.[33]

Philip Cecil regretted a certain weakness in the portion on prayer. Montefiore was aware of the deficiency and later rectified it in a new edition. An earlier booklet *To Help You to Pray*[34] showed a real understanding of the difficulties of praying as well as the ability to teach people how to pray.

Montefiore also contributed to debates on television and radio, some of which appeared later in book form.[35] And there was always interest in his own spiritual journey.[36] There were interviews to be given, books to review and newspaper and magazine articles to be written.

Mervyn Stockwood was at Great St Mary's from 1955 to 1959; Joe Fison from 1959 to 1963. Four years was about the limit in such a cure, certainly in the post-Stockwood era. The 'homosexual' incident had appeared to dish Montefiore's chances of a mitre. He did not want purely academic work. Some of his friends could see him at one of the modern cathedrals – as Dean of Liverpool or Provost of Coventry. But such places would not have satisfied his pastoral instincts. The pastor was never far below the surface.

And it was a human pastor too, not the textbook priest. Barry Till regards him as a very great pastor:

Very wise to go to him in trouble – may not get the best advice but great comfort and pastoral help – e.g. my wife . . . had a zany aunt . . . dying of cancer, not a church woman, [Montefiore] visited her daily, took her Communion and arranged her funeral at Kings. She told me that he had 'taken her across the Jordan'.

In 1968 there was the suggestion that he should succeed
Prebendary Gordon Phillips, who was leaving the University
of London to be Dean of Llandaff. Before any formal offer was
made, news of the possibility reached the trustees of the
University Church of Christ the King (the old Irvingite Catholic Apostolic Church in Gordon Square). The trustees said they
would withdraw the use of their church if Montefiore were
appointed. Montefiore notes 'I told Bishop Robert Stopford of
London that undergraduates would flock to the university
services if I hired a hall, and publicly announced that I had been
victimized; but he sensibly preferred to withdraw the
suggestion.'

By now Montefiore was exhausted and anxious, an unhappy
duet of emotions. There had been suggestions of returning to
Westcott House, where he had been unhappy previously, or of
going to be warden of the Worcester Diocesan Retreat House,
hardly Montefiore's cup of meditation. But he could not continue the unremitting pace he had partly inherited and partly
made for himself. His predecessors had not been writing and
lecturing to the degree that he was. He was feeling the pressure
of 'keeping the circus on the road' at Great St Mary's. By 1969
he was heading towards a crisis. A curate, Barney Hopkinson,
explains:

> It became more and more of an effort to think out new
> courses of sermons, and to find the right preachers to
> preach them. For a while he went through a very low,
> almost depressive, stage. He became more and more
> stressful, and it began to show in his Achilles' heel – his
> back. He began to suffer more and more backaches, until
> one morning we arrived at staff meeting to find him lying
> on the floor of his study with a very pronounced kink in
> his back. We told him he needed a break. 'I know. The
> doctor says the same, but I can't.' It was clear that he had
> reached the stage where he could not even cope with
> making the arrangements for the break he needed.
> Eventually, after fruitless arguments, I stepped over his
> prostrate body, and phoned the bishop. Ted Roberts was
> at his best. 'Tell Hugh that he is off duty as of now, and I
> will come over to see him and arrange his break.' Within

five minutes the *coup d'état* was complete and we drove Hugh back to his house. He remained off duty for nearly three months, most of it, fortunately, during the long vacation.

Montefiore, who has a deep sense of vocation, was waiting for God to show him the next move. By now he was desperate. In the late autumn of 1969 John Robinson, by now Dean of Trinity College, invited him to lunch. Montefiore recalls the occasion:

> After lunch as we were gossiping, he said, 'Oh, by the way, Hugh, would you like to be Bishop of Kingston?' I said, 'Don't be ridiculous. What on earth do you mean?' He replied, 'Mervyn asked me to ask you.' Apparently it had been cleared with Michael Ramsey, the Archbishop of Canterbury. I was dumbfounded. Brought up north of the Thames I had hardly ever set foot in South London. It had never crossed my mind that any such offer could conceivably come.

John Robinson may not have looked like God's messenger, but that is how this proposal came to Montefiore.

10   Mr Johnson Arrives

Mervyn Stockwood had certainly put Southwark and 'South-Bank religion' on the map. He brought all kinds of new men into the diocese, invigorating its life and uplifting its vision. There were then two suffragan sees: Woolwich and Kingston-upon-Thames. With Woolwich he had been fortunate, for Robert William Stannard was appointed Dean of Rochester in 1959 at the time Mervyn Stockwood became Bishop of South-wark. John Robinson succeeded Stannard and when he returned to Cambridge, Stockwood surprised the Church with another unusual appointment. David Stuart Sheppard was the forty-year-old warden and chaplain of the Mayflower Family Centre in Canning Town, who was nationally known as a cricketer; ecclesiastically he was known for his evangelical convictions. He became Bishop of Woolwich.

Kingston-upon-Thames was not as simple. The bishop, William Percy Gilpin, was fifty-seven when Stockwood was consecrated, and Kingston was the end of the line for him. In 1969 he intimated that he would retire in 1970. Another imaginative appointment was therefore likely – but who? Stockwood consulted with his South-Bank coterie.

We have seen how the suggestion was communicated to Montefiore. A great many people had been wondering what was going to happen to him. Would the Church stomach an episcopal Montefiore? Even if Mervyn Stockwood was prepared to take him on, would he be acceptable to the clergy and laity, many of whom had neither forgotten nor forgiven his (in)famous suggestion about Christ's homosexuality.

It was somehow typical that Stockwood did not ask Montefiore himself. There was an aura of theatre and mystery here
which extended to the next stage of the proposal. There must
be absolute secrecy and Montefiore had to communicate with
Stockwood by means of a pseudonym, Mr Johnson! More
sensible was his vetting by Bishop David Sheppard, with
whom he would have to work. David Sheppard writes:

> I had never met Hugh Montefiore before Mervyn
> Stockwood said that he would like to consider him as the
> Bishop of Kingston. Mervyn insisted that I must meet
> him, and say that I would be happy to work with him,
> before he would go ahead with a firm approach. Hugh
> came down to my mother's house in Sussex, where we
> spent half a day together. Soon afterwards Grace and I
> went to lunch with them in Cambridge and we again had
> the chance to talk. It very quickly became clear to me that
> Hugh was someone who knew what it was not to have
> been a Christian and for whom the living Christ was very
> personal and real.

These meetings took place in November 1969 and Stockwood decided to present a petition to the Crown for Montefiore's nomination to be Bishop of Kingston. The Archbishop
of Canterbury, Michael Ramsey, wrote to Montefiore saying
he supported this move. The prime minister's appointments
secretary and leading ecclesiastical figures had no legal power to
prevent the appointment, as they would have been able to do
had the appointment been to a diocesan bishopric. Suffragan
bishops are the choice of the diocesan. In theory the prime
minister could decide not to furnish the name to the sovereign
and the Archbishop of Canterbury could refuse to consecrate.
In practice either step was unlikely to be taken even if a public
furore would be likely to ensue over the nomination.

In this case the Church owed much to the courage of Mervyn
Stockwood in being the only bishop likely to take the risk of
bringing Montefiore into the episcopal fold. History will show
that Stockwood's courage was richly repaid.

For Montefiore there were few doubts about the future. He
needed fresh stimulus and new pastures. Friends were not

uniformly in favour of the move. Whilst allowing that a man's vocation may be to accept that which is offered him and to which he is drawn, the questions 'What is best for Hugh Montefiore?' and 'What is ideal for the Church of Christ?' might elicit different answers.

Would Montefiore's gifts be available to the wider Church? Would he have leisure to speak, travel and write? There were those who felt he was best equipped to be in a position where he would speak to, and, when necessary, against the spirit of the age. Would he do this from Southwark, or should he be in one of the new universities – Essex or East Anglia? There was the possibility of his taking up an appointment at the Open University. The doubters, however, need not have feared.

The formal offer of Kingston-upon-Thames came from the prime minister (Harold Wilson) at the end of December 1969 and confirmation of the Queen's approval came on 5 January 1970. The public announcement was made on 7 January 1970. Montefiore was forty-nine years old.

Predictably, the appointment was greeted with cheers and with abuse. Hysteria came from the extremities, applause from the radicals and 'outsiders' and immense interest from everyone. The Church of England Evangelical Council called on Montefiore to affirm his belief 'that the humanity of our Lord was perfect in every way' and called upon those responsible for making senior appointments

> to take careful account of a candidate's published beliefs, remembering that 'a bishop, as God's steward, must be blameless . . . he must hold firm to the sure word as taught, so that he may be able to give instruction in sound doctrine and also to confute those who contradict it' (Titus 1:7,9). Moreover, 'he must be well thought of by outsiders' (Timothy 3:7).[1]

Montefiore responded to this call by preaching a sermon in May 1970 making plain his convictions. It quenched most of the council's anxieties, but they remained disturbed that Montefiore could not, or would not, give a complete assurance that Jesus' human nature was 'perfect in every way' – a reference to the homosexual question. Montefiore's difficulty with the Evangelical Council was that they did not realize the meaning of *teleios* in connection with Our Lord's nature. The word does not signify his perfection, which is not a biblical doctrine, but his completeness (cf. Psalm 139:15). He had a complete human nature and a complete divine nature. For all their insistence on orthodoxy, they did not know what orthodoxy means.

Mervyn Stockwood thought it important that Montefiore should have an opportunity to give an apologia of his views to the diocese before his consecration. The Diocesan Synod was meeting at Church House, Westminster, in the spring. That would be a suitable occasion. Thus Montefiore was introduced to the diocese of Southwark in a typical cloak-and-dagger way. He was taken to Church House, kept in a lavatory, dramatically produced and invited to speak. He dealt with the Modern Churchmen's Union speech in a careful and candid way to an audience that was touchy, especially after John Robinson. All went well, even if he did not withdraw his speculation. He asked that they should 'join together happily and confidently in proclaiming and living the Gospel of our Lord Jesus Christ in which we are both privileged to share'.

Montefiore's consecration was fixed for September so there was ample time for taking leave of Great St Mary's and for Southwark to become accustomed to his projected arrival. More important, it gave Montefiore time to prepare for his new ministry. Where would he live? His 'area' of 148 parishes stretched from Waterloo to Thames Ditton, from the Thames to Gatwick Airport. There was nothing suitable in the middle of the area so he hired a car and toured the commons of South London, being accustomed to living on the Backs at Cambridge.

He and his wife found the ideal house, overlooking the south side of Wandsworth Common. It was a small detached house with lots of small rooms, in a multi-cultural area and convenient for shops. Wandsworth Common railway station was minutes away and there was a frequent service to Victoria. The multi-cultural environment was important for a bishop whose area included Brixton, Battersea and Balham. They decided this was to be home. When the Second Church Estates Commissioner (Sir Hubert Ashton) went to inspect the property there had been a domestic row next door and furniture was strewn over the garden. The house was pronounced not suitable and too small. The Church Commissioners were about to get another slap on the face. David and Grace Sheppard had already rejected the Commissioners' choice of a large house in Blackheath and had bought their own Georgian semi in Asylum Road, Peckham, with the aid of a grant from the diocese. The Church Commissioners offered the Montefiores a much larger house not far from the one they wanted, but Hugh and Elisabeth Montefiore were not going to have their lifestyle dictated by the Church Commissioners, Montefiore's mother paid for the three-bedroomed late Victorian house they had chosen and helped with the expenses of re-decoration. This residence became a home to which the Montefiores returned years later on their retirement.

The concluding months at Great St Mary's were hectic, but Montefiore was more relaxed. People in the town were beginning to say they would miss him. Amongst the 'gown' population there was sadness and envy. Few clergymen could have achieved as much popularity as he had in just seven years among 8,000 sceptical, critical, twentieth-century undergraduates. This tall, lean figure with his white tie had become a familiar sight, rushing hither and thither. He considered the white tie the proper dress of an English clergyman. The clerical collar and the black stock was an importation from Ireland by Roman Catholics.

Statistically, all evidence was against the Church's institutional survival. But the phenomenon of revival was a continuing one. Montefiore respected freedom and conscience too much to push religion down people's throats. Students in particular did not want to be given the meaning of the universe in the form of a handout. They may have made a conscious decision that the word of God was not relevant to their lives, but they had an enormous interest in the idea, and a desire for some transcendental experience. That is why Montefiore was wary of massive missions and missioners who stoked up emotions to the point where people were pressurized into conversion to the Christian faith. Apart from CICCU missions, which took place every three years, there had been no 'missions to the university' whilst Montefiore was at Great St Mary's. The last had taken place in 1954 when Montefiore was at Caius and Bishop

Michael Ramsey came down from Durham. He was splendid ('Some people think that Bibles came floating down from heaven – some with Apocryphas and some without!') but everyone was so exhausted by the preparations that after the mission attendances actually went down, which is why Montefiore concentrated on courses of sermons when he became vicar.

On 4 July 1970 there was a party for Montefiore in Cambridge. The following day he preached at all three services. Even at the last some remarks in his sermon caused controversy. Recently Mr Justice Melford Stevenson had sentenced six university students to up to eighteen months' imprisonment following some violence at a protest demonstration at the Garden House Hotel against the intolerant and illiberal regime in Greece. Montefiore described the sentences as 'savage' and asked the congregation to imagine the worst conditions that would obtain in Cambridge if 10,000 members of the armed forces lived there in place of a similar number of students. This was too much for Field Marshal Sir Gerald Templer, among others, who fulminated in the columns of *The Times* against the 'slur' on the armed forces. Montefiore could well take care of himself in this matter.

Before his consecration, Montefiore received the gift of a crozier, or pastoral staff, from Great St Mary's. The beautiful crozier was designed and made by Loughnan Pendred a member of Great St Mary's. Carved from English walnut, it shows Christ carrying a small cross with a symbolic lamb beneath. Montefiore's episcopal ring was designed by David Peace of Hemingford Abbots, who worked in association with an independent London silversmith, Michael Murray. In a remarkably successful way David Peace created a modern ring for a mid-twentieth-century bishop which yet achieved an ancient quality. He based his design on the chi-rho symbol, which is repeated on the top and side of the heavy gold ring, while the bottom is engraved with the star of Bethlehem.

When priests become bishops they lose one portion of their personal identity, namely, their surname. Montefiore wrote to his friend Christopher Brooke, Professor of History, Westfield College, University of London, asking for how long bishops – and in particular suffragan bishops – had legally called themselves by the name of their see: 'I would prefer to be known as Hugh Montefiore, Bishop of Kingston, rather than Hugh Kingston' – but he received in reply no ammunition to change the existing practice.

Montefiore's consecration took place on the Feast of St Michael and All Angels, 29 September 1970, in Southwark Cathedral. The chief consecrator was the Archbishop of Canterbury, Michael Ramsey, to whom Montefiore was presented by his old and new 'chiefs' – the Bishops of Ely (E.J.K. Roberts) and Southwark (Mervyn Stockwood). The sermon was preached by his friend Canon Geoffrey Lampe, Ely Professor of Divinity in the University of Cambridge.

Montefiore is grateful for much that he owes to Mervyn Stockwood, not least that he was brave enough to invite him to be his suffragan, and even more for showing him how to be a bishop. Mervyn Stockwood was not everyone's glass of claret, but he remains one of the most interesting and outstanding bishops of his time. Montefiore had been an admirer from the time Stockwood was vicar of Great St Mary's (1955–9). When Montefiore was at Caius, Stockwood used his room for sherry on Sundays between Evensong at Great St Mary's and the 8.30 p.m. university service. Publication of a course of sermons *The Faith Today*[2] marked Stockwood's transition from Cambridge to Southwark. Alec Vidler had this to say about them:

> They constitute a clear and down-to-earth exposition of the Christian faith and its practical implications. It is definite without being cocksure and challenging without being strident. There are no flowers of rhetoric but there is plenty of wit. The preacher is shrewd but not subtle. He may not be an intellectual, but he has a great respect for intelligence and he addresses himself to the intelligence of his hearers. At the same time, he never tires of driving home the truth that a faith which does not issue in action, including political action, is vain.[3]

And the man? He had a strong sense of theatre and knew how to perform 'on stage'. He was always aware that he was playing the leading role and he knew the necessity of having a very strong supporting cast. He was well-known for his 'friends in high places' – Princess Margaret, politicians, artists, writers. His dinner parties were some of the best in London. As a bishop, he was a great encourager as well as a marvellous pastor to those who needed special care. He was more often than not in the pages of the press and in the public eye. He had claimed to be a socialist, and was still saying so in 1968,[4] although he was critical of many of the policies of the Labour Government under Harold Wilson's premiership. His political mentor and hero, from his years as an outstanding parish priest in Bristol (1941–55), was Stafford Cripps. Stockwood was a Labour member of Bristol City Council. By 1975 he was named as one of the 'defectors' from the Labour Party.[5] This does not quite do justice to the 'political' Stockwood. Nicolas Stacey is nearer the mark:

> Stockwood is obviously and painfully torn between heart and head. Intellectually he is a Radical Socialist dedicated to the building of a fairer society with a lively concern for the underprivileged. Emotionally he is a high-church Tory who finds compensation for his bachelor life in the trappings and glamour of episcopal office and the prestige of a seat in the House of Lords. On the one hand he can see through the hypocrisy and cant of much of the Establishment, and yet, on the other, he needs the security it provides. Inevitably the radicals are suspicious of his prelatical heart and the Establishment suspicious of his socialist head. And so his is a lonely life.[6]

There was more than a touch of the prelatical in his manner. Montefiore misjudged the time it took to get to the bishop's house in Streatham for his first staff meeting. 'Bishop,' said Stockwood when Montefiore opened the study door, 'we don't let people in late after the meeting has begun.' Montefiore left – to show that two could play at bluff.

Although Montefiore was responsible for the western part of the diocese, the official wording was careful, indicating that he was 'responsible with the diocesan', as Montefiore confirms:

> There was no system of legal areas. Each suffragan (Woolwich and Kingston) had an area, and the diocesan

bishop had the lot, and one never knew where the other had been, and I might give a ruling the opposite of what Mervyn had said the previous week. But he was a good boss, most lovable and maddening. There were muddles but they were infrequent. By and large with goodwill on both sides the system worked well . . .

Montefiore's responsibility was for the deaneries of Battersea, Tooting, Wandsworth, Merton, Richmond and Barnes, Clapham and Brixton, Lambeth, Streatham, Kingston and Reigate – a total of 148 parishes. His first task was to make himself known to the clergy and they to him. This he accomplished by visiting every vicarage and parsonage house in his area, accompanied by his wife.

There was much hospitality at Montefiore's home, and clergy and their wives felt that they had a bishop and wife who really cared. One evangelical vicar had opposed Montefiore's appointment and had written a strong letter against his appointment in his parish magazine. Then he received a visit from the Montefiores which changed his views completely. Affection and respect was won by love, care and interest.

Above all, there were the 'visitations'. He accompanied Stockwood on one before embarking on his own. These had been started by Stockwood and were as important as they were impressive. Montefiore followed the established pattern. The purpose of the visitations was simple. They were pastoral, not legal, occasions. A bishop visited a parish for thirty-six hours, remaining in the parish throughout and sleeping at the vicarage, sharing in the ordinary life of the parish and visiting the community centres and factories within it, meeting as many people as possible. There might be a confirmation; there was always a service and sermon, when Montefiore tried to be the focus of unity, giving a parish a vision of something larger than itself. The diocese became something more than 'them' to whom dues had to be paid. Stockwood's greatest emphasis was on the diocese. He had no time for Church Assembly and its successor, the General Synod. Montefiore believed in synodical government but wanted to reform it.

Other than archdeacons, the diocese of Southwark had borough deans. One of them was Canon Mick Pinder,

Borough Dean of Lambeth, who describes Montefiore's working methods as well as recording other impressions:

> I had an arrangement of a weekly telephone call at a
> particular time. I never thought that this worked very well
> because Hugh was able to get to the heart of most
> problems and their solution with such incredible swiftness
> one was left with the feeling that there had not been much
> human contact. He did not believe in wasting his time or
> that of others in travelling to meetings when matters could
> be dealt with in some other way. Whenever one was able
> to engineer a meeting the process was still the same. Each
> item was dealt with at lightning speed, although he never
> made you feel that he wanted you out of the door before
> you came in. One was always left with admiration at
> Hugh's ability to address each item with total
> commitment, leaving each as a firmly closed book as he
> passed on to the next . . .
>
> Hugh was a great pastor with a deep concern for the
> clergy and laity who were dependent on him for support
> and guidance. One [quality] which impressed itself on my
> mind was his readiness to place his bishopric on the line to
> help a cleric who had blotted his copy book, not in any
> moral or criminal sense, but who was very much out of
> favour . . .
>
> Before coming to Southwark, having been cosseted in
> Cambridge, Hugh admitted that he had met and spoken to
> hardly any black people. In his area were the boroughs of
> Wandsworth and Lambeth. Lambeth Town Hall is in the
> centre of Brixton. This gap in his education was filled with
> rapidity and it was typical of him that he took considerable
> interest in black and white issues of the seventies and
> became very much at home in those churches which had a
> high percentage of black people.
>
> One of the significant aspects of his intellectual stature
> and academic knowledge was his ability to make himself
> understood by the variety of congregations to which he
> ministered. Hugh's parochial visits were always enjoyed,
> although some of the liturgical purists were dismayed at
> some of the moments at which he chose to clean his glasses

on his rochet. I can remember only one occasion when he was all at sea. He had to preach the sermon when he was licensing a chaplain to a psychiatric hospital and he sounded more confused than any of the patients in the congregation!

One of the many initiatives instigated by Hugh still bearing fruit was the creation of a group whose concern was to be prisons and the penal system, in co-operation with Martin Wright, then the secretary of the Howard League, whom he had known at Cambridge . . . Hugh generously gave the proceeds of one of his books to provide some necessary finance . . . For the past six years [the diocese] has had a priest appointed to give half his time to the work of this group. I think that Southwark is the only diocese in the country which has someone acting in this capacity and is therefore better equipped than any other to keep the Diocese informed of the appalling conditions prevailing in our prisons and what is happening to the large number of people being held in police cells.

Canon J.W.D. Simonson, Rector of St Mary Barnes, refers to another important initiative:

Very soon after his arrival, Hugh started a theological group in his house, which I think met roughly each month . . . This was a typical move on his part. For him theology was exciting and he wanted to share that excitement with some of his clergy. Also he wanted to provide a venue where clergy with theological experience and interest could meet and discuss theological issues together. I had the privilege of being invited to take part in the group. There were about a dozen of us. Normally one of us would read a paper and then a general discussion followed. It was a very happy and stimulating group; alas it came to an end when the bishop left.

Excitement was a word appropriate to life in the diocese of Southwark. The Church may not have been making much impact, but it could not be ignored. The environment was a secular one. Fostering a sense of community was not easy. Old and natural communities were dying. New communities had to embrace a large West Indian population and a small Asian ethnic minority. Montefiore thinks there was some police provocation against them, and later wondered why there had not been Brixton riots years earlier.

Always the emphasis was on diocesan unity. There were residential weekends for deanery chapters at Wychcroft, the diocesan retreat house at Bletchingly. Such occasions, with parties and other diocesan activities, helped to build up a great corporate feeling in the diocese, based on loyalty to the diocesan bishop, who spread prelatical *bonhomie* everywhere. Yet always, at the centre, was pastoral care, and Montefiore learnt almost everything about being a pastoral bishop from Mervyn Stockwood. He and Bishop David Sheppard shared

> the experience of living and working extremely closely with Bishop Mervyn Stockwood. We have rejoiced, chuckled and sometimes fumed together at this experience. Mervyn brought a great deal of celebration and fun to our life. When we had 'three bishops' days' two or three times a year, we would often go to the extremely hospitable home of Lady Kay Robson-Brown in Cheam. It was very important to get any item you cared specially about on the agenda for the morning. When the lunch break arrived, we would go for a swim in the indoor swimming pool. This would be followed by a magnificent lunch.[7] Discussions moved somewhat more slowly in the afternoon! Mervyn had a very high doctrine of the episcopacy. He took both of us very deeply into his confidence over painful disciplinary issues or other serious questions. I don't think either of us felt that, as a suffragan bishop, we did not have any authority.

One central post in the diocese was given to Montefiore – that of chairman of the diocesan Board of Education. He also chaired three of the board's sub-committees – Schools; Finance; and Higher and Further Education. This was very important and difficult work. In the diocese there were two Church Colleges of Education, six Church grammar schools, six Church secondary schools, six Church middle schools, eleven

Church first schools and eighty-seven Church primary schools. Canon Leslie Burditt Tirrell was Director of Religious Education for the dioceses of London and Southwark.

Montefiore entered his new responsibility with deep prejudice against Church schools. He ended by being their champion, powerfully defending the place of religious education when that was being called in question. However, this work involved very considerable trauma.

In the 1960s Mervyn Stockwood saw the need for a new initiative and fresh vision in this sphere. There were some in the diocese who favoured a radical initiative: namely, that the Church schools should be dismantled. Mervyn Stockwood decided to appoint a knowledgeable and innovative person to sort out Church schools for the 1970s and beyond. In 1969 Patrick Miller, a priest who was teaching at Manchester Grammar School, had been appointed independent adviser on religious education to Stockwood. This able and talented priest won the goodwill and the esteem of the secular authorities and had invigorating insights into the work of the diocesan Youth and Children's Councils.

When Montefiore arrived he was uneasy about Patrick Miller's role, which seemed to have no boundaries. It was clear there would be a clash, mostly over terms of reference but a little over personality.

Montefiore knew little about Church schools, but in his usual way he amassed facts from which he could form opinions and express a policy. He discovered that Church schools were very popular with waiting lists. Families would move house to bring their children within the area of a Church school. Headmasters needed their morale boosting as they were on the receiving end of pressure and insinuation – including ones with racial undertones – from the Inner London Education Authority and its new leader, E. Ashley Bramall. Montefiore met a rough reception when he chaired the Standing Advisory Committee on Religious Education (SACRE) where Humanist representation was active, strong and vocal.

Then there was money! There was a very generous grant towards rebuilding, but the diocese had to find 15% which was financed by the sale of the sites of redundant schools. In most parts of England this would not amount to much, but on either side of the Thames a site could be worth more than a million pounds. Montefiore could not discover how much money there was in the diocesan 'kitty' so a finance commission was appointed – and another one million pounds was found!

Before he was consecrated bishop, Montefiore had agreed in principle with Patrick Miller that there should be an enquiry into Church schools. An enquiry into secondary schools took place. In Lent 1971 Montefiore went on holiday to Spain with Mervyn Stockwood, Lady Elizabeth Cavendish and Sir John Betjeman. Montefiore's wife Elisabeth was there too. While they were away the Bishop's Council met, chaired by David Sheppard of Woolwich. A motion for an enquiry into the 104 Church-aided primary, first and middle schools was put through without Montefiore's (and perhaps without Stockwood's) knowledge or authority.

It was agreed that the enquiry would be financed by the Rowntree Trust, with the Acton Society Trust being responsible for its conduct. Professor John Vaizey, educationalist, Professor of Economics at Brunel University and an Acton Society Trustee and former Director, would have oversight of the enquiry.

Montefiore, already troubled by the tensions generated by the secondary school enquiry, was not happy with an enquiry into the other schools which he felt was almost an enquiry into the work of his board. If he were chairman of the board, then the diocesan bishop could not have a 'freelance' educational adviser. It may have been in order in his predecessor Bishop Gilpin's time but it was not so in Montefiore's. The Bishop's Council decision was the last straw. There was to be a meeting on 23 June 1971 of the two delegations of Bishop's Council and Diocesan Board of Education, who were to meet Professor Vaizey and Patrick Miller. Montefiore wrote to Stockwood asking him to chair the meeting in his stead, otherwise he would have to explain his absence and there would be a public row.

Montefiore took the action of the Bishop's Council as a vote of no confidence in his chairmanship. Mervyn Stockwood had a difficult choice to make which in starkest terms rested between losing Patrick Miller, or at least radically altering his job description, or accepting Montefiore's resignation as

chairman of the board. Private agony or public scandal? Stockwood decided the former was preferable to the latter. There
was a very painful period ahead and the wounds were so deep
on either side that they have not healed to this day. Patrick
Miller left the diocese in 1972.

The trauma cast a personal shadow over Montefiore's episcopate in the diocese, but did not affect his achievements. In 1972
Canon Tirrell retired and Prebendary Eric Franklin Tinker,
Senior Chaplain to the University of London, became also
Director of Religious Education for the London and Southwark
dioceses. Montefiore went on to restructure and enliven the
education department, to very considerable effect.

'Enlivening' was one of Montefiore's chief tasks in the diocese. Canon Richard Lewis of St Barnabas, Dulwich, felt Montefiore's impact immediately:

> Hugh's boundless energy and enthusiasm, his rigorous
> pursuit of truth, wherever it was to be found, both
> disconcerted and heartened. Disconcerted, because I
> always felt he had reached the proper end of the argument
> before I had arrived half way through. Yet he did not
> attempt to cut short the wanderings of a less disciplined
> mind. In 1971, having just read his book *Can Man
> Survive?*, I ventured a comment about my own interest in
> environmental issues during a parish visitation. 'What
> have you read?', 'Did you see . . .?', 'Have you visited
> . . .?' He could not have been impressed by my second-
> hand views, although he gave no sign. But he heartened as
> well. Here was a mind not afraid of the truth. His faith in
> the God of all creation was to be shaken neither by biblical
> scholarship nor by secular man.
>
> Mind you, he was not always easy to deal with,
> especially if you disagreed with him or would not see the
> logic of his argument. As a chairman of a meeting he was
> quite ruthless and I have seen him reduce a member of a
> board to incoherent mutterings by his refusal to return to a
> previous point on an agenda. On the other hand I have
> seen him deal most gently and lovingly with a Church
> Council who were convinced Hugh had promised them
> 'their vicar' when he had clearly done nothing of the sort.

His pastoral sensitivity was acute but he did not suffer fools gladly.

Harold Frankham followed that maverick Ernest Southcott as Provost of Southwark in 1970. It was not an easy inheritance, and Provost Frankham came to establish a settled order and yet managed to keep a very talented and sometimes difficult staff together. He recalls Montefiore's boyish attitude to life:

> cheerful, one could almost say insouciant (never indifferent), which brought gaiety and healing to one's situation . . .
>
> He is indeed a pastorally minded bishop, though one must admit that occasionally one wondered if he was really listening to what one said! Also his quicksilver mind could sometimes cause 'off the cuff' remarks which were hurtful . . . he does not always realize that quick judgements can easily appear to be lacking in sensitivity and understanding.
>
> Coming into the cathedral he would greet the stewards at the door with genuine pleasure and friendship, twinkling eyes and obvious enthusiasm for what he had come for . . . Hugh was never, never pompous, neither did he lack a proper dignity. When Church dignitaries are pompous or difficult I came to the conclusion that it was often due to nervousness. Hugh never gave any impression of nervousness! His vestments were usually awry . . . In the pulpit his sermons were those of a man with a great mind but always understandable: they never gave the impression that here was a great man 'talking down' to the congregation.

In 1975 David Sheppard became Bishop of Liverpool. This time it was Montefiore's turn to interview his possible successor. Mervyn Stockwood, who was on sabbatical, wrote to Montefiore and asked him to interview Michael Marshall, vicar of All Saints, Margaret Street. He was not unknown to Montefiore, who had supervised him in the New Testament when he was at Christ's, Cambridge. There was no reason why they should not have a good relationship, although they were very different in temperament, gifts and interests.

It was inevitable that Montefiore should be drawn into the work of the wider Church. He became chairman of the Central Readers' Board and a member of the Board for Social Responsibility, then under the chairmanship of the Bishop of Truro, Graham Leonard.

Mervyn Stockwood set up a colloquy after a suggestion made by Kenneth Woollcombe, then Bishop of Oxford, who felt that theologians and bishops were growing apart. The group met one evening during the meetings of General Synod and papers were read. The theologians included people like Dennis Nineham and Canon John Drury of Norwich. Montefiore contributed the name 'Caps and Mitres' and it died a natural death when they talked one another out. They met at St Matthew's Clergy House, Westminster. David Sheppard recalls one meeting where 'a theologian had put very strongly the argument that people can equally approach God through many religions. Hugh quite passionately asked, "Was I wrong to give up the faith of my fathers, if there is nothing unique about Jesus Christ?" '

It was not always clear what Montefiore would say to a particular audience. When he had been at Kingston for a few months he said to David Sheppard: 'I do love these evangelical clergy in my area. I only wish they would read their Bibles!' David Sheppard reflects,

> That remark brought together two very real features in Hugh. He was very generous about people who thought differently from him in the Church. There was no question that he understood that being a bishop meant serving the whole Church. But he did not duck bringing a challenge to each group. Many will remember his introducing such a challenge by saying, 'I hope you won't mind my saying . . .'

Montefiore was elected to the General Synod in 1976. He had been devastated by the rejection of the Anglican–Methodist Unity Scheme for the second time of asking in 1972 by the Church of England,[8] yet time showed him and others that there was a better way forward. Montefiore tried to get people to face

reality. Reality was that Anglicans were in a spirit of competition with other Christian bodies. There must be a sea-change
from competition to co-operation before any progress towards
Christian unity might be possible. Friendships had to be fostered and formed with Christians of different traditions and
there were churches in the diocese of Southwark, as in any
other diocese, where there was little warmth, sparse friendship
and muted hostility, even between fellow Anglicans of different
traditions or outlooks. Christians must do together all those
things which they do not have to do apart – which is a costly
business. That is why Montefiore welcomed *The Ten Propositions* of the Churches Unity Commission, which came before
the General Synod on 16 July 1976. During the debate he said:

> Our Lord prayed in St John that we might all be one, as he
> is in the Father and the Father is in him. That is not visible
> organic unity; it is a very mysterious unity between the
> Father and the Son, and I for one find it no longer possible
> to say that one particular form of unity is in accordance
> with the will of God.

There were only a few other interventions in debates during
his time as Bishop of Kingston.[9] He had, however, a particular
presence and style of speaking, noted by Peter Dawes, now
Bishop of Derby:

> He has a face which the Bishop of Southwark [Ronald
> Bowlby] described not so long ago as wonderfully
> 'mobile'. He had a habit when disagreeing with anything
> that was being said, which particularly touched on a point
> on which he was concerned, of looking round a bit
> indignantly, and shifting in his seat, and while he has
> always obeyed the Standing Orders and addressed the
> Chairman, yet no one I think has spoken more looking
> around him to the Synod itself.[10]

Moreover, he debated and did not simply read prepared
speeches. Later, when he was chairman of the Board for Social
Responsibility, he had to have well-researched speeches, but
even then he would take up points in the debate.

In early childhood

Recumbent teenager during tour of Greece

Lieutenant Montefiore, Royal Bucks Yeomanry RA, on active service in South-East Asia Command

Oxford freshman camping in Bagley Wood

Theological college student

Westcott House play *The Zeal of Thy House* in St Edward's Church, Cambridge.
Left to right: John Hoskyns, Frank Wright, Hugh Montefiore,
F.G.L.O. van Kretschmar

In conversation, after a dialogue in Great St Mary's, Cambridge

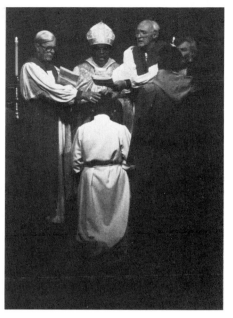

Visiting a junior and infant school during a parochial visitation

At All Angels, off Broadway, New York, assisting at the ordination to priesthood of Susan Cole-King, daughter of a previous Bishop of Birmingham

With Princess Alexandra at the rededication of Birmingham Cathedral after renovation

Blessing the boats at a rally in the canal basin at Rounds Green, near Birmingham

Cardinal Glemp of Poland visits Birmingham; with Maurice Couve de Murville, RC Archbishop of Birmingham

The Bishop of Kingston and his Mini outside his house on Wandsworth Common

Nailing up a derelict house in Handsworth to highlight the housing shortage

On holiday in Spain. Left to right: Elisabeth, Lady Elizabeth Cavendish, Sir John Betjeman, Hugh and Bishop Mervyn Stockwood

The BBC 'Lovelaw' team on location. (On left Germaine Greer and Ken Livingstone)

The 'Urban Bishops' Group'. Back row: Bishops Lunn, Montefiore, Thompson, Bowlby, Sheppard, Young, Booth-Clibborn. Front row: Mrs Montefiore, Mrs Bowlby, Mrs Booth-Clibborn, Mrs Sheppard

With Archbishop Michael Ramsey after consecration as Bishop of Kingston in Southwark Cathedral

Billy Graham visits Bishop's Croft

After preaching at St Aldates, Oxford, with Elisabeth and Canon Michael Green, then the Rector

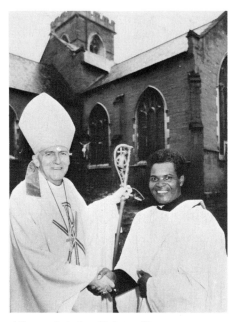

After ordaining Rolston Deson, Birmingham's first West Indian priest

At Dudley Road Hospital, Birmingham, holding a thriving premature baby who could legally have been aborted

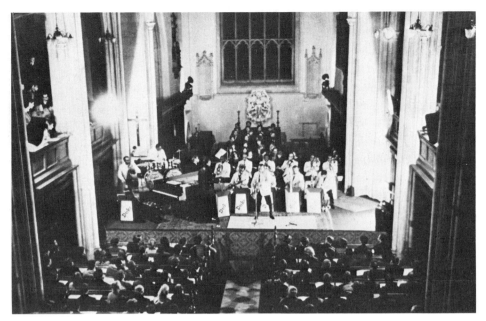

Duke Ellington (centre) conducting his Concert of Sacred Music at Great St Mary's, Cambridge

Blessing the city after enthronement as Bishop of Birmingham

With Pope John Paul II in Canterbury Cathedral. (On left and right, Bishops of Gloucester and Ely)

'You're always so controversial, Bishop': Mrs Thatcher at the National Exhibition Centre, Birmingham

After receiving an Honorary Doctorate of Divinity from Birmingham
University

Acting as press officer of the Boston Conference

As vice-president of the World Council of Churches Conference, 'Faith, Science and the Future', at MIT, Boston, with the General Secretary of WCC

Over 7,000 gather at the National Exhibition Centre for farewell Eucharist

Exeunt Hugh and Elisabeth from Birmingham

After dedicating new buildings at St Mary's School, Temple Balsall, near Birmingham

Whilst he was still Bishop of Kingston, a report, *Authority in the Church: Agreed Statement by the Anglican/Roman Catholic International Commission*, was debated on 18 February 1977. Montefiore made a powerful speech against receiving this report and indicated that he would vote against it. It was the conspicuous beginning that was to lead to lectures, articles and a book.

One of the less than satisfactory episodes which took place during Montefiore's Kingston years concerns the Archbishop of Canterbury's Commission on the Christian Doctrine of Marriage. The commission was chaired by Canon Howard Root, Professor of Theology in the University of Southampton, and the members were Montefiore; A.M. Allchin, Warden of the Convent of the Incarnation, Fairacres, Oxford; J.W. Bowker, Fellow of Corpus Christi College, Cambridge; G.R. Dunstan, F.D. Maurice Professor of Moral and Social Theology at King's College, London; Mrs T.B. Heaton, formerly Secretary and Counsellor of the Oxford Marriage Guidance Council; Lady Oppenheimer, writer on moral and philosophical theology; and Herbert Waddams, Canon Residentiary of Canterbury Cathedral. Dr. J. Dominian, Senior Consultant Psychiatrist at the Central Middlesex Hospital, acted as consultant to the Commission. There was deliberate overlapping with membership of the Doctrine Commission.

The pace at which the commission worked was to an extent determined by the speed of Government legislation: the Divorce Reform Act 1969 was expected to come into operation on 1 January 1971. This Act abandoned the concept of the matrimonial offence. Thenceforce divorce was based solely on the fact of irretrievable breakdown. The commission met ten times. The first draft of their report was written by Montefiore at the Benedictine community of West Malling. The final meeting was held at Lady Oppenheimer's home in Jersey. *Marriage, Divorce and the Church* was published on 22 April 1971. The tensions which came to light and life in the commission found expression at the end of the report:

In the life of the Church there must always be a tension between the settled way and the exploratory way. Only from a basis of stable security is it possible validly to explore; only by exploration can stability retain the pulse of life.

Some members of the commission changed their minds.[11] The controversial conclusion of the commission was that a moral consensus existed in favour of remarriage in church, and that this consensus was theologically well-founded. If such marriage was to be allowed, the commission felt there should be 'due safeguards'. Those suggested were rigid. First, they envisaged a discreet and adequate inquiry by 'the competent authority' to ensure that possible obligations left over from the previous marriage had been met; and an investigation into the circumstances of the divorce and whether the bride and groom were the kind of people capable of a stable and permanent relationship in marriage. It would be conditional that the parties should meet in church with the parish priest for private prayer of penitence for past faults. At the public marriage service, the priest would make to the congregation 'a preliminary declaration', explaining that one or both of the parties had had a previous marriage dissolved, but had discharged or bound themselves to discharge such obligations remaining from the former marriage.

The commission believed that an increasing number of responsible Church people, clerical and lay, found themselves in conscience unable to deny that remarriage could be the will of God. The theological artillery came from Montefiore in one of the eight appendices to the report. The appendix 'Jesus on Divorce and Remarriage' attracted much attention and criticism. After examining the New Testament evidence and placing this in the context of the period, Montefiore argued that Jesus' teaching was not *Halakah,* a rule governing conduct, but *Haggadah*, edifying exaggeration, appealing to the heart by way of the imagination. No certainty regarding the interpretation of Jesus' sayings on remarriage could be attained:

> It is not possible to ground the judgement that all divorce and remarriage is forbidden on the fact that Jesus definitely forbade it. He may not have done so – many, perhaps most, would say he most probably did not. Some criterion other than the clear teaching of Jesus must be found if the

Christian Church is to hold that all marriages are indissoluble and that all remarriages during a partner's lifetime are contrary to God's will. The solution to our problem must be found by an evaluation of factors other than purely biblical considerations.

The commission embraced Montefiore's view in the main body of the report. The report was decanted on a Church that exercised, in the matter of the remarriage of divorced persons, one of the strictest disciplines in Christendom. It could not be said to represent the consistent tradition of the undivided Church, for Eastern Orthodoxy took a different view. However, it had long been the Anglican tradition and in an increasingly secular society many felt it should not abandon its position lightly. The report was on the whole well-received for its main conclusion but criticized for the imposition of the conditions suggested by the commission – 'discreet and adequate inquiries' raise difficult and un-Anglican procedures.

The report was at its weakest and most unconvincing in two areas: the commission did not believe that the marriage vows could be binding on either partner once a marriage had irretrievably broken down. 'Those vows which can never again be honoured obviously cannot be binding.' That applied to some of the marriage vows with more force than to others. The promise not only to love and to cherish but also to forsake all others suggested, perhaps required, the prohibition of remarriage even if it permitted divorce. The commission's answer was that all the vows referred to conduct in married life. The vows were a difficult area, and an appendix, 'Vows', by Lady Oppenheimer and Montefiore was unconvincing and tortuous rather than clear. The case against the report was put most convincingly by J.R. Lucas, Fellow and Tutor in Philosophy at Merton College, Oxford, and a member of the Doctrine Commission, in an article in *Theology*,[12] to which Lady Oppenheimer made an effective reply.[13]

J.R. Lucas concludes his article with these words:

It is one thing for the Church to be a Servant Church, marrying and burying the people, and allowing all who are so minded to pray and praise and give thanks within its walls; it is quite another for it to be an accessory to sin, and to compromise by its compliance the rigour of God's requirements of men. And if the Church makes itself available for those who have made and broken their marriage vows once, to make them in exactly the same words a second time, it will be saying in unmistakable terms that these words do not mean what they say, and that a broken marriage is only a regrettable incident along the road of life.

If we reject the Commission's recommendations, what should we do? I do not know. So far as the argument from witness is concerned, the case would be met by the Orthodox provision for a different penitential rite for second marriages. Certainly the arguments adduced against it are unconvincing. And always the blessed principle of *oikonomia* is at hand to temper the asperities of doctrine to the individual case. But so far as the doctrine of marriage is concerned, I believe the Western rather than the Eastern position is the true one, and that although people whose marriages have broken down may enter into other stable unions, they cannot enter a second time into that state of unqualified lifelong commitment which alone, in Christian eyes, can be called a marriage. The difficulty is partly one of semantics. Divorcees who have been remarried in a Register Office are not Notorious Evil Livers who ought to be excommunicated, and it is not for the Church to say that their unions are not blessed in the eyes of God. But if we are pressed to say they are marriages in accordance with the will of God, and in particular if we are pressed to allow them to be solemnized as marriages in Church, it seems to me that the only answer we can truthfully give is No.

However, the more forceful argument would appear to be from the other side.

If the report was weak in dealing with vows, it was unconvincing when rejecting as unacceptable universal civil registration.

Christian people would register their contract (in the

Register Officer) and then go to church to solemnize holy
matrimony in accordance with the doctrine and discipline
of the Church. The union contracted in the civil ceremony
would be dissoluble; that solemnized in church would be
indissoluble.'

Why was this rejected? It is precisely the situation obtaining
in many countries where the civil and legal ceremony is separ-
ated from the religious act. A contract is made on the one
occasion and vows are made at the other. The fact that vows are
made in church neither adds to nor subtracts from the validity
of the civil ceremony, which, in England, would be the one
recognized by the Inland Revenue. The Church would also
recognize its validity.

In throwing the proposal overboard the commission stated:
'it would follow that the Church would have to regard a large
number of persons who used the register office as living, if not
in sin, then in some form of respectable concubinage'. These
were strangely unctuous and false assumptions. Anglicans did
not, and do not, regard marriages contracted in register offices
as invalid. It would be presumptuous of them so to do. The
commission appeared to add naïvety to insult by stating,
'Engaged couples could put very unfortunate pressures upon
one another to have a church wedding as a safeguard from
desertion, or to have a register office wedding to leave a loop-
hole for escape.' This was a libel on register office weddings.

The commission gave expression to the prominence of folk
religion. Was there nervousness here? If the legal ceremony
took place for all in a register office, would this signal the
removal of the Church still further from the rapids of secular
society? If so, it would have the choice of surviving in a
backwater, rejoining the rapids, or swimming against the tidal
rush. There was a current of opinion which thought the time
had come for all marriages to take place in register offices.
Mervyn Stockwood was amongst those swimming with this
current.[14]

For Montefiore, the motivation for change was pastoral realism. Modern research showed that reasons for marital breakdown were infinitely varied and psychologically complex.
Incompatibilities of temperament may doom a marriage how-

ever sincere the intentions had been at the outset. Neither partner may be to blame: both may be trapped in a situation beyond their control and, in a sense, therefore, out of their responsibiity. A second marriage may be a successful one, rich in spiritual fulfilment. Ought not such a marriage to be solemnized by the Church when the couple are serious and in earnest in their desire to marry according to the rites of their religion?

The commission went right into the heart of marriage, and reflected the Church's pastoral longing to bring healing and reconciliation, declaring its belief that individuals whose marriages had irretrievably broken down should now be free to choose whether or not to remarry: 'The Church's loyalty to Christ requires it to allow this liberty of choice to Christian men and women.' It was a brave assertion.

Once the report was published, many clergy whose marriages had broken down got in touch with Montefiore. Some had divorced and remarried and were no longer exercising their ministry. Montefiore was horrified at the way some of them had been cast on the scrapheap because they had remarried: 'They may be conscientious, devout men to whom the suffering and pain of marriage failure has given a maturity which should help rather than hinder their pastoral responsibility.'

Most disturbing of all was what the Church did with the report. The commission expected the report to be received by the General Synod and referred to the dioceses for discussion. This did not happen. After a cursory glance, General Synod refused even to discuss the report. They did not even receive it. And none of the commission was thanked for their labours until, at the insistence of Howard Root, thanks were conveyed by the Archbishop over a year later. In 1972 General Synod, by a narrow majority after a confused debate, decided not to require from the dioceses a specific opinion on the report.

When that arch-manipulator of Synod, the Bishop of Leicester, R.R. Williams, was asked to chair a working party and to bring a report to Synod on the same subject, it was clear that it would need more weight than Synod could summon to change the existing law. The General Synod debated the 'Leicester' rather than the 'Root' report on 7 November 1973. Bishop Williams made a brilliant speech which both swayed waverers and made converts. He knew how to make a speech full of emotion – the more powerful because it was controlled. There should be no remarriage of divorced parties in church. Unfortunately Montefiore was not at the time a member of General Synod, and there was no member of the Root commission to speak for the sadly forgotten and badly neglected report. Synod voted to reaffirm the traditional ban on church weddings for divorcees, having decided not to accept an amendment from the Bishop of St Albans (R.A.K. Runcie) asking for reference to the dioceses for further consideration before a conclusion was reached.

The Synod proceedings had been unsatisfactory, even 'dubious', Bishop Runcie thought. It was as if the democratic process of consultation before decision making had been snuffed out. Procedural muddle had been evident in the debate and advantage appeared to have been taken of such muddle. Montefiore, who had been sitting in the gallery of Church House during the debate, was quietly incensed. He was not alone, but he was determined to take some constitutional action reflecting the intense dissatisfaction within the Church both at the decision itself and at the way in which it was reached.

He wrote a letter to a senior clergyman in each English diocese asking him, or some other suitable person, to raise the matter in his synod with a view to establishing whether a true consensus of opinion against changing the Church of England's traditional marriage discipline really existed. He referred to the original commission's hope for thorough discussion in the dioceses and said:

> It seems to me (and I hope, that it seems to you) more than a pity, and thoroughly unsynodical, that in the only instance in which General Synod was asked to find out whether or not a consensus existed in the dioceses, it declined to do so.
>
> It would be easy to throw up one's hands in despair at the institutional Church – but not much use. It would be equally easy to wax indignant. The best means of procedure seems to me to behave synodically.

Montefiore asked for a motion to be introduced into each diocesan synod criticizing the action of the General Synod and requesting the Synod to carry out the request of the Archbishop's original commission as soon as possible by referring a question on the subject to the dioceses.

There was a healthy debate in the press, mostly supporting Montefiore's conviction about the subject and his particular stance against General Synod. As Bishop of Kingston, he supported any parish priest who felt in conscience that he could not follow the Act of Convocation of 1956, namely, by refusing to marry in a church anybody who had a former partner still living.

Montefiore's 'campaign' continued through December 1973 and into January 1974. It was a triumph for him that in February 1974 the General Synod acknowledged the disquiet which had been expressed in many quarters and agreed to reopen the matter. Unfortunately, instead of picking up the Root report another commission was appointed under the chairmanship of the Bishop of Lichfield (Kenneth Skelton). The report, *Marriage and the Church's Task*, appeared in 1978. On the major question – remarriage in church after divorce – the commission was divided[15] but unanimous in recommending the rescinding of the regulation forbidding those married after divorce to be admitted to Holy Communion until the bishop had given permission.

When the report came before General Synod on 12 July 1978, Montefiore was Bishop of Birmingham and he spoke briefly in the debate. Once again the Biship of Leicester (R.R. Williams) spoke powerfully against change, as did the Bishop of Truro (Graham Leonard). The Bishop of Durham (John Habgood) endeavoured to unite a warring Synod by commending a service of blessing:

> I believe that what the Church is saying in its present discipline is that we cannot publicly identify ourselves with the act of marrying. We can, however, publicly recognize the new state of marriage, and this is why we can bless it, and this is why we can accept those persons back into Communion.

But the main recommendation, to permit a divorced person to be married in church, failed again.

Montefiore was still a member of the Doctrine Commission. Its chairman, Ian Ramsey, Bishop of Durham, had died on 6 October 1972. Who should succeed him? Montefiore was sure there was only one person with sufficient theological stature, Anglican wisdom and doctrinal conviction who could do it – the Archbishop of Canterbury (Michael Ramsey) himself – and he told him so, but the Archbishop responded by letter, 'On reflection I think it will really be an *impossible* addition to my diary in the coming year!' In the end a strange appointment was made, that of Canon Maurice F. Wiles, Regius Professor of Divinity at Oxford.

The Doctrine Commission had been pursuing trivial matters. When it changed from being an Archbishops' commission into being a commission of the General Synod (a bad move), Archbishop Michael Ramsey told the members to pursue something more fundamental. The commission decided on the basis of belief. Here the commission found itself more than ordinarily divided and it was very doubtful whether it could bring in a unanimous report. Dennis Nineham, then Warden of Keble, and J.L. Houlden, then Principal of Ripon College, Cuddesdon, tended to hold up progress with their persistent brand of radical modernism. In the end there was superficial unity and this only because varying attitudes to the creeds were enumerated – literal belief of necessity; partial reinterpretation allowed; commitment to God rather than to creeds; creeds expressive of the past not the present. What resulted was a forty-two-page report, partly historical, and signed appendices of 112 pages. The report, *Christian Believing: The Nature of the Christian Faith and its Expression in Holy Scripture and Creeds*, was published by SPCK in 1976. Montefiore's own signed contribution was his personal statement of belief, and one which he regards with good cause to be his most important piece of work (see Appendix A).

Christian Believing was received by the Church with a mixture of incredulity and condemnation. The General Synod did not even discuss it. Yet Montefiore feels that if the Church had faced the issues raised in *Christian Believing* it would not have had to deal with the 'Durham affair' years later. The refusal of the General Synod to debate reports from its Doctrine Commissions has been a scandal.

Soon after *Christian Believing* all members of the commission were relieved from further thought, or sacked, with the sole exception of John Austen Baker, Canon of Westminster. The commission was then re-formed under John Taylor, Bishop of Winchester. Montefiore was not a member.

We shall consider Montefiore's theological legacy in a later chapter. A suffragan bishop does not have a ready-built platform from which to proclaim his views. To some extent he is in the shadow of the diocesan in matters ecclesiastical. Fortunately Mervyn Stockwood chose suffragan bishops who already had platforms and audiences reflecting their natural gifts, acquired interests and developed skills. It was in non-ecclesiastical spheres that Montefiore established himself as a national figure.

11 The Future –
Apocalypse or Concorde?

No understanding of Montefiore's passion for the environment is possible or complete without appreciating its source. Preaching the Fourth Gerard Manley Hopkins Sermon in 1972,[1] he said:

> In a letter to Robert Bridges, written in 1889, the very year of his death, [Hopkins] spoke of God as 'the only person I am in love with'. That love lasted life-long: and now it is for eternity.
>
> Out of this love sprang both his relationship to nature and his relationship to man. He saw in nature the footsteps of the Creator.

Montefiore would not put himself on the same plane with Hopkins, yet this has been Montefiore's motivation in environmental matters – seeing in nature the footsteps of the Creator. 'I see God at every point in the evolutionary process.' For Montefiore the doctrine of creation is the Christian response to the questions 'Why is there something, rather than nothing?' and 'Is there a reason for the world's existence?'[2] Montefiore is able to deal with such questions because he does not believe that God works from outside the universe. His view is that the whole wonderful panorama of evolution, from the first explosion of the big bang to the evolution of human life and the amazing cybernetic balance of planet Earth which has enabled such life to exist, is due to God in His creation, to the Holy Spirit acting within matter. What does he mean by this? Simply that matter has a natural tendency to evolve into ever more complex forms and that this tendency, since it can hardly be a brute fact, must have a cause, which is the working of the Holy Spirit. It seeks this complexity so that beings can emerge capable of reflection on the evolutionary process, of self-conscious reflection and of personal relationships with themselves and with their creator – 'made in his image'. God's purpose in this great cosmic experiment, as Montefiore sees it, is to enable people to evolve who are capable of eternal communion with him. As he looks at God at work in creation he is enormously excited by the richness and wealth of the panorama which spreads itself out before him. Excited – but at the same time deeply disturbed.

When *The Question Mark* appeared in 1969 Montefiore was simple enough to believe that all that was required of man was a deepened conviction that all men were accountable before God to solve the looming crisis. Two years later when he gave the Rutherford Lecture – 'Doom or Deliverance?'[3] – he had come to realize how much more was required, because economics is inextricably bound up with questions of environment, and so is politics.

The Rutherford Lecture was a Montefiore *tour de force*, in which he warned of doom unless there were a major reorientation of thought and action. He opened by declaring his hand and formulating some current dogmas of technological culture:

1 Everyone has a right to a rising standard of material living.
2 There is no upper limit to the standard of living that we can achieve.
3 Man has the wit and the power to control his environment. There may be crises, but science and technology can get us through in the end, as they have done in the past.
4 A rising standard of living means greater happiness.
5 The chief aim of government should be material prosperity.

He went on to outline the consequences of a Gadarene rush to live by such dogmas. He ended by showing the way to deliverance and attempted to adapt the biblical Ten Commandments in the form of requirements that were relevant to a technological age:

> *I am the Lord your God: you shall have no other gods but me.*
> *You shall not make to yourself any graven image or idol,* such as GNP or possessions or riches, whether in the heavens above or in the earth beneath or in the waters under the earth: you shall not bow down and serve them.
> *You shall not take the name of the Lord your God in vain* by calling on his name but ignoring his natural law.
> *Remember that you set apart one day in the week* for true festivity, or you will be bored stiff in the technological age you are bringing on yourselves.
> *Honour your father and your mother* but do not seek to prolong their natural term of life so that they are miserable.
> *You shall not murder* future generations by your present greed.
> *You shall not commit sexual sin* by producing more children than is your right.
> *You shall not steal* the inheritance of posterity.
> *You shall not bear false witness* against your overseas neighbours by lying to yourself about the extent of their need.
> *You shall not covet* an ever increasing standard of living.

In between, he referred to Pope Paul VI's *Humanae Vitae* 'with its condemnation of contraception' as 'ecologically speaking, the most disastrous Christian utterance of the century'. The equation of a rising standard of living with happiness was easily disproved. He said in 1971 what was not heard or heeded then but is frightening the world in the late 1980s:

> The most recalcitrant problem of all is thermal pollution. All energy generated by whatever means must end up as heat. There must be a limit to this, if we are not to melt the polar icecaps and flood cities and plains. I understand that this would happen if energy consumption continued to increase at 4 per cent per annum for another 130 years, by which time the temperature of the atmosphere will be

increased by 3–4°C; and that in just thirty years, if trends continue, the American conurbation between Boston and Washington will be releasing through its energy consumption up to 50 per cent of the normal incident solar energy of that area. We shall have to cut down on energy production – and this will mean rationing what we've got. Surely private motor cars will be forbidden.

Such words are heeded so long as the hearer understands them to apply to others. The prophecy of doom remains.

In a similar way Montefiore referred to the difficulties of a mixed economy:

> We have acquisitiveness without scope for initiative; dependency without the high ideals of mutual help. A technological society badly needs some form of economy which can function efficiently, with scope for competition and for private initiative, and which at the same time keeps within the limits necessary for ecological equilibrium . . .
>
> We are responsible to God for our trusteeship over nature. It is part of that trusteeship that we should not waste non-renewable resources. It is part of this trusteeship that we should not abuse the gift of procreation; it is immoral to bring into the world more people than we can reasonably care for. We have a duty to posterity, because all people, past and future, are made in God's image. We have a duty to our neighbours whom we are commanded to love as ourselves, and this applies both to our desperately poor neighbours in developing countries and to our unfortunate neighbours in our own countries. We are commanded to bear one another's burdens and so fulfil the law of Christ. We are taught by Christ that a man's life does not consist in the abundance of things that he possesses; and the Beatitudes inform us in simple language where true happiness is to be found. There is no question at all that if man lived by the Gospel, *homo sapiens* could make the colossal reorientation that is required of him.

The Rutherford Lecture received very widespread notice, and

prompted an interesting first leader in *The Times – Can we afford to be rich?*[4] It criticized British politicians[5] for pursuing higher economic growth and ignoring the perilous path of such a policy:

> (Montefiore) justly observes that if, as he believes, there is a 'ceiling to the global standard of living' imposed by the finite character of the world's resources and capacity to absorb industrial waste products without fatal degradation of the environment, and if that ceiling is rapidly being reached, the problems of distributive justice become immediately more acute, both as between nations and as between citizens within nations . . .
>
> Dr Montefiore supposes that a large loss of customary liberties would be entailed in trying to set limits to consumption and correct maldistribution. The exploitative and individualistic character of capitalism would have to be modified, and he recognizes that it might well be difficult then to preserve its dynamic. Internationally, there would have to be similar restraints on the exercise of national freedom of action . . .
>
> No such redirection of the collective energies of men would be possible without a drastic revision of political and social attitudes. The Bishop does not fail to observe that this appears to give the Christian religion a new secular relevance. To set against the exploitation of nature is the Christian belief that man is 'gifted with intelligence and responsible to God for his trusteeship of this planet, and accountable for the use to which he puts the treasures of the world'. To check the momentum towards the expansion of wealth is the belief that 'man's true happiness lies not in the possession of things but in relationship with people . . . and his earthly goal is the maturation of character to fit him for his final destiny.

These extracts from this very long leader give a judicious opinion of Montefiore's challenge. He had to go on being a prophet of doom, whilst commending the Christian path as the way to deliverance.

The following year, 1972, Montefiore was at the Church

Leaders' Conference in Birmingham.[6] Five hundred leading members of the British and Irish Churches, including a substantial Roman Catholic participation, met to consider the crises which Christianity was facing. All the usual topics came up for airing, but 'In the agenda of the commissions, preference was given to a subject much less familiar to the Churches.'[7] This was the commission on 'Man's Stewardship of God's World', led by Montefiore. There were two consultants, Barbara Ward and E.F. Schumacher, each of them a prophet and pioneer. Barbara Ward[8] had a brilliant and penetrating mind and was well known for a succession of books, including *The West at Bay* (1948); *Faith and Freedom* (1954); *Spaceship Earth* (1966); *The Lopsided World* (1968) and *Only One Earth* (1972). She had been a prominent figure at the 1972 United Nations' Conference on the Human Environment at Stockholm.

Ernst Friedrich Schumacher, economist, conservationist and writer, was an innovator and cult figure. He set up the Intermediate Technology Development Group in 1966 and his philosophy (and his prophecy) was contained in a book of essays *Small is Beautiful* (1973), which became internationally famous. Of him, Barbara Ward said, 'To very few people it is given to begin to change, drastically and creatively, the direction of human thought. Dr Schumacher belongs to this intensely creative minority.'

With such people Montefiore was exhilaratingly at ease. He, with his commission, stung the conference into thinking about issues on which the Churches of all denominations had been either silent or had spoken in whispers. Many people took the view that this commission produced the strongest report – requesting the British Council of Churches to promote further study of the ethical problems of man's impact on the environment, and possible alternatives to the present economic structure. But the commission did not stop at recommending things for other people to do. It produced a short document *Towards Simplicity of Life* which started with questioning one's own lifestyle, not one's neighbours. Were there any rules or guidelines? Yes.

Where you have a choice, resist obsolescence and choose the longer lasting; resist wasteful packaging; support public transport; question advertisements. If possible, work out your way of life with the help of others . . . asking such questions as: 'How can we measure our real needs – by the standards of our neighbours or by the needs of the poor? How can we be joyful without being greedy or flamboyant? How can we be good stewards without being over-scrupulous? How can others benefit from what we have? How far does our personal way of life depend on society's wealth? Can our society's way of life be simpler? Is there any one such change we ourselves can work for?'

And there were slogans to accelerate discussion and heart-searching: 'Happiness is knowing what I can do without'; 'My greed is another's need'; 'Am I detached from worldly goods if I keep what I have, and want to add to it?'

The leaders themselves had to alter their patterns of personal consumption and acquired values. It was not easy. Montefiore was endlessly impressing on individual Christians that adopting a simpler lifestyle did not mean 'going native'. Indeed, he had a warning: 'Individuals and communes who adopt a simpler lifestyle now can be a valuable sign and witness to others. But, like pacifists in time of war, they are in fact parasitic on the community.'[9]

The greatest difficulty of all was changing people's perceptions. In the Judaeo-Christian tradition man is seen as dominating nature rather than living in harmony with it. That is not the case in many other cultures. And when the Western economic disease is added to that tradition, the obstacles to be surmounted before a change can come about are many and mighty. Montefiore knew that, and appreciated that the Church needed educating, re-orientating, before progress could be made.

The Church Leaders' Conference revealed how great was the need for a radical and multi-disciplinary examination of the consumer society. At the time, Montefiore was a trustee of the Ecological Foundation, and before 1972 was out he was asked whether he would organize and chair a Transport Commission. He spent Christmas writing letters to a varied group of people in the hope of achieving a multi-disciplinary commission. To his delight and surprise, he received prompt acceptances from a very diverse set of people.[10] The first plenary session was held on 15 February 1973. It was followed by nine further plenary sessions, supplemented by six committees and by a final meeting on 22 December 1973. The 365-page report was prepared in record time and appeared before the end of 1974. *Changing Directions: A Report from the Independent Commission on Transport*[11] carried ninety-one recommendations. It was clear that almost all of them would need acceptance by Government or by a government agency if they were to be put into practice. Critics of the commission were waiting in the wings ready to pounce on the report. Was it going to be a variation on Lord Longford's report into pornography,[12] which had given self-appointed commissions a bad name? Would it be unreasonably hostile to motor cars? Would it parade broad generalities and banalities and eschew statistical and other evidence? Would it stick to its aim 'to examine the present transport situation in the country, to suggest criteria for national policies and to make recommendations'?

The report was a *tour de force* for Montefiore and his commission. Much credit goes to Stephen Plowden, who was seconded to the commission for a year, and his staff. He wrote the draft report and made the project possible in so short a time. It managed to be both comprehensive and detailed, if breathless rather than measured. *Changing Directions* was successful in bringing reason rather than prejudice to bear on the subject. It concluded that too much public money was being spent on transport when it could be better directed to projects such as housing. It recognized the enormous popularity of the motor car (for those who owned one), but demonstrated unwanted ownership by those enslaved within a self-defeating system. It asked for a reappraisal of the national motorway and trunk-road programme, a moratorium on urban road building, economies on high road maintenance costs and the immediate implementation of rigorous road management schemes. Some of the public money saved by following such a course would be released to expand or restore 'bus services and to attract more passenger and freight rail traffic. Meanwhile, a great deal should be done about pedestrians' and cyclists' rights in the name of natural justice, and steps taken to promote their safety and ease of movement.

Naturally, the commission members, and Montefiore as chairman, were attacked by many vested interest groups. Yet the recommendations were more realistic than radical. One fault of *Changing Directions* was that it failed to place the subject – and in particular the motor car – in true perspective. The vision of some of the members was obscured. Although the subject was complex, there were interrelated themes which did not find sufficient expression. Half the mileage of all cars is driven on city streets. The constant succession of new and ever more expensive measures to relieve traffic congestion is responsible more than anything else for the destruction of neighbourhoods and for the deadly dullness of the streets from which pedestrians have been driven by traffic.

The commission faced the subject of elaborate traffic arteries and motorways in and around towns and cities. The commission in no way wanted to restrict car ownership, because of its many benefits, but it did want to restrict car use.

Perhaps because of vested interest, but mostly because cars are still symbols of mobility and freedom, a government is unlikely to do anything to limit their number. Yet nothing isolates people more than the constant use of cars. They exclude chance meetings and prevent spontaneous sociability by placing each person in their own cocoon, to be hatched out only at the planned destination. They encourage anonymity in a rootless age when we each know more people less well.

The commission was particularly critical of the run-down of public transport. Too many railway lines and stations had been closed. The 'Beeching axe' had much to answer for. The countryside had been abandoned to the wealthy, the elderly and the bindweed. Towns and cities can only be rescued by severely limiting the number of private cars in urban centres. Taxis are more highly taxed than private vehicles yet they carry more passengers per day than private cars and create few parking problems. They are valuable where mass transportation is uneconomical.

The commission was modestly successful in two ways. First, it startled people into questioning what they had accepted blindly because they had never given it serious thought.

The Commission feels bound to conclude that present

transport policies, far from letting people choose what they want, are forcing them into a new way of life which, despite its evident attractions, is in many ways needlessly ugly, brutal and inefficient. Above all it is unjust. Those who chiefly suffer its deficiencies are the old, the young, the infirm and the poor, i.e. all those who do not have ready access to a car; and they comprise over half the population. If our report does nothing else, we hope it will draw attention to the immensity of the injury inflicted by one half of the community upon the other.

Secondly, the commission ensured that its report could not be ignored or demolished because of a lack of evidence to support its views and recommendations.

Within six months of the publication of *Changing Directions* the economy had nose-dived, car sales had flopped and petrol consumption had dropped. But had transport policies changed? Some of the reforms the commission had asked for remained 'on the table' – or in the waste bin. Montefiore was not optimistic when he reviewed developments in the *Guardian*:[13]

We asked for many reforms about which nothing has yet happened; among them, higher taxation for heavy lorries, investigation of town or district goods distribution schemes, a working party on buses, real power to the Transport Users Consumer Councils, the transfer of responsibility for aircraft noise abatement from the Department of Trade to the Ministry of the Environment, a review of the principles of traffic prediction, and the use of cost benefit techniques in a wider frame of reference as an aid and not a determinant in transport decisions.

To these must be added our proposal to review the tax laws about company cars. Only last week someone said to me: 'The price of petrol means nothing to me: I just sign for it for my company car.' At least 19 per cent of all new cars are company cars available for domestic use. (I have one myself – from the Church Commissioners.) Perhaps these fringe benefits should be phased out rather than summarily abolished, or the number of British cars on our roads might suddenly diminish still further.

Montefiore lost no opportunity in bringing to the notice of the public the hypocrisies of government policies and the way in which politicians failed to practise what they expounded. Many of Montefiore's critics did not have the capacity to destroy his argument or to dismantle his statistics, so they lampooned him as best they could. In any case 'a bishop should not be concerning himself with these matters'!

They were wrong. In 1971 the Archbishop of Canterbury appointed a small group to work in connexion with the Doctrine Commission 'to investigate the relevance of Christian doctrine to the problem of man in his environment'. Montefiore was appointed chairman.[14] The group worked from February 1972 and presented its report to the Archbishop in October 1974. The report, with nine appendicized essays, was edited by Montefiore and appeared as *Man and Nature* in October 1975.[15]

Stimulated by the contributions of his colleagues, Montefiore had come to realize that there was much more to be said *theologically* about the whole environmental problem than an appeal to man to exercise his stewardship responsibly. The environmental crisis was a challenge to think not just about man and his problems but about God's creation of the world; not just about creation, but about redemption and sanctification. Deeper changes of attitude than he had earlier realized would be necessary for a successful solution.

Man and Nature was an important book, but was insufficiently influential and studied because it was theological. How uncomfortable the Church feels when faced with theology! Montefiore says, 'We attempted a systematic study of our theme, and developed a trinitarian view of the creation, redemption and sanctification of all things, insisting on a cosmic view of redemption as much as of creation.' The report declared:

We believe that what is needed is a religious world-picture which portrays a common order under which man and his fellow-creatures live, and which gives a framework within which we can relate man, his work and organic and inorganic matter to each other.

Montefiore has always been concerned about the way in

which decisions on energy, transport, noise and the environment are taken. Rarely were the ethical issues discussed in advance of a decision. In reality Montefiore was criticizing government secrecy and his pleas for open government were fervent and frequent.[16] He had many opportunities to prove his point, and nowhere more tellingly than over Concorde. He was president of the Heathrow Association for the Control of Aircraft Noise (HACAN).[17] Heathrow Airport was only fourteen miles from his door. Half of the noise pollution from Heathrow affected Montefiore's half of the Southwark diocese and HACAN worked from Richmond.

When project Concorde began in the 1960s there seemed to be a promise of unlimited technological advancement. In the United States this revolution of expectation sent man to the moon; in Britain and France it found expression in a supersonic passenger aircraft. The United States decided to forgo commercial supersonic transport production but when Concorde was a reality it had to decide if, where, and how often the aircraft could land in the United States.

The United States Transportation Secretary, William T. Coleman Jr., decided to have a one-day hearing of speakers for and against a limited number of movements by Concorde to and from two American airports. The hearing was fixed for Monday 5 January 1976. Montefiore was asked to go as President of HACAN. His expenses were paid. His purpose was to speak of the noise of Concorde. Before he went he had to think carefully about the larger issues involved:

> Was it unpatriotic to speak in a foreign country against the British Concorde? If patriotism means 'my country right or wrong', then yes. But no Christian could support such a view. Back in England HACAN's press releases about Concorde had been almost entirely ignored. The Government, in possession of the monitoring figures for Concorde's noise at take-off and landing at Heathrow, misled Parliament. The Department of Industry had waived its own regulations concerning maximum noise at landing and take-off to enable Concorde to use Heathrow. According to the *Shorter Oxford English Dictionary*, a patriot is 'one who exerts himself to promote the well-

being of his country'. If Concorde diminishes this well-being, then it would be right to exercise freedom of speech by opposing flights from Heathrow. Furthermore, many of those who already suffer from aircraft noise live in Richmond and Kew, within that part of the Southwark Diocese over which I exercise pastoral care: should not their bishop try to help them against the added devastation of Concorde's noise?[18]

At the hearing, Montefiore spoke as a member of the anti-Concorde team shortly after the British and French had put their case for Concorde. With only five minutes at his disposal Montefiore had to make his points cogently and effectively. They were supported by detailed evidence in a written sub-mission. He obtained the biggest cheer of the day with his attack on Concorde's noise levels at Heathrow. He was critical of the way in which the Government had measured noise levels and subsequently misled Parliament. But Montefiore's chief objection to Concorde was the effect of noise on people.

> The noise can be unbearable. It can be above the threshold of pain. It might damage the hearing of the partially deaf who use amplifiers. No sensible mother would feel happy about leaving her baby out in the garden in a pram when Concorde was passing . . . The noise from Concorde is not hell; for hell goes on forever. it is more like a secular form of purgatory. I can best compare it to an inflamed gall bladder; intermittent, but the spasms can leave you speechless.

At the hearing Montefiore pleaded for a 'No' to the application.

> You ask whether the United States has any obligations towards its oldest allies. I believe it has. This is not a matter of political trade-offs but of moral principle. Allow this aeroplane into your country and the ethical basis of your noise abatement collapses. Do not allow us to impose on defenceless people this unbearable noise.

The Secretary of Transportation reserved his judgement.

However, there was no reserve or waiting for the condemnation of Montefiore on his return to England. It was like the homosexuality controversy over again, only this time the missiles came from Parliament and from the aircraft industry.

It was inevitable that Gerald Kaufman, Minister of State for Industry, who had been at the Concorde hearing pleading Britain's case, should misrepresent Montefiore's contribution. Speaking at a press conference on his return from America, he did not disguise his contempt for Montefiore's action. He may have tried to dismiss it as 'a kind of Monty Python sermon . . . a music hall turn' but he was well aware of the support for Montefiore's views in America as well as in Britain.

Lord Boyd-Carpenter, Chairman of the Civil Aviation Authority, and a former MP for Kingston-upon-Thames, claimed that Montefiore was a wrecker of the commercial future of the finest product of the British aircraft industry. In a speech at a luncheon in Coventry he used words which revealed a patronizing unctuousness towards the Church and its clergy:

> Surely in his diocese there is work to be done which could fully engage even his bounding energy? Is there not religious apathy to be fought, lax morality to be countered? Are there not humble homes to be visited and prayed in? Are there no hard-pressed clergy who look for help to their Father-in-God? Would it not have been more useful, not to say more appropriate, if he had devoted his time to spiritual matters rather than to the temporal sort of sky-piloting for which I grant licences?

Robert Adley, MP for Christchurch and Lymington, called Montefiore a 'weirdo'; another MP referred to him as a 'crackpot' and Norman Tebbit, MP for Chingford, told him to concentrate on Church affairs and not 'spend his time on amateurish and ill-informed comments on a matter of which he understood nothing'. The cartoonists were enjoying a new figure and Montefiore is eminently 'cartoonable'.

The way in which people like Kaufman and Boyd-Carpenter expressed themselves brought unexpected support for Montefiore. Everyone was aware of the Government's hidden factor in Concorde – namely, the plane was built in Bristol in the constituency of Anthony Wedgwood Benn. We shall consider later the importance of Montefiore's stance and vocality on many public issues and how far and in what way it is right for a Church of England bishop to 'meddle in politics'.

The American judgement on Concorde did not come until May. William T. Coleman Jr. ruled that France and Britain could operate limited services by Concorde to New York and Washington on a sixteen-month trial basis. This satisfied neither the pro- nor the anti-lobby. Yet it was unlikely to lead to a technological bonanza or an ecological disaster.

For Montefiore it was a further period of limelight, abuse – and some praise. There were local imputations too. The Kingston Borough Council was asked to dissociate itself from Montefiore's statements and to censure him. A local chairman of shop stewards accused him of treachery. Local MPs such as Carol Mather (Esher) were against Montefiore but spoke or wrote in more reasonable terms.

Montefiore responded by asking that his statement at the American hearing should appear in full so that people in the diocese could read what he had said. The *Surrey Comet* obliged.

So far as the national Church was concerned, Hugh Dykes, MP for Harrow East, had written to the Archbishop of Canterbury (Donald Coggan) asking about the propriety of a bishop using his 'official authority to make statements on a high technology subject in which he may not have the necessary expertise'. The Archbishop responded:

> The 'official Church', as you put it, is not morally bound to follow any party line – nor indeed every particular piece of Government policy. The bishop was speaking as president of the Heathrow Association for the Control of Aircraft Noise, which asked him to go to America, and what is really at issue here is surely freedom of speech.

The Archbishop said he was not 'seeking to buttress the bishop's arguments or to express agreement with them' but he pointed out that Montefiore had 'studied ecology rather deeply' and explained that his literary contributions to the field were 'by no means negligible' – which was more than could be said of the majority of the vocal and thoroughly niggled opponents.

Another of Montefiore's interesting and innovative activities concerned nuclear power. The British Council of Churches was asked by the World Council of Churches if it would respond to the challenge of new technology, and especially nuclear technology, by convening a public hearing on the issues involved. The British Council of Churches invited Montefiore and Dr David Gosling, formerly a nuclear physicist, then in the Department of Theology in the University of Hull, to arrange meetings in 1977. An interview took place with the Secretary of State for Energy (Tony Benn), who welcomed the prospect of a public hearing, but indicated that 1977 would be too late if it was intended that government policy could, or should, be influenced. Montefiore swept into action and within five weeks he had recruited a distinguished panel[19] and arranged for expert witnesses to public hearings on the projected fast reactor CFR-1, which were held at the London International Press Centre on 13 and 14 December 1976. Thirty-three expert witnesses provided 500-word statements on which they were cross-examined during the hearing.

CFR-1, if built, would be the first of a new generation of reactors which would be fuelled with a mixture of plutonium and uranium oxides manufactured from the waste of advanced gas-cooled reactors (AGRs). The waste from British and other countries' AGRs was to be reprocessed at Windscale, and British Nuclear Fuels Ltd, the commercial arm of the United Kingdom Atomic Energy Authority, had applied for planning permission to build an oxide reprocessing plant for that purpose.

The fast-breeder system was claimed to be the answer to the world's coming energy shortage. Some very interesting facts emerged from the hearing, and Montefiore noted

> that the construction of a CFR-1 would almost inevitably lead to proliferation, and that an 'energy gap' seems to be probable in the 1990s. Even if permission had been given now for CFR-1, 2005 or 2010 would be the earliest dates by which 33 gigawatts of Fast Breeder Power could be produced. It also appeared likely to be cheaper to build a CFR-1 later under licence if it proved necessary, than to spend millions and millions on pioneering our own,

notwithstanding the claim that in some respects UKAEA leads the world.

The Secretary of State for the Environment later directed that before a licence could be given for a reprocessing plant at Windscale there would be a public enquiry, which took place during the summer of 1977.[20]

The British Council of Churches' hearings persuaded Montefiore that it was vital to master technological complexity before one could make a moral judgement about technological matters. And, impressed by the range, power and clarity of the expert witnesses,[21] Montefiore was convinced that as wide a participation in the decision-making process as was possible was both desirable and necessary, for once the salient issues were set out, ordinary citizens were quite capable of passing a moral judgement. It was only proper that they should, since they would be most affected by any result.

After the hearings, the British Council of Churches agreed that it would be wrong to go ahead with CFR-1 unless and until a safe method of disposal of nuclear wastes had been evolved.

An edited account of the submissions and the cross-examination of the expert witnesses appeared in book form – *Nuclear Crisis: A Question of Breeding,*[22] edited by Montefiore and David Gosling. Montefiore contributed an Epilogue to the book in which he set out some theological reflections, not without a hint of doom:

> Few historians, looking back over the span of history, would say that many countries have been able to control their own destinies. We must of course plan, we must be rational, we must be prudent; but so often men and countries are at the mercy of circumstances. Today we are at the end of an age; indeed, I would say that we are at the end of an epoch. Just as men passed from the nomadic to the agricultural epoch, so it seems we are passing from the industrial to the electronic and nuclear epoch, and it is likely to be a turbulent transition. Stability is likely to be fragile. Theologically speaking, we would express this by saying that all things are in the providence of God, and nothing – not even catastrophe – can prevent the final

fulfilment of His purposes, though it may delay them a few million years. We must accept that the unexpected often happens. We may plan for growth; we may be overruled by events.

This was Montefiore's constant theme. The content of three lectures given at Southwark in October 1976 was published as *Apocalypse: What Does God Say?*[23] In them he drew a parallel between the British plight and the situation of the Jews in the years before the Fall of Jerusalem, in AD 70. The signs were evident – virtual bankruptcy, increasing expectation of material things, lapses in standards of discipline and public behaviour. To continue so would lead to a choice between anarchy and authoritarianism. That part of Montefiore's message sounded like the ramblings of a backwoodsman of the hanging and flogging variety. But Montefiore never stops at judgement. He always passes to grace. That is why he shares in both secular despair and Christian hope – the subject of many of his lectures. For him they are not incompatible. Again and again he says, 'I only wish that the Church of God were not so preoccupied with its own future or so constricted in its idea of redemption that it is unable to interpret to the world the signs of the times.'

In many other ways during the Southwark years Montefiore was trying to direct the gaze of the Church away from itself and to bring to some of the Church's councils insights which he had gained or learned in the secular world.

He was in demand as lecturer and speaker and relied upon to marshal his facts and stimulate the audience. For the National Conference on Population Problems in 1974 he presented a paper on 'Population Control: An Ethical and Theological Assessment';[24] to a management course held by Unilever in 1976 it was 'Questions to a Transnational Enterprise'.[25] The first time Montefiore ever brightened the portals of the Café Royal was to address the Christian Association of Business Executives in 1976 on 'Management and Accountability'.[26] In the autumn of 1977 he was at the British Council of Churches Conference on the Issues of Cultural Pluralism. Montefiore gave the opening lecture on 'A Nation of Many Cultures'.[27]

There was never any doubt that Montefiore was a Christian and that his theme was morality. The RIBA Conference found this out when Montefiore addressed their annual conference at Lancaster University in 1972 under the title 'Designing for Survival'. It is the Christian basis of what Montefiore said here and elsewhere that made the difference, as Anthony Hale noted:

> All the usual anti-tower block, anti-energy intensive, pro-craftsmen and pro-recycling followed, but this time motivated by Christianity. At least it showed the Church was on the side of the angels. When the bishop ended by saying technology was not enough and that man needed to be strengthened by divine grace he was rewarded by loud and long applause.[28]

12   Prince of the Church

Being suffragan Bishop of Kingston had been both a liberating and a constricting experience for Montefiore. It was with a sigh of relief and gratitude that he had moved from seven exciting, exacting and exhausting years at Great St Mary's to the renewing work in Southwark. He had dived headlong into his new work. Its variety was appealing. There was the steady round of visitations and confirmations and much to do with the central work of the diocese, not least in education. But Kingston could not hold the capacity that Montefiore had to offer. For his broader canvas he stepped out of the diocese into other work. In the jargon of the day, had he restricted himself to the work of being a suffragan bishop, he would have been understretched. This is not to criticize those suffragan bishops who devote their full time to the work they have been set. But Montefiore was aware of the dangers of offering a 'nanny' ministry where many priests and some laity would run to him and over-use him for pastoral care as a defence against facing their problems and standing on their own feet. Moreover, the borough deans and archdeacons had much to offer here.

We have seen that he did not have a defined territory into which the diocesan bishop did not venture. Mervyn Stockwood held to the maxim, 'Where a bishop of the diocese is present, there is the bishop of the diocese,' and more than one of the three bishops was present only at ordinations and on very special occasions. None the less, people knew very well where power lay, so that the Bishop of Southwark was much more than *primus inter pares*.

Montefiore was not a member of General Synod when a report of its Standing Committee – *Episcopacy in the Church of England* – was debated on 6 November 1974. During the debate Canon Anthony T. Hanson (Professor of Theology in the University of Hull) made an important speech in which he expressed concern about suffragan bishops:

> The office of suffragan bishop now seems to have been intertwined into our constitution in such a way that it might be difficult to get it out . . .
>   I have always felt that the arguments against suffragans are very strong indeed. The office of suffragan bishop is theologically indefensible. As I understand the office of bishop, a bishop is nothing if he is not representative, but a suffragan bishop represents nobody . . . The suffragan bishop does not exercise any true *episcope* . . . [the] deliberate continuation of the office of suffragan bishop moves us in the wrong direction. It moves us in the direction of building up a hierarchy and of centralization, whereas I am convinced that we need a less hierarchical and more decentralized organization in the Church today.[1]

Anthony Hanson received some vocal support but the heavy artillery for the status quo[2] won the day. Yet his views were not answered. A bishop must have a jurisdiction which puts him in a particular relationship with all the other bishops who have the same jurisdiction. This was not the case with suffragan bishops, and 'area' bishops were in their unestablished infancy. Many suffragan bishops were regarded as 'second-class bishops', substitutes for the real thing. Montefiore recalls being co-opted to the House of Bishops: 'I don't think that most of them took kindly at that stage to suffragans invading their privacy; at least, that is what I felt.'

He was invited to contribute an essay to a volume for the 1978 Lambeth Conference. The essay, 'Nationalism and Internationalism' was one of forty crammed into a volume of 297 pages, *Today's Church and Today's World*.[3] Few of the contributors were able to do justice to their subjects in the compass of a few pages. The book was not well received. A few sentences of Montefiore's catch the theme which, had he had space to develop it, might have been of some significance:

> A nation must believe in itself, must believe in its own
> worth and values and goals, must believe that these are
> worthwhile contributing to the common good. It must
> treasure its culture and its way of life, it must be united by
> ties of loyalty and affection to the symbols of its past, it
> must not only cherish its own spiritual inheritance but also
> the beauties and loveliness of its physical inheritance. A
> country that does not hold the affection and loyalty of its
> citizens will have little to contribute to the well-being of
> the world. Patriotism, in the genuine sense of self-love, is
> as fundamental a good for the well-being of a nation as is
> self-esteem for the well-being of an individual.
>
> We hardly need to be reminded that self-esteem in the
> individual can become self-assertion. The egotist accepts
> no restraint on his own satisfaction, he accepts no moral
> principle other than self-interest, and, rather than the
> enjoyment of genuine personal relationships with others,
> he prefers to dominate and to disparage. So too with
> nations.

Montefiore had become one of the most well-known bishops
in the Church, yet he was still only a suffragan. By 1977 he was
aware of growing a bit stale and, much as he loved Mervyn
Stockwood, he felt the time had come for a change. But what
kind of move was desirable, likely, or possible? A man like
Montefiore makes enemies and there were many in Church and
State who wanted to think that Kingston was as far as Montefiore would travel. Moreover, he was not a man who had
walked in the Church House passages of persuasion with an eye
to the future.

The Archbishop of Canterbury at the time was Frederick
Donald Coggan. The privileges and responsibilities of the
Chair of St Augustine are so great that they throw the incumbent's preceding career into the shade. This is hardly fair, for a
man must already have done substantial, even great, work
before he is chosen to fill so commanding a post. Of few is it
more necessary to remember this caution than Donald Coggan.
The external shape of his ministry and episcopate were never as

important to him as bringing souls to Christ by evangelism, preaching and personal encounters, nourishing the faithful and helping and restoring those who were finding it difficult to be faithful. There were the stern words of duty too, befitting an evangelical. If he did not always seem to fit the spirit of the age, it was because he believed in such old-fashioned ideas as patriotism, the monarchy, liberty (not licence), and the Church and State relationship. Yet his theology was tinged with enlightenment rather than darkened by conservatism. He was a fine biblical scholar. His 'enlightenment' led to his being an ardent advocate of the ordination of women to the priesthood. He was superb at Bible exposition and he preached with a clarity of expression and an unaffected delivery. There was always a feeling that the crusader was just beneath the surface. In his 1975 'Call to the Nation' he was mocked, ridiculed and admired.[4]

Montefiore writes, 'My friends always rather pooh-poohed Coggan, and indeed there was a sense in which he was rather naïve. But he was a real man of God and that came over and influenced me. And a fine preacher too.' And Coggan would have responded to someone who had the heart of the Gospel in him. When Martin Gloster Sullivan retired as Dean of St Paul's in 1977 Coggan wrote to the Prime Minister (James Callaghan) commending Montefiore. Nothing materialized and Alan Brunskill Webster moved from the deanery of Norwich to that of St Paul's.

Meanwhile, there was immense interest in the appointment of a new Bishop of Birmingham. The reason for this was less that it was Birmingham than that it was the first appointment under the new Crown Appointments Commission. The commission was established by the General Synod in February 1977. Its function is to consider vacancies in diocesan bishoprics in the provinces of Canterbury and York and candidates for appointment to them. The commission agrees upon two names for nomination to the Prime Minister by the appropriate Archbishop (Canterbury or York) or, in the case of the archbishopric of Canterbury itself, by the chairman appointed by the Prime Minister. The names submitted are given in the order of preference decided upon by the commission.

The membership of the new commission comprised the

Archbishop of Canterbury *or* York – each ex officio; there were three elected members of the House of Clergy and three of the House of Laity of the General Synod; in addition there were four members of the Vacancy-in-See Committee of the diocese concerned; ex officio members were the appointments secretaries of the archbishops and the Prime Minister.

In 1977 Laurence Ambrose Brown announced that he would retire from the See of Birmingham on 1 November. There were very different views as to what the commission should do and should recommend. A representative hierarchy had been neglected. Some dioceses had thrust upon them a theologian or academic, remote from their needs and their claims. They conveniently forgot that some of the Church's outstanding pastoral bishops had come from such spheres whilst some upgraded parish priests had proved disasters when made diocesan bishops. Another view concerned the undesirability of making safe, uniform appointments, each satisfying the stated aspirations of the diocese, but ignoring the claims of the national Church. Prime ministers had taken risks in nominating the most unlikely of men to bishoprics. There had been some disasters, but more distinct and distinctive successes. Would the Crown Appointments Commission increase, diminish or extinguish the unexpected, the daring and the imaginative appointment?

Laurence Brown had been a popular but not a great Bishop of Birmingham. He had arrived in 1969, already aged sixty-two, with a proven reputation in Church Assembly and General Synod. He was responsible for piloting the 1968 Pastoral Measure through rough, rock-ridden seas. As Chairman of the Advisory Council for the Church's Ministry (ACCM) he had distinguished himself by absorbing or deflecting the arrows which continually were fired in that direction. Yet he was no St Sebastian. He had the gifts of a boy scout and the temperament of a marriage guidance counsellor. Whilst he could be innovative and, like any scout, knew how to get himself out of trouble, he was a reconciler at heart. This may not make for dynamic leadership, but it provides a focus of unity. It was easy to relax with him. The pint in his hand was natural, not affected. The cares of office showed a little, but not overmuch.

Birmingham had had some of the most controversial bishops

in the Church this century. It was a young diocese, whose bishops and the nominating prime minister had been Charles Gore 1905 (A.J. Balfour); Henry Russell Wakefield 1911 (H.H. Asquith); Earnest William Barnes 1924 (J. Ramsay Macdonald); John Leonard Wilson 1953 (Winston S. Churchill).

Following the announcement of Bishop Brown's forthcoming retirement, the Vacancy-in-See Committee started to prepare a statement setting out the needs of the diocese and providing factual information about the diocese for the Crown Appointments Commission. The committee also elected four of its members to serve on the Crown Appointments Commission.[5]

Suddenly the people in the pews thought, mistakenly, that they had a real say in the choice of their new bishop. In June 1977 a poll was taken in four 'typical' parishes to identify the characteristic they sought most in a new bishop. The overwhelming preference was for a godly pastor who could 'get on with ordinary folk'. They seemed to want a man who would have the genuine desire and natural ability to meet and sit and talk with the Midlands' car manufacturers, other craftsmen and tradespeople. Academic and theological worthiness and administrative skill failed to reach the first three places on the mitre-test meter.

All kinds of names surfaced during the Vacancy-in-See Committee's deliberations. There were two bishops with Birmingham connections who would fit some, if not all, of the vocal desires of ecclesiastical activists. In 1958 Bishop Leonard Wilson had invited a forty-three-year-old priest, John Paul Burrough, who had been a missionary in Korea for seven years, to join him in Birmingham, working among immigrants as Chaplain to Overseas Peoples. Paul Burrough responded well to this innovative work and stayed eight years before being elected Bishop of Mashonaland, Zimbabwe, where he was in 1977. Archibald Ronald McDonald Gordon was another priest brought to Birmingham during Leonard Wilson's episcopate. As Vicar of St Peter's, Spring Hill (1959–67) he experimented with ways of removing layers of piety from ordinands by giving them a taste of life in an inner-city urban parish. He left to be vicar of St Mary the Virgin University Church, Oxford, and in 1975 he became Bishop of Portsmouth.

But commendable as these men were, they were not at the forefront of the Crown Appointments Commission's thinking. There *was* a local man: sixty-year-old Mark Green, Bishop Suffragan of Aston. His pedigree was that of a parish priest and one not frightened of new thinking, whether theological, liturgical or ministerial. He was more often than not 'off centre' in his views and had not fully realized his potential as a suffragan bishop. Yet, as Canon H.P. Burgess, Vicar of Wylde Green and Rural Dean of Sutton Coldfield, recalls: 'The name of Hugh Montefiore as our next bishop was mentioned again and again at the Vacancy-in-See Committee.'

Whilst Montefiore's name was mere rumour 'opposition' was muted, even if uneasy. However, by mid-September there was a leak from the Crown Appointments Commission[5] and Montefiore's name was now 'probable', not merely 'possible'. A Tory councillor in Birmingham, Anthony Beaumont-Dark (now MP for Selly Oak), had been consulted and he and other like-minded people paraded their disquiet and anger before the prime minister (James Callaghan) and in the pages of the *Birmingham Evening Mail*. To them Montefiore was 'a clerical Lord Longford who had made an ass of himself and could well do it again'. Montefiore's remarks about Christ and homosexuality were once again brought out for public airing, to which were added his views on Concorde.

A leader in the *Birmingham Evening Mail* was headed 'Not the right man for Birmingham'.[6] Birmingham could well do without a controversial bishop who might have criticisms to make of the motor-car industry. In language which sounds fine, but which simply means 'leave us alone', the editorial concluded that what was needed 'above all is a spirit of unity to bind the community together'.

The newspapers, some Members of Parliament, many citizens and Church people of Birmingham were suffering from an overdose of advance speculation. Canon Keith Walker of Chichester Cathedral wrote a tongue-in-cheek letter to *The Times*[7] in which he said:

It is clearly important that a bishop should be non-controversial. The harmony of the social system might otherwise be threatened. We have only to read the histories of Isaiah, Jeremiah, St Paul and Jesus Christ to realize how inconvenient controversialists are.

In late September and early October the *Birmingham Post* and the *Birmingham Evening Mail* caused a frenetic crisis by carrying each day news items about the Montefiore 'issue'. Basically, there were two worried constituencies. One was the secular one, of which Anthony Beaumont-Dark was the loudest trumpet. There was the fear that Montefiore's conservationist and ecological concerns would damage the city's motor industry.[8] The other constituency was the Church which he would lead. There were anxious strains. Mother Margaret Angela, Mother Superior of the Community of the Nursing Sisters of St John the Divine in Birmingham, refers to one of them:

> The controversial Bishop Barnes continues to be prominent in the minds of those who 'suffered' during that particular episcopate and anyone who has been given a 'controversial' label carries the weight of those unfortunate, and for many acrimonious, years in the history of the Diocese of Birmingham. Bishop Hugh had already acquired a reputation for controversial views and utterances and was therefore regarded with a degree of suspicion as well as being a 'threat' to some people in the diocese.

Another strain concerned his theological views, and there were few apologists for them in Birmingham. That was to change. Fortunately, on the homosexual issue, Bishop Mark Green had been told by the Archbishop of Canterbury (Donald Coggan) that he had read the complete text of Montefiore's Modern Churchmen's Union lecture and had found nothing objectionable in it.

The hubbub was not all angry and negative. Less vocal, but not invisible, were those like the Revd Michael Counsell, Vicar of Harborne, whose 'immediate reaction was one of delight; we thanked the Lord for the possibility of sending us a bishop who would catch the public eye, stand up for worthwhile causes, stimulate our thinking and give us bold leadership'.

The announcement of the appointment was fixed for 11 October 1977. A few days before, Bishop Mark Green was informed that Montefiore's name was the first choice of the Crown Appointments Commission and that his own was the second. (The Birmingham end of the commission leaked like a sieve, despite everyone having taken an oath of secrecy.) When the appointment was announced, he 'issued a statement pledging the loyalty and support of the Church in Birmingham to their new bishop and this turned out to be no empty promise'.

The appointment of 57-year-old Montefiore was greeted by a phenomenal amount of press coverage, the word 'controversial' appearing in most of the headlines. A leader in *The Times* headed 'Joe Chamberlain would not have approved'[9] noted:

The genius of Birmingham, what makes it hum, is dedication to technical progress and its exploitation in manufacturing and trade. It is the city of brass, motors and municipal enterprise. Boulton and Watt are its early and abiding heroes, and their astonishing capacity was unwatered by philosophical second-thoughts about the feasibility of maximum expansion of production or the values implicit in high technology. And here was this priest from Cambridge and the London suburbs, about to be presented to Birmingham, who for years had been blowing the ecological whistle against the very thrusts which have made the place what it is . . .

These views cannot have escaped the attention of the appointments commission. It has chosen either to ignore them or to challenge them, and a case can be made out for either form of rejection. They could be ignored on the grounds that the diocese of Birmingham comprehends a great deal more than its industrial ethos and a lingering belief in sanctification by manufacture; that it contains men and women of all conditions and with the usual variety of motivation; and that the pastoral and intellectual qualities possessed by Dr Montefiore are of much more relevance than the volume of newspaper copy generated by the expression of his views on secular topics. And they could be challenged on the grounds that it is not for the Church necessarily to accommodate itself, by its selection of bishops or by any other act, to the dominant secular preoccupations of any particular place or time; that it is its duty to bring these things before other standards of judgement; and that a man who is inclined to do just that is positively fitted to the post.

If that is the spirit in which the new appointments commission is going to work, the Church of England is in for a lively time. And a troubled time; for its position as the Established Church, its social organization and its comprehensive character set fairly close limits to the pursuit of a policy of stirring thing up in the secular domain.

It was strange of the leader writer to mention Joe Chamberlain in the headline, for he was a Unitarian, a 'heresy' of which Montefiore is innocent.

The *Church Times* seemed nervous and a little hesitant but congratulated the Crown Appointments Commission on having the courage of its convictions.[10] It had not bowed to unanimity in the interests of safety. Indeed, one of the elected Birmingham clergy on the commission, Canon Howard B. Marlow, a well-known Anglo-Catholic,[11] said he would make a last-ditch attempt to prevent Montefiore becoming Bishop of Birmingham. The appointment had to be ratified by the Birmingham Cathedral Chapter 'but I doubt whether I will find myself able to vote for him'.

In a sense, the controversy surrounded Montefiore without actually falling upon him. For him there was a future again, an adventure ahead. From being a theologically indefensible suffragan bishop he was at last moving to a sphere where all his gifts could and would be used in the service of God and his Church. And it would very soon show. The present Archbishop of Canterbury (Robert Runcie) writes:

Once Hugh became Bishop of Birmingham a remarkable consensus of respect was gained amongst his brother bishops for one who had been known as 'Montefiasco' because of his tendency to rush in. He seemed often in his career to give real leadership when not acting under the shadow of someone else. Ken Carey, John Robinson, Mervyn Stockwood – all these people in some ways seemed to overshadow Hugh, not by their skills and abilities, but by being in positions which prevented him flowering as he might. But in the diocese of Birmingham Hugh finally blossomed.

On 4 March 1978 Montefiore was installed in the Cathedral Church of St Philip, Birmingham. Canon H.P. Burgess was one of many sitting in the cathedral, full of apprehension and concern. He knew he would disagree with many of Montefiore's convictions. He was concerned whether Montefiore would 'go down well' with the West Midlands and with the civic authorities. But on 4 March:

> I was impressed, in spite of not wanting to be impressed, by the majestic way this Prince of the Church walked up the aisle of the cathedral. I warmed to him immediately he spoke his first words. What could be wrong with a new bishop when he stands up and says, 'The first priority of the Church is God,' and goes on to remind us that the Church is not primarily in the welfare business, it is about God?

As a diocesan bishop, Montefiore was now theologically defensible!

13   *Style and Substance*

All varieties of Christianity were there – leaders and led alike; leaders of the local Hindu, Muslim and Sikh communities were there, as were the 'descendants' of Joe Chamberlain in their civic ranks. All were intensely interested, many were candidly apprehensive, but all were in the subdued baroque cathedral for the 'enthronement' or installation of Montefiore as Bishop of Birmingham on 4 March 1978. His challenging sermon began and ended with God. He portrayed a Creator God who embraced the whole world and everything and everyone in it:

> The Gospel is not for the chosen few: it is for everyone, whether they hear or whether they don't; and I shall regard it as the first priority of my episcopate to take a lead by preaching, by public addresses and by informal discussions, in sharing Good News about God with the people of this city.

The sermon contained statements and challenges for and to the Church and society. Words of energy to fire the congregation poured forth. 'What we need are new ideals, a new sense of self-esteem which will unite us, energize us and unleash those excellencies of character and creativity latent within us all.' And once he had lifted hearts, raised sights and compelled people to want to act, he was able to direct their minds forward to God. Again and again he was asking for a new lifestyle for a new era.

The sermon worked on two levels – challenging and inspiring. It was wide-ranging – witness the remark made by the

Roman Catholic Archbishop of Birmingham (George Patrick Dwyer) to the Archdeacon of Aston (Donald Tytler) as they walked to Birmingham Town Hall after the service: 'As the cat said when they drew it through the barbed wire, there can't be many points I haven't touched on.'

On moving to Birmingham, the Montefiores decided to let their London home. Bishop's Croft, in Old Church Road, Harborne, is a graceful and lovely house but there were many initial difficulties. Pails hanging from the stairwell, catching water, revealed the state of the roof. The miracle of the appearance of water through normal appliances had to be witnessed to be believed. How it entered the house no one knew. The hot-water system would dry up for reasons inexplicable. If a washer were needed for a tap, the plumber had to bring in refrigerating gear to mend it. The Church Commissioners were not over-generous in providing the wherewithal for all that needed doing.

In a class by itself was the old chapel, reminiscent of the worst kind of pseudo-Oxbridge chapel. A chapel was crucial to Montefiore's spiritual well-being and here he was successful in persuading the Church Commissioners to make some alterations to a large bedroom at the end of a passage so that could be Montefiore's 'upper room'. It held up to twenty people. Each day began with Matins, followed by Holy Communion.

The senior staff of the diocese were Mark Green, Bishop Suffragan of Aston since 1972; Gerald Hollis, Archdeacon of Birmingham; Donald Tytler, Archdeacon of Aston, and Basil Stanley Moss, Provost of the Cathedral.

In Mark Green Montefiore found a suffragan bishop beloved by all, enviably modest and with a versatility that enabled him to be equally at home in church halls, people's homes, the Guild of Students at Aston University or the changing rooms of Aston Villa. The versatility was important, for Montefiore's arrival meant, in Mark Green's words,

a total change of style, pace and organization. It could have been a disaster for me (and him). In fact it was most stimulating. I had been able to give genuine loyalty to Laurence Brown, and now, without strain or disloyalty to the past, I was able to enter into the new regime.

Gerald Hollis had been Vicar of Rotherham for fourteen years before moving to Birmingham in 1974. Donald Tytler was newly appointed but had a long experience in the diocese. He was fifty-two and had an artificial hand as a result of the war. He has about him a certain blend of radicalism and conservatism which gives people the satisfaction of feeling not only that they are keeping up with the times, but that they are also maintaining the traditions of the past. Well-known in the diocese, Donald Tytler had a common-sense approach to issues and his 'dead-pan' sense of humour relieved many a brittle moment. He was a reconciler too. Shortly after Montefiore's arrival, Donald Tytler arranged a dinner party for Montefiore and his arch-critic Anthony Beaumont-Dark. Since then they have been on Christian-name terms.

No one would question Bishop Mark Green's observation:

> Hugh swept in like a tornado. It was obvious that he did not think much of the previous regime, not by what he said so much as by what he did. He immediately scrapped a lot of what he found: for example, almost before he was in he had written a new set of Pastoral Regulations for the diocese. Orders of Service (confirmation, institution of new incumbents, blessing of marriage contracted in a Register Office) followed one after the other.

Yet this hurricane invasion of new ideas was not as innovative as appearance suggested. New to Birmingham, yes. But not originating with Montefiore. As Basil Moss and others testify, many initiatives were merely what Montefiore had been used to in Southwark. For one of such an independent cast of mind, ready to try new ways, this loyalty to what had been imposed on him at Southwark seems very strange. In a way it buttressed a type of prelacy – Montefiore might flinch at such a word, Stockwood might smile – but that is how it appeared. Montefiore was every inch a Prince of the Church, a 'high' churchman in the true sense of having a deep sense of the Church's divine authority, God-given order and discipline. Prelacy was part of this. But he demanded respect and obedience for his office, not for himself. It is by no means easy to keep the two apart, but Montefiore, more than most, succeeded in doing so.

At any service where he was present, the people were left in no doubt that 'Hugh, by Divine permission Bishop of Birmingham,' was with them. He swept in at the end of the procession like an Imperial Caesar come to administer justice and quell warring tribes. But, unlike the emperors of old, he had come to do much more than that: to represent the majesty and the love of God himself. Behind the panache lay an understanding human heart and a mind which was able to interpret the Divine Word to a generation that was often only half-believing, even in the Church. Mother Margaret Angela NSSJD writes:

> The spiritual, mental and physical stature of the man, combined with what sometimes appeared to be boundless energy, left many of us breathless! His commanding presence carried considerable authority and that put many people in awe of him and could fan the flames of the 'public image'. A certain authoritarian trait did go hand in hand with an over-sensitivity to criticism and on occasions he could react to views expressed by others with which he himself disagreed, and he did not always manage to conceal his irritation with people and with situations. He did not suffer fools gladly!

The diocese soon found that they had a bishop of extremes – a rushing mighty wind, an earthquake – and a still small voice. When he was relaxed in his study he was superb, understanding, caring, reassuring. But always there was the limitless energy, with everything done at great speed and with tremendous enthusiasm. He was impulsive, compulsive and a very hard (too hard) worker.

Initially people wondered whether Montefiore would have the tact and the sensitivity needed to avoid destructive confrontation. Would he have the patience and ordinariness needed to capture the energies and hearts of the people of the parishes? The diocese soon knew, but the real regard in which he was held can be measured by the thousands who went to Birmingham's National Exhibition Centre when he retired.

At the opening of his episcopate there was a great deal to be done quickly. Clergy who had been used to slow or cruising speed received an immediate and sustained shock to their systems. Montefiore appeared impatient at times, particularly with clergy who made minor errors in the words or organization of services. He could be insensitive to their nervousness or their difficulties, and his ebullient competence could put a dent in their self-confidence. It was unintentional, but it was there. How little they knew their bishop. Outwardly he gave the impression of being supremely self-sufficient and confident of his own ability and achievements, and yet underneath there were levels of uncertainty. He needed reassurance and encouragement. If ever he unintentionally caused pain to someone and he was told about it, he could be quite distraught. He bore no malice and his flashes of temper were soon forgotten. 'Always look forwards, never backwards' was one of his favourite sayings.

There was much that needed doing, moving and changing. An example was worship in the diocese. No liturgical committee was in existence to advise him. That was soon remedied, and eventually a whole set of services, supplementary to the new Alternative Services Book, was published. However, instant medicine was necessary in some areas to cure liturgical maladies. Montefiore considered that the confirmation service he had inherited was appalling so, as a first step, he introduced the 'Southwark rite' on which he was, as yet, unable to improve.

On Maundy Thursday he wished to have a service with three distinct yet uniting elements – the blessing of oils, the renewal of priestly vows and the Communion of the Priestly College with the bishop. As regards the blessing of the oils there were some rumbles. Montefiore could not see the point in blessing the oils with different formulae for exorcism in baptism and strengthening at confirmation because this seemed to be rather 'magical'. However, when he was assured that this would give offence to some, he caved in and did have different blessings, despite his personal convictions. This is interesting to note in view of the fact that Montefiore effectively intervened in the General Synod on 9 November 1982 to have the Liturgical Commission's draft prayer for the blessing deleted on the grounds that this was best left to the priest who was celebrating.

Ordinations were impressively organized occasions. The prelude to the service was the retreat. Canon Lorys Davies, Director of Ordinands, recalls that Montefiore made a point of visiting ordinands on retreat and interviewing each one: 'All ordinands gained much encouragement and spiritual strength from these encounters.'

In my days as DDO we took time to plan services and all began on time and for the most part ran very smoothly. I totally supported Bishop Hugh that this was important. He himself appeared at rehearsals and acted as CO. They were often tense occasions, sometimes amusing. His obsession with time is best illustrated when on one occasion I reminded him that according to the time schedule for the service it was time he visited the ordinands. He retorted: 'There's thirty seconds to go!'

Punctuality is in Montefiore's genes. It is said that his grandmother at Ramsgate once ordered the coach to arrive at twenty-six minutes past four!

Behind all Montefiore's efforts at preparation was the desire for outwardly dignified and inwardly relaxed worship on the day. Let the concentration be on the service and not on what to do next. Ordinands were not alone in being grateful for being put through their paces beforehand. They benefited throughout the actual act of worship which surrounded their ordination.

Intuitive and intelligent correspondents learned to be concise in letters and to put matters of prime importance into the first paragraph. It is not that Montefiore did not read beyond the first paragraph, rather that he expected to learn the nub of the request without undue verbosity. In any event, woe betide waffling correspondents, unsure of their facts or inaccurate in their presentation. Montefiore's meticulous attention to detail of law and procedure was constantly in evidence. Some people thought this a Jewish trait. Canon Tom Walker, Vicar of St John and St Germain, Harborne, once informed Montefiore that he would miss a meeting of Synod as he was going on a preaching tour in South Africa for a few weeks. Montefiore immediately countered by saying, 'That's all right – an incumbent can legally absent himself from his vicarage for three months in a year.'[1] Canon Walker admired Montefiore's ability to change his mind when necessary:

> On one day I received two letters from him regarding the staffing situation in our parish. I received two letters because I had written two letters. Very early in my acquaintance with Hugh I had decided that he did not read long letters. There was no point in writing about three different topics in one missive. I had consequently written to him concerning my desire to have a man serve his title with me and also I wrote requesting Hugh to ordain our woman parish worker. In both matters he wrote with a blank refusal. I then wrote back to him with twenty-nine reasons why he should both give me a deacon for our parish work, and why my experienced parish worker should not be refused ordination simply because she had chosen not to be a deaconess some years before . . . The following Sunday he came to take a confirmation service for us and with a huge beam on his face gave us the good news that he had completely changed his mind and that he would grant both requests. My admiration for Hugh was that he should be willing to be convinced by the facts of the situation when they were fully presented. He would never be blackmailed into an unjust decision, but he always supported the parochial clergy and furthered the mission of the Church by generous decisions in the light of factual evidence.

Montefiore knew an amazing amount about his clergy. Occasionally he got things wrong by putting tags on people – 'that man who wears a yellow jersey' – but he was quick to learn and to recast his opinion if necessary. It seemed as though anyone who woke up with a bad cough or some threatening sympton was on the intercession list in the chapel at Bishop's Croft within an hour or two. A colleague comments: 'His omniscience seemed superhuman, and I don't know how it happened.'

Any priest who wished to see him urgently knew that, providing he was not away from Birmingham, Montefiore would see him within twenty-four hours, though it might have to be at 10 p.m. or even midnight. This unexpected nocturnal availability sometimes reduced the clergy's troubles to less alarming proportions than they had at first thought.

Montefiore's first task as bishop was to visit all the clergy and their families in their parsonage houses. Thus in the first few months there was a whirlwind tour of the diocese. While visiting he photographed the incumbent – and his family if there was one. These photographs, bound together in deanery packets, became much-thumbed, and were the secret of Montefiore's almost instant knowledge of his clergy and the basis of his constant intercession for them and their families. The whirlwind tour generated a certain amount of cynical mirth, and even a little fear! Few guessed that this costly effort was to be the foundation for an episcopacy of outstanding pastoral care and prayer for the clergy.

Montefiore was fortunate that he had a geographically manageable diocese. There were 176 parishes in an area of 288 square miles. The diocese was heavily populated in and around Birmingham and there was a smell of urban decay which could not be offset by the wealth to be found in Solihull and Sutton Coldfield. The boundaries of the diocese encompassed various parishes in southern Staffordshire, in northern Worcestershire and in Warwickshire. Montefiore was soon a familiar figure, dashing about his diocese. On numerous occasions he made his presence felt to the police by his adventurous driving. A fine for speeding was no deterrent. Bishop Mark Green sums up best what so many people have written:

> God spare me from ever again being driven in a car by him! He is the world's most impulsive driver. I have been with when he was driving down Northumberland Avenue near Trafalgar Square. Suddenly he realized he was going the wrong way, did a U-turn in heavy traffic, shouting rude things at a bus driver who was quite legitimately bearing down upon us. 'Well, well,' he would say, 'the Lord looks after His own.' The astonishing thing is that He does, and we apparently were.

If the pace was hectic around the diocese, it was no less so from the centre. His predecessor had his office in nearby

Church House. Montefiore decided to work from home. Anyone who saw him at work in his study was both impressed and alarmed at the incredible speed with which he worked. He usually wanted everything completed the same day, if not the day before. When he dictated letters one after the other poured out, often in response to quite complicated matters, giving clear, uncomplicated answers, with never a pause or a need to go back and start again. The resulting letters were not gems of English prose, but they were always easily understood, and free from clichés or jargon. Above all, they were decisive. Letters from people criticizing a sermon or speech, or from those seeking advice, received an individual response, never a stereo-typed reply. Three examples are typical of the style:

> I appreciate that you want to share your new-found faith with others. At the same time I hope you won't mind me saying, in as warm and friendly a way as possible, that I really do not think that you ought to pass judgement about other people's faith. My faith was given to me by God through a happy family, and deepened and reinforced when I became a Christian. I have always believed that my motto should be: 'Faith seeking understanding'. Faith must always be distinguished from certitude, since it is precisely faith and not certainty. That does not mean that God does not give us some feelings of assurance, but the distinction must be made and has been made in all classical theology.
>
> I rejoice in your deepened faith, but I hope that you will be tolerant, and learn to understand that God speaks differently to different people.

This was to a lady who had moved to the certainty of the Roman Catholic Church and who was critical of Montefiore's views.

A Lloyds broker who wrote to say that Montefiore should be thoroughly ashamed of himself for remarks made in *The Times* following the scandals at Lloyds (1986) was no doubt surprised at Montefiore's reply:

> I am sorry that you found my remarks in *The Times*

grotesque. I fear I regard original sin as so deeply implanted in human nature that self-regulation is bound to fail. You say that you are not a member of the Church of England. I don't know if you are a Christian who belongs to any other Church, but may I suggest that you read your Bible a little more carefully? In it you will find that: 'The love of money is the root of all evil.' You will find a great deal about the evils of selfish greed in the New Testament, especially in the words of Jesus, when he spoke of the man who had to build bigger and bigger barns in which to put his possessions, and was suddenly told: 'This night your soul is required.' In addition, if you look at the writings of the Prophets, notably Isaiah, you will see that they are constantly inveighing against those rich people who are taking money out of the hands of the poor.

If you regard my statement as disgraceful, I regretfully have to inform you that you must also regard the biblical witness as disgraceful.

And, responding to someone who had written to him about the popular book *Holy Blood and Holy Grail*, Montefiore wrote:

As a matter of fact I did read it rather carefully in 1982 as I went on a television programme in connection with it . . . My expertise lies in the New Testament and the early church, and there is no evidence whatsoever that there was ever a blood line. There could have been – had the dominance of James the Lord's brother continued. There is an interesting incident in Eusebius' *Ecclesiastical History* (Book 3, Chapter 20) about the relatives of Our Lord. I enclose a copy of a translation of this. You will see from this that, far from being a blood line, the collateral descendants of Jesus were humble peasants!

Every day Montefiore was writing letters such as these on every conceivable subject, besides all the official and diocesan correspondence that is the lot of every bishop.

The crisp efficiency with which he organized his correspondence was extended to his chairmanship of diocesan committees. Chairmen come in many guises – the talkative, the pompous, the wanderer, the push-over, the weakling, the muddle-headed. Montefiore was none of these. He was firm, clear and knew what he wanted: occasionally he was ruthless, as a good chairman has to be. Yet anyone who had anything worth saying rarely failed to get the chance to say it, unless they left it too late – for under Montefiore meetings came to a swift end at a pre-determined time. But there was another aspect about which he became sensitive. He seemed to some who did not know him well to be rather fierce and hostile, and, because of his outspoken directness, some were frightened of him. He could stifle debate at Diocesan Synod because ordinary Synod members were often too frightened to speak.

Montefiore's obsession with time was in evidence at meetings and with all appointments. Woe betide any clergy who were late for an appointment without good reason! Two minutes was late! Moreover, to arrive late at a meeting was to receive an episcopal invitation to go to the front where there was plenty of room.

Canon Tom Walker recalls Montefiore's 'remarkable gift of coming out on top in any altercation':

> There was one time when as Chairman of the House of Clergy I was approached by members of the House of Clergy of the Diocesan Synod because they felt that synodical debates were being ruined by Hugh's constant interventions and over-long, over-strong contributions. Plucking up courage, I told him of this criticism at the next Bishop's Steering Committee . . . After I had voiced the criticism Hugh was in silent thought for some moments. He then looked up, gave me a gracious smile and said, 'Thank you for telling me that. It is quite true. I tell you what I'll do. I will stand down from the chair and contribute from the floor on matters about which I feel very strongly. *You* can take the chair in these debates.'
>
> After that time either the chairman of the House of Laity or myself had to chair the most controversial debates on key issues like the marriage of divorced persons, etc. Hugh had graciously accepted the criticism but had ended up turning the tables on us completely.

Soon after arriving in Birmingham Montefiore concluded

that much was wrong. The number of clergy in the diocese had been run down for fear of lack of finance. That must be reversed. A financial crisis was looming. That must be faced. There were few specialist offices in the diocese. That must be changed.

Church leaders were called together and Montefiore made it clear that more clergy were needed, more accredited lay ministers should be appointed. He was appalled at how few women were working full time in Birmingham. He wanted someone who would foster and nourish vocations among women. The talents of lay people should be identified and used. Stewardship should be to the fore if the financial crisis was to recede.

Within a year John Bettinson retired as Chairman of the Diocesan Board of Finance.[2] Who would succeed him, at a time when a very strong man was needed? It was the first significant appointment Montefiore had to make and all eyes were upon him. Would he appoint a 'yes man', or a strong man? He chose the latter in Sir William Dugdale, church warden, patron of a living, well-known businessman and Chairman of the Severn Trent Water Authority. Sir William recalls his experience:

> The first time I met Hugh Montefiore was at the annual meeting of the Lady Katherine Levison Hospital at Temple Balsall . . . I was not too impressed.
>
> About a fortnight later I got a hand-written letter inviting me to be the DBF Chairman in succession to John Bettinson. I went to see him and he said I could have a free hand and he wouldn't interfere as he didn't understand money. As his father had been my father's stockbroker and had amassed a large fortune building up Joseph Sebag and Co., I said laughing, 'Go on, my Lord, you were born to understand it.' Hugh leapt to his feet and said, 'What on earth do you mean?' and I realized my remark had implications which I hadn't intended so I explained and all was quiet. I thought it over and accepted and thereby started a rewarding and interesting, though always fraught, nine years.
>
> However, *à deux*, if faced fair and square with unpalatable facts he never dodged the issue even if the likely solution did not appeal to him. As a 'card carrying'

Liberal he was always conscious that a hard-headed decision might not do his reputation any good but he would always end the conversation, 'Do it if you feel it is really necessary.'

However, it was not long before our first crisis arose. Hugh with great energy fully stocked the diocese with every living occupied and installed seven staff-officer clerics at the diocesan office, who had to have houses bought for them. As a result there was a shortfall of over £150,000 in the diocesan accounts. I went to see him and said there was only one way to put it right and that was to hold the parochial clergy establishment at the same percentage below the establishment as the shortfall was to the total budget. [When told there was not enough money for curates' houses Montefiore wrote to the dioceses of Salisbury and Lincoln which had bulging pastoral accounts, and borrowed a quarter of a million pounds from them at cheap rates.] Hugh was aghast but merely said, 'I have promised to fill all vacancies and keep the diocese fully manned.' I said, 'See you in Carey Street,' and Hugh laughed and said, 'Well, don't make a song and dance about it.' This draconian remedy worked and with full budgeting and the parishes being asked to pay up in full we got straight in about two years. Since then the diocesan office has given a monthly forecast of how fully the diocese can be manned so that after the main ordination dates the diocese can be more over strength and allow numbers to fall back gradually thereafter.

At my first Diocesan Synod I moved towards the platform in Birmingham Town Hall but was neatly headed off by Hugh who said, 'Would you mind sitting as far away as possible, as I don't want my money-bags sitting in my pocket.' God and Mammon, I suppose, and ever since I have always sat in the farthest corner.

Hugh's greatest strength was the way he related to the man in the pew. His sermons ranged from the perfectly marvellous exegesis to the truly awful party political broadcast but he always took so much trouble after the service. No leaping into the chauffeur-driven car and whirling away. He would appear mitre askew and hold court surrounded by parishioners. He invariably struck the right note for his audience and he really became a much-loved figure.

Hugh was always fun. He bullied, cajoled and annoyed to get his way, and prevaricated if he thought he wouldn't. He ruled the diocese like an Old Testament patriarch – greatly loved and slightly feared.

I miss him greatly for the intellectual stimulus and enthusiasm. He never carried over any rancour and however vigorously we argued, the next meeting began with smiles and goodwill. He was a man who needed argument and constructive opposition to bring out the best solution. The more he was stood up to, the better he performed.

Montefiore's visits to parishes revealed much about the man as well as about the bishop. Mother Margaret Angela says:

At baptisms and confirmations he was superb. No doubt this stemmed from his own personal experience of a costly adult baptism and confirmation – costly in personal relationships with his family and friends. His confirmation sermons were always memorable. Baptisms were never to be forgotten – delicate *lavabo* towels were no match for the amount of water used in that great symbolic gesture of 'washing and regeneration'. The clergy were issued with episcopal instructions to fill the font and provide a bath towel – in an aside to me at a clergy chapter a young priest added: 'and a mop and a bucket as well!'

Michael Counsell, Vicar of Harborne, recalls:

The first confirmation Hugh took here we were rather in awe of him. For a start he was so tall that he knocked the sanctuary lamp with his mitre; and he insisted that as baptism is the sacrament of admission to the Church it must take place near the main door. Now the font at St Peter's has been moved in front of the congregation, so we used a silver bowl on a small table at the back. The procession reached this temporary font, and Hugh put the candidates through their promises. Then he said, 'Where's the water?' I had forgotten to provide any, so the two church wardens sprinted off . . . one went into the kitchen in the church hall calling, 'Quick, a jug of water.' They thrust a jugful into his hands, and it wasn't until he got back to a very amused bishop that he realized they had given him water which had been brought to boiling point for making coffee! . . .

Dr Mary Jeavons contrasts Montefiore at meetings and at confirmations:

Bishop Hugh was tall and strongly built, with piercing blue eyes and a fresh complexion. Frequently he appeared to be gazing as if searching for a target. During the coffee interval at the Diocesan Synod he would approach his target at a speed and determination which caused us to step hastily out of the way to avoid being mown down. Yet, by contrast, we were moved to see him after a confirmation service kneel on the floor of the church hall so that he could speak quietly and caringly to a candidate in a wheelchair. He loved confirmation services and his personal interest in speaking to all the candidates afterwards was immensely encouraging to the parishes. He t lked very easily to the ordinary person and he got on ve1y well with children.

Montefiore decided to institute a visitation of the diocese together with the Bishop of Aston, on a similar basis to the Southwark visitations. These were greatly welcomed. A few clergy were sceptical but the congregations were appreciative. The pattern varied, depending on the nature of the parish. After a service on the Sunday evening Montefiore liked 'Question Time', which was like a game of bat and ball the way the questions were answered. The following day might include a visit to a school or a factory or Montefiore might go with the priest on his sick Communion round. Montefiore's files were full of correspondence from individuals he met on his visitations – letters of thanks for a blessing given, a word of healing uttered, a trade unionist wanting to continue a conversation he had started, a doctor sharing his thoughts on medical ethics, a theological query or some aspect of being a Christian today.

Visitations also gave Montefiore the opportunity to see his clergy in action. And despite any criticisms they had of some of his ways and words, they knew, or should have known, that in Montefiore they had a real father-in-God.

Every bishop has occasionally to deal with sad cases of moral failure, scandal or breakdown. Montefiore gave hours of time to these and brought to them a blend of compassion, authority and practical common sense. He was rarely in doubt for long as to what ought to be done. Quite often what needs to be done in such cases is to remove a priest from his parish, either temporarily or for good. Under the English system the latter is not easy to do, but Montefiore managed it with a minimum of fuss, publicity or hurt to the man concerned. He took many such clergy from other dioceses and they 'made good'.

If there was illness, he was there – which might mean that at four o'clock in the morning he would be at the bedside of a priest in a Birmingham hospital. If the family were feeling dispirited and tired, he would do what he could to get the vicar and his wife away for a few days' holiday. When a clergy marriage was in danger, he put an enormous amount of time and effort into sorting things out. If a curate fell foul of his vicar, he would go to endless lengths to find alternative employment, and even if the man had been foolish, h would be given another chance.

And there were times when love, not words, were his gift, as Michael Counsell remembers:

> While [the Montefiores] were away, our five-year-old son Simon was knocked down and killed by a drunken driver near here . . . Bishop Michael Whinney came round immediately to the vicarage to comfort us, having already telephoned the Montefiores to tell them. Within hours of returning to Birmingham, Hugh was at the vicarage, gathering us both into his long arms, weeping and praying with us, and sharing our anguish. It has often been said that Hugh was a big man in every way. To me, the test of a man's greatness is his ability to shut off his major concerns, and for the moment to devote his whole

attention to two ordinary people who need his help. On that day, that is what Hugh Montefiore did, and we shall always be grateful and love him for it.

Behind, beneath and alongside all his activity, were Montefiore's wife and his personal devotional life.

From the start he and Eliza, as she was known by all, decided to entertain. They did this fortnightly in parties of about twenty-five. He also decided that meetings would take place at Bishop's Croft and not in Church House. At these meetings the Montefiores would entertain their visitors: for example, dinner for the Bishop's Council, tea for rural deans' meetings, lunches in the summer; coffee and sherry for staff meetings, after Church House staff Communion and at all other meetings. In Montefiore's words: 'The idea was to warm the place up and to make people feel that they belonged to a family.'

Entertaining can have one drawback. When is it appropriate or necessary to take one's leave? Guests at Bishop's Croft need not have worried. At ten minutes to ten in the evenings Montefiore would say, 'Would you like to say Compline with us before you depart?'

The presence of Eliza Montefiore, unobtrusively near the centre on all occasions, was essential to Montefiore. Her keen and penetrating mind was inextricably linked in an interdependent way with her deeply spiritual life and she helped many people to grow devotionally. One priest recalls visiting her in hospital when she had a hip replacement and coming away feeling that it was he who had been ministered to by the patient. No contributor to this biography has failed to mention the importance of Eliza. They complemented one another in unity: the one providing fire and excitement, the other a penetrating glow that is warm.

What has always been evident is the way they shared everything, starting with daily worship. Here was the still epicentre of Montefiore's faith: the quiet of the chapel, where all his needs and the needs of the diocese were laid before the altar; from here erupted the vision, energy and power that enabled him to lead the diocese he had been called to serve.

There were some raised eyebrows when he appointed a domestic chaplain. Bishop Leonard Wilson had appointed

Canon Henry Fletcher as a domestic chaplain in 1967 and Bishop Laurence Brown had kept him on but he was also rector of the minute parish of Frankley, with a population of 250. He was already sixty-nine when Bishop Brown went to Birmingham but he was not a full-time chaplain and he was not 'domestic' in that he lived in his own rectory.

Montefiore appointed young and energetic priests as his domestic chaplains[3] and their main function was liaison with the clergy. Montefiore's secretary dealt with all other matters.

David Columba was a Franciscan. He recalls the manner of his appointment. He had in fact never met Montefiore:

> Imagine the surprise then when a letter arrived saying that it had been suggested 'that you might like to serve in the Birmingham diocese on ordination and possibly as bishop's chaplain, particularly as I am to be the new chairman of the Board of Social Responsibility . . . I'm wondering whether you would like to come and see me.'
> On a Sunday a week later Eliza produced a splendid lunch of roast pork and superb red cabbage and then Bishop Hugh took me into his book-lined study and as we talked, with me sitting on the end of my seat, he gradually relaxed into an almost horizontal position in a lovely but rather shabby brown leather chair and eventually declared that it seemed right to him in the way things used to 'seem right' when he was in Cambridge. However, we should both think about it for a week or two. It was the first of many 'It seems right's that I was to witness over the subsequent four years.

This chapter has dealt with the 'flavour' of Montefiore. What of his policy?

14 Contrasts

Montefiore was quite sure that pastoral care must not be isolated from the other dimensions of being a bishop, of which teaching was the most important. Here he was on his own ground with his own convictions. In Southwark the teaching voice of the diocesan bishop had been insufficiently heard.

Montefiore started a periodical called *The Bishoprick* (the 'k' was soon dropped). The first issue appeared in January 1979 and the intention was that it would be produced six times a year. In a Foreword to the first issue Montefiore described its purpose:

> I have started it to further my teaching ministry. Of course bishops have many roles. But the role perhaps least emphasized in the more recent past has been their teaching ministry. The normal run of diocesan life gives little scope for this, and I am anxious that it should not lapse.
>
> *The Bishoprick* is meant to stimulate you, not to tell you what to think . . . There will be no academic theology within its pages! Its aim will be to introduce matters of belief, behaviour and prayer within a pastoral context. It is intended as a stimulus to Christian spirituality in its wholeness; biblical, pastoral and above all *relevant*.

The Bishopric continued throughout Montefiore's Birmingham episcopate. Although there were other contributors, it was primarily a journal of the bishop's own work. The majority of articles were especially written for it and were not simply transcripts of lectures or sermons. In its own way it stands as a worthy monument to Montefiore's teaching ministry.[1] There were articles on theological subjects – 'Why Believe in God?'; 'Jesus: The Evidence'; 'The Don Cupitt Show'; 'The Durham Affair'; 'The Credibility of God' – and ecclesiological subjects – 'The Church of England and the Pope'; 'The Tulsa Affair'; 'Christian Ethics and Morality'; 'Conscience and the Clergy'; 'Human Embryos'; 'Divorce'; 'Is Interest Immoral?' – as well as reflections on overseas visits – to California, Lyons, Russia, Malawi.

No one in Birmingham or in the wider Church could say that they were unsure of Montefiore's views. His presidential addresses to the Diocesan Synod were usually about matters of public moment either in the Church or in the State, and were duplicated for all to read afterwards. His first such address (18 March 1978) was on the subject of synodical government. He affirmed his belief in it as a good democrat, whilst saying that the Church is not a democracy where matters can be decided by a mere majority. He was also quick to point out that there are pastoral decisions which a bishop has to make independently of synod. At General Synod level, he was to face increasingly over the years at Birmingham the dilemma of a Church that is episcopally led but synodically governed. The Church is a living organism, not a mere organization. Yet it is also an institution. Montefiore had seen all too clearly what happens to an institution in which the energies of too many Christians lie in the desire to keep the machine going. The fatal characteristic of this danger is in the fact that there is no essential creative life in machine-minding, unlike in any, even the narrowest, form of worship and witness. Under the mechanistic obsession, the life-changing aspect of religion is in danger of being forgotten.

Montefiore is by temperament an hierarchical person. If at times he seemed too big for the organization to contain; if he acted outside it, or even against it, this was a consequence of his character and not a disowning of the Church as an institution. His Jewishness and his Christianity alike prevented such action. The early prophets had criticized the religious institutions of their day and had preached high ideals of faith and morality. But the prophetic religion, by itself, was merely idealism: it never became the religion of the people until it had been embodied in the law of Deuteronomy and in institutional regulations.

The chance for the higher Judaism had not come until Ezekiel united the roles of prophet and priest. Montefiore could make the leap from the Old Testament, so deeply embedded in his psyche, to the New Testament writers. From the first days of the Church, there were rules, hierarchy, organization. St Paul was careful to give 'his' Churches a regimen of administration. He includes 'helps and governments' as operations of the Spirit side by side with 'apostles, prophets and teachers', and he reckoned 'One Body' as a necessity for the Christian fellowship as much as One Spirit, One Lord and One Faith. The early Church distinguished between the serving at tables and the ministry of the word, but it did both and counted both spiritual activities. Those chosen to serve at tables were to be 'full of the Holy Ghost and of wisdom'.

Montefiore had absorbed this, not at once, but gradually, after his conversion. A call for loyalty to the community acted as a bulwark against religious individualism and cliquism. The Kingdom of God in Our Lord's teaching is not an incoherent collection of individual pieties but a social organism.

Montefiore has been strong in fostering (as a priest) and creating (as a bishop) a sense of belonging to a larger whole, developing that catholic spirit, bidding, even compelling, individuals to see beyond themselves and their parishes to the diocese, to the Church at large, and seeing all as one body, one society, one family. He is deeply Pauline and his book *Paul: The Apostle*[2] testified to St Paul's influence on his thinking. In his Introduction he writes:

> Paul holds a special place in my personal affections, partly because I belong to the same race as he did and also came to Christ through a sudden conversion. All 'twice-born' Christians could benefit from remembering that it took Paul many years before he fully matured as a Christian.

Montefiore's optimism and imagination turned problems into opportunities. In 1980 the diocese would be seventy-five years old. There were few plans for celebration, apart from a visit by the Archbishop of Canterbury (Donald Coggan), who in fact retired before 1980. It was difficult to stir up interest. The cathedral was about to be restored. It was not thought of as the 'mother church' of the diocese. A survey showed that of the thousands who lunched outside it in St Philip's churchyard, few were aware that the cathedral even existed. It was Montefiore's wish that the cathedral should become the mother church, and he was determined to use it for all diocesan occasions. That was not all. The cathedral had to be more than the church to which all other churches in the Birmingham diocese looked for example and inspiration in visual art, in music, in singing and in dignified worship. Montefiore held that

> a cathedral does not just belong to the denomination which owns it . . . It is one of the places[3] to which the intelligent layman in search of a faith to live by may look for help. It must have an outreach in reasoned exposition of the Christian faith, an engagement with the world in its many, many problems, a forum where discussion takes place about the great matters of our day, and where citizens of Birmingham may expect to have light shed by Christian thinking on the personal and social perplexities of modern living.

Montefiore compelled movement. He fixed a date and time for the completion of the cathedral renovation before it had begun, and royalty was invited.[4] This was during a period of high inflation and delay meant that the value of the money was diminishing. Montefiore did not allow people to isolate money: 'The need for money [in the diocese] has brought us up against our need for understanding the Gospel, deepened faith and increased commitment of our lives for Christ.' In a leaflet entitled *Call to Faith and Commitment* he prepared Bible readings for Lent 1980. The print of 10,000 copies was soon exhausted.

Every summer there was a bishop's Summer School and over one hundred people would enrol for it. It lasted two days and people brought picnic lunches to the hall of St Martin's-in-the-Bullring. He also reintroduced the triennial residential conferences for clergy and lay workers at Swanwick.

Pastoral letters were issued and published by Montefiore and attracted widespread interest and comment. They were: '*The Kingdom of God in Our Land*' (Advent 1981); '*Risen with Healing in His Wings*' (Lent 1983);[5] and '*Many Shall Come from the East and the West*' (Advent 1984), on inter-faith relationships.

Birmingham was not over-troubled with churchmanship quarrels, but there was growth in the charismatic movement. Montefiore decided that the movement should be kept 'main-line', so he said there would be two renewal Eucharists in the cathedral each year. He would preside at one and the suffragan bishop at the other.

Birmingham was aware that Montefiore would be away from the diocese, not only on official business, but also by request to teach, preach and lecture. In October 1981 he spent twelve days visiting Stanford University and the Church Div-inity School of the Pacific in California. Besides lecturing and preaching, he was expected to be available on the campus for private consultation or debate.[6]

Two trips that made a deep impression on him during the first half of his Birmingham episcopate were to Lyons and to Malawi. He visited Lyons in January 1982 during the Week of Prayer for Christian Unity. Montefiore had been invited by the Roman Catholic Archbishop of Lyons, Albert Decourtray, and by Bishop Vlassios (Greek Orthodox), Pastor J. Kaltemark (Lutheran), Pastor C. Wagner (Reformed), Mgr Zakarian (Armenian) and the Revd B.H.G. Bradley (Anglican chaplain at Lyons with Grenoble and Aix-les-Bains). Here is a brief diary extract:

On arrival at Lyons airport go straight to meet Archbishop, less than a month in office, very friendly, but neither he nor anyone else volunteers speaking in English. Realize I shall have to speak French throughout: hope it will improve. Père Michalon [RC Ecumenical Officer] takes me on pilgrimage to L'Eglise St Irénee, where the saint's bones lay for centuries until the church was vandalized – hadn't realized that the wars of religion were worse in France even than England. Preached (in French) at enormous Mass for Unity in modern church on new housing estate, over 1,100 present. Great occasion, much lay participation and singing, very informal – press wandering around taking flashes throughout. (Can't see this in England!) Archbishop wore simple chasuble – cope and mitre only three times a year, simplicity reigns. He concelebrated with twenty-eight priests, all but one elderly, none with dog collars. Almost all laity received communion by hand (do our Anglo-Catholic brethren *realize* this?), and any lay person who wanted the chalice went to the Altar and helped him/herself, until it ran out. Like home from home when the consecrated bread also ran out! Reception afterwards in the undercroft, with *kir* instead of our 'wine and cheese'. Interviewed by local radio. Dinner afterwards with Archbishop and his priest-secretary. Old palace now municipal library; he lives in an ex-convent, mercifully with good '*chauffage*'. Large urban diocese, 1,000 priests (average age sixty-two), with only 100 ordinations for the whole of France. Also 3,500 *religieuses*, mostly elderly. The city which used to be the most religious in France now has only twenty-five ordinands in training. But the Church was in very good heart. This visit has strangely hit the headlines in the daily as well as the weekly press – very odd.

19 January Attended Archbishop's Mass in private chapel – just like mine, except for meditative silence after Gospel as well as after Communion. Archbishop told me at breakfast that he has many worker priests, without his authorization – tricky situation. Pilgrimage to St Martin, eleventh-century church, consecrated by Pope Pascal II himself, and St Nizier. Then to Amphithéâtre de Gaul where Irenaeus was martyred, only discovered by accident a few years ago. Later we go out to lunch in British Consul's palatial house outside city – sit down twelve at table. In the afternoon a fascinating consultation with theologians. The Catholic Faculty has 500 students compared with 80,000 in the secular university. 400 students in the Dept. of Theology, 50 seminarists (from the whole region), 50 women religious, the rest housewives and people at work who attend in the evening. A bit isolated, I thought; they admitted they were struck by the impact of secular knowledge – I explained that in English depts of theology we had had to live with this for years. They were surprised that our ordinands did not have more grounding in philosophy, and I tried to explain '*la pragmatique des Anglicans*'. Returned to take farewell of Archbishop whom I had grown to like very much – he gave me a present of the *History of Lyons*. (I wonder if he will ever actually use my present of a leatherbound ASB?)

Malawi was as different in every respect from Lyons as it is possible to be. The diocese of Birmingham was linked with the two Malawian dioceses of Lake Malawi and Southern Malawi.[7] There were exchange visits and Birmingham had raised much money for these dioceses, whose bishops were Peter Nyanja (Lake Malawi) and Dunstan Ainani (Southern Malawi). Montefiore's visit was planned for July and August 1983.

In the land-locked country of Malawi, covering 45,747 square miles with a land area of 36,324 square miles, the Anglican presence, which had been there for over a century, was served by two African bishops and over 100 stipendiary and non-stipendiary priests.

Malawi was a place, not an issue, and people in Birmingham were kept fully informed by news items, special events and an annual glossy paper entitled *Mirror on Malawi*.

Montefiore received as much as he gave during his visit. Here he witnessed an unsophisticated and growing Church with a different ethos. He could *feel* the Christianity expressed in singing, rejoicing and praising the Lord, with an equal emphasis being placed on prayer. He had been sent aids to speaking Chichewa, the national language, and spoke it on a number of occasions, to the excitement of his hosts. Everywhere he went, Montefiore was the encouraging bishop, whose impact was great and lasting. And everywhere he went something impressed itself on him – not least the outstanding work being done by the Church in the medical field in a country where infant mortality runs at 40 per cent.

Malawi is strongly Christian, even if there is a Muslim force. Dr Hastings Banda, the president, is an elder of the Presbyterian Church, which is the second largest Christian Church in Malawi. The Roman Catholic Church is the largest and the Anglican Church is in third place.

Montefiore wrote about his impressions in *The Bishopric*:[8]

I asked how people became Christians. Interestingly

enough there is not the great divide between Muslim communities and Christians as there is in this country, or in the Middle East. The Muslim religion is pretty relaxed, and there is intermingling and even intermarriage. People, I was told, become Christians because they attend a Christian funeral and are impressed, or they see how Christians care for one another when one falls ill, or because of the love and care they find in Christian hospitals, or the influence of a Christian headteacher in a school. I found this kind of evangelism very impressive. A European Pentecostalist with whom I spoke derided what he called 'hospital evangelism', but when one sees the crying need for medical help (as opposed to witch doctors) I cannot see that it is unChristian to follow in Christ's steps and help to heal the sick. Non-Christians, too, are impressed by the extent of Anglicans' self-help. The people will themselves build (and often repair) their own churches. Of course there is plenty of earth and water, and there is plenty of wood to burn in a brick kiln. Glass in windows is not necessary, nor is lighting (although it was a near go at one Eucharist which we could not start until 4.30 p.m. and we had to end up holding the altar candle to the book) . . .

The growth of the Church results in large congregations. I myself confirmed eighty-one children and adults at a church in Lilongwe, and also a rather smaller number at Mzuzu (but some kept 'Malawian time' and arrived late, so I had to hold a second one after lunch (Birmingham parishes please don't note). I reckon that more people are confirmed each year in *each* of the two Malawian dioceses than in the diocese of Birmingham. But it really is a question of knowing only 'the ten commandments, the catechism and the Lord's Prayer' – I doubt if they know that. The shortage of books is appalling. There is no instruction book for baptism and confirmation in Chichewa other than an out-of-date one in Mozambiquan dialect. It is the same with prayer and hymn books – perhaps four or five to some congregations, some with less. Fortunately they have a way of singing hymns that depends a lot on the cantor and the choir, and they learn them naturally by heart. I was told that most congregations are forty per cent literate. The children all come to church, and sit there reverently and silently. If a baby starts making noises, his mother gives it the breast: some receive Communion with a baby at the breast. After the rest have received Communion, all the children come up to be blessed. People out there like being blessed. I noticed incidentally that at Communion only about half of the adults present communicated. When I asked why, I was told that they tended to excommunicate themselves, either because they were living together without being married (usually because the man could not afford the bride price) or because the man had more than one wife, which was quite common, or there had been a divorce. The marriage discipline of the Anglican Church is very strict. Incidentally, it is very rare for a couple to be married in church from the beginning: usually the service takes place some time after the 'traditional marriage' with its customary rites.

Montefiore was not used to being greeted on arrival at church with hand-clapping, dancing and choruses and being presented with gifts – so many and so generous and so heavy that he had to spend vast sums for extra freight on his airfare home. On one occasion he was given a monkey and had to explain about quarantine!

The Anglican Church in Malawi was predominantly black, but there were a few whites, including some from Birmingham.[9]

How dreary Church life in Birmingham must have seemed after the Malawian experience. Not that there was any time for pause. Montefiore's pace continued to be extremely fast, and his presence was ever more required on a national scale.

15   National and Ethical

On 25 January 1980 Donald Coggan preached his valedictory
sermon as Archbishop of Canterbury in Canterbury Cathedral.
By this time a new archbishop had been appointed to lead the
Anglican Church through the 1980s. The announcement of
Donald Coggan's successor had come on 7 September 1979. It
was the Bishop of St Albans, Robert Alexander Kennedy
Runcie.

During the period preceding the announcement, speculation
and desire mingled to produce a number of names, including
that of Graham Douglas Leonard, then Bishop of Truro, and,
trailing a little, John Stapylton Habgood, Bishop of Durham,
with Colin Clement Walter James, Bishop of Wakefield, and
Ronald Oliver Bowlby, Bishop of Newcastle, in the more
distant wings. Most of these were mentioned on the assumption that Stuart Yarworth Blanch, Archbishop of York, would
not be translated to Canterbury. A name which did not enter
this speculation was that of Montefiore, yet there were those
wanting vigorous leadership and radical change who pressed his
name.

Not all possible candidates for Canterbury were diocesan
bishops. One suffragan bishop was regarded as outstanding,
noted for combining spiritual depth with evangelistic outreach,
missionary experience (in India) with expository skills, pastoral
effectiveness with dynamic leadership. This was Geoffrey John
Paul, Bishop Suffragan of Hull, later described as a 'leader who
drove himself hard, set visionary goals and encouraged others

to share them'. He became Bishop of Bradford in 1981 and tragically for the Church of England he died two years later.

Montefiore had known Runcie over the years, and there was friendship between them. On some issues they agreed (the remarriage of divorced people in church) and on others they differed (the ordination of women to the priesthood). The recklessness of the one was balanced by the cautiousness of the other. If one was less radical than his detractors depicted, the other was more radical than his supporters suggested. Runcie was to use Montefiore's ability in all kinds of ways.

What were the signs for the coming primacy in 1980? Where would Runcie lead the Church? Rather, where would the Church allow itself to be led? The pressing need would be to find the 'critical point' in real issues, not the manufactured crises produced by purveyors of publicity. He could not know then the problems facing him. It was soon apparent that Runcie was more interested in preserving the Anglican Communion than in propagating belief in the Established Church of England.

There were to be numerous occasions when Montefiore leapt to his support. Equally, Runcie was going to need the heavy-weight theological support which Montefiore could give.

Of the many boards of General Synod which are in the public eye, the Board for Social Responsibility is pre-eminent. Monte-fiore had been a member for many years. He was never an easy member of a committee, as he gave the impression of impatience with the chair, as if he could have done the job better. However, such was not the case with the then chairman of the board, Graham Leonard, Bishop of London. On so many issues they were on opposing sides, but Montefiore admired Leonard's chairmanship, the way in which he presented reports in General Synod and intervened in the House of Lords on those issues which were properly the concern of the Church and the board.

Towards the end of 1982 Leonard accepted the chairmanship of the Board of Education. It was the right appointment – proven more so by the impending Education Reform Bill in which Leonard played a prominent and noble part in the House of Lords. As a result of his persuasive advocacy and conviction the Government had to change its mind on some vital aspects of the Bill.

Who was there to succeed Graham Leonard at the Board for Social Responsibility? Chairmen of boards are appointed by the two archbishops after consultation with the Appointments Sub-Committee of General Synod. A number of diocesan bishops were considered, Montefiore amongst them. There were queries against his name – he was unpredictable and could be volatile. There had been a furore over a report produced by the Industrial Committee of the board in 1977 on *Understanding Closed Shops: A Christian Enquiry into Compulsory Trade Union Membership.*[1] When the draft report had been before the board, Montefiore thought it deficient and biased. The report included a moral judgement in favour of closed shops from which Montefiore disassociated himself. The then secretary of the board, Giles Ecclestone, had invited Montefiore to review the report in *Crucible*, an 'independent' journal of the board, but withdrew the invitation when he heard the kind of things Montefiore would want to say. Accordingly, Montefiore, knowing that his points had not been taken up, submitted an article to the *Church Times*[2] when *Understanding Closed Shops* was published, to the embarrassment and annoyance of the Industrial Committee and particularly its chairman, the Bishop of Worcester, Robin Woods.

The essence of Montefiore's difficulty over the report was this:

> The Report properly calls for a sense of responsibility by unions and management; and, in any case, law should intrude as little as possible in industrial relations . . . But the law (providing it gains general consent) has a vital moral function in safeguarding rights. It is a very grave situation for a man to lose his job (or fail to get one) because of conscientious objection to a particular union, or because of expulsion from it . . . The rights of the individual (nowhere delineated in this Report) are very precious for Christians who hold that a man has a paramount duty to follow his informed conscience . . .
>
> I cannot understand the moral grounds on which this Report accepts the present law which generally restricts exemption for religious reasons. If conscience is 'the judgement of the practical reason at work on matters of

right or wrong', as the Report suggests, there can be genuine and informed conscientious objection against a Closed Shop . . . by an atheist as much as a believer. This Report appears to endorse an unduly privileged position for religion.

On this issue Montefiore asked if he should 'consider his position' on the board, but was told his resignation would not be appropriate. This incident was remembered by some when a new chairman of the board had to be appointed in 1983.

Prebendary John Gladwin (now Provost of Sheffield) was Secretary of the Board at the time of the change. He had only recently settled in under Leonard's chairmanship. At the close of 1982 he heard that the archbishops had invited Montefiore to be the new chairman:

The staff were anxious about this because of Hugh's reputation for firing off in a number of unpredictable directions. However, my own confidence in Hugh was greatly helped when he wrote to me saying that he had been asked and that he did not intend to accept without hearing my views and those of the staff who had been in the department for some time.

I consulted with senior staff and wrote him a long letter setting out their concerns without discouraging him from taking on the chairmanship. From this experience I learnt that Hugh was an open sort of person with a high sense of duty in personal conduct and unafraid of facing hard news.

I count the partnership Hugh and I had as one of the most significant in my ministry. We got on very well together. He was his usual self – wanting about twenty things done at once, often in a last-minute panic, working at incredible speed both of mind and action. The staff here were often terrified of him – expecting him to dump new demands on them at every visit! There were often times when I found him exasperating but one soon got to know that the storm disappeared as quickly as it arose.

His great strengths were his ability to get at the core questions in issues, his willingness to face up to conflict (one of the few bishops in my judgement with this strength), his theological acumen, his capacity for work and his obvious open personality. His weaknesses were sometimes hasty and politically ill-judged decisions, his desire to want the board to do everything, and his personal dominance of meetings (not fully accepting that as chairman he needed to facilitate meetings).

He and I got on because I think he respected my judgement re the process, my capacity to keep pace with him and to help him achieve what he thought was right, and our mutual love of theology.

The issue which immediately preceded Montefiore's chairmanship was the General Synod debate on the controversial report *The Church and the Bomb*.[3] The debate took place with television cameras in place for there had previously been much heated discussion on the subject in the Church and in the country. The Bishop of Salisbury's working party had opted for unilateral disarmament. The board's motion was bland, namely, inviting Synod to urge the Government and its NATO allies to reduce progressively their dependence on nuclear weapons and to seek to strengthen international treaties relating to the possession and control of nuclear weapons.

The General Synod was rescued from these options by a third, proposed by Montefiore. The then Bishop of Durham (John Habgood) referred to Montefiore's amendment as eirenic. Montefiore was convinced that the Church's vital role was 'not to engage in sterile arguments between "doves" and "hawks" but to open up the real issues, to judge moral choices, and to give a creative lead out of our impasse'.

Montefiore's amendment required the Government to provide adequate defence, urged it to negotiate disarmament urgently, and said that nuclear weapons could only be held on the basis of 'no first use'. Personally Montefiore dismissed the idea of Britain alone renouncing nuclear weapons as it seemed likely to be destabilizing and not to be making a proper contribution to NATO.

This amendment on 'no first use', although not as extreme as the Bishop of Salisbury's unilateralism, was (and still is) contrary to NATO's basic strategic policy for the defence of

Europe, which is based on 'flexible response', a euphemism for 'first use' of nuclear weapons in order to repel an aggressor. His argument in General Synod was criticized by some, but more were convinced by the controlled passion with which he pleaded his case. It was a much needed *tour de force* on a difficult day. His amendment was successfully moved and stands to this day as the Church's considered view on *The Church and the Bomb*:

> That this Synod, recognizing: a) the urgency of the task of making and preserving peace; and b) the extreme seriousness of the threat made to the world by contemporary nuclear weapons and the dangers in the present international situation; and c) that it is not the task of the Church to determine defence strategy but rather to give a moral lead to the nations;
> 1 affirms that it is the duty of Her Majesty's Government and her allies to maintain adequate forces to guard against nuclear blackmail and to deter nuclear and non-nuclear aggressors;
> 2 asserts that the tactics and strategies of this country and her NATO allies should be seen to be unmistakeably defensive in respect of the countries of the Warsaw Pact;
> 3 judges that even a small-scale first use of nuclear weapons could never be morally justified in view of the high risk that this would lead to full-scale nuclear warfare;
> 4 believes that there is a moral obligation on all countries (including members of NATO) publicly to forswear the first use of nuclear weapons in any form;
> 5 bearing in mind that many in Europe live in fear of nuclear catastrophe and that nuclear parity is not essential to deterrence, calls on Her Majesty's Government to take immediate steps in conjunction with her allies to further the principles embodied in this motion so as to reduce progressively NATO's dependence on nuclear weapons and to decrease nuclear arsenals throughout the world.

The voting was three hundred and eighty-seven for, forty-nine against, with twenty-nine abstentions.

The major reports or papers initiated or coming to fruition

under Montefiore's chairmanship were:

1983 *The British Nationality Act.*

1984 *Human Fertilization and Embryology*, the response of the BSR to the DHSS *Report of the Committee of Enquiry into Human Fertilization and Embryology* – popularly known as the Warnock Report.

1985 *Personal Origins: Report of a Working Party on Human Fertilization and Embryology*, Foreword by Montefiore.

1986 *Reform of Social Security*, response of the BSR to the DHSS Green Paper. Response written by Montefiore.
Not Just for the Poor: Christian Perspectives on the Welfare State.
Prisoners of Hope, report by the Board on South Africa.
Our Responsibility for the Living Environment, Foreword by Montefiore.

1987 *Changing Britain: Social Diversity and Moral Unity*, Foreword by Montefiore.

1988 (post retirement) *Peacemaking in a Nuclear Age.*

An important initiative by Montefiore concerns AIDS. He saw that the coming AIDS epidemic would bring the question of homosexuality back on to the Church's agenda. In 1986 he asked the House of Bishops to agree that the Board for Social Responsibility should set up a committee to take another look at this controversial subject. The House of Bishops refused.

In a personal communication to the Archbishop of Canterbury, Montefiore said that the Archbishop would get all the flak unless something was done. The Archbishop agreed that a committee should be set up provided that it reported not to the General Synod but to the House of Bishops. The chairman and membership were a closely guarded secret. The committee set to work as much to see how a Church divided on the subject could cope, as to provide an agreed response.

The committee has reported but there is no indication that the report will be published.

If we are to understand Montefiore's actions and influence as chairman of the board, it is important to understand his view of the Church in relation to the world. To him, the Church is not an alternative lifestyle but rather the way to be truly human in the world. Some words he used on many occasions put his view cogently:

The Church is not meant to be a retreat from the world, an oxygen tent where we can escape from the polluted air of the world. The word for church, *ecclesia*, means called out by God. It means an assembly, a coming together, a jamboree. We are called out together to follow Jesus Christ, and that means a re-orientation of our lives, a fresh start, swinging to due north to home on God instead of swinging away to magnetic north to focus on ourselves.

Because Montefiore puts God first, he places his thinking on Church and society in correct perspective. He has a very high view of the Church. He has an even higher view of the Kingdom, and sees that God is primarily interested in all people – perhaps more interested in his world than in the Church.

Behind all his teaching was the desire to equip individual Christians to make them more aware of their faith, more articulate about it and quicker to see its implications for the life of the society in which they live. It was not simply a case of a new Act of Parliament, or of good relations in industry, or a new law about marriage; it was the whole climate of society which Christians ought, by their presence, to be able to influence.

We will consider a few of the Church of England's attempts, led by Montefiore, to influence society. In July 1982 the Secretary of State for Social Security set up, in conjunction with other secretaries of state, a committee to look into matters of human fertilization and embryology under the chairmanship of Dame Mary Warnock, later Lady Warnock. The committee, known as the Warnock Committee, reported in 1984.[4] The report was brilliant and controversial, cogently argued and lucidly expressed, but not unanimous in its recommendations. It dealt with AID (artificial insemination by donor) and IVF (*in-vitro* fertilization). There was a general, though not universal, welcome for many of the recommendations, for example, the suggestion that a new statutory licensing authority should be set up to regulate infertility services, monitor new developments, and vet individual research projects. Clinics which undertake IVF and embryo replacement should be licensed and subject to inspection by the licensing body, as should centres that provide AID.

One of the most contentious parts of the report was the recommendation

No live human embryo derived from *in-vitro* fertilization, whether frozen or unfrozen, may be kept alive, if not transferred to a woman, beyond fourteen days after fertilization, nor may it be used as a research subject beyond fourteen days after fertilization. This fourteen–day period does not include any time during which the embryo may have been frozen.

Two recommendations of significance for the Board of Social Responsibility were:

The form of embryo donation involving donated semen and egg which are brought together *in vitro* be accepted as a treatment for infertility, subject to the same type of licensing and controls as we have recommended with regard to the regulation of AID, IVF and egg donation.
The clinical use of frozen embryos may continue to be developed under review by the licensing body.

The Government did not and could not announce what its legislative proposals would be, except that it allowed a free vote on Mr J. Enoch Powell's private member's bill, *Unborn Children (Protection) Bill*,[5] which was to prevent a human embryo being created, kept, or used for any purpose other than enabling a child to be borne by a particular woman. Although the Bill was heavily supported by MPs and by the organization LIFE,[6] it failed because of parliamentary procedure.

The Board for Social Responsibility had submitted evidence to the enquiry[7] and on the appearance of the Warnock Report it published its nineteen-page response,[8] written and signed by Montefiore as chairman. The board had had its own working party, working concurrently with the Warnock Committee, 'to bring together the threads of moral theology that are relevant to Anglican thinking on the subject, and to apply those to the apparently new problem raised by the scientific developments considered by the Warnock Committee'. Members were: Professor R.J. Berry, Professor of Genetics, University College,

London; Dr Mary Seller, Reader in Developmental Genetics at the United Medical School of Guys and St Thomas' Hospitals, London; Revd Professor Keith Ward, Professor of Moral and Social Theology, King's College, London; and the Revd Professor Oliver O'Donovan, Regius Professor of Moral and Pastoral Theology, University of Oxford. Prebendary John Gladwin, the board's secretary, also attended the meetings.

Before the working party had reported, Montefiore moved a motion in an emergency debate in General Synod on 14 February 1985 asking Synod's support in opposing any moves towards the creation of embryos specifically for research purposes, but supporting Warnock for research under licence on embryos up to fourteen days old for the detection and prevention of inherited disorders or the alleviation of infertility. He had valuable support, including that of the Revd Anthony Dyson, Professor of Social and Pastoral Theology at Manchester University, who was also a member of the Warnock Committee.[9] The board's view was that a human embryo in its first fourteen days, 'is not yet a human person, but it contains all the genetic instructions to develop into a human person and because, when it implants itself in the uterus, it becomes a potential human person, it should be treated with real respect and subjected to strict controls'.

The debate was held at the end of a long day and many Synod members had already left. It lasted under two hours and the motion was lost.[10] Montefiore was so troubled that he tendered his resignation as chairman of the board to the archbishop. The matter became public and a press statement was issued[11] stating that his offer to resign had been refused.

When the board published its own report *Personal Origins*[12] it was obvious that the members of the working party were not themselves of one mind, though they had worked towards unanimity. When General Synod debated the report on 4 July 1985 it was unable to reaffirm its rejection of experimentation on human embryos of up to fourteen days. However, Montefiore's view was that the Church was clearly divided, although moving towards acceptance of the Warnock proposals. In this sense the Church was probably a mirror of the nation.

Although he had presented the board's view in Synod, Montefiore gave a slight hint of his own disagreement with all the findings of *Personal Origins*. His problem concerned the explanation in the report of the status accorded to the human embryo. It seemed to polarize two particular approaches. As he said in Synod:

> On the one hand, it describes those who emphasize *the continuity of the human subject*, and on the other hand it explains the viewpoint of those who major on the human being as *the subject of consciousness*.
>
> At first sight this would seem to leave the impression that, so far as we regard the embryo as a human being, the beginning is either at conception (on the former view) or (on the latter view) at between twenty-one and forty days when a functioning nerve system is establishing itself towards consciousness.

What he did not express publicly was his own view that focused neither on continuity nor on consciousness but on the development of organisms:

> Some biological stability is required in the organism for its individuation to be established. Earlier, the possibility of twinning (and *in vitro* of recombination) still existed, so that individuation had not yet occurred. Until individuation has taken place, and cell differentiation has occurred, the organism has not developed sufficiently to be treated as a human being. The organism has not yet a human soul. On such a view the soul is not infused into a biological receptacle at birth, but wells up within the developing organism at a certain level of complexity, enabling it to relate to its mother emotionally, if sub-consciously, within her womb.
>
> On such a view the continuity of the organism from its first beginnings is sufficiently important to treat the primitive embryo with respect. On the other hand until the stage of individuation and cellular differentiation is reached, it does not deserve the full protection of a human subject. Since organisms develop gradually and not in abrupt saltations, there are no moments in the life of a human embryo when it gains a new ontological status.

But the law requires precise boundaries. Just as the law lays down that a girl cannot give consent to sexual intercourse until a certain age, so also the law needs to lay down a period beyond which it is illegal to interfere with the normal development of a human embryo. In accordance with this view, this period would begin neither from conception, nor after the first appearance of neural structures, but when individuation and cellular differentiation have begun, e.g. fourteen days after conception.

Montefiore was to maintain a close interest in this and in related subjects, one of which was to lead him into prominence in the House of Lords.

No draft report before the Board for Social Responsibility had a safe passage free of Montefiore's pen. Always he was on the watch for woolliness and superficiality. He wanted the board's reports to be credibly received in Government and other circles. If that was to happen, what were the working principles of the board? In some ways Montefiore, more than his recent predecessors,[13] forced the board to consider what its resources were for reflecting theologically and ethically on issues of the day. Here there is a distinction between the Roman and Anglican Churches. The Roman Catholic method of moral theology on social questions is to relate to a long tradition of authoritative statements starting with the Fathers and in more modern times beginning with *Rerum Novarum* (1881) and including *Laborem Exercens* (1981) and *Gaudium et Spes* (Vatican II). The latest is *Sollicitudo Rei Socialis* published in 1987 for the twentieth anniversary of *Populorum Progressio*. There is no similar Anglican tradition.

The Anglican method has been less authoritarian and systematic and more consultative and occasional. That is not to say that it is inferior. Protestant traditions, with their emphasis on man's sinfulness, have tended to ignore the natural law and concentrate on the right intentions of those conformed to Christ. Again, Anglicans have not been so dogmatic. If only they would realize it, they have a distinctive way of reflecting on social responsibility. Montefiore listed seven Bible-based key theological principles which guided his own thinking:

1 God created the world and it is good. The whole world, including the material world, is in itself good: it has intrinsic value.

2 Mankind is created in God's image; that is to say, human beings are bound together in the bundle of life. They have responsible dominion over the material universe and the animal creation. They have the power of choice between what is right and wrong, and humanity has intrinsic goodness. God united himself in Christ with humanity, and thereby sanctified it. Because human beings are made in God's image, they are always to be regarded as ends, not as mere means.

3 God has enabled humanity to evolve so that pairing and bonding are part of human nature, and human beings can attain maturation through stable family relationships.

4 Sin has corrupted all human situations; but because of our redemption, grace is able to overcome and transform any evil situation or relationship.

5 The two great commandments are to love God and to love our neighbour as ourselves. These two laws a) put God first; b) enjoin the service of others; c) require adequate self-love to enable sufficient self-esteem.

6 We live between the times of the Coming of Christ, and the final conclusion of God's purpose when the kingdoms of this world will become the kingdoms of our God and Christ. We can therefore now see only fragmentarily the Kingdom of God: we should not expect perfection, but we should seek for signs of the Kingdom on earth, where justice in society is the corporate expression of love between individual people. Because we live 'between the times' we must seek justice for posterity as well as for our present society.

7 The Church is to be a present sign of the future Kingdom, but the Church, too, is bound to suffer from the fallen nature of humanity.

Many people travelled thus far with Montefiore but parted company when he emphasized that whilst these theological insights helped towards clarifying social responsibility in particular situations, they did not solve particular problems. These are solved by reference first to scripture, to see whether there are any guidelines, for it is unlikely that prescriptions will be found therein to fit a particular contemporary situation; and then to *tradition*, to discover the past and present teaching of the Church, in so far as it bears upon a particular problem. Then one's powers of reasoning are introduced, for this is a tool given by God to use to his glory, although one has to be aware that reason can be corrupted by sin as much as any other aspect of one's being.

In the use of reason three aspects must be considered: the nature of the action or act being considered; the intention of the agents or agent; and the probable consequences of the act or action.

Montefiore's approach – his critics would say 'interference' – resulted in reports being steadied or strengthened. *Not Just for the Poor: Christian Perspectives on the Welfare State*[14] received a long critique from him and he insisted on strengthening the economic sections. He was sensitive to the increasingly articulate and influential voice of the 'new right' in and near the Conservative Government. That voice believed that the Welfare State reduced incentives, reduced freedom of choice, and created dependency while enhancing the role of the State. The 'new right' wanted to make the State interfere as little as possible in people's lives. They believed that it was ademocratic, intrinsically bureaucratic and centralist.

Montefiore made the relevant point that the Welfare State is a function of a capitalist society and could not exist in any other society. It looks to private enterprise to generate the wealth which can then be distributed as benefits. Montefiore held that the whole concept of a Welfare State was a wonderful and noble experiment within capitalist democracy.

In a real sense he was in the tradition of William Temple,[15] who, when asked how Christians should fulfil their moral responsibilities in a Christian spirit, wrote:

> The Church must supply itself with a systematic statement of principles to aid them in doing these things, and this will carry with it a denunciation of customs and institutions in contemporary life and practice which offend against these principles . . . It is bound to seem like an intrusion into politics even when it stops scrupulously short.[16]

The Government had a neurosis about the Church of England which sometimes the Church fostered because of its lack of research and clarity in presenting its case. Many Conservative Members of Parliament (including well-wishers) thought the Church of England was spending too much time on purely political issues, often at the expense of moral issues. When Montefiore heard that kind of remark he knew the process of education had hardly begun. As Chairman of the Board for Social Responsibility as well as a member of the House of Lords, Montefiore had access to Government ministers. Conversations were both 'on' and 'off' the record.

Some of the most vitriolic attacks came from Government ministers who were also Anglicans, notably the Lord Chancellor, Lord Hailsham. Montefiore remembers appearing on *Any Questions* with him. He was perfectly charming throughout supper beforehand but as soon as they were on the air Lord Hailsham turned on Montefiore in a bullying and tendentious way about Concorde, and seemed to imagine he was an expert on the subject because his house in Putney happened to be on the flight path seven miles from touchdown. Again, there was a tremendous furore over the *Matrimonial and Family Proceedings Bill* in 1983. The Bill reduced the time limit to one year from the date of the marriage for divorce petitions. At the time Montefiore was not a member of the House of Lords, so the vitriol appeared in correspondence and at some face-to-face meetings. Later, when Montefiore was in the Lords, the Lord Chancellor apologized for referring to Montefiore as the chairman of the 'board of social irresponsibility'.[17] Montefiore felt that the proposal to allow divorce after only one year was a sanction for yet easier divorce. The statistics were already alarming. In 1968 there were 55,000 divorce petitions filed in England and Wales and by 1979 there were 146,000. The children directly affected by divorce each year amounted to more than half a million. In 1983 there were 1.5 million single-parent families. The need to build stable family life was becoming increasingly important.

When Montefiore, as chairman of the board, wrote to the Lord Chancellor, he was often accused of writing in a slap-happy way and of being ignorant of the facts. Just below the surface was the inference that the bishops should mind their real business. Montefiore was well able to deal with such comments. On the issue of the overcrowding of prisons, for example, he had consulted a wide variety of people – an assistant governor of prisons, a senior probation officer, a chief constable, a professor of criminology, as well as the board's expert criminal justice panel. The comment he made was informed comment, and although Montefiore did not want to exchange statistics, he was able to do so if necessary.

Montefiore was not afraid to take his views to the marketplace. The cover of the December 1984 issue of *Banking World* had a superb reproduction of El Greco's *Christ Driving the Traders from the Temple*. Inside there was an article by Montefiore, 'Is Interest Immoral?' Montefiore considered that there were grave moral objections to some modern loans and rates of interest:

The Old Testament prohibition against usury was aimed against extortion. 'If you lend money to any of my people who is poor, you shall be to him as a creditor and shall not exact interest from him.' . . . The biblical injunctions may no longer be applicable to interest as such, but they are still relevant to all interest which exploits the poor.

Montefiore argued that if interest rates can affect individuals in this way, how much more the poor countries of the world, such as in Latin America, where the debts are astronomical. The banks survived because bankruptcy is avoided by the device of 'rescheduling'.

Nobody seems to question the morality of what is happening. We have gone a very long way down the path that began with the Calvinists and their recognition of interest, capital formation and commercial individualism. Loans to developing countries are partly 'loans for consumption' and partly 'loans for development'. So far as 'loans for consumption' are concerned, the Christian Church (including Calvin) was united for centuries in believing that it was immoral to charge interest for the exploitation of human need. So far as 'loans for development' are concerned, it is immoral to charge such high interest that servicing these loans results in the pauperization of the countries concerned, or the denial of the possibility of further development.

I (merely) wish to state that, according to all the canons of Holy Scripture and the age-old tradition of the Church, the present costs of servicing the poor developing countries are clearly and undeniably immoral.

Montefiore's article led to some heated correspondence, not all of it criticizing his views.

Montefiore made his maiden speech in the House of Lords on 23 January 1985.[18] In 1985 and 1986 he made twenty-two speeches or interventions, many of significance. The former Bishop of Rochester (David Say), who was the respected doyen of the Lords Spiritual, has these reflections:

It was on the abortive Shops' Bill that Hugh made his most important contribution. This was a Bill which occupied the Lords for eight long days. Nine speeches were made by bishops, of which Hugh made three, and a total of seventy-eight episcopal votes were recorded in the division lobby. On one occasion no less than nineteen bishops, including the Archbishop of York, voted in support of an amendment moved by Hugh. This was probably the highest vote by bishops in this century. Hugh took the bold step of putting down an amendment to the motion for the Second Reading, suggesting that the law should be amended so as to rationalize restrictions on trading hours without such extensive deregulation as the Bill proposed. This led to an eight-hour debate. His amendment was rejected by eighty-five votes to 141; the Archbishop of Canterbury and seven bishops supported Hugh. Two months later he returned to the fray and supported an amendment, moved by Lord Denning, designed to preserve the special character of Sunday and to give local authorities discretionary powers over the opening of shops. In his speech Hugh reported that the General Synod had reaffirmed its opposition to total deregulation by 427 votes to six. But once again the

Government refused to listen and the amendment was lost by thirty-one votes. If they had been ready to consider one of the five alternatives put forward by Hugh and others in the Lords, there might now be a Shops' Act 1986 on the statute book. As it was, to the Government's complete surprise, the Bill was unceremoniously thrown out in the House of Commons, a political setback overshadowed by the American attack on Libya the same night.

Montefiore had been personally active over the Shop's Bill. In his original evidence to the Auld Committee, Montefiore said of Sunday: 'It gives space in the midst of a busy week, and it acts as a marker in the rhythm of everyday life.' He asked the Auld Committee to pay due regard to the traditional character of Sunday. It failed to do so.

Unless Sunday is for most people a special day, life is a plateau; it goes on endlessly, like days without sleep, or perhaps life without death. If we are to keep our humanity, society must have reference points for living – which is another way of saying that to disregard a divine ordinance is to court a disaster.[19]

In the House of Lords Montefiore was more successful and persuasive on his feet than in the General Synod. The former Bishop of Lincoln, Simon Phipps, has known Montefiore from Westcott House days and writes about his performance in Synod:

I have never known anyone, with a good case to make and immense gifts with which to make it, so quickly lose the Synod's sympathy! He had a way of seeming to speak in anger, which I think was in fact his way of expressing his profound concern with what he was dealing with and his serious conviction that what he was saying about it was right. His tone would lower and his voice become harsh as he glanced around at his audience. This demeanour would be mistaken by the Synod for bulldozing – which it was not. The Synod's discontent would then be voiced and then he *would* often become angry and strident. It was a shame, when this happened, since he always had good things to say about important matters and it quite belied the very gentle side of his character.

Whilst this is an accurate appraisal of Montefiore in Synod, he could also speak with wit and passion, and some of his interventions in debate were both surprising and effective. One of the most moving occasions in General Synod was Montefiore's speech during a debate on the Arab/Israeli conflict on 12 November 1982. He told the Synod what it felt like to be Jewish and, without disagreeing with the report which was being debated, made it clear it was a Gentile piece of work and would be seen as such. The applause at the end of his speech was prolonged. In a debate on the Charismatic Movement (17 February 1982) he said:

I believe that this new movement must not be forced into the fringes of Church life, where it is bound to generate crankiness and fanaticism, excesses and abuse. It must be kept within the mainstream, where it can enrich the whole and where it can be enriched by the whole. Let us not be frightened by it.

Following a Synod debate in November 1985 on a report *Goals for our Future Society*, a working party was set up under the chairmanship of the Archbishop of York (John Habgood) and produced a report, *Changing Britain: Social Diversity and Moral Unity*, which was published in 1987[20] on the eve of Montefiore's retirement. The report has deservedly sunk without trace. It was, in a word, awful. It was not on the subject about which the board had consulted the dioceses and religious and secular organizations – a future vision for Britain. The board was confronted with the question: could it refuse to publish a report chaired by an archbishop? It decided, wrongly, that it could not. Canon John Atherton of Manchester Cathedral, a member of the board, writes:

Hugh's academic–theological background was important in informing our debates and shaping actual drafting. However, this was far more pertinent to personal and environmental issues (including abortion, Warnock, marriage, sexuality). He was *not* informed about social matters and Christian social ethics – and I believe this is where his style was therefore less than helpful (his interjections, from his theological–academic base and intellectual excitability, were not based on *experience* of complex corporate matters, nor on the disciplines of Christian social thought). *Changing Britain* represents his legitimate concern for the changing nature of work, etc., and his ill-advised pursuit of the issue into a national working party which at least some of us strongly advised against. He got his way and the product was an ill-considered and badly written and formulated report. The draft was introduced to the board by the Archbishop of York and devastating criticisms were brushed aside. His judgement over the issue was too emotionally involved and lacking in good academic/church leadership detachment.

Montefiore almost made history. It all began in 1985 when John Selwyn Gummer, Member of Parliament for Suffolk Coastal, Minister of State for Employment, Chairman of the Conservative Party and General Synod member told Montefiore that as Chairman of the Board for Social Responsibility of the Church of England he ought to be banging on the door of No. 10 Downing Street about abortion. Gummer had passionate views on the subject and thought the Church of England was being less than forceful. Montefiore took the initiative and knocked.

He was told that the Prime Minister would not see him but had asked him to see David Mellor at the Home Office, with whom he subsequently had a good interview. Although David Mellor appeared sympathetic, he said that there was not a ghostly chance of any substantial amendment to the Abortion Act getting through the House of Commons, as it was so polarized. The most he could suggest was for Montefiore to get hold of a private member who had won in the lottery for a private member's bill, and attempt a modest motion to which a controversial amendment might be added. This did not prove feasible. Mellor advised Montefiore not to proceed on his own because there would be no hope of success.

Montefiore knew of many breaches of the existing Abortion Act, and the proportion of abortions to live births was appalling. After seeking the advice of Lord Denham, Government Chief Whip in the Lords, Montefiore introduced his own Bill, the *Infant Life (Preservation) Bill*, on 17 December 1986. He did this after visiting neo-natal intensive care units at Sorrento Hospital and Dudley Road Hospital in Birmingham in the course of pastoral visits. He saw and handled premature babies born of pregnancies between twenty-four and twenty-eight weeks; and he was told by the nurses, who took great pride in their work, that in certain circumstances these babies might have been aborted. This is what determined him that the law should be changed. The simple aim of his Bill was to change the twenty-eight weeks limit for abortions to twenty-four weeks, as the prima-facie evidence indicated that a child was capable at that age of sustaining life.

The moral principle behind the Bill was that any baby that is capable of being born alive should not be killed *in utero*. As he said at the Bill's Second Reading on 28 January 1987: 'If a child can live when it breathes the air of this world, it is wrong to kill it at that stage in its development if it is in its mother's womb.' Montefiore was surprised that the majority of the speakers were against the Bill, some of them speaking with passion. He was distressed that practically none of his colleagues on the bench of bishops turned up to support him, although the Duke of Norfolk had been as good as his word in encouraging Roman Catholic peers to attend. This was almost embarrassing, for Montefiore knew that they would really have preferred a Bill which made all abortion illegal. However, to Montefiore's sudden surprise at the end of the debate, the Government spokesman, Lord Beaverbrook, said that the Bill had the support of the Government. There would be no Government whip, but members of the Government who were in the House would vote in favour of the Bill. Whether for this reason, or, as Montefiore preferred to think, because of the inherent logic of the case, the Bill passed its Second Reading. It appeared that the Bill had a chance of becoming law. How wrong he was:

A few days later I was summoned to see Lord Whitelaw,

the Leader of the House. He told me that three Peers who were violently against my Bill had threatened a filibuster. They would propose amendment after amendment, night after night. Lord Whitelaw said that, although the Government had supported my Bill, it would have to go to a Select Committee . . . After thinking about the matter with regret I acceded to the leader's wishes.

Montefiore was aware that he would have retired by the time the Bill came before the Select Committee, so technically it would no longer be the 'Montefiore' Bill. He was in the unusual position of giving evidence before a Select Committee on his own Bill. Normally the mover of a Bill would be on its Select Committee. Montefiore considered that the Committee[21] under the chairmanship of Lord Brightman was hostile to the Bill. The Select Committee hurriedly published a special report of over 200 pages before the dissolution of Parliament. After the General Election in 1987, Montefiore's chief opponent, Lord Houghton of Sowerby, actually asked to take over the Bill, so that the Select Committee, on which he sat himself, would be able to complete its report in his favour, which is what actually happened. And there the matter rested. The Bill lapsed.

Meanwhile David Alton's private member's bill was being debated in the House of Commons. He asked Montefiore if he would act as Treasurer to the Appeal Fund for his Bill. Montefiore did not really approve of a seventeen-week limit, as it seemed merely a stepping stone on the way to the abolition of all legal abortion, whereas Montefiore did think that legal abortions ought to be allowed. He was sure that seventeen weeks would not get through, but that it would be amended to twenty-four weeks, which was the same as in his own Bill. On those terms he agreed to act as Treasurer. Once again, Montefiore was wrong. David Alton's Bill was talked out. If Alton had agreed to twenty-four weeks, it would probably have been a different story. But Alton wanted to save more foetuses out of the 150,000 killed each year by abortion than the thirty or forty which are aborted over twenty-four weeks' gestation.

Montefiore's Bill had been his first real insight from the inside into the workings of Government. But it was not his first excursion into government waters. Over the years government ministers saw much of Montefiore: he had had dealings with the Secretaries of State for the Environment and for Energy, in connection with pollution and conservation; with the Secretary of State for Transport when he was chairman of the Independent Commission on Transport; with the Secretary of State for Industry when he was Bishop of Birmingham. As Chairman of the Board for Social Responsibility, he saw ministers in the Home Office over the Police Act, over immigration and over abortion; in the DHSS over the Warnock Report; in the Foreign Office over disarmament and over South Africa; he spoke to the Lord Chancellor over divorce law, and the Minister of Defence over 'no first use' of nuclear weapons. Most of these visits were informal and private and all the better for that. Montefiore does not claim to have changed the policy of Her Majesty's Government by any of these talks, but at least it was possible in most cases to discuss the real issues in a relaxed and civilized way, whereas resolutions of the General Synod seemed to provoke a purely defensive attitude on the part of the minister.

Montefiore acted as a bishop of the National Church. He believes in this and shrinks from the notion of disestablishment, which he thinks would marginalize the witness of the Church and turn it into a sect. But he is not tinged with Erastianism. The difficulties of holding his position are neither new nor comfortable. The more frankly a National Church gives expression to purely national moods and emotions, the less distinctively Christian it may be. That does not mean that national moods and emotions ought not to be religiously expressed, but only that their expression, however noble and energizing, is not specifically Christian. Yet it is no small advantage that the expression should be cast into Christian moulds.

Montefiore has walked the delicate path well. On the one hand he has been able to give religious expression to national moods and emotions (moral, social, political); and on the other he has carried to the nation those truths which are properly called 'spiritual' in that they have no lower source than the Divine Spirit Himself. Because of his own inner conviction and direction as a Christian, he has never been dismayed by the most untoward aspects of human affairs. He is fully persuaded that God has a righteous purpose in the universe, and that, in the long run, His purpose will be achieved. In short Montefiore insists upon bringing this outlook into relation with his faith in providence, in the moral law and in the Holy Spirit. That is why he has not been carried away by the currents of public opinion, however vehement, but has had a clear perception of personal duty. Moreover, he has assurance of divine assistance given in response to his prayer in all the secular perplexities with which he is faced.

This makes for a formidable and uncomfortable figure. There is enough of the Old Testament prophet about him to disturb and challenge people. There is enough of the New Testament preacher in him to arrest attention and follow a path of reconciliation. This is not easy in today's world and English society. There is talk everywhere of a crisis in and of authority. When he read Archbishop Robert Runcie's booklet *Authority in Crisis?*[22] he was struck by Runcie's point that the main need today is for the authority of a conductor to harmonize individual and group excellencies in an orchestral symphony – 'a framework of common values which enables personal talents to be co-ordinated for the good of all'.

But Montefiore asks, 'What if there are no common values? What if the strings are playing different pieces in a different style from the brass and wind? What of those who prefer cacophony to symphony?' It is not only liberalism that has to have commonly held moral assumptions to flourish; it is necessary for *any* form of society other than dictatorship. And Montefiore goes on to make an important statement:

> If there is a crisis of authority in Britain today it is because we have no such commonly held moral assumptions. We have privatized values. Nowadays they are neither right nor wrong, simply options for choice, like brands in a supermarket. There is no more urgent need for the wellbeing of our country than to win common acceptance of agreed values which can make possible true community and good relationships between people of different interests and ages.

In all kinds of ways and on all manner of issues Montefiore

distinguished between right and wrong whilst expressing the difficulty in choosing between right and wrong on certain topics. To a lady writing about sex before marriage he replied, 'Let me make it perfectly clear. The teaching of the Church of England is that pre-marital sex is wrong, and that a girl should be chaste and a virgin at her wedding.' But the pastor came into play when faced with a couple who were not virgins wishing to marry in church.

Montefiore supported Victoria Gillick in her 1985 action against West Norfolk and Wisbech Area Health Authority and the DHSS. He believed that in the moral confusion of the age it was beginning to be accepted that girls would have sexual intercourse under the age of consent and this would not be regarded as wrong. Montefiore thought it was deplorable for emotional and physical reasons and considered the time had come to challenge the assumption.

He was severely critical of the Government's advertising campaign over AIDS. The Board for Social Responsibility issued a helpful booklet *AIDS: Some Guidelines for Pastoral Care*.[23] Whatever the topic, Montefiore never remained on the impersonal plane. Everything was rooted and lessons were learnt. He recalls being at the BBC for a programme about AIDS:

> In the reception room beforehand I was introduced to the other participants. One of them I was told had AIDS. I felt an instinctive desire to keep my distance. I knew that I had to force myself to go forward, be friendly and to touch him. It was quite an effort to shake his hand, but I am glad I made the effort. If I, who had a great deal of knowledge about AIDS and knew that it was not infectious – if I had these reactions, is it surprising that others without my advantage feel an instinctive abhorrence?

Pastoral care is always personal and not wholly dependent on or restricted by textbook formulae or ecclesiastical regulations. They are there to guide and suggest the limits of action. But problems have a habit of slipping outside the boundaries. Bishop Stephen Verney, a former Bishop of Repton who had known Montefiore since they were students at Westcott House, has a personal recollection:

> What I chiefly remember is a loyal friend – alive, human
> and impetuous. I remember him coming and taking a
> retreat for me, based on the words 'Holy, holy, holy, Lord
> God of hosts'. After that retreat I remember feeling that
> nothing more could be said! This is one side of Hugh – a
> deep spiritual understanding which goes along with his
> political concern. My most precious memory is of how he
> stood by me at the time of my marriage to my present
> wife, Sandra. She was divorced and her husband still alive.
> I was therefore the first bishop in the Church of England to
> marry a divorced person. It took two years of anguished
> discussion to reach this decision, and Hugh was one of the
> people who helped me most. He didn't advise me one way
> or the other, but pushed me into making a decision, and
> then stood by me in that decision. He came to my
> marriage service, dressed as a bishop and read the gospel.
> This could have led him into hot water during the
> following months, while controversy raged around us. In
> fact our critics did not discover that Hugh had been there,
> though he would have stood up for me if necessary.

16 Theologian – Explorer and Stabilizer

Bishops are chosen for their gifts, not for their deficiencies. Montefiore said his head reeled from the roles expected of him: *alter Christus*, *alter apostolos*, *pastor pastorum*, guardian of the faith, focus of unity, 'true symbol of the personal presence of Christ', sign of the universal Church, representative of the Church. 'Even if I am no longer allowed a monarch's throne, I still have to occupy a teacher's stool, a judge's tribunal, an office armchair, a committee seat, the eucharistic *cathedra*.'[1] He always took heart from Montaigne's warning, 'You will never be seated except on your bottom.'

It takes a strong man to embrace the new without neglecting the old. Would Montefiore have time, as Bishop of Birmingham, to keep up his reading and continue to embark on theological exploration? The answer was an emphatic yes. Could the words of the Bishop of Salisbury, John Austin Baker, be justified? 'If the world lasts long enough for an authoritative assessment to be made of Anglican theology in the second half of the twentieth century, one of the very few figures to be recognized as truly great will be Hugh Montefiore.'[2]

Montefiore continued to write articles and to review books in various periodicals as well as producing pamphlets and contributing to *The Bishopric*. There were books too.

Geoffrey Wainwright, Professor of Systematic Theology at Duke University, North Carolina, was a student at Caius and Montefiore was his director of studies:

As I have read Hugh's later writings, coming from his time in the parish ministry and the episcopate, they have seemed to me to pass with a certain immediacy from the Scriptures to a present application. That is perhaps natural for a biblical scholar and preacher. My own cast of mind leads me on a more circuitous route through doctrinal development, hermeneutical theory and systematic patterning, and I do not always come out at the same point as Hugh. But I always find him refreshing and provocative.

A good example of Professor Wainwright's 'certain immediacy' was Montefiore's book *Jesus across the Centuries: His Relevance to Our Problems*.[3] The basis of the book was articles he had written for theological journals to which access was limited and élitist. They were revised for publication as a book, leavened and lightened by Montefiore's pastoral experience. The approach was that of the teacher, only occasionally marred by broad sweep or slogan. For the most part Montefiore successfully endeavoured to expound and explore the teaching of Jesus and, by careful textual references, to point out the relevance of that teaching to contemporary problems. That is not to say that he was providing answers to intractable problems by reference to biblical texts.

The 1980s were to be a time when talk about God entered the public domain. The decade opened with Don Cupitt's *Taking Leave of God*,[4] which received much notice. Cupitt still functioned as a clergyman because he found Christianity helped him in authentic living. Yet he had reached the conclusion that God did not really exist outside his idea of him. God had for him no objective reality. In sum, he held that science had outdated Christianity.

Three years on another book caused theological tremors, though they were less strong because its authors were less well-known and were not their own publicists. John Hick, formerly Professor of Theology in Birmingham University, and Michael Goulder, a lecturer in the Extra-Mural Department at Birmingham University, wrote *Why Believe in God?*[5] In this book John Hick argued about the existence of God, in whom he passionately believed,[6] with Michael Goulder, who had ceased to believe in God at all. He had been an Anglican priest but had resigned his Orders.

Montefiore used the pages of *The Bishopric*, in November 1983, to consider the arguments and convictions which had led Hick and Goulder to different conclusions. Montefiore explained:

> there are good grounds for believing in God, and . . . it is even probable, on rational grounds, that God does exist. There is no proof, and atheism always remains a possibility. But I would hold that it is wildly improbable. It is always possible that there is no explanation for the universe – it could be just a brute fact, ultimately meaningless.

Don Cupitt's BBC2 television series, *The Sea of Faith*,[7] led Montefiore to write another article, *The Don Cupitt Show*,[8] in which he summed up the Cupitt case – mechanized nature, a demythologized Bible, a totally secular world, no absolute religion, and a pluralist society:

> For him [Cupitt] he prefers the basic Christian ethic without any dogma. God is our value system, the sum of our hopes. I don't know what he would say if someone said they would prefer the principle 'Evil be thou my good', for he is the supreme individualist, averring: 'When I look into the void of the modern situation, and I see that it's entirely up to me what I am to make of myself and my life, then I find I need religion to give me a path.' But someone else mightn't.

Montefiore thought it significant that Don Cupitt's historical thinkers, such as Wittgenstein, Nietzsche, Marx, Kierkegaard, were lonely individualists. Cupitt had been Dean of Emmanuel College, Cambridge, for almost twenty years. Montefiore, with his own experience at Caius, felt that such an atmosphere produces lonely individualism, however combative and convivial high-table conversation might be. There were those who repeatedly called for action to be taken against Cupitt. Montefiore was not one of that number.[9]

The reason why Montefiore devoted, and continues to devote, much time to these matters is quite simple. The question of God is the most important theological question that there is – far more important than questions about heresy or biblical criticism or new forms of worship. He placed before his own clergy in Birmingham, and before much wider audiences by his pen, the commendability of faith leading to belief in God.

In 1984 Montefiore was on a three months' sabbatical at the Church Divinity School of the Pacific in Berkeley, California, getting his own theological thoughts in order ready for an important book, when a volcano erupted in England, the lava flow of which still disturbs. On 14 March 1984 the appointment was announced of David Edward Jenkins, Professor of Theology at Leeds University, to be the new Bishop of Durham in succession to John Habgood, who had been translated to the Archbishopric of York. It was expected that his episcopate would be a lively and innovative one. He was already fifty-nine and was likely to leave no time in making his views known. It was not expected that there would be a heresy hunt before his consecration. Almost too articulate for his own good, and with a penchant for phrase-making that has devastating effects on occasions, there was yet something unusually refreshing about his intellectual candour and theological openness. Dogmas, St Augustine said, are fences round the mystery. In interviews on television it appeared that Jenkins was set on pulling down the fences. This was not the case and, indeed, he was not known as a radical theologian at all. Yet the way in which he presented his thoughts in cascades of words was new to the wider Church.

David Jenkins knew the risks of being misreported or misquoted, but that would not deter him. So he expressed his philosophical convictions and doctrinal doubts with robustness and in illustrative language which rammed home the points he wished to make. Moreover, although there were subtleties in his arguments, he left audience or reader in no doubt about what he believed concerning some of the tenets of faith and doctrine such as the Virgin Birth, the Resurrection, miracles.

That summer between David Jenkins' nomination and consecration, the controversy in the Church – even encroaching on the State – was greater than that surrounding *Honest to God*, twenty years earlier. One perspective was missed. David Jenkins had spent his ministerial 'career' outside the established ecclesiastical network,[10] whilst being well-known inside it as speaker, lecturer, member of working parties and of committees. On moving to Durham he regarded himself as only then 'coming into the Church'. He saw it as an opportunity, but not for keeping the Church of England going. 'The Church of England is so insignificant and unimportant – it doesn't matter.' David Jenkins brought God into the limelight and forced people to reconsider their positions. To those on the evangelical extremities he was a heretic. That did not over-trouble him, except that replying to them in their entrenched positions was time-consuming. More important were those on the fringes of religion, who felt they could respond to his views, even affirm them, who were drawn to the Church.

David Jenkins was consecrated. There was no heresy trial. Instead, it looked as if there would be ordeal by Synod in February 1985 over questions of the Virgin Birth and the empty tomb. The General Synod asked the House of Bishops to reflect on the debate and to report back.

Montefiore did not speak in the debate; he was worried by it. It was as if the Church of England was becoming a sect of the 'You must believe what I believe' variety. Montefiore had joined the national Church of England, not a sect. It should embrace all those who want to be Christians. That is why he was disturbed by the blinkered dogmatism of evangelical and Anglo-Catholic alike. He criticized the Bishop of London (Graham Leonard), who had spoken temperately in the Synod debate but had written in a newspaper article, quoting the words of the Nicene Creed: 'Any bishop who says these words while in his heart allowing room for doubt, fudging or equivocation, should really be somewhere else.'[11]

The House of Bishops grasped the theological nettle in a way that would probably not have been possible earlier. Credit should go to the Archbishop of Canterbury (Robert Runcie). The House of Bishops contained men of strong and opposing views. If there was little meeting of minds on some issues, there was a growing feeling of collegiality, which had not been the case under previous archbishops. Runcie enabled this to happen.

At the Bishops' Meeting in June 1985 it was agreed that a small group should prepare a report. Conflict was built into the group by its membership. The Bishop of Salisbury (John Baker) chaired it; the other bishops were London (Graham Leonard), St Albans (John Taylor), Bristol (Barry Rogerson) and Chester (Michael Baughen). Although Montefiore was not a member of this small group his comments to it via the Bishop of Salisbury (and sometimes direct to the Archbishop of Canterbury) were frequent, forceful and fruitful. He was at all times dissecting the argument and disallowing words which were too ambiguous. His critical appraisal was detailed and thorough; his theological acumen acute. The Bishop of Salisbury was grateful.

Here was an opportunity for the Church to 'declare itself', if it would take it. The Church of England has appeared to sit light to doctrine and belief. The word 'appeared' is correct, for the case is rather that the Church of England has not wanted to face the questions of doctrine and belief. When crises have threatened or engulfed the Church it has reacted, perhaps reluctantly, but none the less it has acted. The 1921 Conference of the Modern Churchmen's Union on 'Christ and the Creeds' was to some more a receptacle for heresy than a container for valid enquiry. Partly as a result of this, the Archbishop of Canterbury (Randall Davidson) had agreed to a theological enquiry which did not report until 1938. The commission, chaired by William Temple (then Archbishop of York), produced *Doctrine in the Church of England*.[12] It was a masterly report, and one in which divergencies of opinion were accepted, considered and explained. William Temple referred to this in his Introduction:

> In view of my own responsibilities in the Church I think it right here to affirm that I wholeheartedly accept as historical facts the Birth of our Lord from a Virgin Mother and the Resurrection of His physical body from death and the tomb. And I anticipate, though with less assurance, that these events will appear to be intrinsically bound up with His Death when the relations between the spiritual and physical elements in our nature are more completely understood. But I fully recognize the position of those who sincerely affirm the reality of our Lord's Incarnation

without accepting one or both of these two events as actual historical occurrences, regarding the records rather as parables than as history, a presentation of spiritual truths in narrative form.

The Church was not put to the test as to whether or not it had the courage to face the major issues contained in the report, for the Second World War intervened. After the war there was no William Temple to move the debate forward. Canon Law became the preoccupation of a Church beginning to turn in upon itself.

Thirty years on, the Church did not pay deep regard to either the 1976 report, *Christian Believing*, or the 1981 report, *Believing in the Church*. The furore over Montefiore's speech to the Modern Churchmen's Union in 1967 had caused an explosion but had not led to action being taken. The catalyst for new action had come in the form of David Jenkins.

Montefiore was thrown back on his own theological resources, and re-examined his own beliefs. This had to be done, not from an academic ivory tower, but from the bishop's study and, ultimately, from the bishop's *cathedra*. Whilst he had been a bishop, Montefiore had wrestled with credal difficulties. On the virginal conception of our Lord he was genuinely agnostic, which did not mean that he denied it. It was a difficult matter for him. He had come to the conclusion that the best and most honest way was to accept agnosticism. If he had reached the conclusion that the Virgin Birth was untrue, he would have resigned. The question was this: is it, or is it not, part of a bishop's freedom of interpretation that he should deny the truth of a belief which is part of the apostolic teaching of the Church? It is not that he is agnostic about it, but that he denies it. Montefiore could not with integrity uphold something about which he was very uncertain. All he could do was to acknowledge it as the faith of the Church of England and affirm the positive aspect of it. He had an *ex animo* belief in the central doctrines of the Church, those of the Incarnation and the Resurrection. He regarded the virginal conception and the physical resurrection as secondary doctrines, although he in fact believes in physical resurrection.

He was out of sympathy with some of Jenkins' utterances,

and even more so with bishops who would not declare themselves, keeping their doubts to themselves. Belonging to the
Church means that individuals are never as independent or
autonomous as they might suppose. The essential facts of
Christianity would not have been known if it had not been for
their transmission through the traditions of the Christian
Church down the centuries. Most fundamental beliefs depend
on a continuing tradition. At the same time any tradition
depends for its vitality on the free criticism of reflective individuals. The challenge for the bishops was to connect the corporate nature of Christian belief and an individual's interpretation
and understanding of his or her faith.

Montefiore considers that the contemporary Church has a
right to question the traditional beliefs which have come down
to us, not rejecting them, but subjecting them to further examination. Why? First, they were produced in a different culture
and may need to be brought 'up to date' in the light of new
knowledge. Secondly, all statements made by the Church fall
short of ultimate truth.

As Montefiore worked with and listened to the conflicting
voices of fellow bishops on the Resurrection, the empty tomb,
the Incarnation and the virginal conception, he became convinced that it was not possible to produce a 'response' which
showed unanimous agreement between the bishops, and that
any honest response must therefore indicate their differences.
Again and again he emphasized his own position that agnosticism in certain secondary doctrines is admissible. He did not say
that it was admissible to deny them.

The Church of England is Catholic (but not Roman) and
Protestant (but not Genevan): this is its particular glory. If there
was to be no liberty of interpretation, the Church was no longer
Anglican. However, it was right that it should be clear what
comprised its core of belief, leaving the boundary fences in
place, but not immovable.

As the bishops moved towards a conclusion, Montefiore
suggested amendments to two paragraphs which to him reflected more honest reporting. Although he withdrew them on
request, they are illuminating:

As regards belief that Christ's Tomb was empty on the

first Easter Day, we accept that belief in the mystery of Christ's Resurrection (to which we are all committed) is not dependent on the Empty Tomb, about which a Christian may in good faith remain reverently agnostic. The Empty Tomb, however, has been part of the received tradition of the Church, derived from the Holy Scriptures, and we acknowledge that it is the teaching of the Church of England. Most of us (almost all of us?) uphold this belief in the conviction that the Tomb was in fact found to be empty, and we hold that this points to the transformation of the material order in the glory of eternity.

On the human origins of Jesus, we accept that belief in the mystery of the Incarnation, to which we are all committed, does not depend on the Virginal Conception of Our Lord, about which a Christian may in good faith remain reverently agnostic. Nevertheless it has been part of the received tradition of the Church, derived from the Holy Scriptures and included in the Creeds, and we acknowledge that it is the teaching of the Church of England. Most of us uphold it in the conviction that Jesus did not have a human father and as affirming the truth that in Christ God acted to unite with himself our human nature.

The report – 'a statement and exposition' – by the House of Bishops was published in June 1986 and was entitled *The Nature of Christian Belief*.[13] It was a brave and admirable document. The statement of the House of Bishops was short, consisting of only six points. First, they were united in their adherence to the apostolic faith the Church had received and in which it lived. Secondly, the Bishops affirmed their faith in the Resurrection of our Lord as objective reality, both historical and divine, not as a way of speaking about the faith of his followers, but as a fact on which their testimony depends for its truth. Thirdly, as regards belief that Christ's tomb was empty on the first Easter Day, the Bishops acknowledged and upheld this as expressing the faith of the Church of England. Fourthly, they declared their faith in the affirmation of the Catholic Creeds that in Jesus Christ, fully God and fully human, the second person of the Blessed Trinity is incarnate. As for the virginal conception of Jesus, they acknowledged and upheld belief in this as expressing the faith of the Church of England, and as affirming that in Christ God had taken the initiative for our salvation by uniting with himself our human nature. Finally, they accepted wholeheartedly their mutual responsibility and accountability as bishops for guarding, expounding and teaching the faith to which God had led them to commit their lives, and for doing so in ways which would effectively proclaim it afresh to each generation, while at the same time distinguishing in their teaching ideas of theological exploration from beliefs which were the corporate teaching of the Church.

The bishops concluded by saying there must always be a place in the life of the Church for both tradition and enquiry. The relation between them is not simple and never settled, and has always meant that there can be a proper diversity of the understanding and expression of the Christian faith. They concluded: 'Providing we are attentive to the Holy Spirit as it glorifies Jesus and leads us into all truth, this variety which our faith not only allows but fosters need not become a cause of division but can deepen our relationship with God and our understanding of the Gospel.'

It was in the exposition that real differences between the bishops surfaced, and which caused anxiety to some readers of the report. It appeared that some bishops believed the tomb was empty and some did not; some thought Jesus was Joseph's natural son and some that Mary's pregnancy was miraculous. In that sense it was both orthodox and liberal – and that unanimously! The critics missed the point. It was a thoroughly Anglican document – which is not a term of reproach. Its importance should not be diminished. It is likely to stand the test of time.

The report was debated at the General Synod on 6 July 1986. The nature of the debate suggested that Synod had come to bury the Bishop of Durham, not to praise him. How different it turned out! It was the first occasion on which David Jenkins had spoken in Synod – on an issue which was primarily about him! His speech in the debate was again controversial, for he appeared to regard the virginal conception of Jesus and his physical Resurrection as 'knockdown miracles', which he somehow compared to laser beams: a striking phrase but hardly justified by the scriptural evidence. The Bishop of Durham seemed to accuse his fellow Christians of believing in a God who is at best a cult idol, and who (if he actually exists) must be the very devil, if he would bring about these knockdown miracles in connection with Christ but would not use such methods to deliver us from Auschwitz, prevent Hiroshima, overcome famine, or bring about a bloodless transformation of apartheid. David Jenkins received an ovation, rare in Synod.

Montefiore did not speak in the debate. He wrote an article about it, *The Credibility of God*,[14] in which he explained why David Jenkins' statement did not hold water. It was as if God in Christ had not identified himself with suffering and vulnerability:

> if he had not opened himself to evil in its most virulent form, if he had not suffered the consequences and yet been found triumphant over death and evil, then (for me at least) God would not be credible as God: then indeed he would be at best a cultic idol or at worst the very devil.

In the middle of this period Montefiore's own book, *The Probability of God*[15] was published. Before considering it, it is as well to look at Montefiore's method, first as perceived by Basil Moss, a former provost at Birmingham:

> In the spring of 1984 Hugh took a three-month sabbatical or 'study-leave' in California, to write a big book. On his return he handed me the MS and asked me to read it and comment. I did as full a 'crit' as I could. The amount he'd managed to read and digest and quote from recent British and American books, about the origins of the universe, the origins of life, evolutionary theory, biology, etc., was truly amazing. The purpose of his book was to defend, or re-establish, at least the possibility of a theistic account of the development of the physical world, of life, and of man. Can the deliverances of science be interpreted theologically, in terms of God's creative activity? Or are we shut in between total scepticism and pre-scientific 'fundamentalism'? Hugh was re-working the traditional

'argument from design', a fairly heroic venture by a non-scientist Daniel in a den of scientists. I remember that, for me, one of the extraordinary achievements in *The Probability of God* was a re-working in terms of modern scientific debate of one of Hume's *Dialogues*, a philosophical classic. I took leave to doubt whether one scientist in a hundred or more would have read it, and be aware of the (unstated) allusion. Nevertheless I was acutely aware (from my own continuing interest in philosophy) that the weak points in the argument were all in the area which I would call 'philosophical' or 'metaphysical'. There was no sign of awareness of the 'sea-change' in the basic way in which the modern world handles the possibility of theistic or theological assertions: I'm referring to the work by the linguistic philosophers about the priority of a critique of meaning in relation to truth, and to the more recent debates about the nature of language itself. Or perhaps I am saying that I could never be a rationalist of Hugh's kind, being more wary than he of a 'God of the gaps'.

I feel that Hugh was a 'loner' in his intellectual work, rapidly formulating with precision what he wanted to say; and having formulated it, the urgent thing for him is not to *discuss* it in continuing tentativeness, but to *communicate* it. On this hypothesis I was not surprised that – having thanked me warmly for my 'crit' and said he would make a few amendments to his MS – he never suggested I might come round and discuss with him some of the issues I'd raised.

And therefore Hugh was always in danger of a degree of unwarranted dogmatism or certainty. He needed for his own sake the sharpest and most forthright criticism of his output (the sort of treatment he was good at dishing out to other people). When he came to Birmingham as bishop, it was plain to me that this most powerful mind was not being challenged enough: and you have to be very alert and very determined to challenge it. More generally, people in Birmingham were a bit scared to disagree directly and bluntly to his face with any opinion strongly held by Hugh. If you did challenge him, and could sustain your challenge, he tended simply to collapse into silence. This has been seen on TV a time or two.

As I got to know him better and better during his Birmingham years, I perceived increasingly that he is in fact more 'trad' in theology than one might suppose from his Liberal profile. He is in fact apt to base 'radical' conclusions on surprisingly conservative presuppositions. So in Christian ethics he holds what seems to me to be an old-fashioned or traditional view about 'law' and 'natural law' and the nature of conscience, but on this basis will argue for decidedly non-conservative views on sexual ethics. For instance, in recent lectures [1988 in partnership with Jack Dominian][16] he has insisted on a very positive view of the unitive and healing power of heterosexual intercourse in marriage: and then (by a 'leap'?) speaks by analogy of the healing power which can belong to homosexual relationships, a view abhorrent to traditionalists. Or again, he holds a high traditional view about priesthood, and on this basis has argued for a long time for the ordination of women.

It may be that I am so aware of this because of my own theological approach, which sees *all* theology as being 'provisional', able to change radically, culturally determined to some degree, a 'process'. I feel that the theologian (my kind) is always on the move, an explorer, prepared for evolution and change in theological understanding. Hugh, as I see it, has a firm basis of strong commitment to theological truth and tradition, from which he moves to attempts at radical restatement. Is this a long-term effect of his personal conversion from Judaism? Or are there simply different kinds of Christian, on the basis of which there are different ways of theologizing?

If we return to Montefiore's contribution to *Christian Believing*,[17] we see that he does believe in the provisional nature of theology in contrast to the firm and improvisational nature of faith, because the expression of one's beliefs in theological systems must change in different cultures and with new insights and knowledge. However, if the criterion of adequacy, outlined in his essay, is taken seriously, the controls which have kept him 'mainstream', as compared with Robinson, Cupitt, Nineham, *et al.*, can be seen.

In *The Probability of God* Montefiore opened up whole areas for discussion between Christians and non-Christians in a way that so much domestic, in-grown theology failed to do. In tracing the development and nature of the world from its origins to our modern civilization, Montefiore drew on religion and scientific evidence and consulted eminent scientists about their views. He rejected the neo-Darwinism hypothesis as the only way in which evolution took place. It was the exclusivity of the Darwinian dogma which he eschewed. There seemed to Montefiore some process at work whereby matter tended to assemble itself in more complex forms of living beings, not in a straightforward line, but in a way which made it probable that sooner or later *Homo sapiens* would emerge. Only *Homo sapiens*, so far as is known, as a living organism, is capable of conscious moral, spiritual and personal activity. Thus man is the end product of the evolutionary process.

For Montefiore the whole key is the Holy Spirit, working within the universe, within the smallest particle of matter, within the galaxies and stars, within the processes of the planet, and within man himself, made as he is in the image of God.

In *The Probability of God* Montefiore managed to convey a sense of excitement and wonderment at the 'grandeur of God'. His God is never too small. He does not believe that modern science, for the book is about religion and science, can prove the existence of God, but he does believe that the findings of modern science make the existence of God more likely than not.

The book received varied treatment from the critics, though all admired the bold style which managed to be erudite, balanced and thought-provoking at one and the same time. Its appeal was wide, winning the commendation of A.J. Ayer and the *Expository Times*. It was the subject of a *Choices* programme on BBC television. Individual reviewers spotted errors here and there: a few dissented from his thesis, but none did other than praise the worthwhileness of the spirited work. Montefiore argued for a more immanent deity conceived to work within the created order. This, he held, was the most *probable* interpretation of the astonishing features of the world as presented by contemporary science.

Professor Keith Ward noted in a fair-minded, critical review:

> it provides a rich source of material for rethinking the nature of scientific investigation and the relation of God and the world. I mean only to suggest that there remain puzzles and obscurities which need to be further explored. I am inclined to think that the case the book does make is that the notion of 'chance' is unhelpful in understanding nature, at least as any sort of basic inexplicable surd; and that some form of purposive explanation is not ruled out by modern scientific knowledge, but is even positively suggested by it. In some sense of probable, perhaps this does make the existence of God more probable than it might be on some other views of the nature of the universe.[18]

One subject which has exercised Montefiore's mind a great deal is that of the Anglican view of authority. This subject had nudged him throughout his membership of the Doctrine Commission. The General Synod may have dodged its own Church reports on doctrine, but it had to face those being presented to it by the Anglican-Roman Catholic International Commission (ARCIC). One cannot discuss authority without considering episcopacy. When the ARCIC report *Authority in the Church*[19] was published, Montefiore criticized it[20] on the grounds that it described a form of episcopacy which was not the same as Anglicanism had received. He quoted with approval the 1920 Lambeth Conference statement ('Appeal to all Christian People'): 'We greatly desire that the office of a bishop should everywhere be exercised in a representative and constitutional manner.' ARCIC appeared to be moving towards a more authoritarian view of episcopacy. He was jumped on by Professor Henry Chadwick, who rebuked him candidly and courteously.[21]

Montefiore would fight against all attempts to dilute or destroy the traditional ethos and doctrine of each Church. Why could not each Church recognize the other, keep its own integrity and retain its own distinctive ways of expressing truth in faith and order?

Friendship between the Churches was real and growing, but the practical realities of division were as great as ever. Anglicans were debarred from Roman altars, Anglican priests (and bishops) were technically laymen. Roman Catholic dogmas such as the Immaculate Conception and the Assumption were anathema to most Anglicans. On sexual ethics there was a deep divide over contraception and a varied one over abortion and divorce. The times were changing, but obstacles remained. Montefiore's Birmingham diocese had a larger Roman Catholic population than an Anglican one. Relations between the Churches were personally friendly but publicly superficial.

Pope John Paul II's pastoral visit to England in 1982 was welcomed by Montefiore. The warmer spirit between the two Churches became closer. Yet Montefiore, who would have been a useful member of ARCIC, would not let his own Church or the Roman Catholic Church assume a relationship that was not true. He continued to exercise himself on the subject.[22] Then in January 1986 he was frustrated from reaching his cottage on the Welsh borders by a car accident in snow and ice some twelve miles out of Birmingham. He returned home, and in the few days available to him roughed out a book on the subject and wrote most of the argument. Tidying up followed in the odd gaps in his exceptionally busy diary. The Preface was dated St Matthias' Day (14 May) and *So Near and Yet So Far – Rome, Canterbury and ARCIC* was published in September that year.[23]

It was an important book, uncharacteristically (for the Church) swimming against the Liberal-Catholic hopeful tide of sympathy with ARCIC and the uncritical desires to resolve, or mitigate, inherited disagreements with Rome. It was a rational voice too little heard in this particular debate. In a way, Montefiore was trying to alter the hierarchical shape of the Roman Church, which is pyramidical. Power flows from the top to the loyal and submissive subjects at the bottom. Anglicanism attempts authority in the round, with, at its ideal best, authority flowing from the centre, serving and enabling the Church to worship and witness.

In a letter to Fr Edward Yarnold, SJ,[24] Montefiore wrote:

I am very sorry to have given the impression of making a

case against Mary. I can assure you that this was at any rate far from my intention. I really do share with others a real love and veneration for St Mary, because she was chosen for the most honoured role that I can imagine, to bear in her womb the Son of God. Further, she had the prime responsibility for the nurture and upbringing of Jesus, so that Christ's human nature was deeply influenced by her at its most formative stage. I find it hard to see how anyone can love and worship Christ without venerating his Mother.

My chapter on the Mother of God Incarnate tried to deal with matters of a different kind, concerning the head rather than the heart. My love of St Mary does not lead me – in company with most Anglicans – to endorse the Roman Catholic dogmas. There seems no New Testament evidence to support them, and some which points perhaps the other way. I felt I must make this clear in my book. (Incidentally, what means most to me personally is the biblical imagery of St Mary as the Ark of God.)

As Basil Moss explains, Montefiore's own debating and teaching methods struck many people as

very much a 'one-way traffic', a one-man exercise of *magisterium*, in the context of the old distinction between *ecclesia docens* and *ecclesia discens* (though I expect Hugh himself would resist this suggestion). The hearer is to say 'yes' to a combination of reason and authority. Reason and reasonableness were for Hugh a very important part of the authority (which is why it is not unfair to call him a rationalist). He would have been supremely at home in the medieval 'schools' where Abelard and Aquinas did their finest work – first argue it through, examine and answer every rational objection, and promulgate authoritatively what is to be accepted and believed.

This comes over as 'paternalist' to those who have been influenced by the revolution during the last thirty years in how the processes of education – and particularly adult education – are to be understood. One cannot here go into the matter fully, but the process of education is now perceived as much more 'discover-through-dialogue' on the part of the learners, who are not *tabulae rasae*, blank pages, on which the teacher simply writes what he has to communicate. The teacher is perceived to be concerned (more than he was on the old model) to work from and to the experience of the 'taught', who are to be encouraged to grasp and interiorize for themselves what is being asserted. In this way of regarding adult education, communication is seen as much more a two-way traffic, 'from below' as much as 'from above' . . . We felt (he will think us unfair) that he really wanted to *instruct* the laity. Theology and theologizing are not the preserve of the theologians.

So Near and Yet So Far contained an Appendix on the subject of the Ordination of Women to the Priesthood. Montefiore has always been an active campaigner for the cause. In 1978 he edited a book *Yes to Women Priests*.[25] His essay was on the theology of priesthood.

At the General Synod on 8 November 1978 he moved the motion asking Synod to prepare and bring forward legislation to remove the barriers to the ordination of women to the priesthood and their consecration to the episcopate. His was the most powerful speech in favour and that of Graham Leonard, then Bishop of Truro, the most powerful against. The motion was lost:

	Ayes	Noes
House of Bishops	32	17
House of Clergy	94	149
House of Laity	120	106

Montefiore spoke again in the 1984 debate, this time on a motion of the Bishop of Southwark (Ronald Bowlby) asking Synod to bring forward legislation to permit the ordination of women to the priesthood. This time the motion was carried:

	Ayes	Noes
House of Bishops	40	6
House of Clergy	131	98
House of Laity	135	79
Abstentions	5	

Proponents and opponents approached the issue from different directions, with different perspectives. As the leading opponent, Graham Leonard's position was clear: a priest represents Christ as head of His Church. In a 1986 statement he expressed his strong case in this way:

[Ordaining women as priests] undermines and questions the way in which God himself has taught us how to speak to him and know him. I do not believe that it was by accident, but by God's deliberate choice that he chose to reveal himself in a patriarchal society and became man in Christ, as a male. The highest role ever given to any human being was given to a woman, Mary, when she responded to God's call to be the mother of Christ. We cannot disregard these facts to suit our ideas today.

Secondly, the Church of England claims to have continued the ordained ministry as given by God and received from the universal Church. I do not believe it has the right or power to alter it fundamentally without destroying that claim.

In my judgement, the whole approach (and the arguments) of those who press for the ordination of women questions and undermines the revealed nature of the Christian faith, as given by God, not devised by man.

Montefiore urged those who would say that a priest represents Christ carefully to consider what is meant by 'represents'. As Professor Geoffrey Lampe once said: an ambassador represents and acts on behalf of the Queen, but this does not mean that therefore an ambassador must be female. As regards the symbolic aspects of gender, not all men are initiators and leaders, and not all women are mild and obedient. Jesus himself acted in a particularly passive manner in his final days on earth. At the Eucharist, Christ is represented not so much in the figure of the priest, but in the symbols of bread and wine. And if the priest must represent Christ by his maleness, why not also by his appearance and by his Jewishness? In so far as the priest has to represent Jesus (male), at the same time he has also to represent the Church (female). There seems to Montefiore no reason why the male aspect should be emphasized.

There is no emphasis in the scriptures on Christ's maleness, only on his humanity. In the Nicene and Epiphanian Creeds *sarkothenta* (being made flesh) and *enanthropesanta* (being made human) are used, rather than 'being made man'. The word *aner* to define gender was never used of Christ. What matters is that the priesthood should represent the humanity of Christ, not his maleness. His humanity can only be fully represented by having both male and female priests. This is the crux of the matter as far as Montefiore is concerned. A male priesthood was appropriate in the days when women really were represented by men, but now it is inadequate. Those who would cite Paul in justifying the authority of men over women must consider his arguments in their cultural setting and take into account his claim that in Christ there is no male or female. Montefiore cannot understand that those who claim it is part of God's plan for women to be subordinated to men are content to have a woman judge, prime minister, or even monarch.

As regards the unity of the Church, considered to be under threat by the ordination of women, we might well wait for ever for the Orthodox, or even for the Roman Catholics, to agree to ordain women, and the Anglican Church has a proud history of witness to the truth being sometimes more important than unity. In any case, as Montefiore pointed out, even our male orders are not recognized by the Roman Catholic Church, so female orders could not be any the less recognized. As Anglicans we look to the scriptures and to tradition. There is nothing in the scriptures to teach us that the Holy Spirit cannot lead us into a new understanding of the truth, or that it is wrong to do something for the first time. The early Church changed its views radically and caused consternation by admitting Gentiles to baptism.

Montefiore felt that those Churches which had already admitted women to their ministry had found themselves greatly enriched by so doing. How can we doubt the fact that there are many devout women who feel a strong call to the priesthood? Are they all mistaken? His advocacy of the ordination of women had been long-standing and persistent. He had never been one of the activists in the Movement for the Ordination of Women, but he was a president[26] of the interdenominational Society for the Ministry of Women in the Church. This society was convinced that women as well as men should be eligible for ordination to the full ministry of Word and Sacrament. It drew its speakers and supporters from all denominations and reported on worldwide developments.

In 1980 a woman priest from the Episcopal Church in the USA (ECUSA) was due to receive hospitality in Montefiore's house. Before she came he took the precaution of finding out from his registrar and chancellor[27] the legality of her celebrating the Holy Communion in his private chapel, which was, of course, unconsecrated ground. He was told that he could not legitimately invite her to do so, but if she asked for his permission he could legitimately give it, providing that she did not use the Book of Common Prayer but one of her ECUSA rites. In fact she did so request, and Montefiore gave her permission.

In May 1987 Montefiore preached at the ordination to the priesthood of Dr Susan Cole-King, daughter of the late Bishop Leonard Wilson, one of his predecessors in the see of Birmingham. The service took place at All Angels, off Broadway, New York.

I conclude this portion with some words of Bishop John Baker:

> If I were to try to identify the golden thread running through Hugh's theology, I would say this. He is a true theologian because the heart of all his concerns is God. He is a Christian theologian, because he finds the key to the mystery of God's work in the universe in the life of Christ.
> In the Orthodox Church to be a 'theologian' is a matter not just of intellectual endeavour but of love and prayer. It is no accident that a phrase which occurs again and again in Hugh's writings to describe the deep centre of God's own being and the destiny of our own sanctification as God's children is 'self-effacing love'. This key concept was there back in the days of *Soundings*, and it has been there ever since, worked out not only in thought but in cogent argument for the infinite value of every human being, whether it be women oppressed by men, or black oppressed by white, or the viable foetus despised and rejected by seemingly everyone. In his 1983 Pastoral Letter, 'Risen with Healing in His Wings', Hugh wrote, 'No Christian can will another human being to suffer

pain.' That has been the demanding issue of his honesty of thought.

It has its roots, dare one say, in his being a child of the ancient, persecuted people of God, for whom he has spoken so eloquently to the Christian world. The human depth of his theology springs, I believe, from his decisive awareness of having been 'laid hold of by Christ'. 'By my realization,' he once wrote, 'that God has done all this for me, just as I am, I can accept myself, just as I am' – and, we may add, accept all others, just as they are, and glorify God for them.

It is to the 'child of the ancient, persecuted people of God' that we now turn.

There is no doubt that Montefiore's conversion was costly. There was a price to be paid. It was not simply a question of severed relationships. Deep down his Jewishness was intact, for that was his birthright, but occasionally he found himself on the horns of a religious dilemma. He had lived through the age of the Holocaust. In 1983 an Auschwitz exhibition was held at the Church of St George in the East, Stepney. Montefiore was asked to give a Lent lecture to the clergy of the Stepney area at the time of the exhibition, on 'The Church and the Jews'. This took place on 24 February 1983 and the lecture was privately printed.

Preparing the lecture made Montefiore search the scriptures as well as the Church's record. Whilst accepting that the Holocaust was carried out by Nazis, whose creed was anti-Christian, he knew that it could never have taken place had it not been for the theological thinking of Christendom from its inception as regards the Jews. In his lecture he traced antisemitism back even to the words attributed to Christ in the Gospels, although he stressed that it was the *interpretation* of the words which was at fault. The lecture received a great deal of publicity from Jew and Gentile alike.

Montefiore feels that it is unreasonable to expect the Jews to convert to Christianity. Christianity has been the cause of too much suffering to the Jewish people throughout the ages. A few individuals like himself may be called to respond explicitly to the Gospel, but the *Logos*, the Word of God, which was incarnate in Jesus Christ, was revealed also to the prophets who preceded Jesus and to those who have lived since:

> Other religions are authentic in so far as they are implicit Christianities, provisional and partial, eventually at the Last Day to be superseded by explicit Christianity. The further they move along the way of divine grace, the closer they come to their incorporation into the Christian Church.

Montefiore's Jewishness is an essential part of his being. He is passionate in his defence of Jews and highly critical of the ways in which they have been treated by the Christian Church. At times he finds it hard to feel at home in a Church which is, seemingly, full of Gentile assumptions, whereas the early Church comprised both Jew and Gentile, and both are essential to its well-being.

As a Christian, he retains his Jewish sense of 'chosenness', as belonging to the chosen people of God. In responding to the draft of *Jewish-Christian Guidelines for the Anglican Communion*,[28] which was to have been considered by the 1988 Lambeth Conference, he urged the removal of passages which seemed to imply that the Jewish religion was a parallel religion and that Christians should pray that Jews should remain faithful to the Torah. He pointed out that the Torah was not of as much relevance to Liberal Jews as to the Orthodox in any case.

Montefiore never minimizes the difference between Christians and Jews. The differences are real and stark:

(a) Jews are offended by the doctrine of the Trinity, which they believe is incompatible with the Unity of God.
(b) Christians believe that God was incarnate in Jesus Christ which Jews believe offends against the Second of the Ten Commandments.
(c) Christians believe that through Christ they have free access to the Father: Jews claim this as their birthright.
(d) Christians believe that the law is no longer binding upon them while Jews (Orthodox ones at any rate) believe that all those who are Jewish, together with proselytes, should keep it.

The New Testament indicates two roads by which people came to Christ. There was the road of the Jew, the road of history, by which disciples of Moses moved out of their ancestral theism into Christianity, finding in the Incarnate the climax of divine self-revelation, the key of Israel's history, the fulfilment of prophecy; and there was the road of the Gentiles, the road of the conscience, which led the victims of polytheism through spiritual bankruptcy and moral despair, to the feet of the Redeemer, in whom was proclaimed the remission of sins and who brought life and immortality to light through the Gospel.

We have seen that Montefiore's faith in Christ was neither a consequence nor a corollary of faith in God. It was more personal, powerful, pervading and profound. There was the vision to which Montefiore's response was compelling and final. Both image and experience remain deep and inviolate, acting as an inner resource and steady inspiration. Yet he is ever mindful that he became a Christian as a fulfilled Jew. He still regards Judaism as a living faith, believing that faithful Jews are very close to the heart of God. But how can he not pray that his brothers and sisters after the flesh will find that more excellent way than the Torah that God has shown him?

17   *Living Tornado with a Human Face*

More than any other bishop in recent times, Montefiore combines qualities that are not often found in a single person. And these were tested at Birmingham. He arrived with a well-established reputation for liberal orthodoxy and wide learning. He was recognized as a stimulating teacher and a learned divine. His counsel, always interesting and often witty, and varied theological learning were at the disposal of the diocese. He soon came to understand the difficult conditions of pastoral work in an industrial diocese. As a speaker, teacher and preacher he was indefatigable. Those in need of personal and spiritual help soon realized that the well ran deep, and there was much on which they could draw.

Those who sought Montefiore's counsel refer to his spiritual realism. He was quick to strip away the protective layers and the mask that is used by those who cannot stand too much reality. His object was not to find packaged solutions or to provide simplistic answers to the problem. If there was a practical remedy it would be identified and pursued. That may avert or conquer an immediate crisis, leaving the spiritual malady awaiting treatment. Here Montefiore was sensitive and tentative. The care and cure of souls is both a privilege and a burden. That is why he took his cares each day to his chapel. It was a place where silence mingled with words. The activity centre of the diocese was Montefiore's study. The sight of him, telephone in hand, desperately searching for a piece of paper, calling for his long-suffering secretary to come and find it for him, is memorable. Here ideas sprang to life and blossomed in a moment, without any visible sign of a seed having been planted, cultivated and nurtured. Suddenly the full-grown plant was there. But the still centre of the diocese was his chapel. Day by day the needs of the diocese and particular people in it were held before God. He really prayed that God's will should prevail – which meant that man's, including his, might not! Giving the Bishop of Norwich's Anne French Memorial Lecture on 'God and Mental Illness' he closed with words that place in perspective his views on the spiritual aspect of pastoral care. Lose this dimension and the bishop, priest or counsellor is left with a series of remedies and advice which rely solely on human resources:

> And so I return to the point from which I set out upon this journey, the vision of our redemption and our eternal destiny, and God's purpose in creating the world and in enabling human beings to evolve who are capable of being with him for ever in heaven. We need to help everyone so far as possible so that each is relieved of excessive pain and distress. But we dare not say that everyone has a right to happiness, nor that the most important thing in life consists of our feelings. The most important thing in life is our fitness for our eternal destiny. Our faith and steadfastness are more important than our immediate feelings and our ability to feel joy and happiness. Of course the Christian does thank God for all happiness and joy that he gives and for the gift of the Holy Spirit which is in earnest for what is to come. But our final destiny lies in eternity, when we are raised up in a different kind of body to the one we have now, and which is not subject to mental illnesses. Meanwhile we do all that we can to overcome this and every form of sickness and ill.[1]

From his study Montefiore was an imaginative innovator. *Festina lente* was a foreign concept to him. Bishop Lesslie Newbigin,[2] Minister of Winsom Green United Reformed Church, recalls one of Montefiore's clergy complaining 'that he "shoots from the hip", but that is not always a bad thing for the Church

Militant to do!' The Church Militant is an appropriate expression. Under Montefiore the Church gained confidence. There
would be celebration and joy; there would be praise and thanks-
giving; there would be a desire to learn more about the faith so
the laity could be God's people in the world.

Once an idea had formed in Montefiore's mind, action was
almost simultaneous. Vision, thought and action were interrelated in his episcopate and resulted in a diocese on the move.

Canon Lorys Davies of Birmingham Cathedral received a
letter from him on 12 July 1984. It read:

> I have a date in June 1986 for a diocesan pilgrimage to
> Canterbury. The Archbishop will be free that Saturday.
> We shall have a Eucharist in the Cathedral. I should be
> grateful if you are willing to be in charge of these
> arrangements . . .

The reply was briefer:

> *Pilgrimage to Canterbury*
> Yes, of course I'll take charge of the arrangements. Should
> be quite an occasion.

The pilgrimage bandwagon was in motion. The planning
was extensive. A sense of excitement had to be fostered. The
Church Militant in Birmingham had to be seen crowding the
streets of Canterbury. The Church quiescent could be van-
quished if the day of pilgrimage matched the fever of antici-
pation. Special stick-pin badges and brooches were designed;
commemorative chalices and patens to be used on the day were
produced by the Bourneville College of Art; a competition for
'a song for Canterbury' was launched; pilgrim crosses would be
worn; Canterbury bells wrought to distribute; commemorative
covers for stamping at Canterbury were issued.

The theme of the pilgrimage was 'Taking our Past into our
Future'. Each pilgrim had a 'pilgrimage passport' and souvenir
wallet containing a brochure, Bible reading pamphlet and other
items. There were journey workbooks and pilgrimage pens for
the children. On the day, 21 June 1986, 3,000 pilgrims travelled
to Canterbury: some on a chartered pilgrim train, others in a

fleet of coaches, a few even walked. All assembled at the
County Cricket Ground for a walk through the streets of
Canterbury to the Eucharist at the Cathedral. Canon Lorys
Davies relates an amusing incident:

> At 1.30 p.m. the pilgrims were due to set off from the
> County Ground, led by the mayor of Canterbury and the
> bishop. Every effort had been made to pace the journey
> but no one could be absolutely certain that every pilgrim
> would get into the cathedral by 2.30 p.m. Perhaps
> fractionally before 1.30 p.m. I went to Bishop Hugh and
> said, 'We're ready to go.' His immediate retort was:
> 'There's still a minute and a half to go.' This time I
> retorted: 'We're off.' And we went. He joined us. We
> started on time.

With Salvation Army band and church banners waving, the
pilgrims marched to the Mother Church of the Anglican Communion. There was something special about the atmosphere in
the cathedral. All seating had been removed so the thousands
crammed into the nave, body to body. There was a tremendous
feeling of unity. The Archbishop of Canterbury (Robert Runcie) was received by spontaneous applause. The worship was
uplifting; the pilgrims were strengthened and renewed. In the
afternoon there were optional activities but the focus of all the
planning following Montefiore's vision was, in some words of
the Pilgrimage Collect, to 'kindle in our hearts gratitude for the
past and hope for the years ahead'.

The day had begun in Birmingham at 7.30 a.m. and finished
there at 12.30 a.m. Canon Lorys Davies has a final memory:

> Pilgrimage evening left me somewhat bewildered and
> punch drunk. It was hard to believe that '*it*' was over. As
> part of the process of unwinding I went to visit a pilgrim
> in the local hospital. He'd fainted in the cathedral and been
> unable to travel home. It was a visit which made that
> special day for others so very special for me.
>
> I'd met him first in Birmingham Cathedral some six
> weeks previously when he told me he was going on the
> pilgrimage and added: 'Are you? I'm wearing the Cross,'

opening his coat.

During the service in Canterbury Cathedral by the strangest of coincidences (or was it?) I presented him with his Canterbury Bell. Now we were meeting again, this time in Casualty. This time he was clothed only in a white sheet and . . . the wooden cross on the gold chain.

Another initiative in 1986 was a diocesan and Free Church pilgrimage to the Holy Land in the September. By coincidence the Roman Catholics in Birmingham would be in Israel with their archbishop at the same time, so there were opportunities for meeting. It was Montefiore's third visit and a memorable one for him and for the other pilgrims. He was in Hebron, the local blackspot, with Israeli troops by Rachel's Tomb, as news of the terrible Handsworth riots came through. It was hard for Montefiore to be so far from his diocese at such a time. He visited Neve Shalom (Oasis of Peace), which is a place where Jews, Arabs and Christians live together in a small community.

Of all pictures one is particularly memorable. It was in the Sower's Bay under the Mount of Beatitudes. If one gets one's feet wet and paddles into the Sea of Galilee in the centre of the bay one can read aloud the parable of the Sower in an ordinary voice and be heard all round the bay. In the Gospels Jesus got into a boat and the people were lining the bay. There is a splendid picture of Montefiore reading the parable there to put this to the test.

Mother Margaret Angela, NSSJD, has another memory of the visit:

I was visiting Jerusalem at the invitation of the RC Sisters of the Congregation of Our Lady of Sion and my private visit coincided with the last few days of an ecumenical pilgrimage to Israel from the diocese of Birmingham. Bishop Hugh telephoned the Ecce Homo Convent and arranged to come over with some of the other 'pilgrims'. The fact that my bishop actually came to visit me rather than vice versa was noted by the RC sisters and has been referred to by them on occasions since! That is just one example of the sort of human touch that Bishop Hugh demonstrated in his ministry.

Another creative initiative was *Live, Learn, Share*, 1984–6. Canon Ian Bennett, Diocesan Training Officer, was responsible for putting flesh on the bones of Montefiore's idea. The purpose of *Live, Learn, Share* was to give confidence and articulacy to lay Christians. Canon Bennett says:

> It was Hugh's idea, and I think it worked because by then a group of diocesan officers had grown sufficiently used to him to be able to argue and negotiate with him about what was practical. Practical plans combined with his very positive and inspirational leadership meant that things happened!

Of the three activities, 'Learning' was the most popular and the most successful. Canon Bennett ponders why:

> Many lay groups had a mental block to overcome when they tried to move to 'Living' because they thought it meant more discussion rather than planning for action on a social/political issue or the life of prayer . . . Our busy church lives tend to exclude the secular world, and often ignore the ministries which Christian men and women perform in and through their secular work.
>
> When it came to 'Share' most people recognized that this meant action. Evangelism is something that many Christians feel we ought to do, and often feel guilty because we are not doing it. 'Share' was the phase of the programme which most left until last and fewest attempted. Perhaps we needed more help to explore why we feel ambivalent towards it. Is it simply sloth, lack of knowledge, or English embarrassment at public displays of enthusiasm, or is there a deeper unease which needs to be articulated and explored? In spite of the fears and inhibitions which discouraged many parishes, some brave ones tackled 'Share'. One parish arranged a full-scale mission, and several months after the programme ended one or two parishes are still asking for leaflets about sharing the Faith. So some healthy seeds have been planted . . .

Although this is the television age, when a picture is said

to be more powerful than a thousand words, one significant lack amongst most church members is our inability to discover faith in non-verbal, non-cerebral ways . . . Many of our controversies in the church and our difficulties in sharing faith with those outside might be greatly eased if we could all learn that religion and religious truth belong to the right as well as the left side of the brain. Music, drama, dance, poetry, painting, sculpture need to be seen as ways of communicating truth and not merely decoration.

The sights of the diocese were always raised beyond Birmingham. The Malawi link was already established when Montefiore arrived. In 1985 he responded to an appeal by the Bishop of North Kigezi (Y.K. Ruhindi) for bicycles and hoes. The hoes were more like mattocks and the bicycles were 'Gazelles' produced in Nottingham. They had double crossbars. £21,511 was raised. Sixty bicycles and ten thousand hoes were sent.

By the middle of his Birmingham episcopate, changes 'at the top' had occurred, and Montefiore was able to appoint his own men to senior positions. In 1982 Michael Whinney, whom Montefiore had known as Archdeacon of Southwark, succeeded Mark Green as Bishop of Aston. His stay was short, for he was appointed Bishop of Southwell in 1985.[3]

Then Montefiore appointed Colin Buchanan, Principal of St John's College, Nottingham, doing what Mervyn Stockwood had done for him. It was a courageous appointment. Colin Buchanan had had public disagreements with Montefiore in the General Synod. He was a leading evangelical, insisting on the primacy of the Bible in Christian theology. He had turned himself into a liturgiologist. The Grove Press was his initiative. Some thought of him as an *enfant terrible*. He was opposed to the Establishment. In two ways he resembled Montefiore: he thought and moved at a very rapid pace. Montefiore invited him to be his episcopal colleague.

There were new archdeacons for Aston and for Birmingham. John L. Cooper (Aston) had been a prison chaplain and parish priest in inner-city Birmingham; John F. Duncan (Birmingham) had been university chaplain at Birmingham and parish priest in suburban Birmingham.

Montefiore has never been what one might call 'churchy'. Being Bishop of Birmingham meant knowledge and interest in everything that the capital of the Midlands represented. One of his moves, after his enthronement, was to write to Michael Edwardes, Managing Director of British Leyland:

> So many of the people under my pastoral care are employed by British Leyland that I wondered whether it would be possible for me to come and meet some of your directors? . . . I am naturally intensely interested in the welfare of your group of companies.

Meetings were arranged with the major members of the group, including Ray Horrocks, Managing Director of Austin Morris, Harold Musgrove, Manufacturing Director, and Pratt Thompson, Managing Director, of Jaguar Rover Triumph. It looked as if British Leyland were going to give Montefiore the routine treatment for 'top' visitors. Montefiore disabused them of any such notion. This was no ordinary bishop. Writing to Ray Horrocks, he said he would like to meet all levels, including trade unionists, 'for it is our job to relate the Gospel to industry and not merely to be concerned with pastoral matters or individuals'.

Birmingham was, and still is, heavily dependent upon the metal manufacturing industries and in particular the motor industry. This was prone to industrial unrest and the word 'Longbridge' became synonymous with strife and strike. Michael Edwardes had been appointed to streamline production. In the autumn of 1984 a number of different issues – pay, conditions and the future of British Leyland – were heading for collision. By the end of October British Leyland was moving inexorably towards a strike. Montefiore wrote to Michael Edwardes offering to mediate. He also issued a press statement referring to the consequences for the West Midlands if British Leyland collapsed. By personal contact, public statement and references in the press, Montefiore did all he could to bring the issues before the public. He was no politician in a mitre. He dealt with the larger issues and no 'side' could claim him for their own. When the Austin Rover pay strike neared crisis point, the moral issues behind the stoppage were paraded by

Montefiore.[4] Should workers have held a secret ballot before striking? Should the law have been used to force the unions to hold a secret ballot? There was a last-minute settlement to the dispute. At the beginning of November the Government's plan to privatize the more successful parts of British Leyland was announced. Montefiore wrote to Patrick Jenkin, then Secretary of State for Industry, in these terms:

> While I can understand that the Government want to privatize industry as a matter of policy, I am deeply disturbed at its implication for BL. In the first place, if a modern motor-car industry is to prosper, it must be big. Secondly, there is a very general desire on the part of the work-force to make BL a success. They feel that they owe it to the community to do this. Indeed, they were only persuaded to take the increase of 3.8 per cent with this in mind, because they knew that the needs of the community required it.
>
> If the Government persist in their plans to privatize BL, the men will feel that they have as usual been betrayed. I am very fearful indeed about the bitterness which will ensue. I think that it will result in a calamitous strike which will bring ruin to the whole of the West Midlands. I cannot believe that the Government want that to happen, resulting in between 30 and 40 per cent unemployment.
>
> Men are not to be bought and sold like serfs. That is the impression that has been given to them.

The famous 'teabreak strike' at Longbridge had taken place in November 1981. Again, Montefiore was active in appealing for compromise.[5] His efforts were well-received by many parties to the dispute. Terry Duffy, President of the Amalgamated Union of Engineering Workers, felt it was right for Montefiore to interfere in industrial affairs, for 'this is part of the fabric of Christianity'. Montefiore used any influence he had with anyone to negotiate in such difficult industrial disputes, but his voice was recognized and his appeals were as usual informed by fact, which helped him to be taken seriously. Unfortunately he was not a member of the House of Lords at that time, where his voice would have carried more weight.[6]

Montefiore was helped in his approach to industry by one of the specialist chaplains he had appointed. Canon Denis Claringbull was Industrial Chaplain and found working for Montefiore an exhilarating experience. 'It was rather like working for an unpredictable, yet lovable, whirlwind!' He organized visits to factories, shops, offices and training workshops and meetings with managers and shop stewards. Canon Claringbull used to accompany Montefiore on these visits:

> He would tour the factory at high speed, sometimes leaving his attendants trailing behind, dashing off into odd corners to talk to people who seemed to be tucked away out of sight. He was not afraid to ask searching questions on these occasions and he recognized expert management when he saw it.
>
> He did not suffer fools gladly nor could he be hoodwinked. On one occasion I took him to a training establishment for young people. In the course of his visit he recognized that the same trainees were reappearing as he visited different classes. 'I have already seen you today,' he said. The manager tried to explain that it was change-over period, and that the trainees were moved on to different classes. The bishop, not convinced, suspected that the training establishment was short of trainees, and that the management were trying to cover up the fact.

Montefiore was still suspect for his views on transport and related subjects. His stand was always independent and his concern was always pastoral. Rather like Pope John Paul II making pastoral visits to countries, it in no way muzzles his speaking on moral issues and most aspects of morality have a political dimension. So, for example, after conducting much research, Montefiore spoke of his anxiety about the amount of lead in petrol.[7] He was said to be attacking the Government. He was! For Whitehall's 'inherent conservatism' and the pressures of the oil lobby had prevented a meaningful reduction in lead pollution. On any technical subject he studied, he went to immense trouble to collect and collate substantiating evidence for his views. He received much help from the University of Birmingham, whose doors were always open to him. One of the city's Members of Parliament, Denis Howell, refers to this:

> I know that he took good care to try to check his facts
> before making public statements. In this connection when
> I was the Minister of State at the Environment and
> responsible for environmental policy and pollution
> matters he consuted me about the problems of lead in the
> atmosphere and lead in petrol, as well as lead in water,
> before making a speech based on statistics gained by
> research projects carried out here in Birmingham, and
> especially close to Spaghetti Junction on the M6, which
> was found to have very considerable deposits of lead in the
> playgrounds of some of the neighbouring schools. His
> work in that area was extremely valuable.
>
> I think the general judgement of people in Birmingham
> about his ministry here would be very positive. He was a
> non-stop go go man. Possibly, he wanted action before he
> tested the ground, and occasionally this led him into some
> difficulties, but certainly no one could ever accuse him of
> doing nothing or of being a bishop concerned with the
> status quo. He was an invigorating and exciting bishop,
> and he certainly stimulated many of us, even if we didn't
> always agree with his detailed comments.

Montefiore was one of the bishops much quoted at the time
of the 1984 Miners' Strike.[8] On 27 June he addressed his Diocesan Synod, calling on the Coal Board 'to show a human face,
and to be open to reconciliation; to spell out the principles of pit
closures; and to explain how help will be given to communities
where pits are closed', and on the National Union of Mineworkers 'to admit the need for change; to show that reconciliation is better than violence; and to ensure that the union represents the wishes of the majority of its members'. He wanted
both 'to have a third party to help both sides to negotiate a
settlement in deadlocked dispute', and asked everyone 'to pray
for wisdom, openness and reconciliation'.

During August 1984 Montefiore had a meeting with the
Energy Secretary, Peter Walker, and wrote letters to Neil Kinnock and Len Murray about the dispute. He urged the TUC to
'condemn in unmistakable terms . . . both violence and un-

democratic practices' and offered the Church's help 'in any way' towards resolving the dispute. The reply indicated a feeling that 'nothing short of direct divine intervention would have any impact on either side', though it was hoped that 'something positive may emerge from our forthcoming Congress'.

On 6 October Montefiore addressed his Diocesan Synod for the second time on the dispute, with a view to looking at some of the deeper issues. Here he was drawing attention to the fear that people have of becoming powerless in a land where those in power don't seem to care. Whether that is or is not a right attitude could not erase the feeling which is always strong in close communities where solidarity has been a prevailing feature. Montefiore knew that the deeper issues concerned the real nature of work as against gainful employment: 'We need to consider the proper distribution of the national income between those who produce it and those who for no fault of their own cannot find gainful employment.' It was a national debate which had hardly begun.

If Birmingham was massively industrial, it was also ethnically mixed. Montefiore encouraged, by word and deed, work amongst those of different ethnic origins. Within a month of arriving in Birmingham he attended a meeting of the Community Relations Council and started a speech with the words, 'I, too, am a member of an immigrant community, an ethnic minority . . .' That was all that needed to be said to convince the ethnic minorities of his understanding of their position. One of the things that pleased Montefiore most on his departure from Birmingham was a special meeting of the Community Relations Council at which he was given a leaving present.

Race and religion mixed in inner cities is a potent brew. When unemployment is added it becomes unstable. In July 1981 there were riots, hooliganism and looting that ravaged Handsworth (Birmingham), Brixton, Toxteth, Manchester, Leicester and Wolverhampton. Montefiore toured Handsworth on his return from the Holy Land and saw the barricades, evidence of violence and looting. Handsworth was a place without hope. The official figures for black unemployed young people were over 60 per cent – unofficial figures were far worse. Montefiore's concern was deep and anguished, even angry. 'if I were in the position of some young people today, I should probably wish to express my dissatisfaction with life . . .'

What should the Church do? Montefiore consulted with Canon Denis Claringbull and in 1981 set up an Unemployment Commission with three working groups. The first undertook to study what advice and guidance ought to be given to unemployed people. A *Guide for the Unemployed* was produced, which circulated in very large numbers and was used in several large companies. The second group investigated what projects could be set up to provide counselling and training leading to employment, self-employment or business enterprise. From this grew a network of centres for unemployed people known as 'Inter-Church Endeavour', which provided training in woodwork, metalwork, car maintenance, computer literacy, pottery, dressmaking, photography and, later, office skills, interview techniques and even sales training. The third group of the commission looked at the long-term economic and technological trends with scope for theological reflection. A booklet was published, *Work, Employment and the Changing Future.*

Montefiore adopted a very high profile on issues of unemployment. He addressed The People's March for Jobs in May 1981 in St Philip's (Cathedral) churchyard, and took part, together with the Roman Catholic archbishop and the Methodist district chairman, in an all-night vigil with unemployed people in Birmingham Cathedral on a cold snowy February night.

One report, *Faith in the City of Birmingham*,[9] had its antecedents within a group of urban bishops. This group was the idea of David Sheppard of Liverpool, who was in an exposed position in Liverpool and felt, rightly, the need to meet with other bishops in similar situations. David Sheppard, David Young of Ripon, whose diocese included Leeds, and Montefiore met and decided to bring a group together. There was nothing official about it. It was a gathering of friends for a meal, discussion and sharing of problems and ideas for mutual sustenance. Other bishops were Stanley Booth-Clibborn of Manchester, who ensured that the political aspect of city life was never ignored; Kenneth Skelton of Lichfield, who was much more radical in his ideas than appeared on first acquaintance; David Lunn of Sheffield, whose enormous common sense and genial outspokenness were a tremendous help; Ronald Bowlby of Southwark, whose presence ensured quiet, level-headed and wise comment. David Young of Ripon was not a frequent attender, as he was often overseas on Partners in Mission business. Jim Thompson of Stepney was a great asset to the group. Always a sensitive person, he combined his strong sense of what was wrong with a sensitive approach to those in a position to put it right.[10] When Kenneth Skelton retired from Lichfield, his successor Keith Sutton took his place and Tom Butler of Willesden also joined.

These friends met three times a year, twice in London during General Synod and once in December, residentially, for twenty-four hours. It was Canon Eric James who persuaded them that it would be a good idea to have a commission on the inner city. The bishops agreed and at a planning meeting in Liverpool they decided to invite the Archbishop of Canterbury to call it his commission. This would give it more standing and authority and might make it easier to obtain the wherewithal to fund it.

This was how the Archbishop of Canterbury's Commission on Urban Priority Areas evolved. The result was the controversial report *Faith in the City*.[11]

If a national report could start to change things, why not a local one? No sooner thought than arranged. Montefiore consulted with the other presidents of the Birmingham Council of Churches and enlisted their support. Sir Richard O'Brien had chaired the national commission. Montefiore secured him for the local one too, and an interesting membership was gathered.[12] The commission did not report until after Montefiore's retirement. It produced a challenging document with detailed recommendations for the public, private and voluntary sectors on housing, economic regeneration, education, poverty and low income, leisure and recreation, social care, health and medical care, order and law.

In the national Church, too, Montefiore had become one of the most influential bishops, not simply the most outspoken. The Archbishop of Canterbury, Robert Runcie, looked to him for advice on many matters. The archbishop has had a rough ride from some sections of the press, where the attacks appear sometimes to have been maliciously motivated and viciously pursued. Montefiore has been a good friend and defender of the archbishop. On one issue and its indirect aftermath, Montefiore was the chief supporter of the archbishop and the chief critic of his 'adversary' (probably not too strong a word), the Bishop of London, Graham Leonard. It is always difficult in any controversy to separate the person from the issue.

If Montefiore were asked what has been the most dangerous development in the Church of England during the years of his active ministry, he thinks he would have to answer 'The Tulsa Affair'.[13]

This concerns the Church of St Michael, Broken Arrow, Tulsa, and its priest, John Pasco. The history of the case need not detain us here.[14] In 1986 the Bishop of Oklahoma, Gerald McAllister, deposed Pasco from the ministry of the Episcopal Church of the USA. Pasco was a traditionalist and considered himself an Anglican. He and his parish had no desire to join any of the break-away Churches in America. He turned to the Bishop of London for counsel and support. In June 1986 Bishop Leonard wrote to Pasco declaring that he was in communion with him, recognized his priesthood and promised priest and congregation 'such spiritual and pastoral assistance as is within our power to give'. Bishop Leonard emphasized he was doing this as a bishop in the Church of God and not as the Bishop of London. There were members of St Michael's congregation awaiting confirmation. Leonard arranged for his suffragan, the Bishop of Fulham, John Klyberg, to go to Tulsa to administer the sacrament of confirmation in October 1986. The Presiding Bishop of the Episcopal Church, Edmund Browning, communicated the fury of the American bishops to the Archbishop of Canterbury. Leonard and Runcie met, the latter half-hoping to dissuade Leonard from sending his suffragan. Leonard did change his mind in one alarmingly unexpected way after the meeting. He decided to go himself to Tulsa for the confirmation and not to send his suffragan. When news of this reached the American bishops they took an unprecedented step by issuing a statement on 25 September 1986 condemning Leonard's action in taking a deposed priest into his care as 'deplorable, destructive and irresponsible'. ECUSA expected Leonard to be challenged, corrected or disciplined.

They knew not Leonard, nor Runcie. It was left to Montefiore to take action. He moved a motion for a meeting of the House of Bishops to be held on 21 October, a week before Leonard's visit to Tulsa. Perhaps it was not too late to persuade him not to go:

> This House believes that, in order to preserve catholic order, the unity of the Anglican Communion and the integrity of its constituent Churches, a Bishop of the Church of England should not exercise episcopal care over a priest in another province of the Anglican Communion who has been deposed by that province through due process of Canon Law; nor should he minister sacramentally or episcopally to the congregation of which the deposed priest is pastor, without the consent of the proper authorities of that province.

In moving the motion, Montefiore said there was nothing personal about it, for he recognized that Leonard was acting from conscientious conviction. In preparing his case against Leonard's proposed action, Montefiore had consulted scholars, including Canon J.N.D. Kelly, formerly Principal of St Edmund Hall, Oxford; Canon Henry Chadwick, former Regius Professor of Divinity, Cambridge; and Canon Gareth Bennett of New College, Oxford. Gareth Bennett, it turned out, had been advising both the archbishop and Leonard! His long letter to Montefiore left no room for doubt that Leonard had no precedents on which to take action, with one reservation. Was the Church of England in full communion with ECUSA? He thought not, for ECUSA had taken the new step of ordaining women to the priesthood and the Church of England had not, nor did it allow women priests to minister as such in England, 'so there is not full interchangeability of ministers, which is one of the tests of full communion. Our communion is impaired on this point.' That was so, yet the 1978 Lambeth Conference, by an overwhelming majority (316 to thirty-seven, with seventeen abstentions) had agreed to respect the autonomy of each of its member Churches and acknowledge their legal right to ordain women to Holy Orders. The Church of England had never reneged on that agreement.

Montefiore noted that

the clearest statement of Early Church practice is Canon 9
of the Synod of Antioch in AD 341. This declared that the
bishop was independent in the administration of his see,
but that he should not act outside his see without the
consent of the metropolitan of his province and the
neighbouring bishops. The only exception to this was if
the Church was in schism or if the rest of the province had
lapsed into grave heresy. For example, Apollinaris, Bishop
of Laodicea, who in his early days was a staunch opponent
of Arianism, when he found that all his neighbouring
bishops were Arians, placed himself under and in
communion with Athanasius – but that was an exceptional
situation of grave heresy.

Leonard's action in Tulsa would be contrary to catholic order as
understood in the Early Church and in the Church of England.
Montefiore did not see how the Anglican Communion could
continue to stay together if it did not respect others' territory
and the integrity of autonomous provinces.

Leonard went to Tulsa and on his return had an interview
with the archbishop on 7 October. The archbishop recognized
Leonard's pastoral concern for a deposed American priest and
his congregation, but still disapproved of the decision to go and
administer confirmation contrary to the wishes of the local
bishop and the clearly expressed mind of the House of Bishops
of the Church of England.

After the debate in the House of Bishops it had been agreed
first that a bishop of the Church of England should not exercise
episcopal care over a priest and congregation situated in a
diocese of another province, except with the consent of the
proper authorities of that province; second that the Archbishop
of Canterbury be invited to take any further steps he thought
appropriate to promote full understanding with the House of
Bishops of ECUSA on this matter and on the pastoral issues
involved. The voting was forty-seven for, one against and two
abstentions. The Bishop of Edmonton, Brian Masters, had
voted against, and the two abstainers were the Bishop of Chichester, Eric Kemp, and Leonard himself.

In a reflective article Montefiore asked:

Should a bishop act unilaterally? St Cyprian wrote (Epistle 33) that 'the Church is held together by the glue of the mutual cohesion of its bishops'. The very concept of Councils in the early Church was rooted in collegiality. If I reckon another Church is heretical or schismatic, I must not take action myself, but I should invite my college of bishops to consider the charges that I make. Once private judgement rather than corporate action (whether about heresy, schism or canonical procedures) becomes the general episcopal rule, the Church dissolves into chaos. It certainly ceases to act as the One Holy Catholic and Apostolic Church.

Have I then no status as bishop apart from my own jurisdiction? A bishop takes part in councils and collegiate discussion. He is set apart both as a focus of unity and for episcopal functions; but he can only exercise these when given due jurisdiction. Once a bishop, always a bishop; but when I retire, I cannot go about the world collecting dissident Anglican congregations and taking them under my wing. By so doing I would damage the integrity of autonomous Anglican Churches. I would become an *episcopus vagans*, against which catholic order has always set its face . . .

I believe there are two [lessons to be drawn from this affair]. In difficult times strong leadership is required. Of course it is easy to speak with hindsight from the sidelines when one does not have to live with the consequences of one's actions; but if the Archbishop of Canterbury had simply told the Bishop of London that he must not go to Tulsa, I feel confident that the bishop would have heeded his vow of due obedience to his metropolitan; and if so, then the troubles would have been averted. Secondly, it may be that the present relationship of mutual consultation and understanding within the Anglican Communion must give way fairly quickly to more definite structures of authority. If we are willing to explore further the concept of a Universal Primate, ought we not here and now to give greater authority to the Archbishop of Canterbury as

Patriach of the Anglican Communion rather than merely *primus inter pares?*

To Montefiore, a breakout of Anglican 'Tulsas' in different parts of the body would be a prescription for endangering the Anglican Communion. The 1989 consecration of a woman to the episcopate could signal the beginning of the end, a plague of Tulsas.

The *Crockford's Clerical Directory* prefaces have provided an opportunity for a commentary on Anglican affairs from an anonymous author. The prefaces have always been thought-provoking and often controversial, causing speculation as to the name of the author. When the 1987/88 edition was published,[15] the Preface was one of the most cogent and pungent polemical writings that had appeared for many years. Instead of attacking traditional policies and people who, it had been said, were endangering Anglicanism, the writer emptied his armoury on the liberal Establishment of the Church and singled out the Archbishop of Canterbury (Robert Runcie) for particular criticism using a phrase of Frank Field MP, 'that the archbishop is usually to be found nailing his colours to the fence,' alleging that 'this makes Dr Runcie peculiarly vulnerable to pressure groups'.

This pointed and personal criticism stung hard and although it appeared after Montefiore's retirement he leapt to Runcie's defence in articles in *The Times* and the *Sun.*[16] The Church was substantially rocked by the Preface and it is now a matter of history that the author was revealed as Canon Gareth Bennett of New College, Oxford, who subsequently committed suicide.

It could be said that in 1986 Montefiore was at the height of his powers. Then, aged only sixty-six, he announced that he would resign the following spring. Why? Quite simply because Eliza was not well and needed his care. She had cared for him all those years, and now it was his turn to care for her.

How was the diocese going to say farewell to Bishop 'Huge' (a misprint which had once appeared on a poster for a Renewal Eucharist)? He had indeed been larger than life. Roger Hooker had arrived in Birmingham after thirteen years in India, and this is how he regards Montefiore: 'He was above all a big man with a touch of greatness about him, yet also something of a holy clown, a rare combination which none of us found easy to live with. I for one would have been the poorer if I had not had to.'

Fortunately Bishop Colin Buchanan, with his own brand of vision and energy, planned another Birmingham 'special' to show that Montefiore had breathed renewed life into the diocese, given it confidence, made it feel it was the Church Militant in Birmingham. First, Colin Buchanan booked the Arena at the National Exhibition Centre for a Farewell Eucharist on 31 March 1987. Then he asked a number of people to contribute to a retirement tribute, a small book reflecting Montefiore's life and work. It is significant that its title was *Bishop Hugh – With Affection*. This biographer was with Montefiore when Colin Buchanan rushed into the study and produced the fifty-page booklet, well-produced and with illustrations. It had been kept secret from Montefiore and his countenance on seeing it was a lovely picture of surprise and joy.

There were farewells all over Birmingham diocese, eventually leading to the Farewell Eucharist. What an event! He had the send-off of a superstar, with singing, dancing and a cascade of balloons. More than 7,000 people attended. No wonder Colin Buchanan had inserted a note on liturgical colour in the programme – Lent had been suspended for the evening. These were Resurrection people. At the end, following the Blessing and Dismissal, Bishop Hugh and Eliza turned to face Bishop Colin, who said: 'Hugh and Eliza, you go with our love to serve the Lord,' to which they replied: 'We go in the name of Christ. Amen.'

Then came a most poignant moment. Montefiore removed his cope and mitre, appearing almost to fling them aside, as if throwing off the Birmingham episcopate. Then, wearing his cassock, he walked hand in hand with Eliza through the arena as balloons descended from above.

The Birmingham episcopate *was* over, and had concluded, as was appropriate, with worship – for prayer and worship enabled the action that made Montefiore a living tornado with a human face. A priest recalls his first visit to Bishop's Croft. He found Montefiore on his knees vigorously poking the fire. This was an authentic picture of his ministry as bishop – he poked the Church into activity, but he did it on his knees.

Notes

1   Enduring Roots

1. Manuscript M69, Mocatta Library, University College, London.
2. *The Cousinhood: Jewish Gentry*, Chaim Bermant, Eyre & Spottiswoode, 1971. This book remains the best guide to the history and influence of the Anglo-Jewish gentry.
3. Address by Denzil Sebag-Montefiore at the Judah Touro College Annual Dinner, June 1980.
4. Israel Finestein QC, circuit judge and honorary research fellow, University College, London, on 'The Uneasy Victorian: Montefiore as Communal Leader' in *The Century of Moses Montefiore*, ed. Sonia and V.D. Lipman, OUP, 1985.
5. 23 October 1883 and 24 October 1884.
6. *Sir Moses Montefiore and His Great-Nephew: A Study in Contrasts*, published by the University of Southampton, 1979. The great-nephew was Claude Goldsmid Montefiore.
7. Speech by Denzil Sebag-Montefiore at the opening of the Montefiore Exhibition in New York, 24 February 1985.
8. *A Family Patchwork* by Ruth Sebag-Montefiore, Weidenfeld & Nicolson, 1987. Ruth's grandfather was the educationalist and politician Sir Philip Magnus and the biographer Philip Magnus is her brother. Denzil Sebag-Montefiore was her second cousin.
9. In *Thinking about the Eucharist*, ed. Ian Ramsey, SCM, 1972.

2   The Vision

1. Essay in *They Became Anglicans*, ed. Dewi Morgan, Mowbray, 1959.
2. Frederick Stephen Temple (Malmesbury) for whom Montefiore was personal fag; John Monier Bickersteth (Bath and Wells); Archibald Ronald McDonald Gordon (Portsmouth, later Bishop at Lambeth); Richard Charles Challinor Watson (Burnley); Patrick Rodger (Oxford) and Montefiore. The leading evangelical, as influential as any bishop, John Robert Walmsley Stott, was also at Rugby at this time.

4   Oxford and Colloquy

1. Nathaniel Micklem in *The Dictionary of National Biography 1941–50*, OUP, 1959.

5   Ordination and Restlessness

1. He had been a fellow of Trinity College from 1915. In 1952 he was appointed Regius Professor of Divinity, Cambridge.
2. *Journal of Theological Studies*, Vol. L, No. 199/200.
3. The Anglican bishops were Arthur Michael Hollis (Madras and the Church of South India's first moderator); Cherakarottu Korula Jacob (Central Travancore); George Theodore Selwyn (Tinnevelly) and Anthony Blacker Elliott (Dornakal).
4. A. & C. Black, 1949.
5. Kenneth Carey became Bishop of Edinburgh; John Robinson, then fellow and Dean of Clare College, Cambridge, went on to be Bishop Suffragan of Woolwich and Dean of Trinity College, Cambridge; Barry Till, fellow and Chaplain of Jesus College, Cambridge, was later Dean of Hong Kong; W.H. Vanstone, Assistant Curate of St Thomas' Halliwell, Lancashire, was later Canon Residentiary of

Chester Cathedral; Alan Webster, Vicar of Barnard Castle,was ultimately Dean of St Paul's Cathedral, and Kenneth
Woollcombe, fellow and Chaplain of St John's College,
Oxford, became Bishop of Oxford.
6. *The Bishoprick*, quarterly magazine of the Diocese of
Durham.
7. Mowbray, 1955.
8. For example, his review of the book in *Theology*, July 1954.

6   Fellow and Dean

1. *A History of Gonville and Caius College*, Christopher
Brooke, Boydell, 1985. Christopher Brooke is Dixie Professor of Ecclesiastical History.

7   'Everything I've Got'

1. *Robertson of Brighton*, Smith Elder, 1916.
2. On another occasion, during a short stay in Rome on
holiday, Montefiore and his wife had a private audience
with Pope Paul VI. Elisabeth wore a splendid mantilla. It
was the last audience after an exhausting morning for the
pope, yet he had still time for a real talk, mostly about
students. When he entered, Montefiore knelt and asked for
his blessing, to which the pope replied: 'Get up! I am a
human being like you.'
3. *New Testament Studies*, Vol. VII, 1961, pp. 220–48.
4. *Studies in Biblical Theology*, No. 35, SCM, 1962.

8   Squalls and Tempests

1. Charles Harold Dodd was Norris-Hulse Professor of Divinity in the University of Cambridge 1935–49 and the first
non-Anglican since the Reformation to hold such a chair at
either of the ancient universities.

2. *The Interpretation of the Fourth Gospel*, CUP, 1953.
3. Charles Francis Digby Moule.
4. Wilfred Lawrence Knox was an Anglo–Catholic priest, son of the wholly Protestant bishop Ronald Arbuthnott Knox of Manchester. His brothers were the famous Father Ronald Knox and Edmund Valpy ('Evoe') Knox, sometime editor of *Punch*.
5. From his contribution 'The Authority of the Church' in *Essays Catholic and Critical*, edited by E.G. Selwyn, SPCK, 1926.
6. David Daube subsequently became Director of the Robbins Hebraic and Roman Law Collections and Professor-in-Residence at the School of Law, University of California.
7. Henry Chadwick was fellow of Queen's College, Cambridge. Then in 1959 he became Regius Professor of Divinity at Oxford. Ten years later he was Dean of Christ Church and ten years after that he moved back to Cambridge as Regius Professor of Divinity. In 1987 he became Master of Peterhouse.
8. William Owen Chadwick chaired the Archbishops' Commission on Church and State (1970), which was responsible for significant changes being made in the system of appointing bishops. He was awarded the Order of Merit and gained a knighthood.
9. William Telfer wrote *The Treasure of Sao Roque*, 1932; *Cyril of Jerusalem and Nemesius of Emesa*, 1955; *The Forgiveness of Sins*, 1959; and *The Office of a Bishop*, 1962.
10. James Franklin Bethune-Baker, Lady Margaret Professor of Divinity 1911–1935.
11. Edward Craddock Ratcliffe had been Professor of Liturgical Theology, University of London. Later he succeeded John Burnaby as Regius Professor of Divinity.
12. Maurice Frank Wiles, Dean of Clare, now Regius Professor of Divinity, Oxford.
13. John Westerdale Bowker, fellow of Corpus Christi, now Dean of Trinity College, Cambridge.
14. Peter Richard Baelz, Dean of Jesus College, later Dean of Durham.
15. Don Cupitt, Dean of Emmanuel College.
16. Roland Charles Walls, fellow of Corpus Christi.

17. Howard Eugene Root was appointed Professor of Theology, University of Southampton 1966–81 and is now the director of the Anglican Centre in Rome.
18. There are similarities in outlook, but perhaps not in character, between W.L. Knox and A.R. Vidler. They had combined to write a book, *The Development of Modern Catholicism* (1933).
19. George Frederick Woods, fellow and Dean of Downing College; university lecturer in Divinity; honorary canon of Bristol Cathedral; later Professor of Theology at Birmingham University.
20. *Soundings: Essays Concerning Christian Understanding*, Cambridge University Press, 1962.
21. *Up and Down in Adria: Some Considerations of Soundings*, Faith Press, 1963. Eric Lionel Mascall was appointed Professor of Historical Theology, University of London, in 1963.
22. November 1962.
23. October 1962.
24. 'Religion and the National Church'.
25. 'Beginning All Over Again'.
26. 'Theology and Self-Awareness'.
27. Editorial in *The Church Quarterly Review*, July-September, 1963.
28. *A Life of Bishop John A.T. Robinson: Scholar, Pastor, Prophet*, Eric James, Collins, 1987.
29. A.R. Vidler (ed.), Constable, 1963. Contributions by D.M. MacKinnon ('Moral Objections'); H.A. Williams ('Psychological Objections'); A.R. Vidler ('Historical Objections') and J.S. Bezzant ('Intellectual Objections').
30. Harry Williams has known what it means to experience the temporary disappearance of Jesus as an object of devotion. Montefiore has never had a crisis over faith in Jesus.
31. *Subscription and Assent to the 39 Articles*, SPCK, 1968.
32. The commission's terms of reference were to consider and advise upon doctrinal questions submitted to it from time to time by the Archbishops and to plan, where desirable, the investigation of questions by other groups.
33. Montefiore was a member of the Cambridge University Society for Psychic Research.

34. Reproduced in Montefiore's collection of sermons, lectures and addresses, *Taking Our Past into Our Future*, Fount/Collins, 1978.
35. The paper was published in the volume *Christ for Us Today*, SCM, 1968.
36. The speakers were E.G. Parrinder, Reader in the Comparative Study of Religion, King's College, University of London; Eric Heaton, fellow and Chaplain of St John's College, Oxford; Dennis Nineham; G.B. Caird, Mansfield College, Oxford; Maurice Wiles; F.W. Dillistone, fellow and Chaplain of Oriel College, Oxford; L.A. Reid of London University; G.W.H. Lampe, Ely Professor of Divinity, Cambridge; P.N. Hamilton of Trinity Hall, Cambridge. Montefiore again was the sole parish priest.
37. Norman Pittenger edited *Christ for Us Today* and was himself to be embroiled in controversy concerning homosexuality some years later.
38. The sermon appeared in *Sermons from Great St Mary's*, edited by Montefiore, Fontana, 1968.
39. Montefiore edited a paperback *We Must Love One Another Or Die* (SCM, 1963, Hodder & Stoughton, 1966) containing lectures on love, sex and morality given by Frank Lake, H.E. Root and V.A. Demant.
40. See the forthcoming biography of Michael Ramsey by Owen Chadwick.

9   Constraining the Waters

1. Horace Dammers, former Vicar of Millhouses, Sheffield, then Canon Residentiary of Coventry Cathedral, later Dean of Bristol; Christopher Driver of the *Guardian*; Sydney Evans, Dean of King's College, London, later Dean of Salisbury; David Faull, lawyer and legal adviser to a number of bishops; Philip Goodrich, Vicar of South Ormsby group of parishes, now Bishop of Worcester; C.F.D. Moule, Lady Margaret Professor of Divinity, Cambridge; Nicolas Stacey, Rector of Woolwich; Alan Patient; Peter Baelz, former Vicar of Bournville, then Dean

of Jesus College, Cambridge, later Dean of Durham; Mollie Batten, Principal of William Temple College; Ronald Bowlby, Vicar of Billingham, now Bishop of Southwark; Simon Burrows, Vicar of Wyken, Coventry, now Bishop of Buckingham.

2. Faber and Faber, 1951. Michael Roberts died in 1948 leaving seven completed chapters of *The Estate of Man* on which he worked from the autumn of 1946 until within three months of his death. These chapters, with notes, form the book.
3. Geoffrey Bles, 1963.
4. University sermon, 29 October 1967.
5. Ed. Edwin Barker, SPCK, 1966.
6. Collins, 1969. Also published in *Can Man Survive? The Question Mark and Other Essays*, Fontana, 1970.
7. Lengthy review in *New Scientist*, 6 November 1969.
8. Review, 30 October 1969.
9. Chaired by G.W. Dimbleby, Professor of Human Environment, University of London. Members included scientists, theologians and a merchant banker; three were Roman Catholics.
10. Tutor-in-Charge of New Hall 1954–64 and first President 1964. She was a chemist.
11. Timothy Wentworth Beaumont was ordained in the diocese of Hong Kong where he served from 1955 to 1959. Combining an honorary curacy in London with writing, he was editor of *Time and Tide* (1960–1) and of *Aspect, Prism, National Christian News* and *Outlook* from 1961. Above all he wanted to start a Christian weekly newspaper – a cross between the *Church Times*, the *Tablet* and the *Spectator*. *New Christian* emerged.
12. Francis Harry Crompton Crick was laboratory scientist at the Medical Research Council Laboratory of Molecular Biology in Cambridge. Although his fellowship of Churchill College lasted only one year (1960–1), he accepted an honorary fellowship in 1965.
13. Sir John Douglas Cockcroft was appointed the first master of Churchill College in 1959 by Sir Winston Churchill himself, a post he held until his death in 1967. He was one of the great creative scientists of the century. His name is

inextricably linked with Harwell and atomic energy. He was awarded the Nobel prize for physics jointly with E.T.S. Walton in 1951, the Order of Merit in 1953 and the Atom for Peace Award in 1961.

14. John Sinclair Morrison had been Professor of Greek in the University of Durham 1945–50 before becoming a fellow, tutor and Senior Tutor of Trinity College, Cambridge, 1950–60. After being Vice-Master and Senior Tutor at Churchill 1960–5 he went on to be President of Wolfson College (formerly University College), Cambridge.

15. Anthony Hewish was a fellow of Gonville and Caius College from 1955–62, lecturer in physics in the university 1962–9, fellow of Churchill College from 1962 and Professor of Radioastronomy from 1971.

16. The plans drawn up by the architect put the chapel in the centre of the college. This was too much for the fellows, and the trustees gave in – the chapel was built on the most remote part of the site.

17. *Novum Testamentum* is an international quarterly for New Testament and related studies based on international co-operation. Two heavily footnoted articles appeared in the journal: 'Josephus and the New Testament', Vol. IV, Fasc. 2 & 4, 1960, which was subsequently printed as a separate pamphlet in the series *Contemporary Studies in Theology*, No. 6, Mowbray, 1962; 'Thou Shalt Love Thy Neighbour as Thyself ', Vol. V, Fasc. 2/3, 1962.

18. 'God as Father in the Synoptic Gospels', 1956. 'Revolt in the Desert', No. 8, 1962. 'Jesus and the Temple Tax', No. 10, 1964.

19. 'When Did Jesus Die?', Vol. LXXII, No. 2, November 1960.

20. 'Does "L" Hold Water?', 1961.

21. 'Sulpicius Severus and Titus' Council of War', XI, 2 April, 1962.

22. 'Roman Catholics and the Bible', Vol. LVII, No. 410, August 1954.

23. *Theology*, June 1955. Review of *The Doctrine of Justification by Faith*, ed. G.W.H. Lampe, Mowbray, and *The Pattern of Christian Truth*, H.E.W. Turner, Mowbray.

24. Collins, Fontana, 1964. This book contains four lectures

given at the Bishop's Hostel, Lincoln, during Passion Week 1964. The 'awkward' questions were: 'The Great Accusation'; 'The Sinlessness of Jesus'; 'Atonement and Personality'; 'The Church – "In Group" or "Out Group"'.

25. Hodder & Stoughton, 1963.
26. Collins, Fontana, 1966. The first section comprises a course of eight sermons which illustrate the sub-title of the book and which were given in the Lent term 1965. The second section contains a course given in the Lent term 1964 under the generic title 'Where the Shoe Pinches' which covers loneliness, parents, the other sex, religion, time, career, cash and status.
27. *Sermons from Great St Mary's*, Collins, Fontana, 1968; *More Sermons from Great St Mary's*, Hodder & Stoughton, 1971.
28. One of four lectures in *God, Sex and War*, Collins, Fontana, 1963.
29. Montefiore also delivered this lecture in Chelmsford Cathedral in September 1966. It was published as *Remarriage and Mixed Marriage: A Plea for Dual Reform*, SPCK, 1967.
30. *Crucible*, November 1964.
31. Adam and Charles Black, 1964, in Black's *New Testament Commentaries* (general ed. Henry Chadwick). This was reprinted in 1969.
32. SPCK, 1968, revised edition, 1984.
33. Review, *Church Times*, 8 November 1968.
34. SCM, 1957.
35. Dialogue between Montefiore and David Tribe, President of the National Secular Society, on London ITV, January 1967, published in *Dialogue with Doubt*, SCM, 1967.
36. Contribution to *They Became Anglicans*, ed. Dewi Morgan, Mowbray, 1959. Also 'In Via' in *Journeys in Belief*, ed. Bernard Dixon, Allen & Unwin, 1968. The book describes how and why eighteen people of different religions and backgrounds changed their beliefs.

10   Mr Johnson Arrives

1. The Church of England Evangelical Council was an important and influential body. Members included MPs Michael Alison and Peter Mills; future bishops Maurice

Wood (Norwich), W.M.D. Persson (Doncaster), Timothy Dudley Smith (Thetford), John Taylor (Winchester); and well-known figures such as Sir Timothy Hoare, Professor Norman Anderson and the Revds John Stott, J.S. Packer, Colin Craston, T.L. Livermore and R.T. Beckwith. It represented the best of Anglican evangelicalism at that time. The council expressed its gratitude to Montefiore for his 'extremely helpful and timely book – *The Question Mark*'.

2. SPCK, 1959.
3. Editorial in *Theology*, 1959.
4. 'Government should broaden its base', *The Times*, 13 January 1968.
5. Profile No. 6 in a series 'The Defectors', *New Statesman*, 28 February 1975.
6. *Who Cares?*, Anthony Blond, 1975. Nicolas Stacey was Rector of Woolwich, Director of Oxfam and then Director of Kent Social Services.
7. On one occasion caviare was flown in from Iran.
8. In a forceful article in the *Guardian*, 2 May 1972, written as the General Synod prepared for its crucial vote on the scheme, Montefiore stated, 'The failure of the scheme would be one more instance of the Church of England's death-wish. To the young – all this kind of ecclesiastical in-fighting is irrelevant to the real problems which men face in today's mad world; and they vote not with their hands but with their feet.'
9. These included 'Marriage Service – Series 3', 3–10 November 1976 and 16 February 1977, and 'Human Rights', 16 February 1977.
10. In *Bishop Hugh – With Affection: A Retirement Tribute*, Birmingham DBF, 1987.
11. e.g. Lady Oppenheimer became convinced of the rightness of remarrying divorced people in church.
12. 'Frustration and Forgiveness', *Theology*, May 1971.
13. 'Marriage, Divorce and the Church', *Theology*, June 1971. The editor of *Theology* was G.R. Dunstan, a member of the commission.
14. Diocesan letter, June 1972.
15. CIO Publishing, 1978.

11 The Future – Apocalypse or Concorde?

1. This took place in the natural setting for the subject but in an unlikely place for Montefiore – the Church of the Immaculate Conception, Farm Street, on 4 June 1972. The sermon was printed by The Hopkins Society.
2. He presented a paper 'Man and Nature, The Theological Assessment' at a meeting of the Science and Religion Forum entitled 'Man's Responsibility for Nature', at Windsor, 7–9 April 1976. Published in *Zygon* (Journal of Religion and Science), September 1977.
3. The lecture was subtitlted 'The dogmas and duties of a technological age'. The lecture, commemorating Lord Rutherford, was delivered on 19 November 1971 at the Polytechnic of Central London and published by Manchester University Press. Previous lecturers were Professor Henry Wright-Baker, Lewis Nichols, Lewis Womersley and Anthony Wedgwood Benn.
4. 20 November 1971.
5. Roy Jenkins and Anthony Barber were mentioned.
6. 11–20 September 1972 at Selly Oak College, Birmingham.
7. *The British Churches Turn to the Future*, David L. Edwards, SCM, 1973.
8. Barbara Ward (later Lady Robert Jackson) was a Roman Catholic. She had studied in France, Germany and England, gaining an honours degree in philosophy, politics and economics. She was Schweitzer Professor of International Economic Development at Columbia University.
9. Letter, 'Towards a Simpler Lifestyle', *Church Times*, 17 January 1975.
10. Members were: Sir John Betjemen (Poet Laureate); Frank Chapple (General Secretary EETPU); Sir James Farquharson (President, Scottish Association for Public Transport, formerly General Manager, East African Railways and Harbours, etc.); John Francis (Director, Society, Religion and Technology Project, Church of Scotland Home Board); John Garnett (Director, The Industrial Society); Michael Graham (Economic Adviser to Overseas Containers Ltd.); Mayer Hillman (Senior Research Officer, Political and Economic Planning); Dick Jones (Local

Government Planner); Gerald Leach (Visiting Fellow, Science Policy Research Unit, Sussex University; formerly Science Correspondent, the *Observer*); Norman Lee, Senior Lecturer in Economics, Manchester University); Ezra Mishan (Reader in Economics, London School of Economics); Jack Parsons (Lecturer in Social Institutions, Brunel University); Gabrielle Pike (Chairman, Women's Group on Public Welfare); Ronald Preston (Professor of Social and Pastoral Theology, Manchester University); Lois Pulling (Chairman, Working Party on Public Transport, National Council of Women of Great Britain); David Rubenstein (Vice-Chairman of the Ramblers' Association; Lecturer in Social History, Hull University); Graham Searle (Director, Friends of the Earth); Colin Speakman (Lecturer in English, James Graham College, Leeds); J. Michael Thomson (Joint Editor, *Journal of Transport, Economics and Policy*); Sir Ralph Verney (Chairman, County Planning Committee of the Buckinghamshire County Council; Chairman, Secretary of State's Advisory Committee on Aggregates for the Construction Industry; member of the Royal Commission on Environmental Pollution); David Wiggins (Professor of Philosophy, Bedford College, University of London); Alfred Wood (County Planning Office, West Midlands' Metropolitan County Council). Consultants were: Lord Ashby (Master of Clare College, Cambridge; formerly Chairman of the Standing Royal Commission on Pollution); Lord Gladwyn; Barbara Ward (Director, International Institute of Environmental Studies); Des Wilson (journalist, formerly Director of Shelter). The executive secretary was Stephen Plowden of Metra Consulting Group Ltd. Montefiore was the chairman.

11. Coronet Books, Hodder & Stoughton, 1974.
12. *Pornography: The Longford Report*, Coronet Books, Hodder & Stoughton, 1972.
13. 'No Way To Go', 3 February 1975.
14. Members were: A.M. Allchin (Canon Residentiary of Canterbury Cathedral); Don Cupitt (fellow and Dean of Emmanuel College, Cambridge); Mary Hesse (fellow of Wolfson College, Cambridge, and Professor of the Philosophy of Science, Cambridge University); John Macquar-

rie (Canon of Christ Church, Oxford, and Lady Margaret Professor of Divinity, Oxford University); A.R. Peacocke (fellow and Dean of Clare College, Cambridge). Montefiore, Allchin, Macquarrie and Peacocke were at the time members of the Doctrine Commission.

15. Collins, 1975. The appended essays were by John Austin Baker, Don Cupitt, Mary Hesse, A.R. Peacocke and Paul Oestreicher.

16. Example: 'Only Months to Plan for 250,000 Years?' *Observer*, 21 December 1975.

17. HACAN was a voluntary association with some two and a half thousand paid-up members, and many thousands more well-wishers. There were thirty-seven amenity associations in the neighbourhood affiliated to it.

18. He wrote up his part in the Concorde controversy in 'Discord on Concorde', *Crucible*, April–June 1976.

19. Members were: Peter Adams (National Officer EETPU, Fuel and Power Industries Committee, TUC, Vice Chairman of Negotiating Committee with UKAEA); Sir Alan Cottrell, FRS (Master of Jesus College, Cambridge, formerly Chief Scientific Adviser to the Government); David Henderson (Professor of Political Economy, University College, London); Alan McKnight (formerly Inspector General, IAEA); Lord Kearton, FRS (Chairman, British National Oil Corporation); Keith Richardson (industrial correspondent, *Sunday Times*); Graham Searle (Director, Earth Resources Research Ltd); James Whyte (Professor of Practical Theology and Christian Ethics, St Andrew's University). Montefiore was the chairman.

20. *The Windscale Enquiry*, report by the Hon. Mr Justice Parker, was published in 1978, as a result of which the House of Commons approved the plans for a reprocessing plant by a vote of 186 to 56 on 15 March 1978.

21. Witnesses from UKAEA included Sir John Hull (Chairman); C.W. Blumfield (Director, Dounreay Experimental Establishment); F.R. Farmer (safety adviser); Dr R. Pease (Director, Culham Laboratory); and Dr R.L. Nicholson.

22. Prism Press, 1977.

23. Southwark Cathedral Publications, 1976.

24. Published in the *International Journal of Environmental*

Studies, Vol. 8, 1975.
25. Published with many of his major addresses, lectures and sermons in *Taking Our Past into Our Future*, Fount/Collins, 1978.
26. Published in *The Month*, July 1976.
27. Published in *Taking Our Past into Our Future*.
28. *Surveyor*, 28 July 1972.

12   Prince of the Church

1. Anthony Hanson had worked in South India and by mouth and pen he defended and commended the episcopate to those who were suspicious of it. He expanded his views in 'The Theology of Suffragan Bishops' in *Theology*, September 1975.
2. Particularly Canon P.A. Welsby, Canon Residentiary of Rochester Cathedral, and the Bishop of London (Gerald Ellison).
3. Church Information Office, January 1978.
4. Mervyn Stockwood chose the *Morning Star* (31 October 1975) as his forum for criticizing the archbishop and for parading his own political and economic predilections. Montefiore wrote to *The Times* (5 November 1975) admitting that he disagreed with Stockwood's prescriptions for the nation's predicament. He declared himself a Liberal and said that neither socialist nor capitalist solutions would remedy the moral malaise.
5. Breaches of confidentiality had been feared by the framers of the commission's terms of reference but it was a risk that had to be taken.
6. 14 September 1977.
7. 22 September 1977.
8. In fact it was grievously damaged later, but in no way by Montefiore, who punctiliously ordered one British Leyland vehicle after another.
9. 12 October 1977.
10. Leader, 'Birmingham and its new bishop', 21 October 1977.

11. Vicar of Stirchley and member of General Synod.

13   Style and Substance

1. See Volume 14 of *Ecclesiastical Law*, paragraph 692.
2. Professionally he was Chairman of the Birmingham Health Authority.
3. Michael Jonathan Russell Tinker 1978–80, appointed at the age of 28; Christopher John Boyle 1980–83, aged 29; David Columba SSF 1983–87, aged 37.

14   Contrasts

1. For complete list see Bibliography.
2. Fount/Collins, 1981. Dedicated to the Readers of the Church of England, with its origin in some open lectures given at Cambridge, it was later adapted for a residential course for Readers in 1979 and rewritten with two additional chapters for publication.
3. Montefiore did not exclude other great city-centre churches: St Chad's Roman Catholic Cathedral, St Martin's, Carrs Lane, and Central Hall – the latter two being temples of vigorous noncomformity.
4. Princess Alexandra attended the service following the cathedral's restoration on 1 November 1980.
5. Adapted from his presidential address given to the Institute of Religion and Medicine in July 1982.
6. His experiences were described in 'Down California Way', *The Bishopric*, November 1981.
7. The link had been established in 1966. By the end of 1982 Birmingham diocese had sent the Anglican Church in Malawi a total of £120,404. The money was used for priests' stipends, pensions and housing, for the education of priests' children and for Christian literature.
8. 'Reflections on Malawi', *The Bishopric*, Vol. 5, No. 4, 1983. He also kept a Notebook (unpublished).

9. John Workman, Treasurer of the Anglican Council and internal auditor for the two dioceses; Tony Cox, Chaplain of the Church School at Mazosa, who went there from Smethwick, and Keith and Jill Gales (priest and doctor, respectively), working at Lilongwe.

15   National and Ethical

1. CIO (Church Information Office), 1977.
2. 18 November 1977.
3. *The Church and the Bomb: Nuclear Weapons and Christian Conscience*, Hodder & Stoughton, 1982.
4. Department of Health and Social Security, *Report of the Committee of Enquiry into Human Fertilization and Embryology*, Cmnd. 9314, July 1984.
5. Bill printed 5 December 1984. J. Enoch Powell was supported by Sir Bernard Braine, Donald Stewart, A.J. Beith, the Revd Martin Smyth, Anthony Beaumont-Dark, Ian Campbell, Sir Gerard Vaughan, James White and Mrs Ann Winterton.
6. LIFE (Save the Unborn Child).
7. General Synod Miscellaneous Paper 172, 24 February 1983.
8. *Human Fertilization and Embryology: The Response of the Board for Social Responsibility*.
9. See his article 'After Warnock: Questions to the Church', *Crucible*, October–December 1984. Montefiore's speech was reproduced in part in *Religion and Medicine*, Journal of the Institute of Religion and Medicine, No. 1, March 1985.
10.

	Ayes	Noes
House of Bishops	14	8
House of Clergy	47	76
House of Laity	67	67
Abstentions 28		

11. 15 February 1985.
12. *Report of a Working Party on Human Fertilization and Embryology*, CIO, 1985.
13. Ronald Ralph Williams, Bishop of Leicester, chairman 1961–76; Graham Douglas Leonard, Bishop of Truro, then

London, 1976–83.

14. Church House Publishing, 1986.
15. Montefiore's article 'Light from the Past', in *Theology and Social Concern*, BSR, 1966, was largely devoted to Temple's teaching.
16. William Temple, *Christianity and Social Order*, Penguin, 1942.
17. During debate of Family Law Reform Bill, 15 January 1987, *Hansard*, p. 669.
18. During a debate on Social and Economic Policies, the first debate in the House of Lords to be televised. Amongst those present who complimented him on the speech was the Earl of Stockton (formerly Harold Macmillan).
19. Montefiore wrote an article in reply to Douglas Hurd, the Home Secretary, in *Church Times*, 24 January 1986.
20. Church House Publishing, 1987.
21. Members of the Select Committee were Lords Brightman (Chairman), Butterworth, Houghton of Sowerby, Hunter of Newington and McGregor of Durris; Baronesses Faithful, Llewelyn-Davies of Hastoe, and Warnock; and the Bishop of Gloucester (John Yates). The Committee was indeed overwhelmingly hostile to Montefiore's Bill. No one could have imagined from the tone of the questions that the Bill had passed its second reading with a 14 per cent majority and with Government support.
22. SCM Press, 1988.
23. Church House Publishing, 1986.

16 Theologian – Explorer and Stabilizer

1. Montefiore's review of *Bishops, But What Kind?* (ed. Peter Moore, SPCK, 1982) in *Theology*, May 1983.
2. Contribution to *Bishop Hugh – With Affection*, Birmingham Diocesan Board of Finance, 1987.
3. SCM, 1983.
4. SCM, 1980.
5. SCM, 1983. John Hick was then working at Claremont University, California.
6. Whilst not ascribing any divinity to the person of Christ, John Hick had a firm, lasting and deep conviction about the

reality of God. He had previously leapt into the headlines when he edited *The Myth of God Incarnate*, SCM, 1977. His fellow contributors were Don Cupitt, J.L. Houlden, Denis Nineham and Maurice Wiles.

7. BBC Publications, 1984.
8. *The Bishopric*, November 1984.
9. In *The Bishopric* Montefiore concluded, 'The last time the Church of England moved against a don who had dangerous thoughts was in 1911 when the licence of G.M. Thompson was withdrawn at Magdalene College, Oxford. It did not help the Church. Cupitt, who says that all Christian postures are corrigible, admits that his own is not unalterable. I only hope that he will wish to alter it.'
10. Deacon 1953; priest 1954; lecturer, Queen's College, Birmingham, and curate of Birmingham Cathedral 1953–4; Chaplain, Queen's College, Oxford, 1954–69; Director of World Council of Churches, Study Department 1969–73; Director of the William Temple Foundation 1973–78; Professor of Theology and Religious Studies, Leeds University, 1979–84.
11. *Mail on Sunday*, 10 November 1985.
12. SPCK, 1938.
13. Church House Publishing, 1986.
14. *The Bishopric*, September 1986.
15. SCM, 1985.
16. *God, Sex and Love,* SCM, 1989.
17. See Appendix A.
18. *King's Theological Review*, Spring 1986. The most substantial and, for Montefiore, the most interesting, review was by John Maddox, editor of *Nature* (*Nature*, 23 May 1985). Whilst admiring Montefiore's honesty to the point of saying that 'the possibility that there is no God remains open' (but is 'wildly improbable'), Maddox considers that readers of the book are asked to make a 'concession to irrationality that most will find impossible'. Maddox is left with the view that, 'Montefiore's God, is not a once-and-for-all God, one who drew up the laws of physics and then left us to it, nor a "God of the gaps", one who may have intervened from time to time, but is instead an immanent God, embedded in the Universe and helping to make it tick from

one instant to the next.'

19. SPCK, 1977.
20. Article 'Authority in the Church', *Theology*, May 1977.
21. *Theology*, September 1977.
22. For example, an article on 'Authority in the Church', following publication of a Roman Catholic report *In the House of the Living God*, *Theology*, November 1983.
23. SCM, 1986.
24. Letter dated 14 January 1987. Fr Yarnold reviewed *So Near and Yet So Far* in the *Catholic Herald* (November 1986) and wrote an 'Open Letter' to Montefiore which was published in the *Newsletter* of the Ecumenical Society of the Blessed Virgin Mary, January 1987.
25. Mowbray/Mayhew McCrimmon, 1978. Other contributions were the Revd. Christopher Evans, Professor Emeritus of New Testament Studies at King's College, London; Canon F.W. Dillistone, Fellow Emeritus of Oriel College, Oxford; Canon Mary Simpson, Canon Residentiary of St John the Divine Cathedral, New York; Gilbert Baker, Bishop of Hong Kong and Macao; Michael Perry, Archdeacon of Durham, with a note by Donald MacKinnon, Norris-Hulse Professor of Divinity, Cambridge.
26. Miss Pauline Webb was the other president. Montefiore's first co-president was Lady Stansgate (mother of Tony Benn MP). The society was founded in 1929.
27. The diocesan registrar was Mr M.B. Shaw; the diocesan chancellor was Judge F. Aglionby.
28. This document was withdrawn and one on Christian–Jewish–Muslim relations was substituted.

17   Living Tornado with a Human Face

1. *God and Mental Illness*, published by Norvicare, was the inaugural Anne French Memorial Lecture, given on 2 November 1984 in the Post-Graduate Centre at Hellesdon Hospital, Norwich. The lecture is a tangible expression of the close links between the chaplains and their colleagues working in psychiatry.

2. Bishop Lesslie Newbigin, author, preacher and theologian, had been Bishop of Madras in the Church of South India.
3. Michael Humphrey Dickens Whinney resigned from the see of Southwell in 1987 as a result of ill health. He is a descendant of Charles Dickens.
4. Article 'Let men vote by ballot', *Birmingham Evening Mail*, 7 November 1984.
5. For example, 'It's time to compromise over strike', *Birmingham Evening Mail*, 24 November 1981.
6. He later made two interventions in House of Lords debates: 'British Leyland Subsidiary Companies' (5 March 1986) and 'The Rover Group' (2 December 1986).
7. A major paper on the subject formed a Presidential Address to the Birmingham Diocesan Synod in 1978.
8. The Bishops of Durham (David Jenkins) and Sheffield (David Lunn) were also active.
9. Paternoster Press, 1988.
10. Many people considered Jim Thompson to be the best choice for Birmingham as Montefiore's successor.
11. Church House Publishing, 1985.
12. Sir Richard O'Brien (Chairman, Policy Studies Institute, formerly Chairman of ACCUPA); Vice-Chairman: The Ven. John Duncan (Archdeacon of Birmingham); Members: Gordon Cherry (Professor of Urban and Regional Planning, Birmingham University; Ken Cure (Executive Council Member, AEUW); Keith Dennis, headteacher, Shenley Court Comprehensive School); Mgr Tom Fallon (parish priest, Handsworth); Revd John Haslam (solicitor and non-stipendiary priest); Peter Houghton (Director, Birmingham Settlement); Dr Mary Jeavons (GP, Chelmsley Wood); Revd Les Milner (Director, St Basil's Centre); Rt Revd Lesslie Newbigin (theologian and Minister, Winson Green); Revd Desmond Pemberton (Wesleyan Holiness Church); John M. Samuels (Professor of Business Finance, Department of Accounting, Birmingham University); Dr John Sawkill (Director, Tube Investments); James Wilson (General Manager, Bournville Village Trust); Hazel Wright (headteacher, Grove Infant and Nursery School, Grove Lane, Handsworth).
13. See article 'The Tulsa Affair', *The Bishopric*, December 1986.

14. The history is partially documented in *Graham Leonard: Bishop of London*, John S. Peart-Binns, Darton, Longman and Todd, 1988.
15. *Crockford's Clerical Directory 1987/8*, Church House Publishing, 1987.
16. 'In defence of Dr Runcie', *The Times*, December 1987; 'How Dare a Failed MP Attack Brave Runcie?' *Sun*, December 1987 (this was a reply to Peter Bruinvels, former Conservative MP for Leicester East).

Appendix A

Christian Believing: 'What I Believe'
Hugh Montefiore

There is a great variety of ways in which people become Christians. Some like myself are introduced to Christianity through a sudden and intimately personal experience irrupting into consciousness; and it is only later that reflection takes place, and intellectual problems of theology arise. The case may not be so very different for some who have been brought up within the Christian Church. From infancy and childhood they may have been nurtured within the community of faith in such a way that they have thought little about their beliefs until adulthood, when (especially if they are intellectuals) they may begin to examine the doctrinal contents of their faith.

It is only natural that this should happen, for curiosity is a characteristic of the higher mammals, and one of the distinguishing characteristics of *Homo sapiens* is a propensity for intellectual curiosity. All intelligent Christians should feel the claim upon them of rigorous intellectual honesty, and when this is combined with a sharpened intellectual curiosity, the result is a passionate search for truth. Christian theology is the product of such a passion.

There are, however, different kinds of truth, and theological truth differs from other kinds. A true statement is usually understood to be one which corresponds to what is the case, or that which is internally self-consistent, and coherent with other truths. But a theological statement cannot precisely tell me what is the case, for the subject of theology is God, and my finite contingent intellect cannot precisely comprehend what is infinite and necessary: I cannot, for example, know just what I mean if I assert that God is love. Even analogical statements about God lack precision (implying, for example, that God's love is to God as human love is to a human being), because by their very nature the precise relationship between God and human beings in such a statement remains mysterious. I can try to describe my relationship to God but I cannot precisely define it.

What then am I doing when I make a statement about God? Theological statements are models, or more usually they contain a combination of differing models in a sophisticated interrelationship, through which different aspects of the reality of God may be conceptualized and thus communicated. I cannot hope that any theological statement that I make about God can be fully adequate to his reality, nor can I necessarily expect a completely logical self-consistency or coherence in a theological statement, or in a series of such statements. For if I am trying to conceptualize a Reality who lies beyond the signification of human language and for whom no adequate human models of thought can exist, then I may have to be content with seeming paradox and inconsistency. Even in the subatomic sciences (in the cases of light and matter, for example) description through analogies and symbols may give rise to apparently paradoxical statements; and *a fortiori* in theological statements, where different aspects of divine activity may require different and to some extent contradictory models, some degree of paradox is to be expected.

How then am I to find some criterion by which I can theologize? How am I to decide what is true from what is false? Can a distinction be made between orthodoxy and heresy, or is the distinction no longer valid?

The ultimate criterion of any theological statement is for me its *adequacy*. It must be adequate to satisfy all the evidence that I can accept, and my interpretation of that evidence. What evidence can I accept? To begin with, a theological statement of belief must be adequate to my experience (such as it has been) and to my interpretation of that experience. For example, I could not accept that the religious experience that inaugurated my Christian commitment was delusory. Although I may interpret it as clothed in the imagery appropriate to my con-

dition at the time, any interpretation which denies its transcendental origin is for me inadequate. Similarly, any expression of
my belief must be adequate to the grace which I have received
as a Christian through word and sacrament.

Again, such an expression of faith must be adequate to my
understanding of the world of nature and of people; that is to
say, it must be congruous with the truth as I understand this
through the natural sciences, and as I encounter it in the world
in which I live. For example, since human personality is formed
through the pairing of twenty-three male and twenty-three
female chromosomes, I find that I can best assert the orthodox
dogma of Jesus' full humanity by interpreting the credal phrases
'conceived by the Holy Ghost, born of the Virgin Mary' in
what are for me very real and meaningful but non-literal and
symbolic senses; and similarly I interpret the phrase 'from
whence he shall come to judge the quick and the dead' in an
equally real but non-literal and symbolic sense in the light of the
scientific hypothesis that in some 10^{10} years the sun will become
a red giant and swallow up the earth.

Again, a theological statement of my belief must be adequate
to what is known through the behavioural sciences about social
and psychological factors affecting belief. Although these cannot prove or disprove the truth or validity of my religious faith,
they can force me into a rigorous self-examination, challenging
me to ask whether my judgement about what is true has been
affected by my psychological needs to assert it as true. These
social and psychological factors themselves produce a criterion
of adequacy: 'What kind of God has created a world in which
laws of this kind operate about our beliefs concerning him?'

One important question to be asked about religious beliefs
focused on an historical person is this: 'Is there an adequate
historical base on which these beliefs about an historical person
can rest?' Although this vast subject must be pursued in detail
with the greatest possible rigour of historical and literary
enquiry, the actual questions that I need to ask myself may be
reduced to two only: 'Is there adequate evidence to establish the
personal character which Jesus must have had to give rise to
these Gospels about him?' and 'Is the evidence of the Gospels
adequate as a base on which to ground the Christian belief in his
crucifixion and resurrection?' I do not have to convince myself

that *proof* can be found from these sources, but simply that other explanations of the Gospel evidence are more inadequate than affirmatory replies to these questions.

Another aspect of the criterion of adequacy assumes particular importance for me because of my Jewish background. I was nurtured with a lively faith in the same one God in whom I still believe, and I cannot deny my origins. In any case I find much evidence of a genuine relationship of faith on the part of members of religions other than the one which I profess; and when (as I wish to do) I assert the uniqueness and exclusiveness of Jesus Christ, what I say must be adequate to the reality of religious experience on the part of those who are not his adherents.

At first sight it might seem that these criteria of adequacy leave me with only a subjective version of the Christian faith. This subjective aspect is inherent in any form of personal belief. A man can only believe what he does believe, and he cannot force himself to accept something that he believes to be untrue, and even if he accepts a belief on the authority of an institution or of another person, there is a subjective aspect to his belief in their authority. But a man's faith is not simply his own. I have received mine through others, and it has been nurtured within the fellowship of the Church. It is intrinsically improbable that the truth about the Christian faith (or of a particular doctrine of the Christian faith) has been hidden down the centuries but has been only lately revealed to me. I share my faith with others, and to disown their fundamental convictions is to cut myself off from the community of faith to which I belong. No doubt the whole question of faith looks very different to someone who lives outside this fellowship of faith; but the existence of unbelievers and agnostics – a factor I must take into account when testing my faith – does not alter for me the adequacy of faith as a response to life.

A crucial test of adequacy is the relationship of my own beliefs to those of mainstream Christianity down the centuries, especially to the theological expressions of belief to be found in holy Scripture. The very possibility of an appeal beyond Scripture rules out the Bible as my only or even my highest guide, for if there is even one occasion when I do not accept its overriding authority, then there must be some criterion higher than Scripture to which I can appeal. On the other hand, the evidence forces me to give a very high authority indeed to the contents of the New Testament, not only as a result of critical study, but also because its words so often speak to my whole self – at the deep levels of will and feelings and imagination as well as at the ratiocinative and discursive levels of mind. When read or heard in a discriminating way, passages from the Bible (including the Old as well as the New Testament) can not only illumine my path but also become for me, as for others, a vehicle of the Holy Spirit. Yet the Bible does not claim inerrancy for itself and I have no reason to suppose it is inerrant. Moreover, I would expect that within a broad spectrum of theological agreement there exists some theological pluralism; and that is what I find even in the New Testament. I cannot suppose that its contents will be free from cultural relativism, so that I may expect to 'translate' or 'remythologize' its thought forms and imagery in order to reformulate for myself the truths which the sacred writers were trying to express when they wrote as they did.

Scripture is the source of Christian tradition, which flows down the centuries to the present, beginning from the original witnesses of the events which were constitutive of the Church. Within this mainstream there have been many different currents and bifurcations, and there are few doctrinal formulations that can claim recognition by a rigorous application of the Vincentian canon *quod semper, quod ubique, quod ab omnibus* (always, everywhere, and by all). None the less, the chief theological affirmations which the Church has held in common far outweigh in importance the differences which are the product of a theological pluralism such as has always existed within Christendom, even when there appeared outwardly to be conformity. Although I may have to reinterpret them afresh for today, I dare not deny these main theological affirmations which the Church has always held without cutting myself off from mainstream Christianity. Yet I cannot expect my own formulated beliefs to be the same as those held in past ages, because I accept the fact of a certain cultural relativism; I think differently from others because I live within a particular context of culture. Nor can I expect to hold the same beliefs as all other Christians, not because I believe that truth is unimportant, but because I realize that the apprehension of truth by each person is determined to a certain extent by his psychological temperament, and also by the environment in which he has been nurtured and in which he now lives.

I must ask myself: is there in fact any substantial subject of faith at all? My basic affirmation is that of Being beyond all being and within all being. It is an affirmation that the world has meaning and value in itself, and is not a mere random concatenation of atoms and energy, unexplained and inexplicable. It is an act of faith in reality at its deepest level and in the rationality and righteousness of the universe. This fundamental affirmation exemplifies the many-sidedness of the criterion of adequacy. It is not for me a matter of mere argumentation – the Five Ways of St Thomas Aquinas cannot prove the existence of God – nor can such a conclusion be read off from the natural or behavioural sciences: signals of transcendence, for example, can be at best 'rumours of angels', not proofs of God. It is a convergence of evidence that justifies my religious affirmation about God: any other attempt to interpret life is not less but more inadequate to explain all the evidence, including the phenomena of man's religious experience and the deepest needs of his psyche for challenge and security. But I do not in fact believe in God because it is reasonable to do so, or even because I find it the least inadequate interpretation of existence, however convincing this way of thinking may appear. I believe because I am caught up in a community of faith which has many aspects. It is when I am assailed by doubt whether I ought to go on believing that I ask myself what is more adequate to the situation, to believe, to disbelieve, or to suspend belief? I must take into account my own religious experience, that of my fellow-Christians from New Testament times down the ages, as well as the theistic beliefs and testimony of adherents to other faiths. I must ask myself whether this experience of God which I share with others is best regarded as illusory or indicative of divine Reality. I evaluate as best I may the evidences of religious psychology, I look at the form and content of contingent existence, the mysteries of energy and matter in subatomic structures and in inter-galactic space. I ask myself about the adequacy of a reductionist interpretation of truth, beauty, goodness, and love. I find that the affirmation of God is a more adequate response to all this than any other.

Out of this basic affirmation about God springs the whole of my doctrinal structure of belief. If I affirm God, I must affirm him as personal or at least as not less than personal, because he cannot be less than his own creation. Insasmuch as he is the creator and sustainer of everything, I would expect to find within his universe the creativity and regularity which the evolutionary process in fact provides. Because there is personality in God and he is transcendent over his universe, I apply to him the human model of fatherhood. Because he is God, he is one; for two Gods form a contradiction in terms. But unity is not necessarily a simple concept. When I contemplate the complexity and dynamism of our evolving universe, together with the suffering experienced by the sentient life within it, a bare static monism which affirms the Unmoved Mover is for me as inadequate as its explanation. A trinitarian faith (whatever be the metaphysical mystery which underlies it) is less inadequate to my experience of God and of his world.

God is almighty in the sense that as Creator and Sustainer he is responsible for everything that is and for all beings who have emerged. He is therefore responsible for the evil in the world; and I would expect him to take special steps on behalf of those beset by it as I find that he has done through Jesus of Nazareth. Because love is the highest experience of human life, and stands at the apex of human values, I must suppose that God's nature is best likened to the model of human love, and that he would use love to overcome evil; and this is what is disclosed to me through Jesus. In fact the very notion of God is so obscure, and so beyond my human comprehension, that it seems congruous with his nature, if he is love, to disclose himself to me through a medium which I can understand; and this too is what is disclosed to me through Jesus. If God used matter and energy as the vehicle for himself, then it seems to follow that these are fundamentally good in themselves, and that God's mode of operation within his universe is likely to be sacramental, i.e. using the physical and material as the medium and means of his spiritual action within his world. If God's nature is love, it would also seem congruous not only that he should disclose himself to all people who are capable of response to him, but that he should also make a personal self-disclosure through the only medium which human beings really understand – that is, through human personality. If God's nature is love, it would also seem congruous that he should wish to share this love with created beings, that in his providence beings capable of participating in his nature should emerge, and that he should enable them to respond. All this I believe to have been disclosed to be the case.

This, in brief, is my formal outline of faith. Christology does not alter my doctrine of God; it clarifies and defines it. The teaching of Christ is not true because Christ taught it: he taught it because it is true. Christ did not reveal a new face of God. He came to disclose the eternal face of God so far as human personality is capable of disclosing it, and by his life, death, and resurrection to effect that reconciliation between God and man which the Divine Will always strives to effect. God wills to be incarnate in all his creatures, and to effect universal reconciliation within his creation: in Jesus his will was fully and uniquely realized.

This historical account of Jesus, in so far as it can be recovered from the Gospels, is subject to strict historical enquiry, and so are the previous events of Jewish history which culminated in his ministry. Although we have not histories of Jesus, but Gospels which interpret his ministry and are coloured by the later experience of the Church, yet in my judgement the character of Jesus shines clear through the records, and the main events of his ministry and the outline of his teaching can be discerned. I cannot explain away the 'miraculous' aspects of the Gospels as fictitious on *a priori* grounds, for the proven existence of paranormal phenomena suggests a more open approach. The idea that the early Church (for the best of reasons, perhaps, and to a large extent unconsciously) may have fabricated the evidence of the Gospels is to me a far less adequate hypothesis than that the historical person of Jesus, with the character depicted in the Gospels, was the creative force which gave rise to the records. His character is to me self-authenticating, as it has been for millions of others. Mere historical reconstruction by itself can only inform us about earlier events and people. It is the coincidence of history and divinely inspired interpretation of it that gives a disclosure of God working within it. So far as the person of Jesus is concerned, this divinely inspired interpretation, shared within the fellowship of the Church, is the combination of three factors: his own self-understanding, expressed in the Gospels and elaborated in the rest of the New Testament; the impact of his character on my consciousness, whereby I acknowledge him as a man uniquely and divinely inspired to disclose God and to make God present; and my personal experience through which I find that he still influences my life today. And so for me he is not only Jesus of Nazareth, but also the risen Lord.

How am I to interpret this mystery to myself and to others? Various models suggest themselves as the least inadequate and provisional modes of explanation. I think of God's energy active throughout his universe, and uniquely active in the life, death, and resurrection of Jesus. The mystery of Christ's divinity can perhaps best be understood by thinking of the moving pattern of divine activity coincident with and focused in the human life of Jesus, and by interpreting the union of human and divine in Jesus after the model of human free will and divine grace. Jesus' death on the cross can perhaps best be understood as God's acceptance of the worst evil of the world which he has created. In the god-forsakenness of Jesus on the cross and in the accursed nature of his death, God was at work so as to open up life and freedom to those whose lives become a desolation and a hell. Through his acceptance of the worst that men can do, God gives an assurance that all men, however bad, are accepted by his love. By his conquest of death on Easter Sunday, God affirmed the ultimate victory of love and truth over evil and falsehood, and embraced all men within this act of redemption.

There remain, of course, many problems and mysteries. For example, in what respects did the particular human nature of Jesus act as the medium of divine self-disclosure? We can only speculate; and such speculations (although regrettably they can cause great distress when distorted by the mass media of communication) are for me a necessary outcome of a genuine search for religious truth; for without speculation there can be no advance in religious understanding.

Christology is the focal element of Christian belief; but it forms only one part of a local doctrinal structure. Whatever may have been the physical manifestations of Christ's ressurection, they attest the power and propriety of his death. The death and resurrection of Jesus give us one of the deepest insights into the nature of reality. Christ died and rose again because the combination of love and faithfulness to truth, when they appear most powerless, are in fact victorious. The resurrection of Christ is not just a past event, but he is alive and active in the world. His Spirit, which is active throughout the evolving universe, and which gives to human beings their special worth, energizes the Church, which despite its human and therefore sinful aspect, is of divine appointment: it is the means through which the Gospel has been made known and the setting in which it is lived. Within the Church grace has been given to needy Christians through word and sacrament. The Bible is not only an essential source book of origins, but also – despite the 'occasional' character of much of its contents and the cultural relativism within its pages – an inspired collection of books through which God can make himself known to me. The gospel sacraments of Baptism and Eucharist inaugurate and continue the Christian's relationship to Christ in a sacramental mode. The apostolic ministry is to represent Christ to the Church and the Church to Christ; and this apostolic ministry, no less than the apostolic scriptures, while not essential to the Church's life, is a gift which the Church cannot afford to be without. None the less, it becomes more dispensable as people become more and more mature. But the immaturity of Christians is a sign that God's purpose is incomplete in this world. The divine intention in creation, redemption, and sanctification embraces the whole world, not just mankind: it includes the fitting of human beings to share eternally in the divine life of love and joy; and for this the process of development continues after death. The Church therefore does not exist for itself, but to serve the true needs of all the world; to help to create a society where men and women can fully develop; and to help individuals within it towards a ripeness of life and character to fit them for everlasting life.

Such, in broad outline, is the particular doctrinal framework to which I myself presently subscribe, and which within the confines of this short paper can only summarily be described. Such a doctrinal position, however, can only be provisional. No interpretation of belief can do justice to the Reality which it seeks to express. Moreover, my understanding of truth can change and (I hope) develop; better models can be employed; a rapidly changing culture can result in changed ways of thinking; errors can be purged and mistakes corrected. What is true for me now was not true for me twenty years ago: and, what is more, it is not true for others now. Without in any way abandoning my own convictions – what is true for me now – I must admit the fact of theological pluralism. All doctrinal systems are therefore only provisional.

Then what security of belief can I have? 'General Councils . . . may err, and sometimes have erred, even in things pertaining to God.' However, dogmas of the Church, which are accepted universally (or nearly universally) within the mainstream Churches, will have very great authority. (I suppose it is possible that I might want to repudiate such dogmas as are contained in the Apostles' Creed or the Chalcedonian Definition, but if I did so, I would not feel able to continue to hold office within the Church.) And yet there are grave difficulties that prevent an unreserved and *ex animo* acceptance of all the Church's dogmas as the personal expression of my own convictions. In the first place, dogmas are written in the language and thought forms of the age that defined them, and these may be different from my own (e.g. the use and meaning of *homoousios*, 'of one substance'). Secondly, every formulation of faith is 'imperfect, incomplete, partial and fragmentary'. Usually they have a polemical bias: they are responses to questions which may be framed very differently today. What a true statement says is true; but what it fails to say may also be true. Theological statements are propositional in form and dialectical in character. The mystery of God is such that any propositional statement which we make about him needs qualification.

The formulation of a dogma, therefore, does not mean that truth has been defined: it means that, through dogmatic assertion, the boundaries of doctrinal formulation have been delineated in such a way as to guard against heresy (that is, an unbalanced formulation of belief), and to open up the possibilities of new doctrinal interpretation. I therefore approach the Church's dogmas with the greatest respect, and (particularly in my episcopal capacity as the Church's representative, which I can never fully divorce from my private life) I can reinterpret but never repudiate or refuse them. That does not mean that I must necessarily assert them *ex animo*. They are a stimulus to my renewed attempts to interpret my belief in a way that is intellectually rigorous, personally satisfying, and pastorally relevant. Dogmas are profoundly important as guidelines to the Church's thinking, and as safeguards against heresy and error.

Yet, even in granting as much as this to doctrine and dogma, I have to enter into the cloud of unknowing, and to assert the Church's apophatic tradition. In the suspension of my critical faculties of mind and in the opening of myself to the living God in an attitude of comtemplative prayer I know him more truly than in any intellectual proposition about him. Before the mystery of the Divine Presence and Energy all doctrinal reasoning seems as inadequate as the babblings of an infant to the apprehension of an adult. We know only the outskirts of God's ways, and in the silence of concentrated attention the soul can grasp what the mind can never comprehend. Whenever the mind affirms that it understands some truth about God, the soul must also cry out that in the abyss of silence and nothingness a man can find a more authentic affirmation of his religious faith.

But something must be said. Truth needs to be communicated. Experience needs to be shared. The facts of an historical faith need to be known. Very well; but my present understanding of God is only provisional, my present and past experience of God may be superseded, the facts of an historical faith may conceivably be disproved. Have I any commitment which is ultimate?

I commit myself wholly to the living God, the divine Reality who confronts me in my own being and in the world around me and who is transcendent beyond it as well as energetic within it. This living Reality demands my total allegiance. And so too does Jesus. 'And he called unto him the multitude with his disciples, and he said unto them: "If any man would come after me, let him deny himself and take up his cross and follow me." ' The call still echoes down the centuries, and with it the power and grace to respond. Following Jesus does not mean primarily believing orthodox propositions about him (although it may involve this); at least it did not mean that during his lifetime. The Apostles did not have to undertake a course of study: they were ordered 'Follow me'. To recite the creed is not the same as to follow Jesus; and in using the creed at baptism we seem to be making a qualifying examination harder than 'finals'. When a young man came to Jesus and wanted to do something more than keep the commandments, he was not ordered to study theology or to learn doctrine: he was told 'Follow me'. To follow Jesus means to adopt his attitudes towards God, towards my fellow men, and towards myself. It has huge implications for my attitudes and practice of prayer and worship, as well as for my deeply held personal and interior feelings of guilt and acceptance, fear and love, anxiety and meaningfulness, disharmony and peace. It has implications too for my outward behaviour, how I react to people and to situations, and what decisions I take. To give my allegiance to God and to follow Jesus affect also my intellectual attitudes. Believing with Jesus that all truth comes from God, I try, like Jesus, to pursue it wherever it may lead me, and I strive to reconcile secular and religious knowledge. Believing that it is unlikely that God has grievously misled his Church in the past, I do not lightly reject past orthodoxies; believing that others are wiser than myself, I accept the fact of theological pluralism.

I accept the Church's dogmas about Christology, in that I greatly respect them and would not dream of disowning them. I have tried to work out my own beliefs about Jesus in a doctrinal system; but I must admit that it is only provisional. The mystery of Jesus is greater than any formulation about him. I find him as a Person compelling and inescapable, and when he calls me to follow, I can but try to obey. I number myself among those who 'in the toils, the conflicts, the sufferings which they pass through in his fellowship' can learn 'as an ineffable mystery, who he is'. All our dogmas are partial and our doctrines provisional. It is not by these, but by my prayers and my life that, as a disciple of Christ, I make my ultimate affirmation about God, creator, redeemer, and sanctifier.

Appendix B

Select Bibliography
Books

Beyond Reasonable Doubt, Hodder & Stoughton, 1963.
Awkward Questions on Christian Love: The Lincoln Lectures 1964, Fontana, 1964.
The Epistle to the Hebrews (Commentary), A & C Black, 1964.
Truth to Tell: A Radical Restatement of Christian Faith, Fontana, 1966.
Remarriage and Mixed Marriage: A Plea for Dual Reform (The Keene Lectures given in Chelmsford Cathedral, September 1966), SPCK, 1967.
My Confirmation Notebook, SPCK, 1968, fifth edition, 1984.
The Question Mark. The End of Homo Sapiens (Theological Lectures in Queen's University, Belfast, 1969), Collins, 1969.
Can Man Survive?: The Question Mark and Other Essays, Fontana, 1970.
Taking Our Past into Our Future, Fontana, 1978.
Paul: The Apostle, Fontana, 1981.
Jesus Across the Centuries: His Relevance to Our Problems, SCM, 1983.
The Probability of God, SCM, 1985.
So Near and Yet So Far: Rome, Canterbury and ARCIC, SCM, 1986.

Communicating the Gospel in a Scientific Age (The Barclay
Lectures 1988, Glasgow),   St Andrew Press,   1988.

Pamphlets, Booklets – sole author

To Help You to Pray,   SCM,   1957.
Josephus and the New Testament,   Mowbray,   1959.
Marriage (Lecture given in Canterbury Cathedral 29 October
1969),   Canterbury Cathedral,   1969.
Fourth Annual Hopkins Sermon (preached at the Church of the
Immaculate Conception, Farm Street, London, 4 June 1972),
                                        Hopkins Society,   1972.
*Doom or Deliverance: The Dogmas and Duties of a Technological
Age* (The Rutherford Lecture, Central London Polytechnic,
19 November 1971),   Manchester University Press,   1972.
Apocalypse: What Does God Say? (three lectures given in South-
wark Cathedral, October 1976), Southwark Cathedral,   1976.
Sir Moses Montefiore and His Great-Nephew (Eleventh Monte-
fiore Memorial Lecture, University of Southampton, 12 February 1979),   University of Southampton,   1979.
Going Places: A Christian Appraisal of Transport Policies (Sixteenth Tawney Lecture),   Tawney House,   1979.
The Kingdom of God in Our Land (Pastoral Letter to Birmingham
diocese, Advent 1981),   p.p.   1981.
Risen With Healing in His Wings (Pastoral Letter to Birmingham
diocese, Lent 1983, adapted from Presidential Address given to
the Institute of Religion and Medicine, July 1982), p.p.   1983.
The Church and the Jews (Lent Lecture given to clergy of the
Stepney Area, 24 February 1983),   p.p.   1983.
'Many Shall Come from the East and the West' (Pastoral Letter to
Birmingham diocese, Advent 1984),   p.p.   1984.
God and Mental Illness (Anne French Lecture, Norwich, 1984),
                                        Norvicare,   1985.
Christian Values in a Technological Society (Eleventh Leggett
Lecture, University of Surrey, 4 November 1987),
                                        University of Surrey,   1987.
The Meaning of Freedom (Annual Froebal Lecture, 5 May 1988),
                                        p.p.   1988.

Environmental Problems (1988 George Williams Lecture),
                                                    YMCA,   1988.

Books, Pamphlets – joint author

Thomas and The Evangelists, Studies in Biblical Theology, No.
35, with H.E.W. Turner,   SCM,   1962.
Can We Covenant?, Correspondence with Bishop Lesslie Newbigin,   John Paul/The Preachers Press,   1981.
God, Sex and Love, with Jack Dominian,   SCM, 1989.

Books – edited by

*We Must Love One Another Or Die: Lectures on Love, Sex and
Morality*, Frank Lake, H.E. Root and V.A. Demant, Introduc-
tion by Montefiore,   SCM,   1963.
Sermons From Great St Mary's (Montefiore's contributions: 'For
God's Sake – Live'; 'Christian Belief – Birth and Rebirth'; 'The
Resurrection – Of What?'; 'Our Lord Jesus Christ'; 'After Mug-
geridge and Davis'),   Fontana, 1968.
More Sermons from Great St Mary's (Montefiore's contributions:
'What is the Resurrection?', unscripted discussion with Bishop
John Robinson; 'Can Mankind Survive?' unscripted discussion
with Lord Ritchie Calder; 'Nothing Really Matters'),
                                               Fontana,   1971.
Changing Directions, Report of the Independent Transport
Commission,   Hodder & Stoughton,   1974.
Man and Nature, Report with appended essays of working
group appointed by the Archbishop of Canterbury in 1971 to
work in connection with Doctrine Commission,
                                               Collins,   1975.
Nuclear Crisis: A Question of Breeding, with David Gosling,
                                               Prism,   1977.
Yes To Women Priests (Contributors: Donald MacKinnon,
Christopher Evans, F.W. Dillistone, Mary Simpson, Gilbert
Baker and Michael Perry; Montefiore's contribution: Foreward,
'The Theology of Priesthood'),
                          Mowbray/Mayhew McCrimmon,   1978.

Books – contributor to

'The Historic Episcopate', in *The Historic Episcopate in the Fullness of the Church*, ed. K.M. Carey,   A & C Black,   1949.
They Became Anglicans, ed. Dewi Morgan,   Mowbray,   1959.
'Man's Dominion', in *The Responsible Church*, ed. Edwin Barker,   SPCK,   1966.
'Personal Relations Before Marriage', in *God, Sex and War*,
                               Fontana,   1963.
'Towards a Christology for Today', in *Soundings*, ed. A.R. Vidler,   Cambridge University Press,   1967.
'Terms of Reference', Dialogue with David Tribe and Peter Snow, in *Dialogue with Doubt*,   SCM,   1967.
'In Via', in *Journeys in Belief*, ed. Bernard Dixon,
                          Allen & Unwin,   1968.
'Jesus, the Revelation of God', in *Christ For Us Today*, ed. N. Pittenger,   SCM,   1968.
'Jesus on Divorce and Remarriage', in *Marriage, Divorce and the Church*,   SPCK,   1971.
'Symbols and the Eucharist', in *Thinking about the Eucharist*, ed. Ian Ramsey,   SCM,   1972.
'Ethical Problems of Geriatrics', in *Death Anxiety*,
                          MSS Inf.Corp.,   1973.
'What I Believe', in *Christian Believing*,   SPCK,   1976.
'Nationalism and Internationalism', in *Today's Church and Today's World*,   CIO,   1977.
'Light from the Past', in *Theology and Social Concern*,
                  Board for Social Responsibility,   1986.
'The Rape of the Earth'; 'On Behalf of Posterity', 'The Richness of Creation', in *My World*, ed. Shelagh Brown,
                  Bible Reading Fellowship,   1989.

The Bishopric

'Review of Reith Lectures' (Christianity and The World Order by Edward Norman),   January   1979.
'Christian Initiation',   January   1979.
'Disarmament',   November   1979.

'Drink!'   July   1980.
'The Church of England and The Pope',   November   1980.
'Hard Sayings, No. 17' ('No one comes to the Father except by
me'),   November   1980.
'Hard Sayings, No. 2' ('So also none of you can be a disciple of
mine without parting with all his possessions'), January   1981.
'Nuclear Defence Forces',   May   1981.
'After One Holocaust',   September   1981.
'Down California Way',   November   1981.
'Conscience and the Clergy',   January   1982.
'Visit to a Spiritual Twin' (Visit to Lyons),   March   1982.
'A Taste of Russia',   July   1982.
'Believing in God',   November   1982.
'Divorce – A National Crisis',   May   1983.
'Shrouded in Mystery' (Turin Shroud),   May   1983.
'Reflections on Malawi',   July   1983.
'Why Believe in God?',   November   1983.
'Jesus: The Evidence',   June   1984.
'The Durham Affair',   September   1984.
'The Don Cupitt Show',   November   1984.
'Is Interest Immoral?',   January   1985.
'A Secret Ballot – The Moral Issues',   January   1985.
'Bishops and Belief',   March   1985.
'On Christian Believing',   March   1985.
'Experiments on Human Embryos',   March   1985.
'Clergy and the Quality Press',   May   1985.
'Sunday Trading',   January   1986.
'Renewal in Lozells',   January   1986.
'Morality of Star Wars',   November   1986.
'Animal Experiments',   November   1986.
'This Joyful Eastertide',   April   1986.
'The Nature of Belief',   July   1986.
'The Credibility of God',   September   1986.
'The Tulsa Affair',   December   1986.
'Illegitimacy and AIDS',   December   1986.

Articles

'The Position of the Cana Miracle and the Cleansing of the

Temple in St John's Gospel', *Journal of Theological Studies*, Vol. L, 199/210, 1949.

'Roman Catholics and the Bible', *Theology*, Vol. LVIII, No. 410, August 1954.

'God As Father in the Synoptic Gospels', *New Testament Studies*, 1956.

'When Did Jesus Die?', *Expository Times*, Vol. LXXII, No. 25, November 1960.

'Josephus and the New Testament', *Novum Testamentum*, Vol. 14, Fasc. 2 & 4, 1960.

'Does "L " Hold Water?', *Journal of Theological Studies*, 1961.

'Thou Shalt Love Thy Neighbour As Thyself', *Novum Testamentum*, Vol. V, Fasc. 2/3, 1962.

'Suplicius Severus and Titus' Council of War', *Historia*, XI, 2 April 1962.

'Revolt in the Desert' (Mark 4: 30ff), *New Testament Studies*, No. 8, 1962.

'Jesus and the Temple Tax', *New Testament Studies*, No. 10, 1964.

'Why I Am a Christian', *Varsity*, 15 October 1955.

'Man's Hope of Survival', *Observer*, 19 December 1971.

'Divorced Vicars', *News of the World*, 27 February 1972.

'Turning Point for the Church of England', *Guardian*, 2 May 1972.

'Economics and Ethics', *Church Times*, 29 December 1972.

'Population Control: An Ethical and Theological Assessment', *Journal of Environmental Studies*, Vol. 8, 1975.

'Only Months to Plan for 250,000 Years?', *Observer*, 21 December 1975.

'Discord on Concorde', *Crucible*, April–June 1976.

'Authority in the Church', *Theology*, May 1977.

'Management and Accountability', *The Month*, July 1976.

'Man and Nature: A Theological Assessment', *Zygon*, September 1977.

'Understanding Closed Shops', *Church Times*, 18 November 1977.

' "Lichfield" Right to Recommend Changing Rules', *Church Times*, 19 May 1978.

'Shattering Vote Against Progress' (ordination of women to the priesthood), *Birmingham Post*, 11 July 1979.

'Mr Botha's Window-Dressing', *The Times*, 18 June 1980.

'Authority in the Church', *Theology*, November 1983.

'It's Time to Compromise over Strike', *Birmingham Evening Mail*, 7 November 1984.

'Let Men Vote by Ballot', *Birmingham Evening Mail*, November 1984

'Is Interest Immoral?', *Banking World*, December 1984.

'Experiments on Human Embryos', *Religion and Medicine*, April 1985.

'From One Bishop to Another: What would happen if drugs and prostitution were legalized?' (response to Richard Holloway, Bishop of Edinburgh), *London Evening Standard*, 17 December 1986.

'Why Durham is Wrong', *The Times*, 16 September 1986.

'Let Not the Constable Judge' (on James Anderton's remarks on AIDS), *The Times*, 21 January 1987.

'Life in the Synod?' *Theology*, July 1987.

'How Dare a Failed MP Attack Brave Runcie?', *Sun*, December 1987.

'In Defence of Dr Runcie', *The Times*, December 1987.

'Putting the Children First', *Daily Telegraph*, 1988.

'Honesty in Updating God', Guardian, 2 May 1988.

'An Issue That Will Not Go Away' (homosexuality), *The Times*, 20 February 1988.

'Wealth is for Giving' – Commentary, *The Times*, 14 June 1988.

'Private Lines, Public Loss' – Commentary, *The Times*, 28 June 1988.

'Crusade for Survival' – Commentary, *The Times*, 11 July 1988.

'Cohabiting Amicably' – Commentary, *The Times*, 25 July 1988.

'Family Life Takes the Strain' – Commentary, *The Times*, 30 August 1988.

'Shadow of a Doubt' (Turin Shroud) – Commentary, *The Times*, 22 August 1988.

'Out, Turbulent Politicians' – Commentary, *The Times*, 30 August 1988.

'AIDS: The Only Answer' – Commentary, *The Times*, 1988.

'Don't Label All Priests as Evil', *Sun*, 7 October 1988.

'Dead-End Signs on the Road to a Free Market', *Sunday Times*, 16 October 1988.

'A Trip to the Wrong Place and It's Late', *Sunday Times*, 30 October 1988.

Index

Abortion, 264–6
Adley, Robert (MP), 198
AID (artificial insemination by donor),
   252–3
AIDS, 251, 269
AIDS: Some Guidelines for Pastoral Care,
   269
Allchin, A. M., 120 175
Allison, Bishop S. Falkner (Winchester),
   77
Amis, Kingsley, 39
Anglican–Methodist Unity, 135, 173
Annan, Lord Noël, 145
Apocalypse: What Does God Say? (1976),
   202–3
Arakan Campaign, 32
Ashcroft, David, 18–19, 22, 25
Ashdown, Bishop Hugh E. (Newcastle),
   135
Ashkenazi Jews, 1–2
Ashton, Sir Hubert, 160
Atherton, John R., 263–4
Auden, W. H., 95
Authority in Crisis (Runcie), 268
Authority in the Church (ARCIC), 175,
   285–6
Awkward Questions on Christian Love
   (1964), 150–1
Ayer, A. J., 284

Baelz, Peter R., 108
Baillie, D. M., 115, 116
Baillie, John, 116
Baker, Bishop John A. (Salisbury), 121,
   184, 249, 276, 291–2
Banking World, 260–1
Barbour, Robin, 18, 21, 22, 25, 38, 99
Bardsley, Bishop Cuthbert K. N.
   (Coventry), 135

Barker, Margaret, 144–5
Barnes, Bishop E. W. (Birmingham), 212
Bates, M. H., 50
Baughen, Bishop Michael A. (Chester),
   276
Beaudesert Park School,
   Minchinhampton, 16
Beaumont, Lord (Timothy) of Whitley,
   114, 146–9
Beaumont-Dark, Anthony (MP), 211,
   212, 219
Beaverbrook, Lord, 265
Believing in the Church (1981), 277
Benn, Tony (MP), 199, 200
Bennett, E. K. (Francis), 60, 61–2
Bennett, G. V. (Garry), 310, 313
Bennett, Ian F., 300–1
Bermant, Chaim, 2
Berry, R. W. J., 253
Bethune-Baker, J. F., 107
Betjeman, Sir John, 170
Bettinson, John, 228
Beyond Reasonable Doubt (1963), 113, 151
Birmingham Evening Mail, 211, 212
Birmingham Post, 212
Bishop Hugh – With Affection (1987), 314
Bishopric, The (Birmingham), 235, 273
Blanch, Lord – Archbishop Stuart W.
   (York), 245
Board for Social Responsibility (General
   Synod), 141, 173, 246–59
Booth-Clibborn, Bishop Stanley E. F.
   (Manchester), 307
Bowker, John, W., 108, 175
Bowlby, Bishop Ronald O. (Southwark),
   174, 245, 288, 308
Boyd-Carpenter, Lord, 198
Boyse, F. V. A., 84
Boys Smith, J. S., 89

Bridge, Anthony C., 94
Brightman, Lord, 266
British Leyland, 302–4
Brockington, Ian, 73
Brook, Bishop Richard (St Edmundsbury
    & Ipswich), 25
Brooke, Christopher, 64, 162–3
Brown, George (MP), 94
Brown, Bishop Laurence A.
    (Birmingham), 209, 210, 234
Broxton, Richard, 25
Buber, Martin, 115, 116
Buchanan, Bishop Colin O. (Aston), 301,
    314
Burgess, Henry P., 211, 215
Burnaby, John, 108, 110, 111, 112
Burrough, Bishop J. Paul (Mashonaland),
    210
Butler, Bishop Thomas F. (Willesden),
    308

Call to Faith and Commitment, 238
Callaghan, L. James (Prime Minister),
    208, 211
Cambridge Inter-Collegiate Christian
    Union (CICCU), 68, 69, 73, 161
Cambridge Theological Faculty, 105–8
Canterbury, Birmingham Diocesan
    Pilgrimage to, 297–9
'Caps and Mitres', 173
Carey, Bishop Kenneth M. (Edinburgh),
    45–6, 47, 52, 53, 54, 55, 86
Casey, R. P., 107
Cavendish, Lady Elizabeth, 170
Cecil, Philip H., 152–3
Central Readers' Board, 173
CFR–1 (Fast Nuclear Reactor), 200–2
Chadwick, Henry, 106, 109, 112, 120,
    285, 310
Chadwick, James, 60, 64–5
Chadwick, Sir W. Owen, 106
*Changing Britain: Social Diversity and
    Moral Unity* (1987), 263–4
Changing Directions (1974), 192–4
Charismatic Movement, 263
Christian Believing (1976), 125, 183–4,
    277, 283, 337–49
Christian Doctrine of Marriage,
    Archbishop of Canterbury's
    Commission on, 175–82
Church and the Jews, The (1983), 292
Church Commissioners, 160–1, 218
Churchill College Chapel, Cambridge,
    145–9
Church Leaders' Conference,
    Birmingham (1972), 189–92
Church of England Evangelical Council,
    159–60

Church of South India, 54
Church Times, 214, 247
Claringbull, Dennis L., 304, 307
Claxton, Bishop Charles R. (Blackburn),
    135
Cleasby, T. W. Ingram, 42–3
Cockroft, Sir John, 146, 147, 148
Coggan, Lord – Archbishop F. Donald
    (Canterbury), 199, 207–8, 212, 237,
    245
Cole-King, Susan, 291
Coleman, William, T., 196, 199
Columba, David (SSF), 234
Concorde, 196–9
Confirmation Notebook, My (1968), 152–3
Conversion, 22–4, 292
Cooper, John L., 301
Corbishley, Thomas (SJ), 94
Counsell, Michael J. R., 212, 230–1,
    232–3
Credibility of God, The, 281
Crick, Francis, 146
Crockford's Clerical Directory 1987/88, 313
Crosland, Anthony (MP), 141
Cross, F. L., 40
Crown Appointments Commission, 208–
    9
Cupitt, Don, 108, 117–8, 272, 273

Dammers, A. H., 55, 109, 110
Dance with the Devil (Schwab), 137–8
Daube, David, 106
David, Bishop, A. A. (Liverpool), 17
Davie, Iain, 41, 44–5
Davies, Enoch, 35
Davies, Lorys M., 222, 297, 298–9
Dawes, Bishop Peter S. (Derby), 174
de Chardin, Teilhard, 140
Decourtray, RC Archbishop Albert
    (Lyons), 239–41
de la Hoyde, Denys R. H., 70–1
Demant, V. A., 130
de Mendieta, E. A. Amand, 76–7
Denham, Lord, 265
Denning, Lord, 95,261
Dennis (née Joseph), Catherine (cousin),
    25, 26
Dennison, Stanley R., 60, 62
de Pass (grandfather), 10–11
de Pass (grandmother), 10–11
Designing for Survival (1972), 203
Dixon, Bernard, 139
Doctrine Commission, Archbishops',
    120–5
Doctrine Commission, General Synod,
    183–4
Doctrine in the Church of England (1938),
    276–7

Dodd, C. H., 105, 108, 116
Dominian, Jack, 175, 283
Don Cupitt Show, The, 273
Doom or Deliverance? (1972), 186–7
Doomsday Book, The (Rattray Taylor
    1970), 140–1
Dragon School, Oxford, 26
Drummond Lectures, Stirling, xii
Drury, John H., 173
Duffy, Terry, 303
Dugdale, Sir William, 228–30
Duncan, John F., 301
Dunstan, Gordon R., 175
Dwyer, RC Archbishop George Patrick
    (Birmingham), 218
Dykes, Hugh (MP), 199

Ecclestone, Giles, 247
Education, Southwark Diocesan Board
    of, 168–71
Edwardes, Sir Michael, 302
Edwards, David, L., 99, 114
Ellington, Duke, 96
Environment, 135–44, 185–203
Epistle to the Hebrews (1964), 83, 152
Estate of Man, The (Roberts), 136
Evans, Christopher F., 120
Every, Edward, 85
Expository Times, 149–284

Faith and Freedom Movement, 133–5
Faith in the City (1985), 308
Faith in the City of Birmingham (1988),
    307–8
Falk, Peter, 20, 21
Farrer, Austin M., 42
Field, Frank (MP), 313
Finestein, Israel, 4
Fisher, Lord – Archbishop Geoffrey F.
    (Canterbury), 77
Fisher, Sir Ronald, 65
Fison, Bishop Joseph E. (Salisbury), 86,
    90, 100, 153
Fleming, Bishop W. Launcelot S.
    (Norwich), 141
Flew, Anthony, 39
Frankham, Harold E., 172
Frend, W. H. C., 126
Fulljames, Owen, R., 24, 25

Gaia Trust, xii
Garden House Hotel, Cambridge –
    demonstrations, 162
Gardner-Smith, Percival, 107
Garrard, 'Nanny' Lucy, 9–10
Garrard, Richard, 92–3
General Synod, xiii–xiv, 173–4, 262–3
Gilbey, A., 72

Gillick, Victoria, 269
Gilpin, Bishop William P. (Kingston-
    upon-Thames), 157, 170
Girton College, Cambridge, 143
Gladwin, John W., 248–9, 254
God and Mental Illness (1985), 296
God, Sex and War (1963), 151–2
Gonville and Caius College, Cambridge,
    59–77, 82–3, 88, 89
Gordon, Bishop A. Ronald M. (Bishop
    at Lambeth), 210
Gore, Bishop Charles (Oxford), 115, 116,
    210
Gosling, David, 201
Gospel and Our Culture, The, xii
Goulder, Michael, 272–3
Graham, Billy, 94
Great St Mary's Church, Cambridge,
    86–155, 161–2
Green, Bishop Mark (Aston), 211, 212–3,
    218, 219, 224, 301
Green, E. Michael B., 120
Green, V. H. H., 52
Greenslade, S. L., 29
Greer, Bishop W. D. L. (Manchester), 45
Grover, General John, 33
Guardian, 139
Guide for the Unemployed, A, 307
Gummer, John Selwyn (MP), 264

Habgood, Archbishop John S. (York),
    109, 110, 111, 112, 182, 245, 249, 263
HACAN (Heathrow Association for the
    Control of Aircraft Noise), 196
Hadley, Patrick, 60, 62–3, 67
Hailsham, Lord, 259, 266
Hale, Anthony, 203
Hanson, Anthony T., 206
Hare, R. M., 42
Hare, Bishop T. Richard (Pontefract), 42
Harris, Barbara (first woman Anglican
    bishop), xii–xiii
Healey, Denis (MP), 30
Heaton, Eric W., 58, 67, 110
Heaton, T. B., 175
Hewish, Anthony, 146
Hewitt, John, 131
Hick, John, 272–3
Historia, 149
*Historic Episcopate in the Fullness of the
    Church, The* (1949), 55–7
Historic Episcopate, The (1949), 56–7
Hodgson, Leonard, 40
Hollis, Gerald, 218, 219
Holy Land, Pilgrimage to, 299–300
Homes for Homeless People Trust, xi
Honest to God (Robinson), 113–15, 274–5
Hooker, Roger H., 313–14

Hopkins, Gerald Manley, 185
Hopkinson, B. J. (Barney), 91–2, 154–5
Horrocks, Ray, 302
Hoskyns, John A. P., 23–4, 25
Houghton, Lord, 266
Houlden, J. L., 183
House of Lords, 259, 261–2
Howell, Denis (MP), 305
Huddleston, Archbishop Trevor (CR), 95

Infant Life (Preservation) Bill (1986), 265–6
'Is Interest Immoral?' (1984), 260–1
IVF (*in vitro* fertilization), 252–3

James, Bishop Colin C. W. (Winchester),
    245
James, Eric, A., 114, 308
Jeavons, Mary, 231
Jenkins, Patrick (MP), 303
Jenkins, Bishop David E. (Durham), 121,
    150, 151–2, 274–5, 277, 280–1
Jenkins, Claude, 40
*Jesus across the Centuries: His Relevance to
    Our Problems* (1983), 272
Jesus and homosexuality controversy,
    125–31, 211, 212
'Jesus on Divorce and Remarriage' (1971),
    176–7
'Jesus, the Revelation of God' (1967),
    125–7
*Jewish-Christian Guidelines for the Anglican
    Communion* (1988), 293–4
Jews and Christians, 292–4
John XXIII, Pope, 83–4
Jones, Cheslyn P. M., 120
Joseph, Anne (cousin), 25
Joseph, Madge Waley (aunt), 26
Judaism 11–15

Kaufman, Gerald (MP), 198
Kaunda, President Kenneth, 95
Kelly, J. N. D., 310
Kelly, Talbot, 19
Kemp, Bishop Eric W. (Chichester), 311
Kerin, Dorothy, 82
Keyte (née Richardson), E., 16
Kingdom of God in Our Land, The (1981),
    238
King's College Chapel, Cambridge, 98–9
Knox, W. L., 105–6
Koestler, Arthur, 140
Kohima Campaign, 33–4
Kunzle, David, 75

Lampe, Geoffrey W. H., 40, 54, 88, 109,
    111, 163, 289
Lausanne University, 26
Leonard, Bishop Graham D. (London),

173, 182, 245, 246, 275, 276, 288–9,
    309–13

Lewis, Richard, 171–2
Lightfoot, R. H., 40
Lindars, Barnabas (SSF), 143
Live, Learn, Share, 300–1
Loveless, William H., 96–7, 128
Lovelock, James, xii
Lucas, J. R., 121, 177–8
Lunn, Bishop David R. (Sheffield), 307–8
Luthuli Cultural and Welfare Services
    Trust, xi
Lyon, P. H. B., 17, 19, 20, 24
Lyons, visit to, 139–41
MacKinnon, Donald M., 41, 107
Man and Nature (1975), 117, 195–6
Malawi, visit to, 241–3, 301
Management and Accountability (1976), 202
Man in His Living Environment (1969),
    135, 143–4
Many Shall Come from the East and the West
    (1984), 238–9
Margaret Angela, Mother (NSSJD), 212,
    220, 230, 299–300
Marks, Anthony W., 69–70
Marlow, Howard B., 214
Marriage and the Church's Task (1978), 182
Marriage, Divorce and the Church (1971),
    175–82
Marshall, Bishop Michael E., 172–3
Mascall, Eric L., 112, 115
Masters, Bishop Brian J. (Edmonton),
    311
Mather, Carol (MP), 199
Matrimonial and Family Proceedings Bill
    (1983), 259
Matthews, W. R., 111
Maunsell, Mark, 32
Mayfield, Bishop Christopher J.
    (Wolverhampton), 68–9
McFarlane, Ian, 67
Mellor, David (MP), 264–5
Merton, Ralph, 31
Mesquita, David Bueno de, 13–14
Meurig-Davies, 29
Milford, T. R. (Dick), 29, 38, 40, 41–3
Miller, Patrick F., 169, 170, 171
Miners Strike 1984, 305–6
Modern Churchmen's Conference,
    Cambridge (1967), 125–8
Monroe, Hubert, 18, 25
Montefiore, Catherine (daughter), 61, 89,
    109
Montefiore, Claude Goldsmid, 14
Montefiore, Elisabeth (née Paton – wife),
    29, 34, 37, 38, 39, 45, 47, 53, 80, 95,
    124, 170, 233, 314

Montefiore, Hugh William, born (12 May 1920), 9; father, 7–10, 11, 39, 80–1; mother, 8–10, 82; Jewish childhood 9–16; keeping of Passover, 11–13, and Day of Atonement, 12; schools: Wilkinson's (1926–9), 15; Beaudesert Park (1929–33), 16; Rugby (1933–9), 16–26; Barmitzvah (1933), 13; idea of being a rabbi, 14; conversion, 23–4; baptism and confirmation, 25; at St John's College, Oxford (1939–40 and 1945–7), 26–9, 39–45; service with Royal Bucks Yeomanry (1940–5): campaigns at Arakan, 32, and Kohima, 33–4; vocation to ordained ministry, 34–5; marriage to Elisabeth Paton (1945), 38–9; Westcott House as student (1947–9), 45–6; curate at St George's, Jesmond, Newcastle (1949–51), 47–9; interviewed for chaplaincy at Lincoln College, Oxford, 52, and for lectureship at Trinity College, Cambridge, 52; Westcott House as chaplain, tutor and then Vice-Principal (1951–4), 52–8; Gonville and Caius College, Cambridge, as fellow and Dean (1954–63), 58–77, 82, 88, 89; founded 'The Church in Caius', 67; Vicar of St Mary the Great with St Michael and All Angels, Cambridge (1963–70), 86–155, 161–2; Thirty-Nine Articles controversy, 118–22; Jesus and homosexuality controversy, 125–31, 211, 212; building of Churchill College Chapel, 145–9; Bishop Suffragan of Kingston-upon-Thames (1970–8), 155–84, 205–6; Chairman of Southwark Diocesan Board of Education, 168–71; member of Commission on the Christian Doctrine of Marriage, 175–82; Chairman of Independent Transport Commission, 191–5; member of Doctrine Commission, 120–5, 183–4; environmental issues, 135–42, 185–203; Bishop of Birmingham (1978–87), 208–315; controversy over nomination and election, 208–15; enthronement, 217–18; Chairman of Board for Social Responsibility, 141, 173, 246–59; in General Synod, xiii–xiv, 173–4, 262–3; in House of Lords, 259, 261–2; *Infant Life (Preservation) Bill* (1986), 265–6; visits to Holy Land, 84–6, 299–300; Rome, 83–4; Lyons 239–41; Malawi, 241–3; America, xii–xiii, 239; major publications and essays: *The Historic Episcopate*, 56–7;

Beyond Reasonable Doubt, 113, 151; *Awkward Questions on Christian Love*, 150–1; *The Espistle to the Hebrews*, 83, 152; *Truth to Tell*, 151; 'Personal Relations before Marriage', 151; 'Towards a Christology for Today', 111; *My Confirmation Notebook*, 152; 'Jesus, the Revelation of God', 125; *The Question Mark*, 139–41, 186; 'Doom or Deliverance?', 186–9; 'Symbols and the Eucharist', 12, 123–4; 'Jesus on Divorce and Remarriage', 176–7; *Apocalypse: What Does God Say?*, 202; 'What I Believe' (in *Christian Believing*), 125, 183–4, 277, 283, 337–49; 'Nationalism and Internationalism', 206–7; *Paul: The Apostle*, 237; *Jesus across the Centuries*, 272; 'The Church and the Jews', 292; *The Probability of God*, 281, 282, 284–5; *So Near and Yet So Far*, 286–7
Montefiore, Janet (daughter), 45, 89
Montefiore (née Cohen), Judith, 2, 3, 6
Montefiore Memorial Lecture, 5–6
Montefiore, Sir Moses Haim, 1–6, 27, 85
Montefiore, Sarah, 6
Montefiore, Teresa (daughter), 43, 89
Montgomery-Massingberd, Field Marshal Sir, 25
Moral Theology, Anglican method of, 256–7
Morris, Colin, 95
Morrison, John, 146, 147, 148
Moss, Basil S., 218, 219, 281–3, 287–8
Mott, Sir Nevill, 65, 75, 88, 146
Moule, C. F. D., 105, 116
Muggeridge, Malcolm, 94
Munby, Denys, 42
Murray, Michael, 162
Murray, Dame Rosemary, 143
Musgrove, Harold, 302

'Nation of Many Cultures, A' (1977), 202
National Church, The, 267–8
'Nationalism and Internationalism' (1977), 206
Nature of Christian Belief, The (1986), 275–81
Needham, Joseph, 76, 139, 142–3
Neill, Bishop Stephen, 43
Newbigin, Bishop Lesslie, 296–7
New Hall, Cambridge, 143
Newnham College, Cambridge, 144
New Scientist, 139
Nicholson, Laurie, 29
Nicoll, Douglas, 28
Niemöller, Martin, 95

Nineham, Dennis, E., 114, 116, 118, 120, 131, 173, 183
Norfolk, Duke of, 265
Not Just for the Poor: Christian Perspectives on the Welfare State (1986), 258
Novum Testamentum, 149
Nuclear Crisis: A Question of Breeding (1977), 200–2

O'Brien, Sir Richard, 308
OCTU (Officer Cadet Training Unit), 30
O'Donovan, Oliver M. T., 254
Ogilvie, Ian D., 90, 100–1
Oppenheimer, Lady, 175, 177
Ordination of Women to the Priesthood, 288–91

Packer, James I., 120
Palmer, Francis H., 98
Parkes, Sir Edward, 64
Pasco, John, 309
Paton, Catherine (sister-in-law), 38
Paton, David M. (brother-in-law), 38–9
Paton, Grace (mother-in-law), 37–8
Paton, James (brother-in-law), 38
Paton, Michael J. M. (brother-in-law), 38, 42, 43, 48
Paton, Sir William (brother-in-law), 38
Paton, William (father-in-law), 37, 38
Paul, Bishop Geoffrey J. (Bradford), 245–6
Paul: The Apostle (1981), 237
Paula, Sister, 49–50
Peace, David, 162
Pedestrian Association, xii
Pendred, Loughnan, 162
People's March for Jobs, 307
Personal Origins (1985), 254–5
Personal Relations before Marriage (1963), 151
Piercy, H. G., 49, 51
Pinder, C. (Mick), 165–7
Plowden, Stephen, 192
Pittenger, Norman, 127
'Population Control' (1976), 202
'Position of the Cana Miracle and the Cleansing of the Temple in St John's Gospel, The', 54, 105
Powell, J. Enoch (MP), 94, 253
Prayer and the Departed, 122–3
Prism, 112
Prisons and the Penal System (group), 167
Probability of God, The (1985), 281, 282, 284–5

Question Mark: The End of Homo Sapiens, The (1969), 139–41, 186
'Questions to a Transnational Enterprise' (1976), 202

Ramsbotham, Bishop John A. (Wakefield), 47, 48, 49
Ramsey, Lord – Archbishop A. Michael (Canterbury), 57, 86, 87–8, 94–5, 98, 114, 125, 127–8, 155, 158, 162, 163, 183
Ramsey, Bishop Ian T. (Durham), 120, 122–3, 183
Ratcliffe, E. C., 108
Raven, Charles E., 60, 107, 115
Remarriage and Mixed Marriages: A Plea for Dual Reform (1967), 151
Responsible Church, The (1966), 139
Riches, Bishop Kenneth (Lincoln), 35
Risen with Healing in His Wings (1983), 238
Ritchie, C. H., 50
Roberts, Colin, 29
Roberts, Bishop Edward J. K. (Ely), 98, 128–9, 154, 163
Roberts, Michael, 136
Roberts, Roger L., 18, 19–20, 21, 29
Robinson, Bishop John A. T. (Woolwich), 55, 56, 103, 108, 112, 113–15, 116, 141, 155, 157, 160
Robinson, Ruth, 114
Robson-Brown, Lady Kay, 168
Rodger, Bishop Patrick C. (Oxford), 17, 18, 21, 42
Rogerson, Bishop Barry (Bristol), 276
Roman Catholic Church, 175, 256
Root, Howard E., 108, 109, 110, 111, 112–13, 120, 175, 180
Royal Bucks Regiment, 30
Rugby School, 16–26
Ruhindi, Bishop, Y. K. (North Kigezi), 301
Runcie, Archbishop Robert, A. K. (Canterbury), xv–xvi, 50–1, 53–4, 181, 214–15, 245, 246, 268, 275, 276, 298, 308, 309, 310, 311, 312, 313

St Catherine's College, Cambridge, 145
St George's Church, Jesmond, 47–52
St John's College, Oxford, 26–9
St Mary the Virgin Church, Oxford, 38, 83
St Michael's Church, Cambridge, 88–9
St Philip's Cathedral, Birmingham, 237–8
Salaman, Esther (cousin), 26
Sanders, Joseph, 109, 110, 111
Sato, General, 33
Say, Bishop R. David (Rochester), 261–2
Schumacher, E. F., 190
Schuster, Bishop James L. (St John's), 35
Schwab, Gunther, 137–8
Sea of Faith, The (Cupitt), 273
Sebag-Montefiore, Arthur (grandfather), 7
Sebag-Montefiore, Charles Edward (father), 7–10, 11, 39, 80–2
Sebag-Montefiore, Denzil (brother), 3–4,

6–7, 9, 11, 81
Sebag-Montefiore, Sir Joseph (formerly
    Sebag – great-grandfather), 6, 7
Sebag-Montefiore, Muriel Alice Ruth
    (née de Pass–mother), 8–10, 81–2
Sebag-Montefiore, Oliver (brother), 9, 81
Sebag-Montefiore, Ruth (sister-in-law), 7
Sebag-Montefiore, Thomas H. (uncle), 30
Seller, Mary, 254
Sephardi Jews, 1–2, 6, 8
Sheppard, Bishop David S. (Liverpool),
    157, 158, 161, 168, 170, 172, 173, 307
Shops' Bill, 262
Sidney Sussex College, Cambridge, 145
Simpson, D. C., 40
Simonson, J. W. D., 167
Skelton, Bishop Kenneth J. F. (Lichfield),
    182, 307
Smart, Ninian, 109, 111, 121
Smith, B. T. D., 107
So Near and Yet So Far (1986), 286–7, 288
Soundings (1967), 111–113, 115
Stacey, Nicolas D., 133, 164
Stannard, Bishop Robert W. (Woolwich),
    157
Stockwood, Bishop A. Mervyn
    (Southwark), 86–9, 100, 108, 114,
    153, 155, 157–9, 160, 163–4, 165, 168,
    169, 170, 173, 179, 205, 207, 219

Strawson, Sir Peter, 39
Sturdy, J. V. M., 88
Styler, Geoffrey, 45
*Subscription and Assent to the Thirty-Nine
    Articles* (1968), 121–2
Sullivan, Martin G., 208
Sun, 313
Sutton, Bishop Keith N. (Lichfield), 308
Sykes, Norman, 57
Sykes, Stephen W., 122
'Symbols and the Eucharist' (1972), 12,
    123–4

Tait, Archbishop A. C. (Canterbury), 17
Taking Leave of God (Cupitt), 272
Tambo, Oliver, xii
Taylor, Gordon Rattray, 140–1
Taylor, Bishop John B. (St Albans), 276
Taylor, Bishop John V. (Winchester), 184
'Teabreak strike', Longbridge (1981), 303
Tebbit, Norman (MP), 198
Telfer, William, 106–7
Temple, Archbishop Frederick
    (Canterbury), 17
Temple, Archbishop William
    (Canterbury), xvi, 37, 115, 134, 256,
    274–5
Templer, Field-Marshal Sir Gerald, 162

Ten Propositions, The, 174
Thatcher, Margaret (Prime Minister), xii
Theological Studies, Journal of, 149
Theology, 112, 149, 150, 177–8
Thinking about the Eucharist (1972), 123
Thirty-Nine Articles of Religion, The,
    118–22
Thomas and the Evangelists (1962), 84
Thompson, Bishop J. L. (Jim) (Stepney),
    308
Thompson, Pratt, 302
Thornton-Duesbery, J. P., 40
Till, Barry D., 55, 145, 153–4
Times, The, xii, 4, 189, 213–14, 313
Tinker, E. F., 171
Tinsley, Bishop E. John (Bristol), 120
Tirrell, L. B., 169
Today's Church and Today's World (1977),
    206–7
To Help You to Pray (1957), 153
'Towards a Christology for Today',
    (1967), 111–12
Towards Simplicity of Life, 190–1
Town and Country Planning Association,
    xii
Transport 2000, xi
Transport, Independent Commission on,
    192–5,
*Truth to Tell: A Radical Restatement of
    Christian Faith* (1966), 151
Tulsa Affair, The, 309–13
Turner, H. E. W., 52, 84, 85, 120, 124
Tytler, Bishop Donald A. (Middleton),
    208, 219

Unborn Children (Protection) Bill, 253
*Understanding Closed Shops: A Christian
    Enquiry into Compulsory Trade Union
    Membership*, 247–8
Urban bishops, 307–8
U Thant, 140

Vacancy-in-See Committee (Birmingham),
    210
Vaizey, Lord, 170
Vanstone, W. H., 55
Verney, Sir Ralph, 30
Verney, Bishop Stephen E. (Repton),
    269–70
Vidler, A. R., 86, 109, 111, 112, 163
'Vows' (1971), 177

Waddams, Herbert W., 175
Waddy, E. F., 24
Wain, John, 39
Wainwright, Geoffrey, 271–2
Walker, Keith, 211–12

Walker, Bishop Peter K. (Ely), 53
Walker, Peter (MP), 305
Walker, Thomas O., 222–3, 227
Walls, Roland, 108, 117
Wand, Bishop J. W. C (London), 113
Wansey, J. C., 98
Ward, Barbara (Lady Jackson), 190
Ward, J. S. Keith, 254
Warnock, Lady, 252
Warnock Report, 252, 253, 254
Webster, Alan B., 45, 52, 55
Westcott House, Cambridge, 45–6, 52, 57, 154
Whinney, Bishop Michael H. D. (Southwell), 232, 301
Whiteley, William (MP), 30, 32
Wicker, Brian, 139–40
Wiles, Maurice F., 108, 116–17, 120, 183
Wilkinson, John, 85
Wilkinson's (Montefiore's first school), 15
Willcocks, Sir David, 51
Williams, Harry A. (CR), 45, 52, 109, 110, 111, 112, 115, 117

Williams, Bishop Ronald R. (Leicester), 110–11, 139, 180–1, 182
Wilson, Bishop J. Leonard (Birmingham), 210, 233
Woods, George F., 109
Woods, Bishop R. W. (Robin) (Worcester), 247
Woollcombe, Bishop Kenneth J. (Oxford), 55, 56, 173
Work, Employment and the Changing Future, 307
World Congress of Faiths, Cambridge Conference (1967), 97–98
Why Believe in God? (Hick and Goulder), 272–3

Yarnold, Edward (SJ), 286–7
Yes to Women Priests (1978), 288
Young, Bishop David N. de L. (Ripon), 307